ISBN 978-0-260-42760-1
PIBN 10947622

PHILLIP WEINBERG,

Appellee,

v.

FRANK C. NICODEMUS, Jr., and NORMAN B. PITCAIRN, Receivers of Wabash Railway Company,

Appellants.

APPEAL FROM MUNICIPAL COURT OF CHICAGO.

286 I.A. 603

MR. PRESIDING JUSTICE HALL DELIVERED THE OPINION OF THE COURT.

This is an appeal from a judgment of the Municipal Court of Chicago against defendants, the receivers of the Wabash Railway Company, for the sum of $150.00. The action is predicated upon a charge that defendants accepted the delivery of a carload of horses at Kansas City, Missouri, for plaintiff, to be transported to Cook, Indiana, and that through the negligence of the defendants, one of the horses was killed, two were blinded, and one was disabled. The trial was before the court without a jury.

Plaintiff testified that on March 19th, 1934, at Kansas City, Missouri, he bought 26 horses and shipped them on the Wabash Railway from Kansas City, and that he received a bill of lading for the same from the Wabash Railway Company. The bill of lading together with the paid freight bill of the New York Central Railway, which latter company received the shipment from the Wabash Railway Company, and delivered the same to the plaintiff, were offered and received in evidence. The bill of lading issued by the Wabash Railway at Kansas City, Missouri, on March 19th, 1934, recited the receipt in apparent good order, of 26 horses from the Kansas City Horse & Mule Company, subject to the classification and tariff in effect, for transportation and delivery to the plaintiff at Cook, Indiana, as ordinary live stock. This bill of lading was signed by the agent of the railway company and the plaintiff as caretaker of the property in transit. Plaintiff travelled with the stock upon

free transportation furnished by the defendants. The conditions in the bill of lading are that the carrier, except in case of its negligence, primarily contributing, should not be liable for loss or damage to the horses caused by the act of God, public enemy, the inherent vice, weakness or natural propensity of the animals, their crowding one upon the other, their kicking, or otherwise injuring themselves, or for the act or default of the shipper or owner; that any person accompanying the live stock, should take care of, feed and water the same while being transported, and that the shipper, meaning plaintiff, should load and unload the live stock into and out of the cars at his own risk and expense, and that before the live stock should be removed from the carrier's possession, the shipper, owner or consignee should inform the railway company in writing, of any possible or manifest injury thereto. The freight bill, called a delivery receipt, of the New York Central Lines, was issued to plaintiff as consignee, and dated March 21st, 1934, at Cook, Indiana. This freight bill is for carrier charges for transportation of 26 horses from Kansas City, Missouri, to Cook, Indiana, and is for the sum of $120.95, and shows the delivery thereof to plaintiff on the day of its date, and upon it is his acknowledgment of the receipt of the horses <u>in good order</u>. Plaintiff testified substantially that he was present at Kansas City when the horses were loaded, and that they were in number one condition at that time; that he rode on the train with the horses, but that he was in the caboose; that the horses were unloaded in transit for feed and water at East St. Louis, where they remained about six hours, being again loaded at 11:00 at night of the day of the shipment; that he went back to the caboose, and that he saw the horses when they reached his barn; that they were unloaded at Cook, Indiana, six miles from the barn at about 8 or 9 in the evening, and that it was then dark; that some of his helpers did the unloading at Cook, Indiana, and that he and his helpers led the horses from there;

and water the same while being transport
meaning plaintiff, should load and unlo
of the cars at his own risk and expense,
stock should be removed from the carrier
owner or consignee should inform the rai
any possible or manifest injury thereto.
a delivery receipt, of the New York Cent
plaintiff as consignee, and dated March
This freight bill is for carrier charges
horses from Kansas City, Missouri, to Co
sum of $120.95, and shows the delivery t
day of its date, and upon it is his ackn
the horses in good order. Plaintiff tes
was present at Kansas City when the hors
were in number one condition at that tim
with the horses, but that he was in the c
unloaded in transit for feed and water at
remained about six hours, being again loa
day of the shipment; that he went back to
the horses when they reached his barn; th

that two hours were required in leading the horses from Cook to the barn; that when he got to the barn, the horses were examined, and it was found that they were bruised and that nearly every one of them was disabled, that there wasn't one which was as perfect as they were when they were put in the car; that some of them were better, and some were worse, but there were a couple of them "we saw no help for"; that the next morning when he came to the barn, he saw one of the horses dead, and that the horse showed evidence of having been bruised, and that the horse was laying in the car when they unloaded the horses at Cook. This witness testified that the horse was worth $150.00; that three other horses were bruised, and one horse had a badly swollen neck; that these three horses were worth from $125 to $135 when put on the car at Kansas City, and that after they were blinded, they were worth $30 to $40. He testified that another horse was damaged in the back, and he sold him for $15, and that this horse was worth $120 when loaded at Kansas City. This witness testified that all told, his damage would be about $700. It was here stipulated that the proper claim had been filed with the railway company. This witness also testified to the effect that he had had experience covering a period of 25 or 30 years in selling horses at Crown Point, Indiana; that the horses were bought by him through the Kansas City Horse & Mule Company, who were the consignors in the bill of lading; that at the time the horses were unloaded at East St. Louis, they were driven out of the car, where they were fed, and that at that time, they were all on their feet and moving around the lot; that he did not see the horses at Danville, where they were transferred from the Wabash Railway to the Big Four Railway; that he was present at Cook at about 8 o'clock at night, when the horses were unloaded. He testified that he signed a receipt for the horses in a book kept by the railway for that purpose. He

identified the book and his receipt, and stated that he, with his men, drove the horses from the railroad to his barn, that they were tied together, and that they did not have to help any of the horses at that time, and that the horse which subsequently died, was laying down in the car at the time the witness went to the car to unload these horses.

Several employees of the plaintiff who assisted in unloading the horses from the car and in taking them to his barn, testified substantially to the same effect as the plaintiff.

The agent of the New York Central Railway Company, a witness produced by the defendant, testified that he was present when the horses were unloaded, and that after the horses were unloaded, plaintiff paid the freight and signed a receipt for the freight, and stated in this receipt that the horses were "received in good order", and that the plaintiff Weinberg had ample opportunity to inspect the horses before they were unloaded.

Another witness for the defendant testified to the effect that he was a track operator for the New York Central Railway Company at the time the horses were received at Cook, Indiana, and that it was his duty to take care of all freight that came in while he was on duty; that he assisted in the unloading; that it was dark when the horses were unloaded, and that he furnished lanterns so that the defendant and his helpers could see them taken from the cars, and that he saw the whole proceeding; that the horses travelled down the chute from the car, and that they showed no evidence of having been blinded or crippled, that Weinberg and his helpers put halters on the horses and led them away, and that Weinberg told the witness that they were a pretty fair bunch of horses. This witness further testified to the effect that he heard no complaint about the condition of the horses

until two months later, and that at the time of the unloading, there was sufficient light so he could tell whether any of the horses were crippled or blind.

A live stock agent of the defendant company who stated that he was a resident of Kansas City, testified that he, as such agent, signed the contract with plaintiff for the shipment of the horses at Kansas City on March 19th, 1934, the date of their shipment; that he saw Weinberg about three months after, and that Weinberg said nothing about the shipment, nor that the horses were injured in transport.

In view of the provisions in this contract, and after taking into consideration all of the evidence, we reach the conclusion that plaintiff has not established his right to recover by the manifest weight of the evidence. His contract clearly provides that he, the person accompanying the shipment, should feed and water the horses, and otherwise care for them during their shipment. There is no proof that the carrier was guilty of negligence. The undisputed fact that the horses were received by plaintiff in apparent good order, and that he made no complaint as to their alleged condition at that time, nor until some weeks later, has also been considered.

The judgment is reversed and the cause is remanded.

REVERSED AND REMANDED.

HEBEL, J. AND DENIS E. SULLIVAN, J. CONCUR.

38396

GEORGE PLACZKIEWICZ,
Appellee,
v.
WILHELMINA K. BORGMEIER and ADOLPH J. BORGMEIER, her husband,
Appellants.

APPEAL FROM CIRCUIT COURT COOK COUNTY.

286 I.A. 603[2]

MR. PRESIDING JUSTICE HALL DELIVERED THE OPINION OF THE COURT.

This is an appeal from a decree of foreclosure entered in the Circuit Court of Cook County on May 22nd, 1935. The bill of complaint filed in the cause on January 20th, 1934, alleges that on May 22nd, 1927, the defendants, Wilhelmina K. Borgmeier and Adolph J. Borgmeier, her husband, executed a principal note, of date May 2nd, 1927, for $8,000.00, payable in five years after date, with interest at the rate of 6% per annum, the interest payments being evidenced by coupon notes of even date with the principal note, secured by a mortgage on real estate, and that on May 14th, 1932, an extension agreement was entered into between the parties, which was executed by Wilhelmina K. Borgmeier in person, and as attorney in fact for Adolph J. Borgmeier. The bill also alleges defaults in the payment of both the principal note and interest, together with defaults in the payment of taxes agreed to be paid by the makers of the trust deed and notes, and that on November 25th, 1933, Wilhelmina K. Borgmeier and Adolph J. Borgmeier conveyed the title to the mortgaged premises, which they had previously held, to H. A. O'Connor, one of the defendants. On March 22nd, 1934, the appearances of Wilhelmina K. Borgmeier, individually, and as administratrix of the estate of Adolph J. Borgmeier, deceased, and H. A. O'Connor, together with a demand for a jury trial, were filed. On April 2nd, 1934, a document

entitled an answer and counter claim was filed by Wilhelmina K. Borgmeier, as administratrix of the estate of Adolph J. Borgmeier, in which the death of Adolph J. Borgmeier is suggested, together with her appointment as administratrix of his estate, and in which she denies that Adolph J. Borgmeier executed the notes and trust deed, as set forth in the bill of complaint, denies that Adolph J. Borgmeier entered into the extension agreement as recited, denies that there were any defaults in the payment of the principal note and interest, and that there has been any default in the payment of taxes. In this document it is further recited that the extension agreement between the parties, entered into on May 14th, 1932, provides that of the principal amount agreed to be paid, the sum of $7,500.00 was extended as follows: $500.00 to become due May 15th, 1933, and the balance of $7,000.00 to become due May 15th, 1935; that simultaneously with the extension agreement, Adolph J. Borgmeier, by Wilhelmina K. Borgmeier, his alleged attorney in fact, executed six interest coupon notes numbered 1 to 6 inclusive, with interest at 6% on the sum of $7,500.00, payable on November 15th and May 15th in each year, until the maturity of the principal sum should be paid; that in consideration of the extension, Wilhelmina K. Borgmeier,his attorney in fact for Adolph J. Borgmeier, was compelled to pay the complainant $713.00 in cash, that is to say $500.00 to be applied on the principal sum of $8,000.00 then matured, leaving a balance of $7,500.00, which was extended by this agreement, and the further sum of $213.00 as a commission. It is charged in this answer that the contract for the payment of $213.00 made the whole agreement usurious, and that thereby the complainant forfeited the whole amount of the interest agreed to be paid, and that at the time of the execution of the original mortgage, and of the power of attorney under which the extension agreement was executed, that Adolph J. Borgmeier was incompetent, and that the principal note, trust deed, extension agreement,

and all of the documents upon which the foreclosure proceeding is predicated, are null and void. Defendants prayed that all these documents be ordered cancelled, and that certain moneys be ordered paid to them.

A motion was made by plaintiff to strike the answer and counter claim, but no order was ever entered upon such motion. A motion was made by plaintiff to refer the cause to a Master in Chancery to hear evidence on the bill of complaint and answers, to which defendants objected. The cause was thereupon ordered referred to a Master in Chancery to take testimony on the issues made, and upon notice to the defendants, the cause came on for hearing before the Master. Defendants appeared and objected to the taking of any proofs upon the ground that a demand for a jury trial had been filed by the defendants, and that they refused to participate in the hearing before the Master because of such jury demand. Without further objection, plaintiffs offered proofs to sustain the allegations in the bill of complaint, and no evidence was offered on behalf of defendants. The Master heard the evidence and prepared and filed a report, to which the defendants filed objections and exceptions. The Master's report found that the note, trust deed, extension agreement and extension coupons were executed by the defendants, as hereinbefore recited, that the defaults have occurred, as alleged, and recommended that a decree of sale of the mortgaged premises be entered. Defendants objections and exceptions were overruled, and the decree appealed from was entered on May 22nd, 1935, ordering the sale of the property, and dismissing the counter claim.

As recited in the brief filed by defendants in the cause, the grounds for reversal urged are that they were entitled to have the issues of fact concerning the affirmative defenses raised in their answers and counter claim, tried by a jury; that the cause was not

at issue, and should not have been referred to a Master in Chancery; that Adolph J. Borgmeier was incompetent to execute the principal note, trust deed, extension agreement and extension coupons, and his name should be expunged therefsom; that usury existed in the extension of the principal note and trust deed herein foreclosed, and that plaintiff must forfeit all interest contracted to be received under the extension, and is entitled to recover only the principal; that after deducting the usurious amounts alleged to have been paid, no default existed under the terms of the trust deed, and that the master's report and the decree are at variance with the allegations of the complaint.

As already stated, these defendants appeared before the master, where evidence was introduced by plaintiff which proved the giving of the notes and mortgage, as alleged in the bill of complaint, the execution of the extension agreement, and the defaults charged in the bill, and no evidence was offered by defendants to controvert this proof, or to sustain the charges made in their answer. So far as the right to a trial by jury is concerned, which seems to be the principal contention of defendants, the Supreme Court in Weininger v. Metropolitan Fire Insurance Co., 352 Ill. 584, page 590, said:

> "The right of trial by jury guaranteed by the constitution is only in such actions as were known to the common law. Where equity takes jurisdiction the defendants are not deprived of their constitutional right to a trial by jury. A trial by jury is not a matter of right in an equity proceeding. Riehl v. Riehl, 247 Ill. 475; North American Ins. Co. v. Yates, 214 Ill. 272; Turnes v. Brenokle, 249 Ill. 394; Keith v. Henkleman, 173 id. 137; Barton v. Barbour, 104 U. S. 126, 26 L. ed. 672."

The contentions of the defendants here are without merit, therefore, the decree of the Circuit Court of Cook County is affirmed.

AFFIRMED.

HEBEL, J. AND DENIS E. SULLIVAN, J. CONCUR.

38437

GENEVIEVE ARGENTINA DEL BOCCIO, Appellee,

v.

LESLIE MARINGER and VIRGIL MARINGER, Appellants.

APPEAL FROM SUPERIOR COURT COOK COUNTY.

1017

286 I.A. 603[3]

MR. PRESIDING JUSTICE HALL DELIVERED THE OPINION OF THE COURT.

This action was brought by plaintiff against defendants to recover damages for injuries said to have been received through the negligence of the defendants. The cause was submitted to a jury, which returned a verdict for the plaintiff in the sum of $3,500.00, upon which judgment was entered. From this judgment, this appeal is being prosecuted. It is defendant's contention that defendant was not negligent, and that plaintiff was guilty of contributory negligence. It is also claimed by defendants, that the damages are excessive, that the court erred in allowing plaintiff to inform the jury that defendant was protected by liability insurance, and in giving and refusing certain instructions.

The record discloses that on the night of January 3, 1933, plaintiff was walking along the dirt shoulder east of a two lane paved highway on Harlem Avenue in Cook County, and that defendant, while proceeding south on the west lane of such paved highway, suddenly turned directly towards the east and towards plaintiff and struck her. Defendant's statement, as set forth in their brief filed here, is as follows: "The accident out of which this litigation arose occurred on Harlem Avenue about a block and a half north of Irving Park Boulevard, shortly after midnight on January 3, 1933.

At that time, Harlem Avenue, which runs in a north and south direction, was a two lane concrete highway, approximately eighteen feet wide. Both east and west of the pavement there was a shoulder six to eight feet wide. To the east of the east shoulder, there was a ditch four or five feet wide and six feet deep, and beyond that were open fields. On the night in question, the plaintiff, who was then eighteen years old, attended the dance with three of her friends at the Yellow Lantern Ballroom, which was located on the east side of Harlem Avenue about three blocks north of Irving Park Boulevard. The plaintiff testified that she and her three friends, Anita, Jack and Mildred, left the dance hall together shortly after twelve o'clock, and proceeded to walk toward Irving Park Boulevard, where they expected to board a feeder bus. She stated that she walked with Anita, and that Jack and Mildred were about fifteen or twenty feet ahead of them, and that at all times they were walking on the dirt shoulder about three feet east of the east edge of the pavement on Harlem Avenue. Before the plaintiff left the dance hall, she had had a conversation with Nick Russo, who wanted to take her home in an automobile. She told Nick that maybe she would go with him, but while he and his friends were getting their wraps, the plaintiff and her friends started on. When the plaintiff had reached a point about a block away from the dance hall, a whistle called her attention to an automobile in which Nick and his friends were riding. Nick asked Anita if she and the plaintiff wanted to go home. This discussion continued for about four or five minutes, with the plaintiff and Anita walking along, and the car in which Nick and his friends were seated, driving slowly along the dirt shoulder on the west side of Harlem Avenue. The plaintiff remembered nothing from the time they were standing talking to the boys in the automobile,

until she found herself in the Belmont Hospital. There was no dispute that the pavement was dry and free from ice, snow and sleet." It is in evidence that when plaintiff was struck, she was thrown about five feet into the air, and a distance of about ten feet from where she was struck, and that she was then picked up and taken to a hospital. Defendant's statement proceeds as follows: "The automobile involved in the accident was a four door model A Ford Sedan, owned by the defendant, Virgil Maringer. At the time of the occurrence, the defendant, Leslie Maringer, was driving the car, having obtained his brother's permission to take a friend, Roy Walker, to his home. Prior to leaving the dance hall, three other persons who had attended the dance, got into the car for the purpose of being taken to the feeder bus on Irving Park Boulevard. As Leslie Maringer drove the Ford south on Harlem Avenue from the dance hall, he drove at a speed of twenty to thirty miles an hour. There was one car ahead of him. About a block south of the dance hall it began to slow down. There was no car on the west shoulder of the road at the point where the accident occurred. When the car ahead started to slow down, Leslie was about twenty feet in back of it. He then decreased the speed of his car until he was less than ten feet behind the other car. As Leslie swerved his car to pass the car in front of him, about five feet separated the two cars. At that time, he was going from fifteen to twenty miles an hour. As he swerved into the northbound lane, there was no traffic coming from the south closer than a block or a block and a half away. As he got his car parallel with the one he was passing he had increased his speed to about twenty two miles an hour, and at that time, the plaintiff and her friends loomed up before him. They were walking

side by side holding hands, one on the pavement, and two on the shoulder of the road. The plaintiff and her friends were then about six feet in front of Leslie's car. Leslie, in an effort to avoid striking them, thereupon swung his car sharply to the left into the ditch on the ease side of Harlem Avenue. Before starting to pass the car in front of him, Leslie sounded his horn long and loud. As he was headed directly east after making the turn toward the ditch he heard a very dull thud, and later found that it had struck the plaintiff."

It is defendant's contention that when Leslie Maringer, the defendant who was driving the car which caused the accident, turned to pass a car which was in front of him, that the three girls mentioned were walking along the highway on the east side, and that two of them were walking on the dirt shoulder, and one of them on the pavement, and that in order to avoid hitting the one who was walking on the pavement, he was obliged to drive straight east, and in so doing, struck and injured the plaintiff. He insists that he was not at fault in what he did.

Mildred Capece, the Mildred referred to in defendant's statement of the case, testified to the effect that as the three girls mentioned, including plaintiff and one Anita Conforti, walked along, the witness and one Jack Cupella walked behind them, and that Genevieve and Anita walked ahead, and that at no time were either of these persons on the concrete pavement, but on the contrary, that they were all walking on the dirt shoulder.

Anita Conforti testified to the same effect, and we find nothing in the record to refute this testimony, except the evidence of the defendant Leslie Maringer.

As to the extent of plaintiff's injuries, her attending physician testified that prior to the accident, he had treated plaintiff for minor ailments, including a cold and the "flu"; that prior to the accident, he had occasion to make a general examination of the plaintiff, and that he "found her general condition good"; that on January 3, 1933, he was called to treat the plaintiff at the Keystone Hospital, and that he found her in a semicomatose condition, her pulse weak and rapid, and that she had a bandage on her head; that he found a scalp wound about 2½ or 3 inches long, which was brought together by three clips; that there was an abrasion in the region of the right shoulder blade near the arm pit, which had dressing on it; that there was a contusion in the region of the right hip, or sacro-iliac region near the spine, evidenced by discoloration, and some swelling and tenderness in that region, right at about the level of the crest of the hip bone or ilium; that there was a marked flatness which extended from the symphysis pubis up to the level of the umbilicus, evidencing a marked distention of the bladder; that the symphysis pubis is the lower bounding of the abdomen anteriorly; that he examined all of the reflexes; that the deep reflexes of the upper limb or upper extremity were normal; that the reflexes of the abdomen muscles by superficial stimulation made by stroking the skin of the abdomen, were not normal; that he attended the patient commencing on the occasion mentioned, and for some time thereafter; that he observed the absence of the normal reflexes, and that this condition indicated an injury to the nerve system; that he sent the patient to the Belmont Hospital by ambulance, and that she remained in that hospital for three weeks; that x-rays were made of the plaintiff; that he had had experience with x-ray pictures, and that the x-rays introduced in evidence represented the region referred to in his examination. From these x-ray pictures, the witness testified that there was a zigzag line of fracture with saw-like

edges extending clear across the inferior articular process of the vertebra; that the inferior process is a process extending from the lateral and posterior aspects of the vertebrae and forming part of the arch of the vertebral canal. He described and testified to other conditions of the vertebrae; that he found a comminuted fracture, which is one that is splintered; that he found from the x-ray picture an enormous dilation of the bladder; that it indicated that the pelvis was twisted, and that the two sides are not symmetrical, and that in his opinion the condition found was permanent. This doctor testified that in his opinion, plaintiff's condition, as described, was permanent.

As to her injuries, plaintiff testified to the effect that during the time she was in the hospital, she suffered much pain in the lower part of her spine; that she had a bruise on her head and received treatment for that; that she could not pass urine for several days; that she had x-ray pictures taken; that the doctor placed a cast around her body, which started from her chest all around her body to her left knee and up to her right thigh; that the cast remained on her body for two months; that when she left the hospital, she went home in an ambulance; that when she had the cast on her body, she lay in bed for a month or so, and then gradually got up with her mother's support with the cast still on; that during the time she had the cast on, she suffered pain in the lower part of her spine and all through her back; that before the accident, she was in good health, but that after the cast was removed, she suffered pain in her back and spine, and continued to suffer for some time, that she suffered a constant pain; that at the time of the trial, her condition was such that after the least bit of work, she was compelled to lie down and rest, and that then she had pains in her back and spine; that she had done some housework from the time she got out of bed; that she worked for the

Curtiss Candy Company for two months; that she started to so work in July, 1934, approximately 1½ years after the accident, but that she left the work for the reason that she could not stand it, because of the pains in her back; that her work there was wrapping candy bars; that she had been under Dr. Weinberg's care since she got out of bed, and after the cast was taken off; that about one year after she left the hospital, she had to go to Dr. Weinberg because she could not urinate, and that she had seen him with referance to this condition several times since.

Dr. Charles Pease, a witness for the plaintiff, testified to the effect that he had examined the plaintiff shortly before the trial, that he had her take off all her clothes and examined her back and legs; that she had limited motion of her back, lumbar region of lower back, loss of lower lumbar lordosis, and she had left lumbar scoliosis; that the motion of her back was limited in all directions, also, that he found some structural shortening of the muscles in the lumbar region; that scoliosis is a curvature of the spine; that he took x-ray pictures of the plaintiff, which were introduced in evidence; that he had had experience in the reading of x-ray films; that from this reading he found, among other things, a crack in the vertebra on both the right and left sides, and that he found other cracks of the vertebrae. He described other conditions found in the x-ray pictures, which, in his opinion, indicated that an injury had occurred to these organs.

Another doctor who examined the plaintiff on October 31, 1934, testified as to conditions which were similar to those found by Dr. Pease. He stated that chronic cystitis means inability to control the urine. This doctor gave his opinion that the fractures which he found, together with the other conditions, could have been caused by the injury described.

Dr. E. C. Duval, a witness for the defendant, testified in substance that on January 3, 1933, on behalf of the defendants, he examined the plaintiff at the Keystone Hospital; that when he arrived at the hospital, the plaintiff was in bed, and that she then had a circular bandage around her head, that he did not see the wound underneath, it having been freshly dressed; that there was nothing of a traumatic nature or any manifestation of any injury to the parts examined; that his examination disclosed no other injuries in the way of contusions, lacerations, bruises or discolorations of any part of the back; that there was no bruise, contusion or edemic swelling on the lower part of the back in the region of the hip, or anywhere below the shoulders when he examined this young woman; that she could flex her limbs readily, that her pulse was of good quality and the rate of 80, and that is normal for a person of the age of 19; that he had had experience treating patients with cystitis, which is an inflammation of the bladder, and that such inflammation is an abnormal condition produced either by trauma or by infectious process, and that by trauma, he meant injury. He gave his opinion that, as to some of the conditions shown by the x-ray and testified to by the other physicians, they were congenital.

A Dr. R. T. Vaughn, produced by the defendant, testified that he had examined the x-ray films concerning which Dr. Weinberg testified, and disagreed with Dr. Weinberg concerning his testimony to the effect that the x-rays indicated fractures.

Defendant insists that the trial court erroneously allowed the plaintiff to deliberately bring before the jury the fact that a liability insurance company was interested in the case on behalf of the defendants, and that this was prejudicial to the defendant.

Dr. Duval, who, as stated before was produced as a witness by defendant, testified that on the day of the accident he visited the Keystone Hospital, where plaintiff then was, and examined her.

On cross-examination, he was asked at whose request he visited the hospital at the time to make such examination, to which objection was made, which objection was overruled. His answer was that he represented a Mr. De Shields, who was at that time with the Bankers Indemnity Insurance Company, and that he was paid $10.00 for the examination made by him. Objection was made to the answer, and a motion to strike the testimony. The objection was overruled, and the motion was denied.

The precise question was presented in the case of Wrisley Co. v. Burke, 203 Ill. 250, and the Supreme Court said:

> "In the cross-examination of a physician who testified in behalf of the appellant company as to the condition, physically, of the appellee soon after the injury was received, it was developed that the physician had been employed to make the examination for the purpose of becoming a witness in the case, and had been paid for his services in so doing. The fact the physician had been engaged and paid to make the examination and for the purpose of giving testimony in the case was proper for consideration, as bearing upon the weight and value of his testimony. (Jones v. Portland, 88 Mich. 64.) The fact that in developing the proof that the witness was employed and paid to make the examination it indidentally appeared he was paid by an accident company does not constitute error demanding the reversal of the judgment."

See also Kiewert v. Balaban & Katz Corp., 251 Ill. App. 342, where this court said:

> "Dr. Otto Ludwig, who treated the plaintiff immediately after the accident, was asked on cross-examination as to who paid him for the services and answered, 'the Zurich Insurance Company.' No objection appears to have been made at the time nor was an exception taken to the answer; nor can we see any reason why the witness might not be asked, as it might have a bearing on the credibility given his testimony if it should appear that he had been paid by or on behalf of the defendant."

Also, in Taber v. Wittelle, 230 Ill. App. 653, Abstract Opinion No. 28099, a similar situation was presented, and in passing upon the question, this court said:

"That it may be reversible error, either in the preliminary examination of jurors or durkng the course of the trial, to endeavor to create prejudice by any means tending to bring information before the jury that the defendant is insured against liability on the cause of action, is undoubtedly true, but we are not aware of any case which holds that pertinent and material evidence should be exaluded because it might incidentally thereby be made to appear that the defendant carried insurance."

Defendants complain because of the refusal of the court to give the following instructions submitted under the provisions of the Civil Practice Act:

"If you believe from the evidence under the instructions of the court that on the occasion in question as the defendant's automobile approached the place of the occurrence, it was being operated with ordinary care and caution, and that just prior to the occurrence in question an emergency presented itself, then if the defendant, Leslie Maringer, did not act with such perfect judgment as would be exercised under other and different circumstances, he might still not be negligent, provided he acted as a reasonably prudent person would act under similar circumstances. When a driver of an automobile is confronted with a sudden emergency, then failure on his part to exercise the best judgment the case renders when considered after the event, such fact does not necessarily establish conduct inconsistent with the exercise of ordinary care."

"If you believe from the evidence that the defendant, Leslie Maringer, immediately prior to the accident in question without fault on his part, was confronted by a sudden emergency, then you are instructed that under such circumstances, if you believe it to be the fact, the defendant Leslie Maringer would not be required to use the same degree of self-possession, coolness and judgment as when there is no eminent peril or emergency; but if under such circumstances, the defendant Leslie Maringer acted as an ordinarily prudent person would have acted under the same circumstances, he would not be guilty of negligence."

"If you believe from the evidence that as the defendant, Leslie Maringer, turned to pass an automobile proceeding south on Harlem Avenue that he was confronted by the vision of persons standing or walking upon the east side of the paved portion of Harlem Avenue, that such persons were so close to the front of his automobile that he could not stop the same before striking one or more of said persons, and could not turn to the right on said highway to avoid said persons on account of the presence of the automobile which he was then passing, and if you believe from the evidence that in turning to the left and running into the ditch at the east side of

"That it may be reversible error, either in the preliminary examination of jurors or during the course of the trial, to endeavor to create prejudice by any means tending to bring information before the jury that the defendant is insured against liability on the cause of action, is undoubtedly true, but we are not aware of any case which holds that pertinent and material evidence should be excluded because it might incidentally thereby be made to appear that the defendant carried insurance."

Defendants complain because of the refusal of the court to give the following instructions submitted under the provisions of the Civil Practice Act:

"If you believe from the evidence under the instructions of the court that on the occasion in question as the defendant's automobile approached the place of the occurrence, it was being operated with ordinary care and caution, and that just prior to the occurrence in question an emergency presented itself, then if the defendant, Leslie Maringer, did not act with such perfect judgment as would be exercised under other and different circumstances, he might still not be negligent, provided he acted as a reasonably prudent person would act under similar circumstances. When a driver of an automobile is confronted with a sudden emergency, then failure on his part to exercise the best judgment the case renders when considered after the event, such fact does not necessarily establish conduct inconsistent with the exercise of ordinary care."

"If you believe from the evidence that the defendant, Leslie Maringer, immediately prior to the accident in question without fault on his part, was confronted by a sudden emergency, then you are instructed that under such circumstances, if you believe it to be the fact, the defendant Leslie Maringer would not be required to use the same degree of self-possession, coolness and judgment as when there is no eminent peril or emergency; but if under such circumstances, the defendant Leslie Maringer acted as an ordinarily prudent person would have acted under the same circumstances, he would not be guilty of negligence."

"If you believe from the evidence that as the defendant, Leslie Maringer, turned to pass an automobile proceeding south on Harlem Avenue that he was confronted by the vision of persons standing or walking upon the east side of the paved portion of Harlem Avenue, that such persons were so close to the front of his automobile that he could not stop the same before striking one or more of said persons, and could not turn to the right on said highway to avoid said persons on account of the presence of the automobile which he was then passing, and if you believe from the evidence that in turning to the left and running into the ditch at the east side of

> Harlem Avenue and in operating his automobile prior to the occurrence here in question, Leslie Maringer was acting as a reasonably prudent person would have acted under the same circumstances, then you are instructed that there can be no recovery in this case."

The defendant Leslie Maringer alone testified that as he turned out to pass the car in front of him, he was confronted by one of the girls, who, he stated, was walking on the paved portion of the highway, and these instructions proceed upon the theory that with the peril before him of striking one of the girls, he was justified in turning his car at a right angle and striking the plaintiff, who was at all times walking along the unpaved portion of the shoulder of the road. The two witnesses who were walking with plaintiff both testified that prior to and at the time of the accident, neither of them were walking on the paved highway. The clear preponderance of the evidence is to the effect that the defendant had no such peril before him as these instructions suggest, and as would justify the court in giving them to the jury. We have examined other objections made to given and refused instructions, and from an examination of the instructions given, we are of the opinion that the jury was fully and fairly instructed and that all questions of fact were fully and fairly presented to the jury. We can see no reason for disturbing the verdict and judgment. Therefore, the judgment of the Superior Court is affirmed.

AFFIRMED.

HEBEL, J. AND DENIS E. SULLIVAN, J. CONCUR.

Harlem Avenue and in operating his automobile prior to the occurrence here in question, Leslie Maringer was acting as a reasonably prudent person would have acted under the same circumstances, then you are instructed that there can be no recovery in this case."

The defendant Leslie Maringer alone testified that as he turned out to pass the car in front of him, he was confronted by one of the girls, who, he stated, was walking on the paved portion of the highway, and these instructions proceed upon the theory that with the peril before him of striking one of the girls, he was justified in turning his car at a right angle and striking the plaintiff, who was at all times walking along the unpaved portion of the shoulder of the road. The two witnesses who were walking with plaintiff both testified that prior to and at the time of the accident, neither of them were walking on the paved highway. The clear preponderance of the evidence is to the effect that the defendant had no such peril before him as these instructions suggest, and as would justify the court in giving them to the jury. We have examined other objections made to given and refused instructions, and from an examination of the instructions given, we are of the opinion that the jury was fully and fairly instructed and that all questions of fact were fully and fairly presented to the jury. We can see no reason for disturbing the verdict and judgment. Therefore, the judgment of the Superior Court is affirmed.

AFFIRMED.

HEBEL, J., AND DENIS E. SULLIVAN, J. CONCUR.

38458

EDWARD E. KLEINSCHMIDT,
Plaintiff - Appellee,
v.
FLORENCE OTIS,
Defendant - Appellant.

APPEAL FROM
SUPERIOR COURT
COOK COUNTY.

286 I.A. 604

MR. PRESIDING JUSTICE HALL DELIVERED THE OPINION OF THE COURT.

Plaintiff brought suit against defendant to recover for injuries alleged to have been sustained through defendant's negligence in the operation of her car. The trial was by a jury, which returned a verdict in favor of plaintiff and against defendant for the sum of $2,181.30, upon which the judgment appealed from was entered.

The accident out of which the claim arises occurred shortly after 10 o'clock on the night of March 24th, 1933. Plaintiff was driving south on the west driveway of a two lane highway near Lake Bluff, Illinois, and defendant was driving north on the east driveway of the same highway. At the time of the accident in question, a heavy snow was falling.

Plaintiff testified to the effect that as he was driving along, two cars going north, passed "quickly in succession", and that as he saw the lights of the second car, it came towards him, and that this second car struck plaintiff's car just back of the front fender, and again toward the rear by the rear wheel on the running board, and that plaintiff immediately felt his car swerve to the left, that he attempted to turn to the right putting his foot on the pedal to stop the car, and that his car kept going to the left and ran into a truck on the east driveway of the road in question.

From the evidence, it appears that shortly prior to the accident, the defendant, going north, had turned her car to the left and had passed a truck proceeding in the same direction as defendant. It was with this truck that plaintiff's car collided after defendant's

38458

EDWARD E. KLEINSCHMIDT,
Plaintiff - Appellee,
v.
FLORENCE OTIS,
Defendant - Appellant.

APPEAL FROM
SUPERIOR COURT
COOK COUNTY.

286 I.A. 604

MR. PRESIDING JUSTICE HALL DELIVERED THE OPINION OF THE COURT.

Plaintiff brought suit against defendant to recover for injuries alleged to have been sustained through defendant's negligence in the operation of her car. The trial was by a jury, which returned a verdict in favor of plaintiff and against defendant for the sum of $3,181.50, upon which the judgment appealed from was entered.

The accident out of which the claim arises occurred shortly after 10 o'clock on the night of March 24th, 1933. Plaintiff was driving south on the west driveway of a two lane highway near Lake Barry, Illinois, and defendant was driving north on the east driveway of the same highway. At the time of the accident in question, a heavy snow was falling.

Plaintiff testified to the effect that as he was driving along, two cars going north, passed "quickly in succession", and that as he saw the lights of the second car, it came towards him, and that this second car struck plaintiff's car just back of the front fender, and again toward the rear by the rear wheel on the running board, and that plaintiff immediately felt his car swerve to the left, that he attempted to turn to the right putting his foot on the pedal to stop the car, and that his car kept going to the left and ran into a truck on the east driveway of the road in question.

From the evidence, it appears that shortly prior to the accident, the defendant, going north, had turned her car to the left car had passed the truck, and after it had come in contact with plaintiff's car.

The driver of the truck testified on behalf of plaintiff to the effect that the truck which plaintiff's car struck, consisted of a tractor and trailer, and that together they weighed about 13,000 pounds gross, that they were about 30 feet long and 7½ feet wide, that he had a load which weighed about 18,000 pounds, and that the load and truck together weighed about 31,000 pounds; that he was headed north on his way to Waukegan, and was just coming to the north limits of Lake Bluff when a Ford Coupe (defendant's car) passed him going north, and that this coupe went over the road to the left, and that one set of its wheels went off the road to the left and then went back on the road. This witness further testified in substance, that he then slowed down, and that the car which passed him, which was a Ford, disappeared, and that he did not see the collision between the Ford and the Cadillac, plaintiff's car. He further stated that the Cadillac car then collided with the car of the witness; that at the time of the collision, he was coming to the top of a hill, that he saw the headlights of plaintiff's car and immediately put on his brakes, but before he could come to a dead stop, plaintiff's car hit him; that as a result of the collision, the front end of plaintiff's car was smashed, and was partly underneath the witness's truck, and that plaintiff's car came to rest over on the right side of the north driveway of the road; that the car of the defendant passed his truck 4 or 5 minutes before the collision between the Cadillac and the truck of the witness. He further stated that after the car of the defendant had passed the truck, it was on its own side of the road, and that he did not see it again until after the collision with his truck. He stated that when the car of the plaintiff collided with the truck, it was going with sufficient force so that when it hit the end of

the truck, it bounced around on the road to the south and gave him a good bump, and that he, the witness, was thrown into the front part of the truck. He stated that at the time he first saw the lights of plaintiff's car coming towards his truck, the Ford car of the defendant had gone out of his vision north on its own part of the road; that the last he saw of the Ford car (defendant's car) "it was ahead of me on its own side of the road going north".

Several witnesses testified for the plaintiff to the effect that as defendant's car approached, plaintiff was driving entirely within the west driveway of the road going south, and that at no time did he go over the center of the highway dividing the two driveways. Several witnesses for the defendant testified to the same effect as to defendant's driving, and as to the position of her car, stating that at the time in question, it was well within the east driveway.

The evidence is conflicting as to which of the parties was responsible for the accident. The fact remains, however, that the undisputed evidence shows that plaintiff's car was driven with such force against the heavy truck, which, at the time of the collision, according to the testimony of the driver was practically at a standstill, that plaintiff's car was almost demolished, and that the heavy truck was badly damaged.

Defendant testified that at a dinner shortly prior to the accident, she drank a cocktail. In the course of the argument to the jury by counsel for plaintiff, the following occurred:

> "Mr. Jones: (Counsel for plaintiff) * * * There are a great many safety campaigns going on continuously. Some are effective and some are not."
>
> "Mr. Vogel: (for defendant) If the court please, I think this argument, this type of argument, is wholly improper and I object to it."

"The Court: I didn't heax it."

"Mr. Vogel: What is done with reference to safety campaigns throughout the country is certainly an improper subject."

"Mr. Jones: There will be nothing said about what is being done in safety campaigns."

"Mr. Vogel: I object to it."

"The Court: Objection overruled."

"Mr. Jones: There is one campaign for safety on our highways which is going on quietly day by day, which is the most effective campaign which has ever been inaugurated, and that is the campaign that is going on in a jury box of this kind and all kinds in Illinois. If, as and when carelessness on the highway is expensive, then carelessness on the highway will cease to be a menane. These people are going to keep on driving cars. You may meet them. I may meet them. This defendant is going to keep on driving a car. The next time a situation of this sort - "

"Mr. Vogel: I submit, if the Court please, this is a highly improper form of argument."

"The Court: Your objection is overruled."

"Mr. Vogel: I want to note an exception, Your Honor."

"Mr. Jones: If these circumstances occur again, the defendant is going to know it is a matter of a day in court, where the defendant is going to know there is compensation at the end of the trial, compensation for the man who is injured by the carelessness of the careless driver, and I submit to you gentlemen that the carless driver, had a few drinks, or had at least one drink, and thereafter starts down the road through a snowstorm which encrusted the windshield so you can't see through it except through the opening made by the windshield wiper, who goes up a perfectly strange road, follows another car around a 30-foot truck, is careless, and in this instance carelessness brought it s result. There are lots of times when you can do that and an accident does not follow. But if an accident does follow from it, and an accident did follow from it, and this accident is now in your hands. * * * Those are the elements of damage which we are asking you gentlemen, at this time in your particular portion of this campaign for safety on the highways, to award to this plaintiff."

Counsel's remark has in it a suggestion that defendant's drinking liquor had to do with the accident. One witness for plaintiff testified that shortly after the accident, defendant's breath smelled of liquor. Another witness for plaintiff, evidently produced for the

purpose of showing defendant's condition, testified that she, with the other parties involved in the accident, together with the witnesses and police officers, proceeded to the police station at Lake Bluff, Illinois, and arrived there about 10:30 o'clock, and after the accident. Her testimony was to the effect that she saw defendant there, and that "there was nothing peculiar about her manner". There is nothing in the record to indicate that defendant was intoxicated at the time of the accident.

As stated, a number of witnesses were produced by each side as to the position of the two cars immediately prior and subsequent to the happening of the accident, and the evidence as to whose negligence caused it was about evenly divided. Under the circumstances, the argument of counsel should have been confined to a discussion of the issues in the case.

In Lindenberger v. Klapp, 254 Ill. App. 192, an action was brought by a husband for damages based upon the charge of the alienation of the wife's affections. Counsel for plaintiff, in his closing argument to the jury, said:

> "Boys, the question that you have to determine is, whether a rich man like Klapp can break up a poor man like Lindenberger's home and enjoy his wife, or whether the poor devil has any rights in this world."

In its opinion in reversing the case, the court said:

> "We think this argument was improper and the trial court very properly sustained an objection to it and instructed the jury to disregard this statement. The purpose of an argument to a jury is to enlighten them what the evidence is in the case and the law applicable thereto, and any argument that tends to inflame or prejudice the jury is objectionable. Both our Supreme Court and Appellate Courts when their attention has been called to the same have not hesitated to reverse a case on this ground alone, when an objection has been made to the improper argument in the trial court. The attorney in this case was not talking about the evidence, but was attempting to create prejudice, and a judgment founded on a verdict tainted with such an argument cannot be permitted to stand. In the case of Nicklich v. Schnitker, decided

> by this court at the October term, A. D. 1928, (not reported in full), we held: 'If counsel persisted in an improper argument to the jury and an objection is made and sustained, said argument coming from counsel of ability, age and experience in the practice of law, and if it tends to excite the passions and prejudice of the jury, neither the attorney nor his client may complain if the verdict is set aside for that reason alone.' (Illinois Power & Light Corp. v. Lyon, 311 Ill. 123; City of West Frankfort v. Marsh Lodge, 315 Ill. 33; Wabash R. Co. v. Billings, 212 Ill. 37, 42; City of Centralia v. Ayres, 133 Ill. App. 290, 294.)"

In Weil v. Hagen, (Ky.) 170 S. W. 618, counsel for plaintiff in his argument said:

> "You should find a verdict against the defendants in order to protect the lives of citizens in traveling on the highway, and that would be a warning to the drivers of automobiles on the highway."

and in reversing the judgment, the court said:

> "If as a matter of fact plaintiff and his property were injured by reason of defendant's negligence, he was entitled to such a sum as would reasonably compensate him for the damages actually sustained, but no more. * * * * We therefore conclude that an argument like the one in question, which was evidently designed to play on and increase this natural prejudice, and therefore to arouse the passions of the jury, was not within the bounds of legitimate argument. Where an automobile owner or driver is negligent and injures another, he should answer only for the reasonable consequences of his own acts. He should not be mulcted in damages in order that a verdict in his case may operate as a warning to others. As the language complained of was not within the range of legitimate argument, we conclude that the trial court should have sustained defendants' objection thereto and admonished the jury not to consider it."

We are of the opinion that the argument of counsel for plaintiff was of such a highly prejudicial character, that the cause should be and it is reversed and remanded for a new trial.

REVERSED AND REMANDED.

HEBEL, J. AND DENIS E. SULLIVAN, J. CONCUR.

No. 38467

In the Matter of the Estate of JOHN FARSON HESLER, a Minor,

CARL R. HESLER, GUARDIAN, Appellant,

v.

JOHN FARSON HESLER, MINOR, Appellee.

APPEAL FROM CIRCUIT COURT COOK COUNTY

12A

286 I.A. 604[2]

MR. PRESIDING JUSTICE HALL DELIVERED THE OPINION OF THE COURT.

Carl R. Hesler, guardian of his minor son, John Farson Hesler, presented his final report of guardianship to the Probate Court of Cook County, for approval. Objections were filed to this report by the ward, who, at the time of filing such objections, had attained his majority, in which he alleges that certain loans made on his behalf amounting to $11,100.00, were made contrary to law, and that the guardian should account to the ward therefor; that the guardian is the father of the ward, and that on November 19th, 1925, the guardian applied to the Probate Court for, and was granted, an order authorizing the payment of $50.00 a month from the funds of the estate of the ward to be expended by the guardian for the support and education of the ward, without any representation in the petition that the guardian was financially unable to furnish support and education for the ward, and that during the period of guardianship, the guardian had ample funds to provide for the support and education of the ward without resorting to the funds of the ward. On March 7th, 1934, after a hearing in the Probate Court, the court entered an order to the effect that all orders theretofore entered granting leave to the guardian to invest the funds of the ward in real estate mortgage loans, which as originally made or as extended, matured beyond the minority of the ward, be vacated and set aside, and that the guardian account for and pay to the ward in cash the sum of $11,100.00, the same being the amount of the principal notes repre-

sented by certain real estate mortgage loans, together with interest on the principal amount of said loans from the date of investment of the funds of said ward in said loans to the date of payment of such interest by said guardian to the said ward at the rate of 5 per cent per annum, and that the guardian be allowed credit on account of the total amount of such interest to be paid to the ward, an amount representing all interest obtained from said loans theretofore paid into the funds of the estate of the ward by the guardian; that all orders theretofore entered authorizing the guardian to make expenditures from the funds of the ward for the support and education of the ward be vacated and set aside and that the guardian account for and pay to the ward the sum of $3,225.00, the same being the amount expended by the guardian from the funds of the ward for the support and education of the ward in excess of the amount found by the court under the evidence to be justified for such purposes, and that the guardian pay to the ward within thirty days the several amounts found to be due him. From the order of the Probate Court, an appeal was taken to the Circuit Court, and after a hearing, that court found, among other things, that Carl R. Hesler, as guardian, had filed an inventory of the assets of the estate of John Farson Hesler, minor, which was approved by the order of the Probate Court; that from time to time the guardian filed reports and accounts in the Probate Court, showing receipts and disbursements; that the guardian from time to time petitioned the Probate Court for authority to invest the funds of the ward in certain real estate mortgage loans, which investments at the time of the filing of the final report and account of the guardian on January 20th, 1934, amounted to the sum of $13,300.00. The court then made certain findings regarding loans made by the guardian, and further found that on November 19th, 1923, the guardian had applied to the court for an order authorizing the payment of $50.00 a month from the funds of the ward to be expended by the guardian for the support and education of the ward, without any

representation in the petition that the guardian was financially unable to furnish support and education for the ward from his own funds; that pursuant to this petition, orders were entered granting leave to the guardian to expend from the funds of the ward the sum of $50.00 per month on account of his support and education, which sums at the time of the filing of the final report and account, aggregated the total sum of $6,450.00, and that from the evidence presented upon the hearing of the objections and the petition, the income of the guardian during the period from the time of his appointment to the date of the filing of his final report and account was such as to justify expenditures from the funds of the ward for the support and education of the ward of a sum not to be in excess of $25.00 per month, or a total of $3,225.00 for the entire period. The court ordered that the guardian account for and pay to the ward in cash the sum of $5,600.00, that being the amount of the principal notes represented by certain real estate mortgage loans, together with the interest upon the principal amount of such loans from the date of the investment of the funds to the date of the payment of the interest by the guardian to the ward, and that the guardian be allowed credit on account of the total amount of interest paid to the ward. It was further ordered by the Circuit Court that the orders theretofore entered by the Probate Court, authorizing the guardian to make expenditures from the funds of the ward for the support and education of the ward, be vacated and set aside, and that the guardian be directed to pay the ward the sum of $3,225.00 on such account, and that the guardian be ordered to pay to the ward, in addition to the sums mentioned, the sum of $1,455.31, the amount shown by the guardian in open court to be held by him as funds of the ward. From this order, the appeal here is being prosecuted. Also, a cross-appeal has been taken by the ward. It is asserted by him that the father should not be allowed any credit for moneys expended by the father, as guardian, on his son's account.

The errors assigned here by the guardian are as follows: "That the court erred in finding that the income of the guardian during the period from the time of his appointment to the date of the filing of his final report and account was such as to justify expenditures from the funds of the ward for the support and education of said ward, of a sum not in excess of $25.00 per month during said period, or a total sum of $3,225.00; that the court erred in vacating and setting aside all orders entered by the Probate Court authorizing the guardian to make the expenditures from the funds of the ward for the support and education of the ward; that the court erred in holding that the guardian should account for the sum of $3,225.00, being the amount expended by the guardian from the funds of the ward for the support and education of the ward in excess of the amount found due by the court to be justified for such purposes."

Counsel for John Farson Hesler, the ward, state in their brief here, that "there are but three questions of fact that are determinative of the issues raised by appellant. First, the income of the father during the period of the guardianship. Second, the expenditures by the father as guardian for the support, maintenance and education of the minor during the period of the guardianship. Third, the expenditures by the father for his own maintenance during the period of the guardianship." The record shows, as is hereinafter indicated, that the facts as to the first two questions are undisputed. The only question before us for consideration and determination is whether or not the trial court erred in requiring the guardian to pay over to the ward the sum of $3,225.00, this being just one half of the amount of $6,450.00 which he had expended, and which he seeks to retain.

The evidence discloses that some time prior to the death of Marguerite LaRos, formerly Marguerite Hesler, the mother of the minor,

The errors assigned here by the guardian are as follows:

"That the court erred in finding that the income of the guardian during the period from the time of his appointment to the date of the filing of his final report and account was such as to justify expenditures from the funds of the ward for the support and education of said ward, of a sum not in excess of $25.00 per month during said period, or a total sum of $3,225.00; that the court erred in vacating and setting aside all orders entered by the Probate Court authorizing the guardian to make the expenditures from the funds of the ward for the support and education of the ward; that the court erred in holding that the guardian should account for the sum of $3,225.00, being the amount expended by the guardian from the funds of the ward for the support and education of the ward in excess of the amount found due by the court to be justified for such purposes."

Counsel for John Carson Hesler, the ward, state in their brief here, that "there are but three questions of fact that are determinative of the issues raised by appellant: First, the income of the father during the period of the guardianship. Second, the expenditures by the father as guardian for the support, maintenance and education of the minor during the period of the guardianship. Third, the expenditures by the father for his own maintenance during the period of the guardianship." The record shows, as is hereinafter indicated, that the facts as to the first two questions are undisputed. The only question before us for consideration and determination is whether or not the trial court erred in requiring the guardian to pay over to the ward the sum of $3,225.00, this being just one half of the amount of $6,450.00 which he had expended, and which he seeks to retain.

The evidence discloses that some time prior to the death of Marguerite LaHos, formerly Marguerite Hesler, the mother of the minor, the parents of the ward had been divorced, and that until her death, he had been living with his mother, and that at the time of her death, he was about the age of ten years; that at that time, the father, now the guardian of the minor, was residing with his brother in Chicago; that the father is a salesman, and was compelled to be absent from Chicago for a large portion of the time involved in his guardianship; that in the Fall of 1923, the guardian placed his son and ward in the Morgan Park Military Academy, and that the son attended such school as a student, for a period of seven years, when he completed, what would correspond in the public schools, to a grammar school education, together with four years of high school; that upon his graduation from the Morgan Park Military Academy, he entered Denison College, where he remained for a period of one year, and that he then entered Beloit College, where he was a student for two years prior to reaching his majority, and where he continued and was still a student at the time of the trial of the cause in the Circuit Court. The evidence further shows that on November 19th, 1923, the guardian filed his petition in the Probate Court, in which he set up the income received from the trust estate already created for the minor; that there had been received from such trust estate monthly payments of $150.00, and that at the time of the death of the mother of the ward, he, the ward, had no one to care for him but his father, and that since the father's appointment as guardian on March 13th, 1923, the father had entire control and charge of both the person and estate of ~~him~~ his son. The evidence shows that in placing the child in the Morgan Park Military Academy, and his entire action in connection with his guardianship, the father acted for the best interest of his child. It was stipulated in the trial that the income of the father and guardian for the years 1923 to 1932 inclusive, and up to September 6th, 1933, amounted to $58,878.17 - gross. The evidence is rather vague as to the father's cost of living during the

period of the guardianship. The father, as guardian, has made no claim for compensation for his services.

Both parties to this litigation seem to rely largely upon the case of Bedford v. Bedford, 136 Ill. 354, to sustain their contentions here. In that case, the Supreme Court said:

> "At common law the father was bound to support his children, and the strict rule was that he was entitled to no reimbursement for his outlays in providing such support. As a general rule, no allowance will be made him out of the property of his infant children, if his own means are adequate for their maintenance. If he is able to take care of them out of his own estate, he must do so. Where, however, the father is without any means, or is without sufficient means to maintain and educate his children suitably to their condition and prospects, equity will make him an allowance out of their estates for such purpose. In the matter of granting such an allowance courts are more inclined to be liberal than was their practice in the early history of the law. It is not necessary that the father should be actually bankrupt or insolvent in order to justify a charge against the property of his infant children for their support. The welfare and happiness of the children must be considered, and if the means of the father are inadequate to the promotion of their welfare and happiness, their own property may be resorted to for their maintenance either in whole or in part. Each case will depend largely upon its own circumstances. In determining whether the estate of the children shall be drawn upon and to what extent it shall be drawn upon, the amount of their fortune, their condition and expectancies, the means of their father, and the just claims of others upon his bounty, will all be taken into consideration. (Shouler's Domestic Relations, sec. 238; 3 Pom. Eq. Jur. sec. 1309, note 4; Newport v. Cook, 2 Ashm. 332; Gilley v. Gilley, 79 Me. 292; Fuller v. Fuller, 23 Fla. 236)."

We are of the opinion that this case is decisive and controlling here.

In view of all the circumstances in the case, and taking into consideration both the income of the child and the income of the father, we can see no reason why the judgment of the Circuit Court should be disturbed. Therefore, the judgment is affirmed.

AFFIRMED

HEBEL, J, and DENIS E. SULLIVAN, J, CONCUR.

period of the guardianship. The father, as guardian, has made no claim for compensation for his services.

Both parties to this litigation seem to rely largely upon the case of Bedford v. Bedford, 136 Ill. 354, to sustain their contentions here. In that case, the Supreme Court said:

> "At common law the father was bound to support his children, and the strict rule was that he was entitled to no reimbursement for his outlays in providing such support. As a general rule, no allowance will be made him out of the property of his infant children, if his own means are adequate for their maintenance. If he is able to take care of them out of his own estate, he must do so. Where, however, the father is without any means, or is without sufficient means to maintain and educate his children suitably to their condition and prospects, equity will make him an allowance out of their estates for such purpose. In the matter of granting such an allowance courts are more inclined to be liberal than was their practice in the early history of the law. It is not necessary that the father should be actually bankrupt or insolvent in order to justify a charge against the property of his infant children for their support. The welfare and happiness of the children must be considered, and if the means of the father are inadequate to the promotion of their welfare and happiness, their own property may be resorted to for their maintenance either in whole or in part. Each case will depend largely upon its own circumstances. In determining whether the estate of the children shall be drawn upon and to what extent it shall be drawn upon, the amount of their fortune, their condition and expectancies, the means of their father, and the just claims of others upon his bounty, will all be taken into consideration. (Shouler's Domestic Relations, sec. 258; 3 Pom. Eq. Jur. sec. 1309, note 4; Newport v. Cook, 2 Ashm. 332; Gilley v. Gilley, 79 Me. 292; Fuller v. Fuller, 23 Fla. 236)."

We are of the opinion that this case is decisive and controlling here. In view of all the circumstances in the case, and taking into consideration both the income of the child and the income of the father, we can see no reason why the judgment of the Circuit Court should be disturbed. Therefore, the judgment is affirmed.

AFFIRMED

HEBEL, J., and DENIS E. SULLIVAN, J., CONCUR.

No. 38477

H. E. WACKERLE,

Appellee,

v.

GLOBE INDEMNITY COMPANY, a corporation,

Appellant.

APPEAL FROM SUPERIOR COURT COOK COUNTY

13 4

286 I.A. 604[3]

MR. PRESIDING JUSTICE HALL DELIVERED THE OPINION OF THE COURT.

This is an appeal from a judgment of the Superior Court of Cook County against defendant, entered on July 11th, 1935, for the sum of $11,840.18. The action is upon an appeal bond given by one Louis Nies, as principal, and by the defendant herein as surety in the case of Wackerle v. Nies, et al., said bond having been filed in the Municipal Court of Chicago in case No. 1434970 in that court, wherein a judgment was obtained against Nies. An appeal to this court from the judgment in Municipal Court case No. 1434970, was perfected, the judgment appealed from was here affirmed, and on appeal to the Supreme Court of the state, the judgment was there affirmed. After the mandate of the Supreme Court had been filed in the Municipal Court in Wackerle v. Nies, et al, No. 1434970 in that court, a petition under Section 21 of the Municipal Court Act, in the nature of a bill for review, was filed in the Municipal Court by Nies, seeking to have the judgment against him vacated, and the pendency of the petition in that case is urged as a defense in this suit. There is no question as to the amount of the judgment. After a hearing in the Municipal Court on the petition to vacate the judgment against Nies, a motion to strike the petition was granted, and the petition was dismissed. From that order, an appeal is being prosecuted here, case No. 38421 in this court.

Contemporaneously with the filing of the opinion herein,

this court is filing an opinion in case No. 38421, in which the judgment of the Municipal Court, in dismissing the petition filed in the Municipal Court, is affirmed.

This case is governed by the opinion in case No. 38421, inasmuch as all pertinent questions raised here as to the liability of defendant on the appeal bond are there determined. The judgment of the ~~Municipal~~ Superior Court against the defendant, Globe Indemnity Company, is affirmed.

AFFIRMED

HEBEL, J, and DENIS E. SULLIVAN, J, CONCUR.

No. 38492

THE PEOPLE OF THE STATE OF ILLINOIS ex rel, OSCAR NELSON, as Auditor of Public Accounts of the State of Illinois,

Complainant,

v.

CITIZENS TRUST AND SAVINGS BANK, a Corporation, et al.,

Defendants.

CONTINENTAL ILLINOIS NATIONAL BANK AND TRUST COMPANY OF CHICAGO, a Corporation, as Executor of the Last Will and Testament of Ossian Cameron, Deceased,

Appellant,

v.

WILLIAM L. O'CONNELL, Receiver of Citizens Trust and Savings Bank, a Corporation,

Appellee.

APPEAL FROM SUPERIOR COURT COOK COUNTY

14A

286 I.A. 604[4]

MR. PRESIDING JUSTICE HALL DELIVERED THE OPINION OF THE COURT.

In a proceeding brought for the purpose of liquidating the affairs of the Citizens Trust and Savings Bank, Ossian Cameron, now deceased, filed a petition in which he sets forth that he had advanced and paid to the Citizens Trust and Savings Bank on June 14th, 1921, the sum of $3,000.00, and on September 23rd, 1922, the sum of $831.44. In this petition he prays that his claim be allowed as a preferred claim against the assets of the bank, with interest from June 14th, 1921, on the $3,000.00 so alleged to have been advanced, and interest on the amount of $831.44 from September 23rd, 1922, at the rate of 5% per annum from the dates mentioned to August 5th,1930. He alleges that the amounts referred to were advances made by Cameron to and were received and retained by the bank as a trust fund.

The record indicates that at a meeting of the directors of this bank held on June 7th, 1921, which was attended by Cameron as one of the directors, a resolution was adopted by these directors,

by which it was agreed to collect a fund called a "Directors Fund", of $50,000.00, with which to pay certain overdrafts of certain firms and corporations then standing on the books of the bank, in which Oliver F. Smith, the bank's president, was interested, and that on June 15th, 1921, Cameron contributed $3,000.00 by check to this fund. This check, dated June 14th, 1921, was drawn upon the Citizens Trust and Savings Bank, made payable to its order, and was marked paid on June 15th, 1921, as shown by the check which was introduced in evidance. The overdrafts were liquidated and the accounts were closed. While petitioner alleges that the amounts of these overdrafts were afterwards collected, this is denied, and there is no showing that either the bank or its receiver ever collected a cent on these accounts. As to the item of $831.44, the record shows the following: On May 24th, 1922, a note for the sum of $22,000.00 was drawn by Oliver F. Smith, president of the Citizens Trust and Savings Bank, payable four months after date to the Chatham-Phoenix National Bank of New York. This note was endorsed by five directors of the bank, including Cameron, the claimant. As we understand the record, and from the testimony of various uncontradicted witnesses, this note was used for the purpose of borrowing money from the Chatham-Phoenix National Bank for Smith, and that it was his obligation and not that of the bank; that as security for its payment, there was deposited with the Chatham-Phoenix National Bank of New York as collateral, 180 shares of the stock of the Citizens Trust and Savings Bank. This note was endorsed by Oliver F. Smith. Joseph P. Smyth, one of the directors of the bank, testified that certain of the directors, including himself and Cameron, paid $3,000.00 on this note, together with certain expenses, and that on November 15th, 1922, they signed a renewal note for the sum of $19,000.00. Joseph P. Smyth wrote Oliver F. Smith, the president of the bank, a letter which was produced in evidence in the trial, without objection, in which he states, among other things, that:

"Note for $22,000, Oliver F. Smith obligation due at Chatham-Phoenix National Bank, New York, on September 25th, 1922. He was unable to pay it; it devolved on four other directors, Hagamann, Zuber, Cameron and Smyth to take care of it. We paid $3,000.00 on principal plus interest, and revenue stamp, and got four months renewal of $1,900.00.

Paid on principal----------------	$3,000.00
Interest------------------------	321.94
Revenue Stamp-------------------	3.80
	4)3,325.74
Amount paid by each	831.43

My check for $831.43 made payable to O. F. Smith and given to Mr. Woodrow, Cashier."

Cameron, the claimant, was alive at the time of the hearing of this cause, and admitted writing the following letter to Smith, the president of the bank:

"Pursuant to conversation with you last evening, I am enclosing herewith a statement of the moneys advanced or expended on your account and to accommodate you in connection with certain of your notes to date.

To amount as per check June 14, 1921	$3,000.00
" interest on said amount from June 14, 1921, to Sept. 14, 1922, @ 7%	262.50
" interest on said amount from Sept. 14, 1922, to Nov. 14, 1922, @ 6%	30.00
" amount advanced on account of interest, principal and war tax, your N. Y. note of $22,000 to Chatham-Phenix Nat. Bank of N.Y. Sept. 25, 1922	831.44
Total	$4,123.94

It is understood that you will personally take care of any of your notes on which I appear as accommodation endorser as well as any guarantees collateral or otherwise which I may have given to aid and accommodate you in financing your affairs, as I explained I am unable to meet any of these. I have prepared a note for this amount, payable on or before one year after date, which is herewith enclosed and which I will thank you to sign and return to me."

The claimant insists that the fund of which the $3,000.00 was a part, was a trust fund, and that, therefore, the bank and the receiver of the bank became trustees of a fund which belonged to the contributors, and that there was some obligation on the part of the receiver to treat these contributions as preferred claims and pay them. We fail to see where there was any trust relation created. While the

signers of this agreement were directors of this bank, the fact is that they voluntarily contributed money to liquidate overdrafts in the bank of certain concerns in which the president of the bank was interested, in order to make a better showing to the auditor of public accounts. Claimant volunteered to pay another's debt to the bank, and we can see no reason why the bank, or the receiver thereof, should be made liable for the payment of these moneys. If collections had been made from the persons or concerns owing this money to the bank, perhaps claimant would be entitled to have any amounts so paid, paid to him and to the other contributors, but, as stated, there is no showing that any such collections were made. As to the item of $831.44, it is clearly demonstrated that this money was paid on account of the president of the bank, and in so far as the record indicates, the bank had nothing whatever to do with it. Therefore, the judgment ~~xxxxxxxxxx~~ disallowing the claim, is affirmed.

AFFIRMED

HEBEL, J, and DENIS E. SULLIVAN, J, CONCUR.

38369

/13 #

MAUD HARTLEY,
Appellee,
v.
METROPOLITAN LIFE INSURANCE COMPANY, a corporation,
Appellant.

APPEAL FROM
SUPERIOR COURT
COOK COUNTY.

286 I.A. 605[1]

MR. JUSTICE HEBEL DELIVERED THE OPINION OF THE COURT.

This is an appeal by the defendant insurance company from a judgment for $1725. entered in the Superior Court of Cook County in an action by the plaintiff as beneficiary named in a life insurance policy issued by the defendant company. There was a trial before the court without a jury.

Plaintiff alleges that the defendant issued a policy of insurance payable upon the death of Robert Hartley to Maud Hartley, the beneficiary named, upon the terms therein stated, and that "the insured kept, performed, and complied with the provisions of the policy during his lifetime". Plaintiff further alleges that she filed proof of death, with the defendant, as required by the policy.

The defendant filed a plea of not guilty, together with an affidavit of merits wherein it is stated that the policy sued upon lapsed for non-payment of the premium, which became due February 2, 1932, and that on March 25, 1932, Robert Hartley executed an application for reinstatement in which he made false representations as to his health and medical treatment since the date of the policy. The company reinstated the policy on the basis of these false representations, and alleged that after the death of Hartley (sixteen days after the application for reinstatement was signed) the company learned of the fraud. It is also alleged by the defendant that the application

38369

MAUD HARTLEY,
Appellee,

v.

METROPOLITAN LIFE INSURANCE COMPANY, a corporation,
Appellant.

APPEAL FROM SUPERIOR COURT COOK COUNTY.

286 I.A. 605

MR. JUSTICE HEBEL DELIVERED THE OPINION OF THE COURT.

This is an appeal by the defendant insurance company from a judgment for $1725, entered in the Superior Court of Cook County in an action by the plaintiff as beneficiary named in a life insurance policy issued by the defendant company. There was a trial before the court without a jury.

Plaintiff alleges that the defendant issued a policy of insurance payable upon the death of Robert Hartley to Maud Hartley, the beneficiary named, upon the terms therein stated, and that "the insured kept, performed, and complied with the provisions of the policy during his lifetime". Plaintiff further alleges that she filed proof of death, with the defendant, as required by the policy.

The defendant filed a plea of not guilty, together with an affidavit of merits wherein it is stated that the policy sued upon lapsed for non-payment of the premium, which became due February 2, 1932, and that on March 25, 1932, Robert Hartley executed an application for reinstatement in which he made false representations as to his health and medical treatment since the date of the policy. The company reinstated the policy on the basis of these false representations, and alleged that after the death of Hartley (sixteen days after the application for reinstatement was signed) the company learned of the fraud. It is also alleged by the defendant that the application for reinstatement by its terms created no liability on the company under the circumstances and therefore the policy was never reinstated. Defendant admitted liability for the premium paid which was tendered and refused.

The facts are that the defendant issued its policy of life insurance to Robert Hartley, dated February 2, 1926, wherein the plaintiff Maud Hartley was named beneficiary, and the sum of $1500 was payable to her upon the death of the insured. The premiums were paid to February 2, 1932. There was a default in the payment of the premium due on February 2, 1932, nor was the premium paid within the grace period of 31 days thereafter. Under the terms of the policy of insurance here in litigation, a loan was made to the insured of $85.46. Subsequently, on March 25, 1932, the insured executed an application for reinstatement and paid the past due premium, which was received by the defendant company, and on April 10, 1932, the insured, Robert Hartley, died.

In the application for reinstatement signed by the insured, the pertinent parts are as follows: In reply to question 4. "Are you now in sound health?" the answer is "Yes;" to 6. "Have you since date of issue of the above policy (a) had any illness or injury? If yes, give date and particulars," the answer is "No;" (b) Consulted any physician or physicians? If yes, give date, and name and address of physician or physicians, and state for what illness or ailment." The answer to this question is "No." also as part of the application appears the following:

> "Application is hereby made for the reinstatement of the above stated policy which lapsed for non-payment of premium due as stated above. I hereby certify that the foregoing statements and answers are correct and wholly true and have been made by me to induce the Metropolitan Life Insurance Company to reinstate the above policy, and I agree that if said Company shall grant such reinstatement the same shall be deemed to be based exclusively upon the

for reinstatement by its terms created no liability on the company under the circumstances and therefore the policy was never reinstated. Defendant admitted liability for the premium paid which was tendered and refused.

The facts are that the defendant issued its policy of life insurance to Robert Hartley, dated February 2, 1926, wherein the plaintiff Maud Hartley was named beneficiary, and the sum of $1500 was payable to her upon the death of the insured. The premiums were paid to February 2, 1933. There was a default in the payment of the premium due on February 2, 1933, nor was the premium paid within the grace period of 31 days thereafter. Under the terms of the policy of insurance here in litigation, a loan was made to the insured of $95.45. Subsequently, on March 25, 1933, the insured executed an application for reinstatement and paid the past due premium, which was received by the defendant company, and on April 10, 1933, the insured, Robert Hartley, died.

In the application for reinstatement signed by the insured, the pertinent parts are as follows: In reply to question 4. "Are you now in sound health?" the answer is "Yes;" to 6. "Have you since date of issue of the above policy (a) had any illness or injury? If yes, give date and particulars," the answer is "No;" (b) Consulted any physician or physicians? If yes, give date, and name and address of physician or physicians, and state for what illness or ailment." The answer to this question is "No." Also as part of the application appears the following:

"Application is hereby made for the reinstatement of the above stated policy which lapsed for non-payment of premium due as stated above. I hereby certify that the foregoing statements and answers are correct and wholly true and have been made by me to induce the Metropolitan Life Insurance Company to reinstate the above policy, and I agree that if said Company shall grant such reinstatement the same shall be deemed to be based exclusively upon the

representations contained in this request and upon the express condition that if the foregoing statements be in any respect untrue said Company shall, for a period of two years from the date of such reinstatement, be under no liability by reason of the attempted reinstatement of the policy except that the Company shall return to the insured or his personal representative all premiums paid since the date of said reinstatement.
Dated at Chicago, Ill. this 25th day of March, 1932.
Signature of
Applicant: Robert Hartley."

It appears that the insured was treated by Dr. C. R. Steinfeldt from June 2, 1931, to July 16, 1931, for pulmonary tuberculosis. The death certificate shows that he had pulmonary tuberculosis for six months prior to his death, and that the doctor who made out the statement certified that Hartley admitted in a history given that he had pulmonary tuberculosis for three months prior to the date of his death. The Municipal Tuberculosis Sanitarium records show that he had received treatment there in 1931, which was admitted by the attorney representing the plaintiff.

Plaintiff objected to the admission of any of the evidence which showed misrepresentation by Hartley as to matters of health and medical treatment, and further objected to the introduction in evidence of the reinstatement application. The trial court sustained plaintiff's objection and entered judgment against the defendant company for the amount of the policy, plus interest.

On this appeal the plaintiff calls to our attention paragraphs 3 and 4 of the insurance policy.

Paragraph 3 is headed, "Incontestability", and is as follows:

"This policy shall be incontestable after it has been in force for a period of two years from its date of issue, except for non-payment of premiums, and except as to provisions and conditions relating to benefits in the event of total and permanent disability, and those granting additional insurance specifically against death by accident, contained in any supplementary contract attached to, and made part of, this Policy."

Paragraph 4 is headed, "Entire Contract," and is as follows:

representations contained in this request and upon the express condition that if the foregoing statements be in any respect untrue said Company shall, for a period of two years from the date of such reinstatement, be under no liability by reason of the attempted reinstatement of the policy except that the Company shall return to the insured or his personal representative all premiums paid since the date of said reinstatement.
Dated at Chicago, Ill. this 25th day of March, 1932.
Signature of
Applicant: Robert Hartley."

It appears that the insured was treated by Dr. C. R. Steinfeldt from June 2, 1931, to July 15, 1931, for pulmonary tuberculosis. The death certificate shows that he had pulmonary tuberculosis for six months prior to his death, and that the doctor who made out the statement certified that Hartley admitted in a history given that he had pulmonary tuberculosis for three months prior to the date of his death. The Municipal Tuberculosis Sanitarium records show that he had received treatment there in 1931, which was admitted by the attorney representing the plaintiff.

Plaintiff objected to the admission of any of the evidence which showed misrepresentation by Hartley as to matters of health and medical treatment, and further objected to the introduction in evidence of the reinstatement application. The trial court sustained plaintiff's objection and entered judgment against the defendant company for the amount of the policy, plus interest.

On this appeal the plaintiff calls to our attention paragraphs 3 and 4 of the insurance policy.

Paragraph 3 is headed, "Incontestability," and is as follows:

"This policy shall be incontestable after it has been in force for a period of two years from its date of issue, except for non-payment of premiums, and except as to provisions and conditions relating to benefits in the event of total and permanent disability, and those granting additional insurance specifically against death by accident, contained in any supplementary contract attached to, and made part of, this Policy."

Paragraph 4 is headed, "Entire Contract," and is as follows:

> "This policy and the application therefor constitute the entire contract between the parties, and all statements made by the insured, shall, in the absence of fraud, be deemed representations and not warranties, and no statement shall avoid this policy or be used in defense of a claim hereunder unless it be contained in the application therefor and a copy of such application is attached to this policy when issued."

In the consideration of the questions which necessarily follow, it is well to have in mind paragraph 10 of the policy, which is entitled, "Reinstatement" and is as follows:

> "If this policy shall lapse in consequence of default in payment of any premium, it may be reinstated at any time, unless the Cash Surrender Value has been paid or the non-participating Paid-up Term Insurance period has expired, upon the production of evidence of insurability satisfactory to the company and the payment of all overdue premiums with interest at six per centum per annum to the date of reinstatement. Any loan which existed at date of default, together with interest at the same rate to the date of reinstatement, may be either repaid in cash, or, if not in excess of the cash value at date of reinstatement, continued as an indebtedness for which this policy shall be security."

The defendant contends that the plaintiff must proceed both under the insurance policy and the reinstatement contract in order to recover, and where the undisputed evidence shows that defendant was induced to reinstate the policy through fraud there can be no recovery. To this contention the plaintiff in this action replies by stating that the defendant by reinstating the policy of March 25, 1932, waived forfeiture of the policy and the policy, including the incontestable clause, was revived in its entirety; that the policy was therefore incontestable.

The important question to be considered is whether the defendant was induced to reinstate the policy in question by the fraudulent act of the insured. The general rule upon this question, and it hardly needs citation of authorities, is that in order to establish fraudulent representations, the representations complained of must have been made with respect to a material matter, and must not only have been false, but must also have been known to be false

by the person making them at the time, and have been relied upon by the other party entering into the contract sought to be enforced.

In the case of Joseph v. New York Life Ins. Co. 219 Ill. App. 453, the court in passing upon a similar question to the one now before us, said:

> "From a consideration of the authorities to which we have referred and of many others which we have examined, we think the law is that where it is sought to avoid a policy on the ground that the insured made false answers in his application, the question of the good faith of the applicant in making his answers (in the absence of an express provision that they are warranties) is always a material one, and as Mr. Justice Harlan said in the Moulor case: 'If it be said that an individual could not be afflicted with the diseases specified in the application without being cognizant of the fact, the answer is that the jury, in that case, would have no serious difficulty in finding that he had failed to communicate to the company what he knew or should have known was material to the risk, * * * and the policy was, by its terms, null and void.'
>
> While there is some apparent conflict in the language used in the reported opinions, yet we think upon a careful analysis of each case it will be found that there is no real conflict; that the question in each case is whether the answers made by the applicant were knowingly false. Other authorities sustain this view. Donahue v. Mutual Life Ins. Co., 37 N. Dak. 203; Baer v. State Life Ins. Co., 256 Pa. 177; Oplinger v. New York Life Ins. Co., 253 Pa. 328; Sharrer v. Capital Life Ins. Co., 102 Kan. 650; Reserve Loan Life Ins. Co. v. Isom, 173 Pac. (Okla.) 841; Mutual Life Ins. Co. v. Morgan, 39 Okla. 205; Guarraia v. Metropolitan Life Ins. Co., 90 N. J. L. 682; Suravitz v. Prudential Ins. Co., 244 Pa. 582."

It must be admitted that the policy in the instant case had lapsed because of the non-payment of premium due February 2, 1932, and in order to revive his interest in this policy it was necessary for the applicant to apply for reinstatement, as provided by Paragraph 10 of the lapsed policy, and in complying with the provisions of this paragraph it was necessary for the applicant to produce evidence of insurability satisfactory to the insurance company and to pay all overdue premiums. For this purpose the defendant company provided a form known as an "Application for Reinstatement", which the insured signed, and in which he was required to answer certain questions. In

answer to one of these questions the applicant stated that he was in sound health on March 25, 1932, at the time he signed the application for reinstatement, and that he was not afflicted with any illness or injury from the date of the issuance of the policy, nor was it necessary for him to consult any physician regarding his condition of health. Therefore the question is: Did the applicant knowingly make fraudulent answers to induce the reinstatement of the policy by the defendant company?

In a further discussion of this question, it is to be noted from the application for reinstatement signed by the applicant, that according to its provisions the defendant company shall not be under any liability by reason of any attempted reinstatement for a period of two years from the date of reinstatement if founded upon fraudulent representations by the applicant. For this reason where fraudulent conduct is discovered such as would nullify reinstatement of the policy, the insurance company must return to the insured or his personal representative all premiums paid since the date of the application. In other words, the insurance company, upon discovery of fraudulent representation within a period of two years from the date of the application, may offer that as a defense.

As to the question whether there was fraudulent representations knowingly made by this applicant when he filed his application, there is evidence that he was afflicted with the disease of pulmonary tuberculosis; that he was treated by a physician for a period of about 45 days from June 2, 1931 to July 16, 1931, and it appears from the death certificate that the attending physician certified that the assured died of pulmonary tuberculosis and was suffering from the disease six months prior to his death, and in 1931, was treated at the Municipal Tuberculosis Sanitarium in Chicago.

It is claimed from the facts as they appear in the record that applicant was afflicted with tuberculosis and died of this disease sixteen days after he filed his application for reinstatement with the defendant company. We think this was an important question for the trial court, and that the court erroneously entered an order striking out the evidence offered by the defendant upon the question as to whether there were fraudulent representations knowingly made by the applicant at the time he filed his application for reinstatement. This was a proper issue in this case and should have been considered by the court in passing upon the questions involved in this litigation.

Plaintiff contends that the defendant waived forfeiture of the policy by reinstating the same on March 25, 1932, and by reason of such reinstatement the policy, by all of its terms, was in full force, which included the incontestable clause.

We are of the opinion that if the trial court, upon further consideration of this question should conclude from the evidence there were fraudulent representations knowingly made by applicant and relied upon by the defendant company, then the court would also conclude that this application is not binding upon the defendant because of such fraud, and no reinstatement of the policy was made.

From the record as it appears in this case it will be necessary to reverse the judgment and remand the cause for another trial in order that the court may have before it the evidence relating to the questions raised by the defendant that was erroneously stricken out by the court, and it is so ordered.

JUDGMENT REVERSED AND CAUSE REMANDED.

HALL, P.J. AND DENIS E. SULLIVAN, J. CONCUR.

38471

CORNELIUS ROTTIER,

Appellant,

v.

DOUGHNUT EQUIPMENT CORPORATION, a corporation, PETER KIRBACH and W. D. PIERSON,

Appellees.

APPEAL FROM SUPERIOR COURT COOK COUNTY.

286 I.A. 605[2]

MR. JUSTICE HEBEL DELIVERED THE OPINION OF THE COURT.

The plaintiff instituted a proceeding for an accounting against the defendants, which action was referred to a Master in Chancery, who filed his report, upon which a decree was entered by the ~~Circuit~~ Court of Cook County finding that the Doughnut Equipment Company, the defendant herein, is an Illinois corporation, having its principal place of business in Chicago, Illinois, and is engaged in the business of mixing and selling doughnut flour to various restaurants, bakeries, business houses and doughnut shops throughout the State of Illinois and other states; that on September 15, 1927, the plaintiff, Cornelius Rottier was employed by the defendant corporation, as general sales manager and agent in charge of the distribution of the products of this corporation; that he remained in the employment of the defendant corporation from September 15, 1927 until June 2, 1932.

The decree further finds that the plaintiff was employed by the defendant corporation during the period beginning September 15, 1927, and ending January 1, 1930, upon a weekly salary, and that there was no agreement for the payment of commissions or any sum in addition thereto for said period; that thereafter the plaintiff was employed by the defendant corporation during the period beginning January 1, 1930, and ending June 1, 1932, at a salary of $6,000 per year and in addition thereto was to receive a sum equal to

one-eighth of the net profits of the business of said defendant corporation at the expiration of each business year.

From the court's finding it further appears that the plaintiff received the sum of $7,432.80, representing one-eighth of the net profits for the year 1930, and that the defendant corporation admitted by its answer herein that the plaintiff was entitled to an accounting for the period beginning January 1, 1931, and ending June 1, 1932; and that this cause was referred to one of the Masters in Chancery of said court to take an accounting between the plaintiff and the defendant corporation for a period beginning January 1, 1930 and ending June 1, 1932, and it is from this decree, which was entered after the court overruled the exceptions filed to the Master's report, that the plaintiff is here on appeal.

From the facts in this case it appears that on September 15, 1927, plaintiff commenced working for the defendant corporation, and worked constantly until June 2, 1932. Plaintiff received $30 a week from September, 1927 to March, 1928, when the amount was increased to $50. In September of 1928 it was increased to $60. On November 1, 1928, it was increased to $75 and finally in September, 1929 it was made $100. From January 1, 1930, the plaintiff was to receive a salary of $6,000 a year, and in addition, one-eighth of the annual net profits of the corporation. During this time the plaintiff was engaged in carrying on the business of the defendant company. He made sales of flour produced by this defendant, sold and repaired equipment, and also installed equipment used in the business. He was empowered to hire employees.

The plaintiff contends that the proper determination of the appeal rests upon the decision as to whether the plaintiff and a witness named H. H. Leary were telling the true account of the meeting between Peter Kirbach, president of the defendant company, Mr. Leary and the plaintiff, held on July 27, 1927, at the Raddison

Hotel in Minneapolis. The plaintiff claims that it was at this meeting he was employed by the defendant company upon a commission basis of $1.80 a barrel for flour sold by him and ten per cent on the price of all equipment sales made by him. He was also to be allowed a drawing account of $30 a week.

On the other hand, the defendant contends that while the defendant offered to employ the plaintiff on a commission basis upon the terms stated at the time the parties met in Minneapolis, the plaintiff desired to consider the matter, and finally, on September 15, 1927, met the defendant Peter Kirbach, an officer of the corporation, at Kirbach's home in Crystal Lake, Illinois, and plaintiff was then employed at a fixed salary.

Plaintiff in support of his bill for an accounting introduced evidence to the effect that at a meeting in July, 1927, at the Raddison Hotel in Minneapolis, between Mr. Kirbach, Mr. Leary and the plaintiff, the question of plaintiff's employment was considered, and, after a discussion, he was employed by the defendant company on a commission basis of $1.80 a barrel for flour of the company sold by him, and 10% on the price of all doughnut equipment of the company sold by him; and that he was to be allowed a drawing account of $30 a week. It also appears that Mr. Leary, who was employed on a commission basis for the sale of products handled by the defendant, testified that Mr. Kirbach stated to him that plaintiff was to devote his entire time to the sale of the defendant's products, for which he was to receive $35 a week and a commission of $1.80 on all sales of flour made by the plaintiff, and 10% on all equipment sold by him, such as cartons, doughnut boxes, and the like.

On the other hand, the evidence of the defendant is that when the plaintiff in July, 1927, met the defendant company's officer Kirbach at the meeting in Minneapolis, he stated he would take

the matter of the commission offer under advisement and see Kirbach later; that subsequently when Mr. Kirbach called on the plaintiff in Minneapolis he was informed by plaintiff that he had a prospective buyer for the doughnut stand that plaintiff was operating, and if he sold it he would get in touch with Mr. Kirbach. Mr. Kirbach testified that about 30 days after the last mentioned meeting, the plaintiff called on him at his home in Crystal Lake and told him that if the company would pay him a salary he would be glad to consider working for the Doughnut Equipment Corporation. Plaintiff then spent three or four days with Kirbach going over the matter of selling doughnut flour, and when the plaintiff was ready to go out on the road selling flour, Kirbach told him he would send his wife a check for $30 every week as salary, until he had established his ability to sell the flour handled by the defendant company.

As we have already stated in this opinion, the plaintiff was engaged in the work of selling products handled by the defendant company, and the amount paid to him was increased from time to time, as above stated, until finally he was engaged at a salary of $6,000 a year and one-eighth of the net profits of the business of the corporation at the expiration of each business year for his services.

It is a part of the record, too, that plaintiff at a subsequent period was in charge of the office of the company and empowered to employ such help as was necessary, but that he at no time directed the bookkeeper of the company to make up a statement of his account showing the amount due.

It does appear from the record that the plaintiff desired to buy a house in Elgin, Illinois, and wished to obtain money to make the purchase. The evidence shows that Mr. Kirbach offered to loan plaintiff $5,000 toward the payment of the home, but wanted a

mortgage or trust deed executed to secure repayment of his money. This was not satisfactory, and shortly thereafter the plaintiff tendered his resignation.

During the time plaintiff was employed by this company, he received $6,000 a year salary, and one-eighth of the net profits of the corporation for the year 1930, and was given a check for the profits, amounting to $7,432.80, which money the plaintiff applied to the payment of stock of the defendant company, and at that time made no complaint about commissions being due him for the period in question, nor did he demand any commissions when he accepted the check and applied it toward the purchase of the stock.

There is some evidence in the record that the plaintiff testified that before leaving the firm he did ask Mr. Kirbach, for an accounting, but not at any time while at the office.

All the facts in the record were for the Master to pass upon, and as the question of credibility of the witnesses is one of importance in this case, we must assume that when the decree was entered from which this appeal is taken, the court believed the evidence justified the findings of the Master, and where, as in this case, there is a conflict in the evidence, the Master is in a better position than the trial court to judge of the credibility of the witnesses appearing before him, and from their manner to determine the truth of their several statements.

This court in the case of Wechsler v. Gidwitz, 250 Ill. App. 136, upon a like question said:

> "The master both heard and saw the witnesses, privileges denied the chancellor, and therefrom was the better enabled to judge of the credibility of the several witnesses than the chancellor or this court. The decision of the master under these circumstances would be disturbed with reluctance and not at all unless we are able to say that the master's findings of fact are manifestly contrary to the probative force of the proofs found in the record. This we are unable to do after a careful examination of all the proofs. The findings of the master on controverted questions of fact are entitled to the same consideration as accorded to the

verdict of a jury. Story v. De Armond, 179 Ill. 510."

In the case of Brooks v. Gretz, 323 Ill. 161, wherein it was pointed out by appellants that at the time of the execution of the deed of Frank J. Gretz and wife of parcel 1, on July 24, 1908, it did not contain the name of a grantee, and that the name of Catherine L. Ernst was inserted after the delivery of the deed to Ignatz Gretz without the knowledge or consent of the grantors, and upon this question the court said:

> "Neither of these witnesses had any interest in the present litigation. The master in chancery saw and heard the witnesses and in addition thereto had the benefit of a personal inspection of the deed, the ink with which it was written and the character of the handwriting, from which he might be able to judge whether or not the writing in the instrument was all done at one time, with the same pen and ink, or whether it was done at different times. Upon this record we would not be justified in disapproving the finding of the master upon this question of fact."

In determining the question of fact in this case, we agree with the theory of the plaintiff that the Master's report is entitled to the same consideration as accorded to the verdict of a jury. The only ground upon which this court could disregard the finding would be if it was against the manifest weight of the evidence heard before the Master. Such is the rule in the consideration of objections offered by the plaintiff.

The plaintiff urges as a further ground that where a party alters, changes or destroys evidence, every presumption will be indulged in that the evidence in its original form would have been detrimental to the destroyer, and points to certain evidence, Defendant's Exhibit 77, which it is claimed the defendant's own witnesses admit had been very materially altered and changed. Although it is admitted that some testimony had been offered for the purpose of explaining the change, yet it is contended the testimony failed to carry any weight, and our attention is called to the evidence of Frederick C. Laird, a witness for the plaintiff, who was a public

accountant and who testified he frequently had occasion to note the possibility of erasures and irregularities of different kinds appearing in instruments, and that he examined defendant's Doughnut Equipment Corporation Exhibits 75 and 76, and plaintiff's Exhibit 1, and from such examination it appeared that the words, "Draw Acct." had been erased from each of the exhibits.

While it appears from the heading of the books of account of the defendant that in the account entitled, "C. Rottier, Salesman," a line was drawn through the words "Drawing Account" and after these words the word "Salary" written, still according to the evidence this was done at the request of the auditor of the defendant's books and without effort to conceal by means of erasure.

The question here involved was a controverted question of fact to be passed upon by the Master, and the evidence having been submitted to him, it of course was his duty to determine from the witnesses whether the evidence heard by him would justify the conclusion that the purpose of the change was to alter, conceal or destroy, and the Master having passed upon this question and finding that the purpose was not as contended for by the plaintiff, we are of the opinion that under all the facts and circumstances appearing in the Master's report and included in the decree of the court, the decree was a proper one, and it is therefore affirmed.

DECREE AFFIRMED.

HALL, P.J. AND DENIS E. SULLIVAN, J. CONCUR.

38481

THE PRUDENTIAL INSURANCE COMPANY OF AMERICA, a Corporation, (Plaintiff) Appellant, v. CARRIE JOHNSON, (Defendant) Appellee.	)	APPEAL FROM CIRCUIT COURT COOK COUNTY.

17 A

286 I.A. 605[3]

MR. JUSTICE HEBEL DELIVERED THE OPINION OF THE COURT.

This is an action by the plaintiff to cancel a life insurance policy issued by the plaintiff in the sum of One Thousand Dollars on the life of Myrtle Waffenschmidt, in which policy Carrie Johnson is named as the beneficiary.

The defendant filed a cross-bill to recover on said policy, and a trial was had before the court and a jury, which resulted in a decree in favor of the defendant and against the plaintiff company in the sum of $843, from which the plaintiff has taken this appeal.

The plaintiff's bill of complaint alleges that it issued its policy No. M-2326511, dated January 2, 1933, upon the life of Myrtle Waffenschmidt, in consideration of a written application and certain premiums to be paid, in which it agreed to pay upon receipt of due proof of the death of the insured, to Carrie Johnson, her mother, the sum of $1,000.

The policy contains a clause which provides that it shall be incontestable after one year from its date of issuance. The action in question was instituted on December 7, 1933.

It appears from the bill of complaint that the policy was issued and delivered upon the application of Myrtle Waffenschmidt, dated December 16, 1932, in which she declared all the statements and answers to the questions therein were complete and true; that certain of her answers enumerated with reference to her health,

attendance by physicians and treatments in any hospital or sanitarium were false; that she had tuberculosis and had received treatment therefor at the Municipal Tuberculosis Sanitarium and had been treated by Dr. Samuel H. Rosenblum prior to the application signed by her.

Further and other allegations are contained in the bill of complaint, but to the allegations above stated the defendant filed an answer denying that the application is the original application of Myrtle Waffenschmidt, and stating that the answers contained therein are not her answers but the answers of plaintiff's agent; that the agent of the plaintiff advised the insured to sign the application and have the policy issued in lieu of two other policies which she already had upon her life in the plaintiff company, being policies Nos. 83714894 and 83714895; that the agent who solicited the insurance had known the defendant and her family for a long period of time and induced the insured to convert the policies into a new policy.

The answer of the defendant further denies that the deceased, Myrtle Waffenschmidt, had been treated by Dr. Rosenblum, and alleges that she was in good health for two and one-half years prior to her death.

The defendant, Carrie Johnson, filed a cross-bill, which alleges among other things the issuance of the policy sought to be cancelled by the bill of complaint; that the insured had died; that during her lifetime she kept and performed all the conditions of the policy. In the cross-bill the defendant prays that the plaintiff be ordered to pay the sum of $1,000 with interest and in the alternative, asks that she be paid the sum of $385 on each of the policies, Nos. 83714894 and 83714895. An order was thereafter entered allowing the bill of complaint to stand as the answer to the cross-bill of complaint of Carrie Johnson.

There is evidence in the record that Myrtle Waffenschmidt was the daughter of the deceased, Carrie Johnson, and lived with her in 1932; that Myrtle Waffenschmidt was a patient in the Municipal Tuberculosis Sanitarium from October 15, 1930 until July 3, 1931; that when she entered this sanitarium, and while a patient, Dr. Samuel H. Rosenblum examined her and made a diagnosis of pulmonary tuberculosis; that he saw her after she left the sanitarium on December 10, 1931, April 22, 1932, January 4, 1933, and on several other dates, including the date of her death, which was June 26, 1933. The doctor testified he examined the sputum of this patient each time he saw her after she left the sanitarium and found that it was positive each time, and that he told her she had tuberculosis. There is also in the record evidence that Dr. Joseph J. Singer also examined Myrtle Waffenschmidt at the Municipal Tuberculosis Sanitarium on October 4, 1930; that he found she had a cough and that she had lost twenty pounds during the preceding six months; that he diagnosed her case as pulmonary tuberculosis; that when this patient left the sanitarium in July, 1931, her condition was improved; that after leaving the sanitarium she returned to the home of her mother, the defendant, and on December 16, 1932, Mr. O'Brien, who was substituting for Mr. Fritsch as the agent of The Prudential Insurance Company of America, in that immediate vicinity, visited Mrs. Johnson's home and solicited the insurance policy sought to be cancelled; that previously two policies were issued by this plaintiff company on the life of Myrtle Waffenschmidt, which were dated September 15, 1930; that each of these policies provided for the payment of $385 to the executors or administrators of the insured, and each of the policies required a weekly premium payment of twenty-five cents; and that the premiums were paid on these policies until July 4, 1932, on which date the last payment was made. This fact, however, is in dispute, for

defendant contends that she had made the payments to Mr. Fritsch and upon the issuance of the new policy Fritsch destroyed the receipt book which showed the payments, and that she thereafter continued to make payment of the premium on the policy for one thousand dollars. However, upon this question the plaintiff offered its books in evidence that on July 4, 1932 the policy had lapsed for non-payment of premium.

The agent of this company, Mr. O'Brien, talked with Mrs. Johnson about insurance and she told him, which appears from his evidence, that she owed so much on these policies on Myrtle's life she was not able to reinstate them. Mr. O'Brien suggested to her that Myrtle apply for a policy for $1,000 at a monthly premium rate which would enable her to have a larger amount of insurance for slightly more than she had previously been paying on the two small policies, to which the defendant Carrie Johnson agreed. The application was thereupon prepared and signed on December 16, 1932, and sent to the Home Office of the Company and the policy was issued dated January 2, 1933. The plaintiff forwarded the policy to the branch office of the Company in Chicago and Mr. Fritsch, who was the regular agent in that territory, delivered the policy on or about the 10th or 12th of January, 1933. The application signed by Myrtle Waffenschmidt was in blank and the answers to various questions contained in the application were inserted by agent O'Brien, who took the three other applications at that time for $1,000 policies for members of this same family.

There is also evidence in the record that Mr. Fritsch collected premiums and had been acquainted with members of the family for seven years, and knew of the condition of Myrtle's health at the time she signed the application for the $1,000 policy. But to offset the evidence offered upon this question, he testified he knew she had been in a hospital, and when the question was

finally put to him, it developed that it was a maternity hospital. Facts of this kind are for the jury, and upon hearing and considering the evidence it found the issues for the defendant, on her cross-bill, for the amount fixed by the two policies for $385 each, together with interest at five per cent from June 26, 1933; whereupon the Judge entered a decree in which the court dismissed the plaintiff's bill filed for cancellation of the policy for want of equity, and fixed the amount due from the plaintiff to the defendant in accordance with the verdict of the jury.

The defendant - the cross-complainant, admits that Myrtle Waffenschmidt had been a patient in the Municipal Tuberculosis Sanitarium from September, 1930 to June, 1931, for tuberculosis, but that she had recovered and was discharged therefrom, and enjoyed good health for a period of two years until about a month before her death on June 26, 1933; that she was in good health on December 16, 1932, when the application was procured for the policy sought to be cancelled.

The evidence of Dr. Rosenblum, which was before the jury, is that in December, 1931 her health was good, and also in April, 1932, that plaintiff's agent O'Brien and its agent Fritsch testified Myrtle's health appeared to be good in December, 1932. Several other witnesses called to the stand testified to the same effect, and the defendant points to an exhibit offered in evidence showing that Dr. Singer charted a "negative" condition of the insured for each successive month for a period of five months before the insured left the sanitarium July 3, 1931. It was for the jury to determine whether the evidence disclosed that defendant was in good health, or whether at the time she signed the application her condition was such as would indicate that the replies to this application were false. We must bear in mind however, that the answers in the application were the answers made by Myrtle Waffenschmidt but written in by finally put to him, it developed that it was a maternity hospital. Facts of this kind are for the jury, and upon hearing and considering the evidence it found the issues for the defendant, on her cross-bill, for the amount fixed by the two policies for $335 each, together with interest at five per cent from June 28, 1933; whereupon the judge entered a decree in which the court dismissed the plaintiff's bill filed for cancellation of the policy for want of equity, and fixed the amount due from the plaintiff to the defendant in accordance with the verdict of the jury.

The defendant - the cross-complainant, admits that Myrtle Weiffenschmidt had been a patient in the Municipal Tuberculosis Sanitarium from September, 1930 to June, 1931, for tuberculosis, but that she had recovered and was discharged therefrom, and enjoyed good health for a period of two years until about a month before her death on June 28, 1933; that she was in good health on December 16, 1932, when the application was procured for the policy sought to be cancelled.

The evidence of Dr. Rosenblum, which was before the jury, is that in December, 1931 her health was good, and also in April, 1932, that plaintiff's agent O'Brien and its agent Fritsch testified Myrtle's health appeared to be good in December, 1932. Several other witnesses called to the stand testified to the same effect, and the defendant points to an exhibit offered in evidence showing that Dr. Singer charted a "negative" condition of the insured for each successive month for a period of five months before the insured left the sanitarium July 3, 1931. It was for the jury to determine whether the evidence disclosed that defendant was in good health, or whether at the time she signed the application her condition was such as would indicate that the replies to this application were false. We must bear in mind however, that the answers in the application were the answers made by Myrtle Weiffenschmidt but written in by plaintiff's witness O'Brien. Upon this question the plaintiff calls the attention of the court to the fact that as the insured had possession of the policy the presumption is that she was familiar with its contents; that it was her duty if anything untrue was included to advise the Company of the fact. The defendant seems to have had possession of this policy from the date it was delivered until the time of the death of Myrtle Waffenschmidt, and there is no evidence indicating that the insured had possession of the policy so as to be able to examine it, but if she was in good health - and there is evidence that she was - at the time the application was signed, then there would be no need of making false answers and, as we have said before, this was entirely a question of fact for the jury and they have found for this defendant.

The plaintiff contends that the verdict of the jury was advisory, and therefore if the weight of the evidence sustains the bill of complaint the court should have entered a decree finding that fraudulent answers were made, and for that reason the defendant did not have a right of action and the policy should have been cancelled. It was for the trial court to determine whether from the facts presented the jury, was justified in finding for the defendant. The trial court having passed upon it, the question before this court is: Was the decree entered against the manifest weight of the evidence?

It does appear from the evidence that the defendant was in good health at the time she signed the application, and this was testified to by Dr. Rosenblum. The evidence shows that when she left the sanitarium her ailment appeared to be "negative", so that there is evidence which would justify the jury in returning the verdict it did return.

The plaintiff contends that the evidence regarding the policies issued to several members of defendant's family was plaintiff's witness O'Brien. Upon this question the plaintiff calls the attention of the court to the fact that as the insured had possession of the policy the presumption is that she was familiar with its contents; that it was her duty if anything untrue was included to advise the Company of the fact. The defendant seems to have had possession of this policy from the date it was delivered until the time of the death of Myrtle Waffenschmidt, and there is no evidence indicating that the insured had possession of the policy so as to be able to examine it, but if she was in good health - and there is evidence that she was - at the time the application was signed, then there would be no need of making false answers and, as we have said before, this was entirely a question of fact for the jury and they have found for this defendant.

The plaintiff contends that the verdict of the jury was advisory, and therefore if the weight of the evidence sustains the bill of complaint the court should have entered a decree finding that fraudulent answers were made, and for that reason the defendant did not have a right of action and the policy should have been cancelled. It was for the trial court to determine whether from the facts presented the jury was justified in finding for the defendant. The trial court having passed upon it, the question before this court is: Was the decree entered against the manifest weight of the evidence?

It does appear from the evidence that the defendant was in good health at the time she signed the application, and this was testified to by Dr. Rosenblum. The evidence shows that when she left the sanitarium her ailment appeared to be "negative", so that there is evidence which would justify the jury in returning the verdict it did return.

The plaintiff contends that the evidence regarding the policies issued to several members of defendant's family was erroneous. From the record it appears that when the application was signed for the policy now in litigation, applications were also signed by two brothers and a sister of the defendant for insurance in the same amount, and it was due to the conversation with the agent of the Company at that time with respect to the several policies that the statements were made. We are unable to find in what way this plaintiff has been injured. His own agent testified to the occurrences at the time, and in view of the fact that during the conversation other applications were signed, it would appear that no harm was suffered by the plaintiff, and we are of the opinion that the court did not err in refusing to strike from the record the evidence complained of.

Other objections are called to our attention by the plaintiff, but in view of the conclusion we have reached, we feel it is unnecessary to pass upon them.

The real question here is as to the condition of Myrtle Waffenschmidt's health at the time of her application. It is a controverted question of fact, but if she was in good health, then the question of false representations is not a proper one to be considered in this case, and we feel from all the facts and circumstances that the court should have entered a decree for the cross-complainant for the amount due under the $1,000 policy.

For the reasons stated in this opinion, the decree here on appeal is modified and an order entered that the plaintiff pay to the defendant the sum of $1,000, together with interest at five per cent (5%) from June 26, 1933. The decree is affirmed as modified.

DECREE AFFIRMED AS MODIFIED.

HALL, P.J. AND DENIS E. SULLIVAN, J. CONCUR.

erroneous. From the record it appears that when the application was signed for the policy now in litigation, applications were also signed by two brothers and a sister of the defendant for insurance in the same amount, and it was due to the conversation with the agent of the Company at that time with respect to the several policies that the statements were made. We are unable to find in what way this plaintiff has been injured. His own agent testified to the occurrences at the time, and in view of the fact that during the conversation other applications were signed, it would appear that no harm was suffered by the plaintiff, and we are of the opinion that the court did not err in refusing to strike from the record the evidence complained of.

Other objections are called to our attention by the plaintiff, but in view of the conclusion we have reached, we feel it is unnecessary to pass upon them.

The real question here is as to the condition of Myrtle Waffenschmidt's health at the time of her application. It is a controverted question of fact, but if she was in good health, then the question of false representations is not a proper one to be considered in this case, and we feel from all the facts and circumstances that the court should have entered a decree for the cross-complainant for the amount due under the $1,000 policy.

For the reasons stated in this opinion, the decree here on appeal is modified and an order entered that the plaintiff pay to the defendant the sum of $1,000, together with interest at five per cent (5%) from June 28, 1932. The decree is affirmed as modified.

DECREE AFFIRMED AS MODIFIED.

HALL, P.J. AND DENIS E. SULLIVAN, J. CONCUR.

18 A

38507

WILLIAM B. UIHLEIN, (Plaintiff) Appellant,

v.

M. FAITH McAULEY, (Defendant) Appellee.

APPEAL FROM THE MUNICIPAL COURT OF CHICAGO

286 I.A. 605[4]

MR. JUSTICE HEBEL DELIVERED THE OPINION OF THE COURT:

This is an appeal by the plaintiff from a judgment entered against him in the sum of $11,990.01 upon a statement of claim on set-off filed by the defendant in a suit instituted by the plaintiff to recover the balance of $11,942.70 due upon a contract of purchase of real estate in Chicago, Illinois. The case was tried before a jury and the court entered judgment on the verdict of the jury.

On November 16, 1932, plaintiff filed his statement of claim in the Municipal Court setting forth that on August 22, 1927, defendant had entered into a written contract with the plaintiff for the purchase by the defendant of certain lots in Edward G. Uihlein's subdivision in the southerly part of Chicago, lying south of 103rd Street and west of Lake Calumet for a total price of $18,600, and setting forth that there was a balance due upon the contract in the sum of $11,942.70.

The defendant joined issue by filing her amended statement and affidavit of merits in which she denied that she was indebted to the plaintiff as set forth in his statement of claim, and in her set-off alleged that the plaintiff falsely and fraudulently represented to the defendant that Calumet Harbor, lying east of said lots, was being improved at great public expense

and that Lake Calumet was then being dredged and deepened; that the Calumet River was being widened and deepened at great public expense; and that factories and mills were then being erected on the Calumet River and Lake Calumet and in the general neighborhood then known as the Calumet District. The statement also alleged that plaintiff represented that a great number of people were interested who desired to purchase lots upon which to build homes, and that sales were then being made and that resales would be made of the lots in question; that the defendant relied upon the statements, which were false and that no purchasers had been produced for said lots. Defendant during the trial of the case filed an amended statement, in which she alleged that she paid taxes on the lots for the years 1927, 1928, and 1929, in the total sum of $1,301.70, and that she had expended $11,990.01.

On November 5, 1934, the plaintiff filed his reply to the amended statement and affidavit of claim on set-off, denying the allegations of false and fraudulent statements, and stating that if any such representations had been made, they were part of the negotiations carried on by the defendant with real estate agents or brokers with whom the plaintiff had listed the lots for sale and that all such negotiations were merged in the written contract under seal.

The defendant admits that the facts are substantially as set forth in plaintiff's brief, from which it appears that the plaintiff was the owner of a number of lots in Edward G. Uihlein's subdivision, the legal description of which is set forth in the brief, and that the property lies east of

the right-of-way of the Illinois Central Railroad, and south of 103rd Street, east of Cottage Grove Avenue, and west of Lake Calumet.

The defendant in this case has been a resident of Chicago for some years, and has been a teacher in the public schools and since the fall of 1918 she has been engaged as a teacher at the University of Chicago, teaching Institution economics.

It also appears from the evidence that at the time in question there was some activity in the Greater Chicago Subdivision, a large subdivision of about 3,100 lots, extending from 95th Street to 108th Street and from Indiana Avenue to the Illinois Central tracks, which lie west of the property herein question.

Mr. Bergtold, ~~a witness~~, called the defendant's attention to Fred C. Hagstrom, a real estate broker who had been engaged in the business on the South Side of Chicago for some twenty years. Mr. Hagstrom advised her of the property in question and told her that he was able to obtain a price on the lots of either $900 or $1,000, but after some negotiation he obtained a price of $775 per lot, and after a discussion at the office they went to view the property, and after giving the matter consideration, the defendant finally made a deposit of $200 toward the end of August, 1927, and agreed to purchase the property, consisting of 24 lots, at a price of $18,600. Thereupon the contract was drawn on a form prepared in Milwaukee, and filled in on the typewriter in the office of Edgar J. Uihlein, and this contract was presented to the defendant by Mr. Bergtold. She executed it and it was

returned to the office of Edgar J. Uihlein, who forwarded it to Milwaukee for execution by William B. Uihlein. Neither Edgar J. Uihlein nor any one in his office, nor William B. Uihlein, had met the defendant at this time.

The defendant examined the contract before executing it and made some criticism. The contract as executed by her was forwarded to William B. Uihlein for execution, and contained the following paragraph:

> "The buyer expressly represents to the seller that no promises nor representations of fact other than contained herein have been made to or relied upon by said buyer, and that no promise nor representation has been made to the buyer by any person whosoever as to the condition of building upon said premises or as to the transferability of this contract, or as to any waiver or forfeiture that may hereafter accrue hereunder, or as to any other conditions of this sale or contract."

From the evidence offered by the defendant it appears that the property in question was in Edward G. Uihlein's subdivision, and that the first eight lots numbered from 3 to 10, both inclusive, were in Block 1 of Uihlein's Addition, facing Corliss Avenue, and lay south of 103rd Street. The second block of 8 lots numbered 11 to 15, both inclusive, in Block 2 of the subdivision faced Corliss Avenue also and were south of 103rd Place; the third block of 8 lots faced south on 104th Street. The lots were 25 feet in width and 125 feet in depth, with the exception of two corner lots which were slightly larger, and one irregular shaped lot on 104th Street. This latter lot lay next to the alley immediately east of Cottage Grove Avenue. There was a large laundry facing Cottage Grove Avenue immediately on the other side of the alley. The

Illinois Central Railroad ran along Cottage Grove Avenue; east of Corliss Avenue was low swampy marsh land, which the City of Chicago was using as a dump; west of Cottage Grove Avenue was the Greater Chicago Subdivision, also known as the Bartlett subdivision, zoned for three flat buildings.

It also appears that Bergtold informed Hagstrom that the defendant had some money to invest, and they succeeded in getting her in Hagstrom's office at 40 East 112th Street, and from there they took her through the Bartlett Subdivision, then across Cottage Grove Avenue and along Corliss Avenue to the location of the lots in question; that Hagstrom at the time told the defendant Bartlett's Subdivision was zoned only for three flat buildings, with the necessity for property suitable for small homes and indicated that the Uihlein subdivision could be handled in the same way. He told her of the widening and boulevarding of 103rd Street and the advantages of this street. He told her also of the great traffic that would come across 103rd Street and the enhanced value to the lots in question; told her about Calumet Harbor being a world center for shipping, and that it was being deepened and lined with wharves and docks, factories and plants of all character; he told of Calumet River being improved and deepened and of the great influx of workmen into that locality and the scarcity of land suitable for small homes and cottages; that this work was all in progress at the time.

The defendant objected to making an investment in unimproved property because it had to advance at such extreme rates to keep from absorbing her interest therein. Hagstrom, however, persisted, met her at her home on the campus of the

University of Chicago and talked to her over the telephone, repeating his statements regarding the property, and finally succeeded on August 19, 1927, in getting a payment of $200 earnest money, and stated to her that she need not worry about the payments to become due under her contract, as it was a wonderful buy, and resales would be made more than sufficient to take care of all interest and prepayments. The defendant finally raised the first down payment of $2300 at the time of the execution of the contract by borrowing funds from Hagstrom, the agent.

Following the execution of the contract in 1927, the defendant repeatedly in 1928 and 1929 called upon Hagstrom for resales and pointed out to him again the necessity of resales in order to meet the payments under the contract. No purchasers were produced, so in 1930 she visited Edgar J. Uihlein and pointed out to him the promise of resales and the necessity thereof in order to make payments under the contract.

The evidence in the record on behalf of the defendant is that Uihlein's reply was they would do everything they could and that resales were hard to make, but probably things would improve and the thing to do was to see what the developments were.

In June or July, 1933, defendant discovered for the first time that all the representations made were false and untrue. Defendant immediately called upon Uihlein, reported her findings, tendered to him her abstract and contract and said the only fair thing for him to do was to return her

University of Chicago and talked to her over the telephone, repeating his statements regarding the property, and finally succeeded on August 19, 1927, in getting a payment of $200 earnest money, and stated to her that she need not worry about the payments to become due under her contract, as it was a wonderful buy, and resales would be made more than sufficient to take care of all interest and prepayments. The defendant finally raised the first down payment of $2300 at the time of the execution of the contract by borrowing funds from Hagstrom, the agent.

Following the execution of the contract in 1927, the defendant repeatedly in 1928 and 1929 called upon Hagstrom for resales and pointed out to him again the necessity of resales in order to meet the payments under the contract. No purchasers were produced, so in 1930 she visited Edgar J. Uihlein and pointed out to him the promise of resales and the necessity thereof in order to make payments under the contract.

The evidence in the record on behalf of the defendant is that Uihlein's reply was they would do everything they could and that resales were hard to make, but probably things would improve and the thing to do was to see what the developments were.

In June or July, 1933, defendant discovered for the first time that all the representations made were false and untrue. Defendant immediately called upon Uihlein, reported her findings, tendered to him her abstract and contract and said the only fair thing for him to do was to return her money, to which Uihlein replied that "his brother wanted the contract completed and did not want the lots back and did not want to make that type of adjustment." He said further that no money would be returned and suggested that she make a counter proposition. She thereupon did make such a counter proposition, namely, the letter of October 8, 1932, to accept a deed for lots to the extent of the money paid to the plaintiff by the defendant. This counter proposition was refused by Uihlein's letter of October 11, 1932, and suit was instituted in the Municipal Court of Chicago on November 16, 1932.

It also appears that during the period of the succeeding five years, each of the payments, including the payment due July 1, 1931, and a part of the payment due January 1, 1932, was made by the defendant. She was delinquent at that time in making her payments and claimed that this delinquency was due to her inability to collect sums due her. She wrote numerous letters addressed to the plaintiff. It does not appear that in any of her written communications in evidence she charged the agents with having misrepresented the property to her or with having promised to make any resale. In her last letter of October 8, 1932, in which she was seeking settlement, she did not make any reference to any such matters. The letter in substance is that she was writing it in an effort to salvage something from a contract which she felt was not going to be profitable. She started the letter by saying she was in arrears on the contract and anxious to make some adjustment of the matter, as it was impossible for her to meet money, to which Uihlein replied that "his brother wanted the contract completed and did not want the lots back and did not want to make that type of adjustment." He said further that no money would be returned and suggested that she make a counter proposition. She thereupon did make such a counter proposition, namely, the letter of October 8, 1932, to accept a deed for lots to the extent of the money paid to the plaintiff by the defendant. This counter proposition was refused by Uihlein's letter of October 11, 1932, and suit was instituted in the Municipal Court of Chicago on November 18, 1932.

It also appears that during the period of the succeeding five years, each of the payments, including the payment due July 1, 1931, and a part of the payment due January 1, 1932, was made by the defendant. She was delinquent at that time in making her payments and claimed that this delinquency was due to her inability to collect sums due her. She wrote numerous letters addressed to the plaintiff. It does not appear that in any of her written communications in evidence she charged the agents with having misrepresented the property to her or with having promised to make any resale. In her last letter of October 8, 1932, in which she was seeking settlement, she did not make any reference to any such matters. The letter in substance is that she was writing it in an effort to salvage something from a contract which she felt was not going to be profitable. She started the letter by saying she was in arrears on the contract and anxious to make some adjustment of the matter, as it was impossible for her to meet the payments of principal, interest, taxes, and assessments. She then lists her arrearage, not counting payment due August 1, 1932, and also her total payments of $11,735.29, and says:

> "Since my income is further reduced this coming year due to the non-payment of interest and principal due me, I am asking if you will be willing to deed me lots for the amount paid in and allow me to cancel the contract for the balance of the lots. This seems the only way out for me and would involve no loss for you, only the deferred sale of the balance of the property.
> I very much hope you will give this proposal favorable consideration."

The question in this litigation is largely one of fact and controlled by law in relation to fraudulent representations made at the time the defendant signed the real estate contract, and upon which contract plaintiff seeks to recover the balance of the purchase price on the lots therein described. As we have already stated in this opinion, the defense is that fraudulent representations were made by an agent of the plaintiff which induced her to sign the contract, and she therefore is making a claim on set-off against the plaintiff for the return of the part payment price made by her.

To determine the question of the right of plaintiff to recover under the issues controlled by the law germane to the question now before us, it is well to have in mind that in order to establish fraudulent representations which will avail at law or in equity, the representations complained of must have been made with respect to a material matter. They must not only have been false but even if not known to be so by the person making them at the time of being untrue, still such affirmation of what one does not know to be true is not justifiable. The

the payments of principal, interest, taxes, and assessments. She then lists her arrearage, not counting payment due August 1, 1932, and also her total payments of $11,735.39, and says:

> "Since my income is further reduced this coming year due to the non-payment of interest and principal due me, I am asking if you will be willing to deed me lots for the amount paid in and allow me to cancel the contract for the balance of the lots. This seems the only way out for me and would involve no loss for you, only the deferred sale of the balance of the property.
> I very much hope you will give this proposal favorable consideration."

The question in this litigation is largely one of fact and controlled by law in relation to fraudulent representations made at the time the defendant signed the real estate contract, and upon which contract plaintiff seeks to recover the balance of the purchase price on the lots therein described. As we have already stated in this opinion, the defense is that fraudulent representations were made by an agent of the plaintiff which induced her to sign the contract, and she therefore is making a claim on set-off against the plaintiff for the return of the part payment price made by her.

To determine the question of the right of plaintiff to recover under the issues controlled by the law germane to the question now before us, it is well to have in mind that in order to establish fraudulent representations which will avail at law or in equity, the representations complained of must have been made with respect to a material matter. They must not only have been false but even if not known to be so by the person making them at the time of being untrue, still such affirmation of what one does not know to be true is not justifiable. The representations must have been relied upon by the other party and induced him to enter into the contract sought to be set aside. Brennan v. Persselli, 353 Ill. 630.

It is also the established rule of law in this State that where parties are dealing with each other, and one makes a positive and material statement upon which the other, to his knowledge, acts, and such statement is known or should have been known to him who makes it to be false, his conduct is fraudulent and he can have no benefit therefrom; but the mere expression of an opinion as to a material fact is not equivalent to positive affirmation, and this rule is followed in the cases considered by the court.

It appears that mere expressions of opinion employed in urging or importuning another to engage or invest in any matter are regarded as mere inducement, and form no ground upon which to base fraud, and in the determination of the question of whether the plaintiff in this case is bound by reason of the fact that he did not participate in the fraudulent representations made by his agent, the rule is that one who has not participated in the perpetration of the original fraud becomes a party thereto by insisting upon availing himself of the fruits thereof. Brennan v. Persselli, 353 Ill. 630.

Now, what have we here in the way of facts such as would justify the entry of the judgment for the defendant upon her counterclaim?

The defendant entered into the contract and continued to make payments for the purchase of the lots described

therein under its terms until June or July, 1932, when she tendered to plaintiff's representative in Chicago her abstract and contract and stated to him that the only fair thing for the plaintiff to do was to return the money. However, this representative of the plaintiff suggested that she make a counter proposition, which she did at that time, namely, by the letter of October 8, 1932, in which she agreed to accept a deed for the lots to the extent of the money paid to the plaintiff by the defendant under the terms of the real estate contract. This counter proposition, however, was refused on October 11, 1932.

It is well to remember that the contract here in question was delivered to the defendant in August, 1927, and from that time she continued to make the payments required by the terms of the contract, although at times she was unable to pay promptly the amount due.

It is further to be noted that in the discussion of the facts no question is raised by the defendant as to the fairness of the price at which she contracted for the purchase of the lots. The whole question is as to whether the representations made by these agents were false and made for the purpose of inducing defendant to purchase the lots. The defendant complaint that no resales have been made of any of the lots, notwithstanding she spoke to these agents, as well as to the agent of Uihlein, in regard to resales of the property. Although the defendant contracted for the lots in 1927, she took no steps whatsoever to learn what was being done in the way of improvements, until, as she says, in 1932. There is no evidence in the

record that she was prevented from investigating and examining the property described in the contract before the signing thereof. Some objection was made to the form of the contract before it was signed, and at her suggestion this was changed, and the contract according to its terms was approved by her.

The defendant is an educated woman, and it is not claimed that she did not understand the terms of the contract, or that any advantage was taken of her because of lack of knowledge, except that it was suggested by her lawyer that she was not familiar with real estate deals. As to the fraudulent representations complained of by her, they are denied by the agents who appeared as witnesses on the trial of the case. The conflicting evidence was passed upon by the court and the jury and the question now is whether the judgment entered upon the verdict of the jury was against the manifest weight of the evidence.

Assuming that the factual evidence of the defendant in support of her set-off is true, we find that the sum paid for the lots, as well as the location, is not questioned. The purphase price of the lots was to be paid by supplemental payments, and the payments as called for were made and continued until June or July, 1932, a period of five years from the date of the contract. During all this time the defendant made no complaint regarding representations that were not true. Her only complaint was that no resales of lots were made by the plaintiff during the time the defendant was making payments.

Purchase of the lots was made evidently with the

expectation of the possible profit that might be realized through resales. The only time the defendant questioned the honesty of the transaction was, as we have stated before, in June or July, 1932, when for the first time it was claimed by the defendant that all of the representations made were false, such as the dredging of the lake, river and harbor, the building of docks and factory buildings, the improvement of 103rd Street, and the enhancement in value of the land by the influx of workmen in that locality.

Having considered the facts and applying the rules contained in this opinion, we think it is necessary that further trial be had, as from the record it appears the judgment entered is manifestly against the weight of the evidence; and, the issues having been tried before the court and a jury, we remand the case for further hearing.

We cannot, however, agree with the plaintiff's contention that the alleged false representations made to the defendant which induced her to sign the contract cannot be urged as a defense for the reason that in this contract there is a provision, which is quoted in this opinion, to the effect that the defendant did not rely upon any representations that were not contained in the contract. This question was passed upon in the case of Ginsburg v. Bartlett, 262 Ill. App. 14, contrary to plaintiff's contention, and we adhere to what we said in our opinion in that case. See also Miller v. Nydick, 254 Ill. App. 584.

For the reasons indicated in this opinion, the judgment here for the defendant upon her set-off is reversed and the cause is remanded for retrial.

REVERSED AND REMANDED.

HALL, P. J. AND
DENIS E. SULLIVAN, J. CONCUR.

38560

LILLIAN M. MARTIN,
Appellee,

vs.

AMANDA K. STRUBEL, ET AL.,
Appellants.

APPEAL FROM CIRCUIT COURT COOK COUNTY.

19 H

286 I.A. 606[1]

MR. JUSTICE HEBEL DELIVERED THE OPINION OF THE COURT:

This is an appeal by Amanda K. Strubel and Clarence J. Strubel, defendants, from a decree entered by the court in a foreclosure proceeding filed by the plaintiff. In this decree of foreclosure the court finds that certain promissory notes were signed by the defendants, which were on the date thereof, for value received, delivered to the plaintiff, who became the owner of the notes; that there is due the plaintiff upon the principal and interest notes the sum of $8,168.93, and adding to this amount $73 allowed to the Chicago Title and Trust Co. for minutes of title, $10.15 for stenographer's fee, and $600 for attorney's fees, makes a total sum of $8,852.08.

No questions are raised as to the pleadings, and only two errors have been called to our attention; namely, that the court erred in allowing the sum of $73, which was paid to the Chicago Title and Trust Company for minutes of title to the property in question, and in allowing the plaintiff's attorney the sum of $600 for services rendered in the preparation of the pleadings and in the trial of the litigation in this foreclosure proceeding.

The principal point made by these defendants in regard to the bill of $73 paid to the Chicago Title and Trust Company is that the amount was paid for services rendered as attorney and that this Company was not qualified to act in that capacity, citing in support of this proposition the case of People v. Motorists Association, 354 Ill. 595, and The People v. Real Estate Tax-payers in the same volume, page 102. These authorities support the general rule that no corporation can be licensed to practice law, whether the corporation was organized for profit or not for profit. From an examination of the record we find the evidence is that the Chicago Title and Trust Company furnished minutes showing the state of the title to this property, which were used for the purpose of preparing the bill to foreclose in this case. Counsel for the plaintiff was not retained by this Company to appear for it in the foreclosure matter, and from the authorities cited by the defendants it must appear that the Company was organized for the purpose of furnishing lawyers to act for members of the association in matters in which they were retained to carry on. Such is not the case in the matter now pending here on appeal.

It is generally known that the Chicago Title and Trust Company furnishes minutes to practicing attorneys who prepare bills to foreclose, showing the condition of the title to the property involved in the litigation, but we are unable to find from this record that the Chicago Title and Trust Company holds itself out as furnishing lawyers for the purpose of taking care of litigation.

The remaining question is whether the solicitor's fees allowed by the court were excessive. It is to be noted that

the defendants did not offer any evidence, and the only evidence in the record upon which the court may determine the amount to be allowed is that of the plaintiff in her foreclosure proceeding. The amount allowed and fixed in the decree was $600, so that we are unable to say from this record that the amount is exorbitant, when we consider the services rendered by plaintiff's attorney in this foreclosure proceeding. We have had no assistance from the defendants, as they offered no evidence as to what would be a reasonable amount, and viewing the evidence as the trial court did, we are of the opinion that the amount allowed is not unreasonable.

For the reasons stated the decree is affirmed.

DECREE AFFIRMED.

HALL, P. J. AND
DENIS E. SULLIVAN, J. CONCUR.

20 A

38485

THE LIVE STOCK NATIONAL BANK OF CHICAGO, a Corp., Administrator of the Estate of James J. Drymiller, deceased,
Appellee,

v.

ALBERT HILBERG, et al., On Appeal of ALBERT HILBERG,
Appellant.

APPEAL FROM SUPERIOR COURT, COOK COUNTY.

286 I.A. 606[2]

MR. JUSTICE DENIS E. SULLIVAN DELIVERED THE OPINION OF THE COURT.

This is an appeal from a verdict and judgment entered in the Superior Court of Cook County for $10,000 against the defendant Albert Hilberg, because of an automobile collision which resulted in the death of James J. Drymiller. It is claimed that the accident occurred due to the negligence on the part of the defendant through his agent James Paul Richter, who was driving what was claimed to be defendant's automobile when it collided with the automobile driven by James J. Drymiller. The accident occurred on July 7, 1933, at the intersection of Milwaukee avenue and the River road in Cook County, Illinois.

It appears from the evidence that Drymiller, the deceased, was driving a Ford automobile north on the River road and that his family was with him in the automobile; that when he approached Milwaukee avenue he stopped at the south side of the intersection, there being a stop light at that point; that whilst the Ford automobile was at a standstill, another automobile, a LaSalle, was being driven by James Paul Richter, claimed to be an agent of A. W. Hilberg, the defendant, in a southeasterly direction on Milwaukee avenue; that said Richter while so driving turned said automobile off Milwaukee avenue in a southerly direction and on to the right hand lane of

traffic of the River road and collided with the automobile of James J. Drymiller, as a result of which Drymiller was killed; that James Paul Richter, the driver of defendant's car, was also killed.

The contention of Albert Hilberg, the defendant, is that he was the business representative of the International Union of Operating Engineers, Local 150; that James Paul Richter was a subordinate employee of the same union; that the union is a voluntary association and is not liable for the torts of its agents.

The evidence shows that Hilberg was paid a salary and had an oral agreement with this unincorporated union to be their business representative; that he acted as a sort of arbitrator between contractors and union members and if any of the men had grievances he was to settle their differences, - in a general way looking out for the men and the union; that he was never told to hire a man or not to hire one; that if the men sent in their dues and wanted to send their due books to him he would pick them up and take them to the office.

Richter, the driver of defendant's automobile, had been a former member of the union and had been in the habit of going with the defendant on business trips. On the day of the accident the defendant was in Lake County and had to go over to a village in McHenry County; that he instructed Richter to take the LaSalle automobile and drive to Chicago and pick up some due books which were at his home and to meet him at Maywood; that he gave Richter $5.00 with which to buy gas and oil and he gave him an extra dollar in case he had a puncture. The defendant stated that he always gave Richter money to take care of whatever was needed for the automobile; that he occasionally gave Richter a dollar or so and while on these trips would pay for his meals and lodging. The defendant said that he sent Richter to pick up the books on the day of the accident "to

save me a trip back to my house so I could save time coming down here to the loop." The defendant further stated that Richter was not on the union payroll; that he, the defendant, had the privilege of hiring and discharging anybody that he wanted to.

Plaintiff contends that Hilberg was not an employee of the union, but that he was an independent contractor. The evidence shows no instructions were given to him and that he had no specific work except to look after the interests of the men, using his own judgment as to how he should perform his work.

In the case of Besse v. Industrial Commission, et al, 336 Ill. 283, at page 285, the court said:

> "One who contracts to do a specific piece of work and hires and controls his assistants and executes the work entirely in accordance with his own ideas or with a plan previously given him by the person for whom the work is done, without being subject to the latter's orders in respect to the details of the work, is not a servant or employee but is an independent contractor. * * * An independent contractor is one who renders service in the course of an occupation representing the will of the person for whom the work is done only as to the result of the work and not as to the means by which it is accomplished. * * * The right to control the manner of doing the work is an important consideration in determining whether the worker is an employee or an independent contractor."

In Ferguson & Lange Co. v. The Industrial Commission, 346 Ill. 632, at page 635, the court said:

> "It is impossible to lay down a rule by which the status of a person performing a service for another can be definitely fixed as an employee or as an independent contractor. Ordinarily no single feature of the relation is determinative but all must be considered together. (Bristol & Gale Co. v. Industrial Com. 292 Ill. 16). An independent contractor has been defined as one who renders service in the course of an occupation and represents the will of the person for whom the work is done only with respect to the result and not the means by which that result is accomplished. (Hartley v. Red Ball Transit Co., 344 Ill. 534; Lutheran Hospital v. Industrial Com. 342 id. 325."

In this case the defendant was not under the control of any one. He was the business representative of the defendant's

union, in control of his own time as to when, where and how the same was spent and apparently not responsible but for results. Hilberg had exclusive control of the automobile and the evidence does not show that the union in any way directed or controlled in what manner the automobile should be used; that in a legal sense he was an independent contractor and his hiring of the driver was an individual responsibility of his own and not that of the union. Trust v. Chicago Motor Club, 276 Ill. App. 289, 298 and 300; Burster v. National Refining Co. 274 Ill. App. 104, and cases cited. We think under the evidence and the law applicable thereto that Richter, the driver of the LaSalle automobile, was the agent of Hilberg.

It is contended by defendant that the manifest weight of the evidence shows that Drymiller drove into Milwaukee avenue without stopping at the stop sign and was guilty of negligence which proximately caused the accident, and that the beneficiary, Drymiller's widow, was also negligent at the time, and that Richter was free from fault.

As usually happens in cases of this kind, witnesses testifying in relation to the accident gave varying statements with regard to what took place. We think that the statements of the witnesses who testified on behalf of plaintiff as to the physical condition of the automobiles after the accident, both as to the position of the automobile in which Drymiller was riding and as to the side of the automobile which was damaged, tend to prove that Richter who was driving the LaSalle automobile on Milwaukee avenue in a southeasterly direction, suddenly swerved on to the River road, striking the automobile in which Drymiller and his family were seated, while their automobile was standing still, and that the negligence of the said Richter was the proximate cause of the accident

which resulted in Drymiller's death. It is such a case of conflicting evidence that a jury is particularly well fitted to determine wherein lies the truth of the testimony and the weight to be accorded the same.

Defendant's claim that the wife of Drymiller as a beneficiary of his estate was guilty of contributory negligence and consequently cannot recover in this action. The evidence is that she was sitting in the car with the rest of her family when Richter, driving the LaSalle car, suddenly swerved from Milwaukee avenue and struck the Ford car and killed her husband. She was in the exercise of due care and certainly nothing she did or failed to do contributed to the death of her husband.

We think the jury was properly instructed and that no error was committed either in the giving or the refusal of instructions. The cause was tried before a court and jury and we think the trial judge and the jury who saw the witnesses and heard them testify, were in a much better position to judge as to their credibility than is a court of review.

There being no prejudicial error and for the reasons herein given, the judgment of the Superior Court is hereby affirmed.

JUDGMENT AFFIRMED.

HALL, P.J. AND HEBEL, J. CONCUR.

38540

ISABELLE BARGER,
Appellee,
v.
NATIONAL PAINT & WALL PAPER COMPANY, a corporation,
Appellant.

APPEAL FROM CIRCUIT COURT, COOK COUNTY.

24 A

286 I.A. 606[3]

MR. JUSTICE DENIS E. SULLIVAN DELIVERED THE OPINION OF THE COURT.

This is an appeal from the Circuit Court of Cook County, wherein a judgment for $22,500 was entered in favor of plaintiff, Isabelle Barger, for personal injuries sustained by her through claimed negligence of the defendant, National Paint & Wall Paper Company.

Plaintiff's complaint alleges that on May 18, 1933, she was struck by a truck owned and operated by the defendant at or near the southeast corner of Crawford and Armitage avenues in the City of Chicago, while she was in the exercise of due care and caution for her own safety and was attempting to cross the street; that defendant's servant drove the truck past a standing street car and that said truck was so constructed that the body of the truck projected two feet; that the space between the standing street car and the east curb of Crawford avenue did not exceed 13 feet; that defendant's servant in carelessly and negligently driving said truck between the standing street car and said curb caused the projection of the body of said truck to strike the plaintiff.

The answer denied that plaintiff was in the exercise of ordinary care for her own safety and the charges of negligence made by the plaintiff.

Plaintiff's theory of the case is that the driver of defendant's motor truck attempted to pass a northbound Crawford avenue street car and struck plaintiff while she was on the south crosswalk of Crawford avenue.

38540

ISABELLE BERGER,
Appellee,
v.
NATIONAL PAINT & WALL PAPER
COMPANY, a corporation,
Appellant.

APPEAL FROM
CIRCUIT COURT,
COOK COUNTY.

286 I.A. 606

MR. JUSTICE DENIS E. SULLIVAN DELIVERED THE OPINION OF THE COURT.

This is an appeal from the Circuit Court of Cook County, wherein a judgment for $32,500 was entered in favor of plaintiff, Isabelle Berger, for personal injuries claimed sustained by her through the negligence of the defendant, National Paint & Wall Paper Company.

Plaintiff's complaint alleges that on May 10, 1933, she was struck by a truck owned and operated by the defendant at or near the southeast corner of Crawford and Armitage avenues in the City of Chicago, while she was in the exercise of due care and caution for her own safety and was attempting to cross the street; that defendant's servant drove the truck past a standing street car and that said truck was so constructed that the body of the truck projected two feet; that the space between the standing street car and the east curb of Crawford avenue did not exceed 13 feet; that defendant's servant in carelessly and negligently driving said truck between the standing street car and said curb caused the projection of the body of said truck to strike the plaintiff.

The answer denied that plaintiff was in the exercise of ordinary care for her own safety and the charges of negligence made by the plaintiff.

Plaintiff's theory of the case is that the driver of defendant's motor truck attempted to pass a northbound Crawford avenue street car and struck plaintiff while she was on the south crosswalk of Crawford avenue.

Defendant's theory of the case is that plaintiff was directly and solely responsible for the accident; that at the time its truck started up the traffic light was green for north and south traffic; that no cars were parked at the east curb, permitting one to pass the street car as there was ample space; that plaintiff was not on the crosswalk nor in the street; that plaintiff had just purchased a newspaper and was looking at it and proceeded westward, took a step off the curb into defendant's truck as it was passing, coming in contact with the truck just back of the cab on the right-hand side.

No error is assigned as to the pleadings.

Byron G. Gremley, a witness called on behalf of the plaintiff, testified that he was a surveyor and that he was familiar with Crawford avenue, now known as Pulaski Road, at its intersection with Armitage avenue; that both streets are approximately 40 feet in width; that the former street runs north and south and the latter runs east and west; that there are street car tracks for traffic in each street; that the distance from the east rail of the northbound street car track on Crawford avenue to the curbstone is 14 feet and there are stop and go lights on the four corners of this intersection; that the stop light at the southeast corner is located approximately 9 1/2 feet west of the east building line of Crawford avenue and 6 feet 3½ inches south of the south building line of Armitage avenue; that the south crosswalk of Armitage avenue from Crawford avenue is 7 feet north of the stop and go sign, and that it is indicated by a raised gutter and the distance to the east edge is 6 inches; that the east curb is 12 inches high and 3 inches above the surface of the crosswalk at the center; that the crosswalk rises from the street as it approaches the edge of the gutter; that it has a rise of about 9 inches from a point a foot south of the south curb of Armitage avenue to the center of the walk.

Defendant's theory of the case is that plaintiff was directly and solely responsible for the accident; that at the time its truck started up the traffic light was green for north and south traffic; that no cars were parked at the east curb, permitting one to pass the street car as there was ample space; that plaintiff was not on the crosswalk nor in the street; that plaintiff had just purchased a newspaper and was looking at it and proceeded westward, took a step off the curb into defendant's truck as it was passing, coming in contact with the truck just back of the cab on the right-hand side.

No error is assigned as to the pleadings.

Byron G. Gremley, a witness called on behalf of the plaintiff, testified that he was a surveyor and that he was familiar with Crawford avenue, now known as Pulaski Road, at its intersection with Armitage avenue; that both streets are approximately 40 feet in width; that the former street runs north and south and the latter runs east and west; that there are street car tracks for traffic in each street; that the distance from the east rail of the northbound street car track on Crawford avenue to the curbstone is 14 feet and there are stop and go lights on the four corners of this intersection; that the stop light at the southeast corner is located approximately 3 1/2 feet west of the east building line of Crawford avenue and 6 feet 2½ inches south of the south building line of Armitage avenue; that the south crosswalk of Armitage avenue from Crawford avenue is 7 feet north of the stop and go sign, and that it is indicated by a raised gutter and the distance to the east edge is 6 inches; that the east curb is 12 inches high and 3 inches above the surface of the crosswalk at the center; that the crosswalk rises from the street as it approaches the edge of the gutter; that it has a rise of about 8 inches from a point a foot south of the south curb of Armitage avenue to the center of the walk.

Plaintiff testified that on the day of the accident she left her home at 1817 North Crawford avenue about 8 o'clock in the morning to go to her work at Mandel Brothers where she was employed as a saleslady; that she was 32 years old at the time of the accident and had been previously married; that she usually boarded a northbound Crawford avenue street car at Bloomingdale road and rode two blocks north to Armitage avenue, where she would board an eastbound street car for downtown; that the intersection in question is a business area; that on the morning of the accident she got off the Crawford avenue street car and walked over to the newsstand located on the southeast corner of Crawford and Armitage avenues and bought a newspaper; that she intended to take the eastbound Armitage avenue street car; that in order to get that street car she would have to cross Crawford avenue; that the newsstand faced south and while buying the paper she was facing north; that after she bought the newspaper she started to cross the street and had one foot off the curb when she saw a truck swing from behind the street car and that she stopped and cannot remember anything that happened after that until ten or twelve days after the accident when she regained consciousness while in the West Suburban Hospital where she had been taken; that her right arm was numb and that she could not use it and her right side was sore; that one eye was bandaged and that she could see faintly out of the other; that her teeth were all loose; and at the time of the trial she was having a plate made; that the vision of her left eye is completely gone; that her right leg was paralyzed and that her left side is paralyzed; that she always has to have someone with her; that her shoulder comes out of the socket and she has difficulty when combing her hair.

Paul Abraham, the motorman who was operating the northbound Crawford avenue street car at the time of the accident, testified that he recalled the occurrence; that when he got the bell to go

Plaintiff testified that on the day of the accident she left her home at 1817 North Crawford avenue about 8 o'clock in the morning to go to her work at Mandel Brothers where she was employed as a saleslady; that she was 32 years old at the time of the accident and had been previously married; that she usually boarded a northbound Crawford avenue street car at Bloomingdale road and rode two blocks north to Armitage avenue, where she would board an eastbound street car for downtown; that the intersection in question is a business area; that on the morning of the accident she got off the Crawford avenue street car and walked over to the newsstand located on the southeast corner of Crawford and Armitage avenues and bought a newspaper; that she intended to take the eastbound Armitage avenue street car; that in order to get that street car she would have to cross Crawford avenue; that the newsstand faced south and while buying the paper she was facing north; that after she bought the newspaper she started to cross the street and had one foot off the curb when she saw a truck swing from behind the street car and that she stopped and cannot remember anything that happened after that until ten or twelve days after the accident when she regained consciousness while in the West Suburban Hospital where she had been taken; that her right arm was numb and that she could not use it and her right side was sore; that one eye was bandaged and that she could see faintly out of the other; that her teeth were all loose; and at the time of the trial she was having a plate made; that the vision of her left eye is completely gone; that her right leg was paralyzed and that her left side is paralyzed; that she always has to have someone with her; that her shoulder comes out of the socket and she has difficulty when combing her hair.

Paul Abraham, the motorman who was operating the northbound Crawford avenue street car at the time of the accident, testified that he recalled the occurrence; that when he got the bell to go ahead and started on the green light he got to the north side of Armitage avenue when he got the stop signal from the conductor; that the front end of the street car was about fifty feet or so past the north curbstone of Armitabe avenue; that between the time he started and received the signal to stop he saw the truck on his right side.

Charles E. Jelinek, a witness called on behalf of plaintiff, testified that on the day of the accident he was seated on the east side of a northbound Cfawford avenue street car and witnessed the accident; that the car was waiting for the green light and as it started up a truck flashed by hitting the plaintiff and knocking her into Armitage avenue and cutting the street car off about in the middle of the intersection, stopping about 100 feet north of the corner; that when he first saw plaintiff she was about a foot off the sidewalk; that the truck was an open stake truck and that the side of the truck away from him hit her; that when the street car came to a jar stop he got off and saw the body lying on the eastbound Armitage avenue car track, right off the corner.

Don Barger, a brother of the plaintiff, testified that after the accident he saw the truck that hit plaintiff and that there was blood on the truck right behind the driver's cab on the side of the body.

Joseph L. Hodgins, called as a witness in behalf of defendant, testified that he was a chauffeur for the defendant and on the day of the accident was driving a Ford stake body truck which had a wheel base of 131½ inches and that the widest part of the truck was 72 inches; that he had been following a northbound Crawford avenue street car and that upon reaching Armitage avenue the street car stopped and he stopped and he brought his truck between the curb and the tracks on the east side of the tracks; that the rear end of the street car was about eight to ten feet from the front end of the truck; that he stopped there for the lights to change from red to green; that

at the time the street car started up the light was green and that he started with his truck in first speed and was going along close to the street car; that he was only two or two and a half feet away from the street car; that as he passed over the crosswalk he heard a bump some place behind the cab on the right side; that he pulled over to the north side of Armitage avenue so as to clear the traffic and looked back and saw a woman lying in the street; that when he stopped his truck was ahead of the street car. Hodgins further testifying denied that he cut over in front of the street car from the time he started up until he came to a stop after the accident.

Leo Pasowicz, a witness called in behalf of defendant, stated that on the day of the accident he was standing on the corner of Crawford and Armitage avenues near the newsstand; that plaintiff was buying a newspaper and that she looked down at it and started to walk towards the west side of the street and walked into the side of the truck.

William Steele, a witness called on behalf of defendant, testified that on the day of the accident he had a newsstand at the southeast corner of Armitage and Crawford avenues; that he had been selling papers there for about a year or a year and a half; that plaintiff bought a paper from him on the morning of the accident and that she started toward the curb and the lights changed for "go" and just as she stepped off this truck was coming by and she walked right into the side of it.

It is claimed that the evidence does not sustain the judgment; that the court erred as to the instructions given and refused; that the conduct of the attorney for the plaintiff was highly improper and prejudicial to defendant; that the court erred in the exclusion of certain evidence offered by defendant.

As to the first assignment of error; As usual in this type of case, the statements made by the witnesses are conflicting. The

evidence tends to show that the body of the truck in question was more than six feet wide and extended out on each side of the front of the cab; that it struck the plaintiff and injured her. While some of the witnesses stated that plaintiff walked into the truck and was thereby guilty of contributory negligence, others testified that she had just stepped from the curb when the lights changed and that before she could retrace her step to the sidewalk, the truck suddenly dashed from behind the street car and struck her before she could reach a zone of safety. In this case the jury was in a position to weigh the evidence and judge as to the credibility of the witnesses and we believe there is sufficient evidence to sustain their verdict. The question of contributory negligence is settled by the verdict of the jury.

As Mr. Justice Wilson said in the case of Hill v. Richardson 281 Ill. App. 75, in quoting from the case of Cleveland C. C. & St. L. Ry. Co. v. Keenan, 190 Ill. 217;

> "The question whether Kerr was guilty of contributory negligence was a question of fact to be passed upon by the jury, and while the burden of proof was upon the plaintiff to show that Kerr was in the exercise of due care for his own safety, it did not devolve upon him to establish such due care by direct and positive testimony, but such due care might be inferred from all the circumstances shown to exist immediately prior to and at the time of the injury, and in determining such question the jury might properly take into consideration the instincts prompting to the preservation of life and avoidance of danger. (Terre Haute and Indianapolis Railroad Co. v. Voelker, 129 Ill. 540; Illinois Central Railroad Co. v. Nowicki, 148 id. 29; Baltimore and Ohio Southwestern Railway Co. v. Then, 159 id. 535."

In the case of Gore v. O'Keefe Bros. Co. 280 Ill. App. 163, the court at page 165, said:

> "It is urged that defendant was not negligent and that plaintiff was guilty of contributory negligence. Both these questions are settled by the verdict of the jury."

It is claimed that error was committed by the court in the giving of the following instruction:

"The driver of an automobile is bound to anticipate that at public street intersections or crossings people may be crossing said streets and is bound to keep a proper lookout for them and to use ordinary care to keep his machine under such control as will enable him to avoid a collision with a pedestrian rightfully upon said street and in the exercise of due care and caution for his safety, and, if necessary, he must slow up and even stop. In other words, he must use all the care and caution which an ordinarily careful and prudent driver would have exercised under the same circumstances, and if you believe from the evidence in this cause that the driver of the automobile saw the plaintiff or by the exercise of due care could have seen the plaintiff and had a full view of the situation before the accident, and by the exercise of reasonable and ordinary care could have avoided and prevented the injury; and if you further believe from the evidence that he failed to exercise such care and in consequence of the want of such reasonable care, if you believe from the evidence there was any want of reasonable care on his part, the plaintiff received the injuries complained of, then you should find the defendant guilty provided you further believe from the evidence that the plaintiff was in the exercise of due care and caution for her own safety at and just prior to the time of the accident in question."

We cannot say that this instruction is subject to the criticism or to the construction insisted upon by the defendant. We do not believe this instruction could be construed as saying that the plaintiff was rightfully upon the street or that there was an obligation upon the defendant's driver to stop. Rather, we think it merely points out that if the driver of an automobile sees a person at a street intersection, where people usually are when attempting to cross a street, it is the duty of the driver to use reasonable care to avoid hitting that person. The instruction complained of was one of a series of instructions given and as the Supreme Court said in the case of Reivitz v. Chicago Rapid Transit Co., 327 Ill. 207, at page 213:

"The office of instructions is to give information to the jury concerning the law of the case for immediate application to the subject matter before them. The test, then, is not what meaning the ingenuity of counsel can at leisure attribute to the instructions, but how and in what sense, under the evidence before them and the circumstances of the trial, ordinary men acting as jurors will understand the instructions. (Chicago Union Traction Co. v. Lowenrosen, 222 Ill. 506; Funk v. Babbitt, 156 id. 408.)"

Complaint is made to that part of the instruction in which the court explains to the jury the declaration and what it contains. We have held this to be proper practice. As was said in the case of Central Ry. Co. v. Bannister, 195 Ill. 48, at page 49:

> "Had the instructions copied the allegations no objection could have been urged to them."

See also West Chicago R. R. Co. v. Lieserowitz, 197 Ill. 607, 610. The part of the instruction criticised by defendant, reads:

> "It is charged in the fourth count of plaintiff's complaint that on said date both of said avenues, to-wit, Crawford avenue and Armitage avenue, passed through a closely built up business portion of the said City of Chicago, and said defendant then and there carelessly and negligently drove and operated its said automobile truck northward along said Crawford avenue and over said intersection and through said closely built up business portion of the City of Chicago at a rate of speed which was greater than was reasonable and proper, having regard to the traffic and the use of the way, so as to endanger the life or limb or to injure the property or any person on said public highway and at a rate of speed in excess of fifteen miles per hour, contrary to and in violation of the statute of the State of Illinois in such case made and provided, and that as a direct and proximate result of the negligence of said defendant, said automobile truck struck the plaintiff violently throwing her into the air and causing her to fall violently to and upon the pavement of Armitage avenue."

Defendant contends that this instruction is erroneous in that it tells the jury that a rate of speed in excess of 15 miles an hour is contrary to and in violation of the statute of the State of Illinois. We do not construe this instruction as telling the jury anything about the speed. The court was merely telling the jury what was contained in the fourth count of plaintiff's complaint. If this statement was improperly in one of the counts of the complaint, it should have been eliminated on a motion by defendant to strike before the hearing. Defendant having seen fit to permit it to remain in the complaint, we do not think it was error for the trial judge to tell the jury, among other things, what the declaration contained.

Complaint is made to that part of the instruction in which the court explains to the jury the declaration and what it contains. We have held this to be proper practice. As was said in the case of Central Ry. Co. v. Bannister, 195 Ill. 48, at page 49:

"Had the instructions copied the allegations no objection could have been urged to them."

See also West Chicago R. R. Co. v. Lieserowitz, 197 Ill. 607, 610.

The part of the instruction criticised by defendant, reads:

"It is charged in the fourth count of plaintiff's complaint that on said date both of said avenues, to-wit, Crawford avenue and Armitage avenue, passed through a closely built up business portion of the said City of Chicago, and said defendant then and there carelessly and negligently drove and operated its said automobile truck northward along said Crawford avenue and over said intersection and through said closely built up business portion of the City of Chicago at a rate of speed which was greater than was reasonable and proper, having regard to the traffic and the use of the way, so as to endanger the life or limb or to injure the property of any person on said public highway and at a rate of speed in excess of fifteen miles per hour, contrary to and in violation of the statute of the State of Illinois in such case made and provided, and that as a direct and proximate result of the negligence of said defendant, said automobile truck struck the plaintiff violently throwing her into the air and causing her to fall violently to and upon the pavement of Armitage avenue."

Defendant contends that this instruction is erroneous in that it tells the jury that a rate of speed in excess of 15 miles an hour is contrary to and in violation of the statute of the State of Illinois. We do not construe this instruction as telling the jury anything about the speed. The court was merely telling the jury what was contained in the fourth count of plaintiff's complaint. If this statement was improperly in one of the counts of the complaint, it should have been eliminated on a motion by defendant to strike before the hearing. Defendant having seen fit to permit it to remain in the complaint, we do not think it was error for the trial judge to tell the jury, among other things, what the declaration contained.

Further objection is made to the instruction in that it uses the language of the pleader. We do not think in that respect that error was committed.

Defendant further complains that the trial court erred in refusing certain instructions. We do not think error was committed in this regard as the subject-matter of these instructions was fully covered by other instructions given and the defendant's contention fairly presented to the jury.

It is next contended by the defendant that the conduct of the attorney for the plaintiff was improper and prejudicial. We have examined the abstract in this regard and we are unable to find that defendant's contention is sustained by anything contained therein. The court properly ruled on the objections that were made and the record is free from error in this regard.

It is further claimed that error was committed in sustaining objections to the offer of proof by the witness Glene Steele; that it was stated she would testify as to what her son Willie Steele told her about the accident when he came home out of the presence of the plaintiff. We think the court rightfully sustained the objection to this evidence.

No error was assigned as to the extent of the injuries sustained by plaintiff nor as to the amount of the verdict, so we will not refer to them except to state that from the injuries sustained, the amount allowed by the jury does not appear to be excessive.

For the reasons herein given the judgment of the Circuit Court is affirmed.

JUDGMENT AFFIRMED.

HALL, P.J. AND HEBEL, J. CONCUR.

Further objection is made to the instruction in that it uses the language of the pleader. We do not think in that respect that error was committed.

Defendant further complains that the trial court erred in refusing certain instructions. We do not think error was committed in this regard as the subject-matter of these instructions was fully covered by other instructions given and the defendant's contention fairly presented to the jury.

It is next contended by the defendant that the conduct of the attorney for the plaintiff was improper and prejudicial. We have examined the abstract in this regard and we are unable to find that defendant's contention is sustained by anything contained therein. The court properly ruled on the objections that were made and the record is free from error in this regard.

It is further claimed that error was committed in sustaining objections to the offer of proof by the witness Olene Steele; that it was stated she would testify as to what her son Willie Steele told her about the accident when he came home out of the presence of the plaintiff. We think the court rightfully sustained the objection to this evidence.

No error was assigned as to the extent of the injuries sustained by plaintiff nor as to the amount of the verdict, so we will not refer to them except to state that from the injuries sustained, the amount allowed by the jury does not appear to be excessive.

For the reasons herein given the judgment of the Circuit Court is affirmed.

JUDGMENT AFFIRMED.

HALL, P.J. AND HEBEL, J. CONCUR.

38626

MARY SCHALLER,
Appellee,

v.

METROPOLITAN LIFE INSURANCE COMPANY,
Appellant.

APPEAL FROM CIRCUIT COURT, COOK COUNTY.

22

286 I.A. 6064

MR. JUSTICE DENIS E. SULLIVAN delivered the opinion of the court.

This is an appeal from the Circuit Court wherein a judgment for $2,000 was entered on the verdict of a jury in favornof the plaintiff Mary Schaller, named as beneficiary, and against the defendant Metropolitan Life Insurance Company, upon a group insurance policy issued by the defendant on the life of Abel Schaller, husband of the plaintiff.

Plaintiff's theory of the case is that Abel Schaller was employed at the time of his death and the defendant's claim is that the insurance on the life of Abel Schaller was canceled almost three months prior to his death and that his certificate was not in force when he died. No question is raised upon the pleadings.

The proof shows that on or about May 1, 1931, the policy of insurance here sued upon was issued by defendant to Abel Schaller, wherein his wife, who is the plaintiff here, was named as beneficiary and that the said Abel Schaller died on April 27, 1934.

From the evidence it appears that Abel Schaller was a carpenter and for many years worked for the Becker-Ryan and Company store, a branch of Sears, Roebuck and Company. The

38838

MARY SCHALLER,
Appellee,

v.

METROPOLITAN LIFE INSURANCE COMPANY,
Appellant.

APPEAL FROM CIRCUIT COURT, COOK COUNTY.

286 I.A. 606[4]

MR. JUSTICE DENIS E. SULLIVAN delivered the opinion of the court.

This is an appeal from the Circuit Court wherein a judgment for $2,000 was entered on the verdict of a jury in favor of the plaintiff Mary Schaller, named as beneficiary, and against the defendant Metropolitan Life Insurance Company, upon a group insurance policy issued by the defendant on the life of Abel Schaller, husband of the plaintiff.

Plaintiff's theory of the case is that Abel Schaller was employed at the time of his death and the defendant's claim is that the insurance on the life of Abel Schaller was canceled almost three months prior to his death and that his certificate was not in force when he died. No question is raised upon the pleadings.

The proof shows that on or about May 1, 1931, the policy of insurance here sued upon was issued by defendant to Abel Schaller, wherein his wife, who is the plaintiff here, was named as beneficiary and that the said Abel Schaller died on April 27, 1934.

From the evidence it appears that Abel Schaller was a carpenter and for many years worked for the Becker-Ryan and Company store, a branch of Sears, Roebuck and Company. The

Becker-Ryan and Company store closed and as a result thereof Schaller, the insured, did no work from February 5, 1934 to March 20, 1934; that from March 20, 1934 to April 25, 1934, excepting the first week of April, 1934, he worked for Sears, Roebuck and Company at two of their several stores and worked for them on April 25, 1934, the day on which he received the fatal injury from which he died two days later.

Defendant contends that when Abel Schaller ceased working on February 5, 1934, and came back to work on March 20, 1934, that he was a new employee and defendant further contends that the money he received between the dates when he was laid off was not regular compensation.

There appears to be no question that Schaller, although ostensibly employed by Becker-Ryan and Company, was in reality an employee of Sears, Roebuck and Company and that they were one and the same employer. The certificate of insurance described Schaller as an employee of Sears, Roebuck and Company and it is admitted that Becker-Ryan and Company was operated by Sears, Roebuck and Company.

It is further contended by defendant that Abel Schaller was not eligible for insurance because the insurance policy provides that in no case shall any employee be eligible until he has completed six months of service and is then actively at work on full time and for full pay. This contention is based on the clause of the policy which reads as follows:

> "Eligibility - All employees except those excluded below, who are actively at work on full time and for full pay on the effective date of the policy and those employees then absent upon their return to active work, and new employees shall be eligible for insurance hereunder - except that in no case shall any
> ~~(present or future new)~~
> (future new) Employee be eligible until
> he has completed six months of continuous service and is then actively at work on full time and for full pay."

Another clause of the policy that bears upon the relation of Schaller and Sears, Roebuck and Company, reads as follows:

> "Lay-off or leave of absence of three (3) months or less shall not be considered, and retirement on pension shall not be considered a termination of employment within the meaning of this policy unless notification to the contrary shall have been given by the Employer to the Company within thirty-one (31) days after the date when such lay-off, leave of absence or retirement shall have commenced."

It is further contended by the defendant that the report of Sears, Roebuck and Company to the defendant insurance company shows that Abel Schaller was dropped from the roll of employees. It does not appear from the evidence, however, that the defendant received any notice that Sears, Roebuck and Company had finally discharged Schaller from their employ. The records of Sears, Roebuck and Company on the question of notice to the insurance company were excluded by the court and the defendant has not assigned error because of this exclusion.

It is contended here that the premium was not paid on the policy in question. No such defense was set up in the answer of the defendant and, as this is an affirmative defense, evidence concerning the same could not be presented unless it was affirmatively alleged in the pleadings. Smith-Hurd's Rev. Stat., Chapter 110, Par. 157; Benes v. Bankers Life Ins. Co., 282 Ill. 236; Union Trust Co. v. Chicago, etc., Ins. Co. 267 Ill. App. 470.

In this case it appears that the main issue to be decided is as to whether or not the evidence shows that the employment of the deceased permanently terminated on February 5, 1934, and that notice thereof was given by the company as provided by

the policy. Whatever the company's intention was, it finally developed that plaintiff's leave was but temporary because he later resumed his duties with them. The policy provides that a "lay-off or leave of absence of three (3) months or less shall not be considered, and retirement on pension shall not be considered a termination of employment within the meaning of this policy unless notification to the contrary shall have been given by the Employer***" As heretofore stated, no notification was given and the defendant produced no notice which had been received by it.

We think the jury properly found from the evidence that the deceased was an employee of Sears, Roebuck and Company at the time of his death and, therefore, his rights were not forfeited under the terms of the policy.

Complaint is further made that the court committed error in refusing the instructions offered by the defendant, the effect of which would have been to instruct the jury to find for the defendant. The instructions that were given on behalf of defendant presented the law fairly to the jury and we do not think that in refusing the instructions complained of the court committed error. The remaining assignment of errors not having been argued will not be considered here.

We are of the opinion that the evidence clearly shows that at the time of his death the defendant was an employee of Sears, Roebuck and Company and, although his work had been interrupted on account of the Becker-Ryan and Company store having been closed, yet he could not have been considered as a new employee as no application was required of him for the purpose of obtaining work and he was still insured under the policy inasmuch as the insurance company had received no notice to the contrary.

For the reasons above set forth the judgment of the Circuit Court is hereby affirmed.

JUDGMENT AFFIRMED.

HALL, P.J. AND HEBEL, J. CONCUR.

38729

ALEX and PEARL LEVINSON, Plaintiffs,
Appellees,
v.
HARRY L. TIRSWAY, Defendants,

HARRY L. TIRSWAY, Plaintiff,
For the use of ALEX AND PEARL LEVINSON,
Appellees,
v.
CONSOER TOWNSEND & QUINLAN, INC., a corporation, Garnishee below,
Appellant.

APPEAL FROM MUNICIPAL COURT OF CHICAGO.

2317

286 I.A. 607[1]

MR. JUSTICE DENIS E. SULLIVAN DELIVERED THE OPINION OF THE COURT.

This is an appeal from the Municipal Court wherein a judgment was entered in an attachment and garnishment suit against a nonresident defendant and a resident garnishee. Judgment by default was entered against the defendant and later, after a trial without a jury, a judgment was entered against the garnishee.

One of the grounds of the appeal involves the pleadings. The attachment affidavit was filed June 17, 1935. An attachment bond was filed on the same day. The obligee in the bond was the defendant. A condition of the bond erroneously stated that the plaintiffs would indemnify themselves and not the defendant and other persons interested. The attachment writ shows on its face that it was issued June 15th, two days before the affidavit or bond were filed. As to the defendant Tirsway the writ was returnable three days later, June 20th, and as to the garnishee Consoer Townsend & Quinlan, Inc., on June 28th. An attachment notice was posted by the bailiff and he mailed a copy to the defendant in care of his employer in Chicago instead of mailing same to him at his address in Indianapolis as

disclosed by the affidavit in attachment. It is quite evident from an inspection of the abstract that many errors were committed in suing out this writ of attachment. In order that a writ of attachment be valid, the provisions of the statute concerning its issuance must be strictly complied with, otherwise the attachment is subject to be quashed on proper motion. The defendant was not personally served and did not at any time appear. He was defaulted July 24th, and judgment entered for $180.00 and a conditional judgment against the garnishee. A writ of scire facias was served on the garnishee who filed an answer on August 4, 1935, setting up the facts and claiming the wage earner's exemption and also claiming that nothing was due and owing from the garnishee to the defendant and stating that they had already paid him all his salary. To this answer of the garnishee no traverse was filed.

The trial court denied the motion to dismiss for want of jurisdiction and entered a judgment against the garnishee for $138.45 and costs.

We are not aided in our consideration of this cause by any briefs filed in this court on behalf of plaintiffs.

The answer filed by the garnishee in the trial court disclosed that the defendant was a resident of Indiana, living with his wife and family in Indianapolis and was working for Consoer, Townsend & Quinlan, Inc., which corporation was engaged in supervising the construction of a waterworks system at Savanna, Illinois, being employed by the city and being paid out of Federal PWA funds; that for the purpose of insuring the prompt payment of the employees of the garnishee at Savanna when salaries were due, checks for salaries were mailed in advance of the due date so that the government would have time to check the amounts.

The answer of the garnishee further shows that during the

month of June, 1935, three checks were mailed to Tirsway at 400 Main street, Savanna, Ill., one on June 15th for $46.15, one on June 21st for a like amount and one of June 29th, covering services from June 27th to June 29th, at which time his services were dispensed with, the excess pay being considered as a bonus in lieu of notice.

The answer of the garnishee further states that on June 19th, it was not indebted to the said Harry L. Tirsway at the time the writ was served on it; that though it had been indebted to him, said funds would not in any event be subject to garnishments under the laws pertaining to the Public Works Administration.

As we have already stated no traverse was filed to this answer and no appearance entered in this court by plaintiffs.

In the case of Wabash R. R. Co. v. Dougan, 143 Ill. 248, it was said:

> "Where the answer of a garnishee is not traversed it must be taken as true, and on appeal by the garnishee the only question will be whether the plaintiff will be entitled to a judgment on the facts disclosed by the answer."

From the answer of the garnishee it appears there is nothing due and owing and, secondly, that under the law the money being the property of the United States Government, it could not be garnisheed. This was admitted by the plaintiffs in failing to traverse the answer. The trial court should have found for the garnishee instead of finding for plaintiffs.

There being nothing due from the garnishee, there is no necessity for remanding the cause. For the reasons given in this opinion the judgment of the Municipal Court is reversed with costs to be taxed against plaintiffs.

JUDGMENT REVERSED WITH COSTS TAXED AGAINST PLAINTIFFS.

HALL, P.J. AND HEBEL, J. CONCUR.

38737

24A

LORETTA DRYMILLER, JAMES DRYMILLER AND DELBERT DRYMILLER, minors by LORETTA DRYMILLER, their mother and next friend,

Appellants,

v.

ALBERT W. HILBERG,

Appellee.

APPEAL FROM CIRCUIT COURT, COOK COUNTY.

286 I.A. 607[2]

MR. JUSTICE DENIS E. SULLIVAN delivered the opinion of the court.

This is an appeal from an order and judgment entered in the Circuit Court directing a verdict for the defendant, Albert W. Hilberg, and against the plaintiffs, Loretta Drymiller, James Drymiller and Delbert Drymiller.

This action is one to recover for personal injuries sustained as the result of two automobiles colliding. The plaintiffs, a mother and her two children, were sitting in a northbound automobile on River road at its intersection with Milwaukee avenue. While the Ford automobile in which they were seated was standing still at that intersection, a LaSalle automobile traveling in an easterly direction on Milwaukee avenue suddenly pulled out of the line of traffic and made a sharp turn into the River road, striking the automobile in which the plaintiffs were passengers. Both automobiles tipped over and the drivers of both automobiles were killed and the plaintiffs injured.

Plaintiffs contend the evidence shows that defendant was an independent contractor and therefore liable for the wrongs

of his servant.

Defendant contends that the driver was a sub-agent of an unincorporated labor union and that defendant is not liable.

The trial judge held as a matter of law that the defendant was not an independent contractor as the plaintiffs contend, but was an agent of the owner of the automobile which caused the injuries to plaintiffs.

We have this day failed an opinion in case No. 38485, entitled, The Live Stock National Bank of Chicago, a corp., Administrator of the Estate of James J. Drymiller, deceased, appellee, v. Albert Hilberg, appellant, which was a cause of action growing out of the same accident, wherein the driver of the Ford automobile was killed, he being the husband and father of the plaintiffs herein. In that case we held that the driver of the LaSalle automobile, Richter, was the agent of Drymiller and was performing services for him at his request. and The facts in that case and the law applicable thereto are identical to those involved here. Therefore, what we have already said in case No. 38485 is controlling here and there would be no need of writing another extended opinion covering the same subject-matter.

We are of the opinion that the trial court should not have directed a verdict but should have submitted the issues to the jury.

For the reasons herein stated the judgment of the Circuit Court should be and the same hereby is reversed and the cause remanded for a new triall.

JUDGMENT REVERSED AND CAUSE REMANDED.

HALL, P.J. AND HEBEL, J. CONCUR.

38634

HATTIE GREENBERGER (Complainant)
Plaintiff in Error,

vs.

BARBARA O'NEILL, Individually and as Trustee and Executrix of the Estate of Terence J. O'Neill, Deceased, (Cross Complainant), Defendant in Error,

and

HENRY FRIEDMAN, (Cross Defendant), Defendant in Error.

ERROR TO SUPERIOR COURT OF COOK COUNTY.

25

286 I.A. 607[3]

MR. Presiding JUSTICE MATCHETT DELIVERED THE OPINION OF THE COURT.

February 7, 1924, Allen W. Selby, being indebted to the amount of $75,000, made his principal promissory note of that date for that amount, due and payable February 7, 1929. He also executed ten interest coupons for $2250 each, representing the interest which would become due and payable upon this note until maturity. On the same day he executed a trust deed, in and by which he conveyed certain premises in Cook county, Illinois, to secure the payment of the note and coupons. The trust deed was duly acknowledged and recorded. Henry Friedman thereafter became the owner of a second mortgage on the same premises, which, default having been made, he foreclosed, became the purchaser at the master's sale August 12, 1926, and on November 14, 1927, the period of redemption having expired, he, by a master's deed, became the owner of the premises subject to the lien of the trust deed first described. December 20, 1932, complainant, Hattie Greenberger, a niece of Henry Friedman, filed her bill in the Superior court of Cook county against Barbara O'Neill and others. She alleged in her bill that she was the owner of interest coupons Nos. 4 to 9, representing interest which had matured on the $75,000 loan; that these coupons were payable to bearer, were past due and unpaid; that

Barbara O'Neill was the holder of coupon No. 10 of the same series for a like amount and also the owner of the principal note for $75,000, interest upon which was represented by these coupons; that payment of the principal note and coupons was secured by a trust deed, as above described, and that Henry Friedman held title to the premises. She prayed foreclosure and that the coupons and costs, expenses, etc., of foreclosure might be declared a first lien on the real estate, and that in default of payment the same should be sold.

Barbara O'Neill, individually and as trustee and executrix of the estate of Terence J. O'Neill, deceased, answered and filed a cross bill, in which she averred that she was the owner of the note for $75,000 and coupon No. 10 representing the last instalment of interest due and payable thereon; that coupons Nos. 4 to 9 had been paid by Henry Friedman, and that the interest of complainant, Hattie Greenberger, was subordinate to the interest of cross-complainant. Cross complainant also alleged defaults in payment of principal, interest and taxes, and prayed foreclosure, etc.

Hattie Greenberger answered the cross bill, denying that the coupons held by her were paid or that her rights were subordinate to those of cross complainant. She alleged that the $75,000 principal note and coupons Nos. 4 to 9, inclusive, had been deposited in an escrow with the Lake View Trust & Savings Bank, as escrowee; that said escrow was a subterfuge to cover a deal in which cross complainant was to sell the $75,000 mortgage to Henry Friedman for $72,000; that $15,000 of the amount was received by Barbara O'Neill and ought to be credited against the indebtedness due and owing on the $75,000 note. She denied that cross complainant was entitled to relief as prayed.

The cause was put at issue and referred to a master, who reported in favor of cross complainant, finding that she was the

owner of the $75,000 note and coupon No. 10, and that she had a valid lien on the mortgaged premises for $104,205.89. The master also found that on August 7, 1928, F. J. Klauck, as the owner and holder of the principal note and interest coupons, executed an order on the Lake View Trust & Savings Bank then in possession thereof to deliver to Henry Friedman interest coupons Nos. 8 and 9 due February 7, 1928, upon payment of interest; that on November 21, 1927, Henry Friedman executed his receipt to the Lake View Trust & Savings Bank for interest coupons Nos. 4, 5, 6 and 7, and on August 30, 1928, executed his receipt for interest coupons Nos. 8 and 9; that on the respective dates Henry Friedman received these interest coupons, they were not cancelled or marked paid, and that at said dates Friedman was the owner of the premises described in the bill of complaint; that shortly after receiving the interest coupons Henry Friedman delivered them to complainant, Hattie Greenberger as collateral security for a loan; that the coupons were then long past due; that there was no evidence that complainant purchased the interest coupons from Frank J. Klauck or the Lake View Trust & Savings Bank; nor evidence that there was any agreement between the owners of the interest coupons and Hattie Greenberger. The report said:

"I therefore find that the said interest coupons four (4) to nine (9), both inclusive, were paid to the owner and holder thereof by HENRY FRIEDMAN, the owner of said premises, after their maturity, and were not purchased by the Complainant, HATTIE GREENBERGER. I therefore find that said interest coupons have been paid and are no longer secured by said Trust Deed."

Complainant filed objections to the report of the master, which were overruled and the cause was heard by the chancellor upon exceptions to the report. These exceptions were overruled and a decree of foreclosure entered in favor of cross complainant as recommended by the master. This decree also found that interest coupons Nos. 4 to 9, inclusive, held by complainant had been paid

and were therefore no longer secured by the lien of the trust deed. The decree further (inconsistently) found that by filing her bill complainant elected to subordinate her lien to that of cross complainant. Complainant sued out this writ of error for the purpose of having these interest coupons declared to be on a parity with the principal note and interest coppon of cross complainant and to have the proceeds of the foreclosure sale distributed accordingly.

Complainant cites authorities to the effect that where the owner of a greater estate purchases a lesser estate to the same premises, the question of whether the lesser estate merges in the greater depends upon the intention of the parties to the transaction. Robertson v. Wheeler, 162 Ill. 566, and similar cases are cited. She contends that in the instant case the intention of the parties was that there should be no merger and says, therefore the interest coupons held by her because of their earlier maturity may be entitled to priority over the principal note and coupon held by cross complainant. As to the priority of the coupons maturing at the earlier dates she cites Gardner v. Diedericks, 41 Ill. 158, and contends that in any event her coupons were entitled to parity with the principal note and coupon. She also contends upon the authority of Peoples National Bank v. Johnson, 271 Ill. App. 507, that the proceeds of the foreclosure sale ought to have been distributed pro rata to complainant and cross complainant in proportion to their respective holdings.

There is a preliminary question which seems to us to be controlling. That question is whether Henry Friedman at the time he received the coupons which were afterward delivered to Mrs. Greenberger, in fact paid the same. If he did in fact pay them, all questions concerning merger of estates become wholly immaterial, as complainant in her reply brief admits. The master found as a

fact that Henry Friedman paid these coupons at the time he received them from the bank on the order of the then owner. The chancellor approved that finding. Complainant did not in her original brief argue that the finding of the decree in this respect was against the weight of the evidence, although the argument in her reply brief is based upon the contention that it is. We cannot agree with her contention. Henry Friedman at the time he received the coupons was the owner of the premises upon which the mortgage securing the coupons was a first and valid lien. It was, so far as the evidence shows, the only outstanding lien. The coupons were due and payable. He gave money for them; how much, the evidende does not disclose. The fair inference is that he paid the coupons, although the same were not formally cancelled. There is some evidence to the contrary, but the master saw and heard the witnesses, and his finding is prima facie correct. It has been approved by the chancellor.

Complainant, in her reply brief, cites Chicago Title & Trust Co. v. Bidderman, 275 Ill. App. 457, which is clearly distinguishable, since the bonds there received and reissued by the owner were not yet due at the time of their receipt and reissuance. Walker v. C. M. & N. R. R. Co., 277 Ill. 451, cited in the reply brief is also distinguishable. In that case a surety purchased a note secured by mortgage after maturity, and it was held that the note and the mortgage were not extinguished by reason of the purchase. Jones v. Taylor, 261 Ill. App. 403, is likewise distinguishable. It was there held that the possession of uncancelled mortgage notes by one who was a co-maker and also a part owner of the premises was prima facie evidence that he was the owner thereof.

There were in all these cases equitable reasons requiring the notes to be kept alive. There are no such reasons here. The

master held Friedman paid the notes at the time he took them up. The chancellor approved the finding. We hold that the finding is sustained by the evidence, and this finding is controlling.

The decree is therefore affirmed,

AFFIRMED.

McSurely, P. J., and O'Connor, J., concur.

38679

FRANK C. KUHN and ANNIE BARTELS, Appellees,

vs.

SPIEGEL'S HOUSE FURNISHING COMPANY, (formerly known as Spiegel May Stern Company) an Illinois Corporation, SPIEGEL MAY STERN COMPANY, INC., a Delaware Corporation, and BURLEY & COMPANY, an Illinois Corporation, Appellants.

APPEAL FROM MUNICIPAL COURT OF CHICAGO.

26

286 I.A. 607

MR. PRESIDING JUSTICE MATCHETT DELIVERED THE OPINION OF THE COURT.

In and prior to the year 1928 plaintiffs were the owners of premises in the city of Chicago described as Nos. 2023-2035 Milwaukee avenue, which were improved and were under lease to Spiegel May Stern Co., an Illinois corporation, (afterward known as Spiegel's House Furnishing Co.), which conducted on the premises a business of selling household furniture.

In February of that year plaintiffs executed an indenture in writing under seal, whereby they demised these premises to this Illinois corporation, then in possession, for a term of ten years, beginning May 1, 1929, ending December 31, 1939, for a total rental of $151,000, payable in 128 monthly instalments, the first sixty of the amount of $1100 each and the remaining sixty-eight $1250 each. The lease was a lengthy, partly written and partly printed document, containing provisions which, so far as they are material, we will later discuss. May 14, 1928, the Illinois corporation, lessee, assigned its interests in the lease to Spiegel May Stern Co., Inc., a corporation organized under the laws of the state of Delaware, with the consent in writing of the lessors, which was endorsed upon the lease. The Delaware corporation went into possession and afterward assigned all its right, title and interest (with the consent of the lessors) to Burley & Co., another Illinois corporation, - in fact a subsidiary

of the Delaware company.

June 1, 1933, Spiegel's House Furnishing Co., an Illinois corporation, Spiegel May Stern Co., a Delaware corporation, Burley & Co., and plaintiff lessors, entered into an agreement under seal by which the rent for the eleven month period beginning June 1, 1933, and ending April 30, 1934, was reduced to $900 a month, all the parties further agreeing that:

"Except as herein expressly amended and modified, all of the terms, covenants and conditions of said indenture of lease shall remain in full force, virtue and effect and the parties of the first, second and third parts respectively severally covenant and agree that except as by this agreement expressly modified their liability under said lease shall in no wise be affected, altered or abrogated by virtue of the execution of this agreement."

November 29, 1933, plaintiff lessors began in the Municipal court a suit to recover from defendants unpaid rent for November, 1933. Thereafter suit was begun also to recover unpaid rent for December, 1933. The statements of claim in each case were identical except as to the month for which rent was claimed to be due, and the affidavits of merits filed in both cases were likewise similar. The cases were consolidated and tried in the Municipal court before the same jury, which in each case returned a verdict for plaintiffs to the amount of their claim, and the court overruling in each case motions for a new trial and in arrest, entered judgment for plaintiffs and against defendants upon each of the verdicts. From both judgments defendants appealed and, the issues being identical as heretofore explained, the causes in this court also have been consolidated for hearing.

The defendant Delaware corporation undertakes to interpose a defense applicable to it alone. It made a motion for an instructed verdict in its favor at the close of all the evidence, upon the theory that by reason of the language of the assignment from it to Burley & Co., and particularly by the language of the consent of the lessors thereto, it was released from its obliga-

tion to pay rent under the lease.

April 28, 1930, the Delaware corporation assigned this lease to Burley & Co., by a writing under seal, as follows:

"The Undersigned, * * a Delaware corporation, * * does hereby sell, assign and transfer unto Burley & Company, an Illinois corporation, all of said Delaware corporation's right, title and interest in and to the following described leases:
* * *
Said sale, assignment and transfer is made subject in all respects to the terms and conditions of said lease.
Said Illinois corporation does hereby assume and agree to perform all of the terms and conditions of said lease therein provided to be performed by the lessee thereunder to the same extent and under the same conditions as if said Illinois corporation had been the original lessee thereunder. ***"

The consent of plaintiffs is as follows:

"The undersigned hereby consents to the assignment of the within lease to Burley & Company, an Illinois corporation, on the express condition, however, that the assignor (<u>the lessee under the terms of said lease</u>) shall remain liable for the prompt payment of the rent and performance of the covenants on the part of the Second Party therein mentioned, and that no further assignment of said lease shall be made without the undersigned's written consent first had thereto."

This consent is also under seal. The Delaware corporation contends that the plain construction of the words of the writing, which it insists is not ambiguous and must therefore be taken as found, following the rule laid down in <u>Green v. Ashland State Bank</u>, 346 Ill. 174; <u>Decatur Lumber Co. v. Crail</u>, 350 Ill. 319, shows that the lessors retained only the liability of the Illinois corporation and not the liability of the Delaware corporation. Defendants say:

"There were two assignors of the lease, the Illinois and the Delaware corporations. The lessors, by inserting the words in the parentheses, indicated and described which of the two assignors they meant, namely, that assignor which was the lessee under the lease. It is undeniable that only the Illinois corporation was the lessee under said lease."

We have not been able to bring ourselves to accept this construction. There were, as a matter of fact, several lessees: the original or first lessee; the second lessee, which became such when by a prior agreement the Delaware corporation promised to pay the rent and perform all the other covenants of the original lessee of the lease; and a third lessee when Burley & Co., with consent of the

lessors, also assumed these obligations. The taking possession of the premises, the consent of the lessors and the acceptance by them of the rent, was sufficient to create the relationship of landlord and tenant and lessor and lessee. The plain language of the written consent leaves no doubt as to which of these three is meant. It says: "* * the assignor (the lessee under the terms of said lease) shall remain liable," etc. The assignor referred to is, of course, the assignor, who by that very writing is making an assignment. This is not only the reasonable construction of the language as we read it but also the construction which, the evidence shows, up to the time of the beginning of this litigation was put upon the writing by the defendant Delaware corporation. This is shown by recitations in an agreement made for the reduction of rent on June 1, 1933, to which the Delaware corporation voluntarily became a party. It is also shown by the fact that the Delaware corporation, subsequent to the making of the assignment and after the assignee, Burley & Co., ceased to pay rent for more than five months, paid the rent of these premises according to the terms of the lease, thus giving to the writing a construction which it now repudiates. We hold that by becoming a party to the agreement for the reduction of rent and by paying the rent after the assignee ceased to do so, the Delaware corporation has put a construction upon the writing which it cannot now be permitted to deny. Moreover, the mere assignment by the Delaware corporation of its lease, with the consent of the lessors, would not, as a matter of fact or of law, release the Delaware corporation from the obligation, which it assumed, to pay the rent. The assignment terminated the privity of estate between the lessors and the Delaware corporation but did not destroy the privity of contract. Springer v. DeWolf, 194 Ill. 218. It is still liable on the contract. This special defense

interposed by the Delaware corporation cannot be allowed, and the court properly denied its motion for an instructed verdict on that ground.

All the defendants, by their affidavit of merits, interposed the defense of constructive eviction, upon the theory that plaintiffs failed to repair the premises and failed to keep them in repair as provided by the terms of a rider attached to the lease. This rider provided:

"The lessors shall proceed at once, at their own expense, to repair the roof upon the premises, and put it in reasonably good condition and repair; and they will during the term of this lease keep and maintain the said roof in reasonably good condition and repair, at their own expense.

The lessors further agree that they will at once, at their own expense, make whatever repairs are necessary to the heating plant to put it in reasonably good operating condition; and that they will, at their own expense, during the term of this lease, make all necessary repairs to the heating plant on the premises which may be required to keep it in reasonably good condition for proper operation; provided, however, that in case repairs to the heating plant are required which are occasioned by the freezing of the pipes or radiators, due to the negligence of the lessee, such repairs in such case shall be made at the lessee's expense. The lessee shall use reasonable care to avoid grates being burned out through negligent operation by its employees."

Defendants offered evidence tending to show that plaintiffs did not comply with these agreements; that they permitted the roof to leak to such an extent as to make the premises untenantable for the purpose for which they were rented; that the heating plant was also allowed to come into such a state of disrepair that it was impossible to secure heat necessary to conduct on the premises the business in which they were engaged and for which the premises were leased. Defendants rely on the doctrine of constructive eviction, as stated in Gibbons v. Hoefeld, 299 Ill. 455; Kinsey v. Zimmerman, 329 Ill. 75; Auto Supply Co. v. Scene, etc. Co., 340 Ill. 196. Defendants say that these cases hold that upon constructive eviction of the tenant by his landlord the tenant is exonerated from paying rent under the lease, and that he may abandon the property; that a clear case of constructive eviction was made out by the

testimony offered in behalf of defendants, and that the right of plaintiffs to recover rent as claimed in their pleading is therefore defeated.

The original lessee was in possession of the premises under a prior lease at the time of the execution of the present lease and at the beginning of the term. That lessee expressly acknowledged in the lease that it had received the premises in good condition. Plaintiffs contend that defendants are precluded from interposing this defense based on failure to repair because the covenant of the lessees to pay rent and the covenant of plaintiffs to repair are "independent not dependent" covenants; that the lessees covenanted to pay rent in consideration of the demise alone and not in consideration of both the demise and the agreement to repair, and they cite Rubens v. Hill, 213 Ill. 523, and Gelz v. Stafford, 284 Ill. 610, which seem to sustain the contention of plaintiffs that if there was a breach of any covenant on the part of lessors, the lessees were limited to their rights to sue the lessors for damages in a separate suit, or in a suit brought by lessors for rent to recoup their damages, not exceeding the amount of the rent claimed. In this case defendants made no claim by way of recoupment and therefore cannot defeat plaintiffs' claim for rent on that theory. The cases cited we think accurately state the law applicable in this commonwealth. Defendants cite a line of cases, such as Lloyd v. Bissell, 100 Ill. 214; Nelson v. Eichoff, 158 Pac. 370, which are, we think, clearly distinguishable upon the facts, the holding in these cases being that where the lessee has not yet gone into possession and the landlord covenants to make repairs before the beginning of the term and fails to make such repairs, the lessee may then refuse to enter into possession and when sued for rent defend upon the ground that he was justified in not taking possession. As already pointed out, that is not the case

here, since the lessee was in possession when the lease was made and covenanted in the lease that it had received the premises in a good state of repair.

Without undertaking to discuss all the cases in detail, we think it is sufficient to say that the general doctrine announced in all of them is to the effect that a tenant cannot take and remain in possession of premises and at the same time refuse to pay rent upon the ground that the premises have not been repaired as agreed. In other words, if the tenant wishes to plead constructive eviction, he must abandon the premises within a reasonable time and must pay rent for the time in which he has occupied. Patterson v. Graham, 140 Ill. 531; Keating v. Springer, 146 Ill.481.

The issues of fact in this case, as to whether plaintiffs did in fact repair as agreed and as to whether defendants in fact abandoned the premises, were submitted to the jury which found for plaintiffs on these issues. Defendants contend that the verdict of the jury is against the manifest weight of the evidence, and that a new trial should have been granted for that reason. We have given careful attention to the evidence as presented in defendants' abstract of the record and are unable to agree with their contentions, either that plaintiffs failed to repair or that defendants in possession abandoned the premises as untenantable. Burley & Co. vacated the premises in the latter part of September, 1931, but there were signs in the window reading, "Liquidation Sale" some time before the business was closed out. No claim was made to plaintiffs at that time nor until just before this suit was brought that the removal was due to the fact that the building on the premises had become untenantable. Burley & Co. subleased the premises to Denenholz Bros., who remained in possession and conducted their business there until they were closed out by bankruptcy proceedings. It is clear from the evidence that the reasons defendant Burley & Co.

ceased to occupy were economic in their nature. Mr. Gatzert, secretary of the Delaware corporation, negotiated for release of defendants from their obligations under the lease and asked the assistance of plaintiffs, as the correspondence shows, in endeavors to find other tenants, and we think he stated the key to the solution of this whole controversy when he said, "When no agreement was reached between us subsequent to that reduction of $200, we began to look around to see if there was a way out." He testifies that in the latter part of October, 1933, in a telephone conversation he told one of plaintiffs that no more rent would be paid, and that they had not kept the agreements made in the lease as to repairs, but this conversation is denied. As already stated, the jury has rendered a verdict for plaintiffs, which we do not think should be disturbed. As a matter of fact, long after that time the agents and servants of defendants looked after the premises, and even now defendants retain the key, which has never been surrendered but which the lease expressly provided should be surrendered upon the termination of the lease. We cannot overlook that upon these issues of fact a jury has found in favor of plaintiff lessors. We must hold therefore on this record that the evidence does not disclose such failure to repair as would make the building untenantable nor any abandonment of the premises by these defendants such as is necessary to enable them to defend upon the theory of a constructive eviction.

Defendants contend, however, that the court erred in giving, over their objection, certain instructions requested by plaintiffs. One of these is as follows:

"The court further instructs you, Gentlemen of the Jury, that as to the defense of constructive eviction, the burden of proof is upon the defendants to show the following things by a preponderance or greater weight of the evidence. (1) That on or before December 1, 1933, the premises were unfit for use for the purposes for which they were rented; (2) that the cause of such unfitness was a lack of repair of the roof or heating plant; (3) that the landlords had notice or knowledge of the unfitness of the

premises for the use for which they were rented; (4) that the defendants abandoned the premises before the first of December, 1933; and (5) that such abandonment was on account of the unfitness of the premises (if there was such unfitness.)

"If the defendants have failed to prove any one of these things by a preponderance or greater weight of the evidence, your verdict must be in favor of the plaintiffs.

"Even if you find from the evidence that all of these things enumerated above have been proven, yet if you further find from the evidence that the defendants by their conduct waived any right to abandon the premises on account of said condition, you must find the issues in favor of the plaintiffs."

The criticism of this instruction is that while the evidence for defendants tended to show that the premises were unfit for use during October, 1933, and that the lease was cancelled and terminated by defendants on notice to plaintiffs prior to October 31, 1933, the instruction was misleading because it stated that defendants must show the abandonment of the premises before the first of December, 1933. As we have already stated, these two suits were tried together. In one of them plaintiffs claimed rent for November, 1933, the other for December, 1933. We do not think the jury would have been confused through a statement that the premises should have been in fact abandoned prior to December 1, 1933. Any other statement would have been inaccurate. We must presume that the jury was intelligent.

Defendants also complain of this instruction because, they say, there is no evidence in the record upon which to predicate any claim of waiver. We have already indicated our opinion that there was such evidence, and the jury has so found. The instruction was not inaccurate in view of the pleadings in this case which did not claim by way of recoupment.

Other objections are made to some of the instructions which we think it quite unnecessary to discuss in detail. The issues in this case are comparatively simple. The instructions given were substantially accurate, and those given cover fully the propositions of law that it was necessary for the jury to know in order to decide the case. We think there was no substantial error

either in the giving or of the refusing to give instructions.

Defendants also contend that a certain letter written by the attorney for plaintiffs to defendant Spiegel May Stern Co. on October 24, 1933, was erroneously excluded from the evidence. The letter stated that the lessors had given consideration to certain letters of the defendant company and had reached the conclusion that a cash settlement of $90,000, while it would represent a substantial loss to the lessors, would be accepted by them. The letter was written after the controversy had arisen and by way of trying to reach a compromise settlement. The court, however, permitted it to go in evidence with the amount "$90,000" deleted. The court did not err in this ruling.

Defendants also contend that plaintiffs under the terms of the lease did not have any remedy against defendants by reason of a provision in the lease to the effect, "if said party of the second part shall abandon or vacate said premises, the same shall be re-let by the party of the first part for such rent, and upon such terms as said first party shall see fit; and if a sufficient sum shall not be thus realized, after paying the expenses of such reletting and collecting, to satisfy the rent hereby reserved, the party of the second part agrees to satisfy and pay all deficiency." Defendants contend that the lease having thus defined the remedy that the lessors should have against the lessees in case the premises should become vacated, the lessors are restricted to such remedy, and plaintiffs therefore have no right to elect another remedy. Defendants cite no authorities. The Supreme court and this court have held directly to the contrary, although at one time divergent views were entertained on that question. Humiston, Keeling & Co. v. Wheeler, 175 Ill. 514; Rau v. Baker, 118 Ill. App. 150; Hirsch v. Home Appliances, 242 Ill. App. 418.

In a fair trial before a jury, which could not have been

prejudiced against defendants' cause, verdicts were returned for plaintiffs, and the Judge, who saw and heard the witnesses, entered judgments on these verdicts. We think the judgments just, and they are affirmed.

JUDGMENTS AFFIRMED.

O'Connor and McSurely, JJ., concur.

prejudiced against defendants' cause, verdicts were returned for plaintiffs, and the judge, who saw and heard the witnesses, entered judgments on these verdicts. We think the judgments just, and they are affirmed.

JUDGMENTS AFFIRMED.

[illegible] and [illegible], JJ., concur.

38680

FRANK C. KUHN and ANNIE BARTELS,
Appellees,

vs.

SPIEGEL'S HOUSE FURNISHING COMPANY, (formerly known as Spiegel May Stern Company), an Illinois Corporation, SPIEGEL MAY STERN COMPANY, INC., a Delaware Corporation, and BURLEY & COMPANY, an Illinois Corporation,
Appellants.

APPEAL FROM MUNICIPAL COURT OF CHICAGO.

27

286 I.A. 607[5]

MR. PRESIDING JUSTICE MATCHETT
DELIVERED THE OPINION OF THE COURT.

The issues of fact and law of this case are identical with those presented in case No. 38679 between the same parties, in which an opinion has been this day filed. For the reasons stated in that opinion, in this case also the judgment of the trial court is affirmed.

AFFIRMED.

McSurely and O'Connor, JJ., concur.

38759

GORDON A. RAMSAY, as Receiver for the ALBANY PARK NATIONAL BANK AND TRUST COMPANY,
Appellant,

vs.

JACOB J. PRICE,
Appellee.

APPEAL FROM CIRCUIT COURT OF COOK COUNTY.

28

286 I.A. 608[1]

MR. Presiding JUSTICE MATCHETT DELIVERED THE OPINION OF THE COURT.

In an action of assumpsit upon a written guaranty and upon trial by the court, there was a finding for defendant with judgment. The defense interposed was that after the execution and delivery of the written guaranty on March 10, 1930, defendant on October 1 of that year served a notice on plaintiff revoking the guaranty, and that the notes for which it was claimed defendant was liable by reason of the guaranty were executed after the revocation.

Plaintiff contends for reversal, first, that the finding that notice of revocation was served on plaintiff is against the manifest weight of the evidence, and, second, assuming that notice was actually served as alleged under the terms of the written guaranty, such notice was wholly ineffectual as a matter of law.

Plaintiff is the receiver of the Albany Park National bank. For some years prior to the transaction in question the Price Realty Securities Co., a corporation, engaged in dealing in real estate securities, was a customer of the bank and on or about March 10, 1930, had become indebted upon two promissory notes for several thousand dollars. One of these notes by its terms would become due March 31, 1930, and the other May 5, 1930. The Securities Co. was a family corporation. Howard Hurwith, nephew of defendant, was secretary of the corporation and owned, as he says, from 10 to 15 per cent of its capital stock. The rest of the stock was owned by defendant and his wife. Defendant was president

of the corporation. The notes taken by the bank for the indebtedness of the corporation were collateral notes and, apparently, a number of second mortgages upon real estate had been delivered to secure the indebtedness. The depression was under way, and the bank requested further security. In compliance with this demand defendant on March 10, 1930, executed and delivered to the bank a guaranty in substance as follows:

"For and in consideration of the sum of $1.00 the receipt whereof is hereby acknowledged, the advancement of moneys, the giving and extending of credit by The Albany Park National Bank and Trust Company of Chicago to Price Realty Sec. Co., and of other valuable considerations, on demand I promise to pay The Albany Park National Bank and Trust Company any and all sums of money which the said Albany Park National Bank and Trust Company may at any time loan or advance to Price Realty Sec. Co., or on.... account including obligations now existing to the amount of Forty-Five Hundred dollars, together with interest on such loans and advances from the time the same are made, or have been made respectively, at the rate of 6 per cent per annum until paid.

This agreement and guarantee applies to the payment of all notes and obligations to be made by said Price Realty Sec. Co., to the said Albany Park National Bank and Trust Company, and any renewals thereof or continuances of same, whether in full or in part for the amount not to exceed Forty-Five Hundred Dollars."

The notes held by the bank, as the same thereafter matured, were at the request of the Securities Co. from time to time renewed for the balances respectively remaining due thereon, and plaintiff now holds unpaid two of these renewal notes, one for the sum of $1132.68, dated December 29, 1930, and due March 30, 1931, and another for the sum of $1132.60, dated November 3, 1930, and due February 2, 1931.

The burden of proving his affirmative defense was assumed by defendant. On the trial he served notice upon plaintiff to produce a letter alleged to have been delivered by him to the bank on October 1, 1930, notifying the bank that he was cancelling and terminating his guaranty as of that date. The letter was not produced. Defendant then produced a copy of this supposed letter and testified that he dictated it to his stenographer, who was still employed by him; that she wrote it, and he signed it and

took it over to the bank and gave it "to the man at the desk; the man was sitting at the desk at the bank on the main floor." Defendant said that he walked into the bank with the letter and asked for Mr. Nagel, a vice-president of the bank, who was not there. He does not remember exactly with whom he talked. Mr. Nagel was the only officer of the bank he knew. He gave the letter to a man who was back of the counter and never heard from the bank after he delivered it. He said that the carbon copy in evidence was a true and correct copy of the letter. Defendant further said that he did not have knowledge of any loan or note signed by the Price Realty Securities Co. in any transaction with the bank after October 1, 1930. On cross examination he testified that he drove alone to the bank in his automobile. He says that as he walked in, the cages were on the right.

> "I could not tell you whether there were cages on the right and left side of the bank. I believe there were cages on both sides. I was in the bank fifteen or twenty minutes. I had a conversation with the man I gave the paper to. I asked him where Mr. Nagel was, and he told me he was either out to lunch-- I don't remember where he told me at that time. I told him I was going to leave this with him and he said he would see that the proper party got it."

He says he did not ask the man his name and the man didn't tell him his name; that he has never seen him since, has never looked for him and has never heard from him. He did not know Mr. Masterson, the discount teller. He never wrote any letter to the bank in connection with this visit of October 1, 1930, never received any acknowledgment from the bank and never asked for nor got a receipt for the letter.

Defendant also produced as a witness Mr. Pancoe, a real estate man, who said he knew Mr. Camp of the bank, and that he used to do business there; that in the early part of October he went to the bank with Mr. Hurwith, who called him that morning, and that in the bank they met Mr. Camp, another vice-president;

took it over to the bank and gave it "to the man at the desk; the man was sitting at the desk at the bank on the main floor." Defendant said that he walked into the bank with the letter and asked for Mr. Nagel, a vice-president of the bank, who was not there. He does not remember exactly with whom he talked. Mr. Nagel was the only officer of the bank he knew. He gave the letter to a man who was back of the counter and never heard from the bank after he delivered it. He said that the carbon copy in evidence was a true and correct copy of the letter. Defendant further said that he did not have knowledge of any loan or note signed by the Price Realty Securities Co. in any transaction with the bank after October 1, 1930. On cross examination he testified that he drove alone to the bank in his automobile. He says that as he walked in, the cages were on the right.

"I could not tell you whether there were cages on the right and left side of the bank. I believe there were cages on both sides. I was in the bank fifteen or twenty minutes. I had a conversation with the man I gave the paper to. I asked him where Mr. Nagel was, and he told me he was either out to lunch-- I don't remember where he told me at that time. I told him I was going to leave this with him and he said he would see that the proper party got it."

He says he did not ask the man his name and the man didn't tell him his name; that he has never seen him since, has never looked for him and has never heard from him. He did not know Mr. Masterson, the discount teller. He never wrote any letter to the bank in connection with this visit of October 1, 1930, never received any acknowledgment from the bank and never asked for nor got a receipt for the letter.

Defendant also produced as a witness Mr. Pancoe, a real estate man, who said he knew Mr. Camp of the bank, and that he used to do business there; that in the early part of October he went to the bank with Mr. Hurwitch, who called him that morning, and that in the bank they met Mr. Camp, another vice-president;

that there was talk by Mr. Camp about the drawing of the guaranty; that Mr. Camp took a letter from his desk drawer and showed it to Mr. Hurwith, who said that Mr. Price was withdrawing the guaranty but that he, Mr. Camp, did not particularly care as long as the notes were collateralized and no collateral would be reduced and as long as the notes were being paid off. He did not remember the wording of the letter, but the substance of it was that Mr. Price was withdrawing his guaranty and he didn't want anything further to do with it. Mr. Pancoe further testifies, "Nothing else was said. We just had a friendly chat, were kidding along about business and about the stock market, and we left;" that they drove out to the bank in Hurwith's car; that he didn't talk to anyone in the bank besides Mr. Camp, and he has not seen Mr. Camp since that time, and he did not know where Mr. Camp lived but used to see him and knew him well.

Howard Hurwith (who was secretary of Price Realty Securities Co.) for defendant testified that prior to the date of the guaranty, the Realty corporation had a line of credit with the bank for about $15,000, which was secured by mortgages on loans made and owned by the Price Realty Securities Co.; that the company collected on the second mortgage notes up as collateral and paid the proceeds to the bank, and that this was the practice also after the guaranty was given; that Mr. Camp asked him in October, 1930, to come to the bank and he went there with Mr. Pancoe; that Mr. Camp showed him a letter he had received from defendant and that he saw it in Mr. Camp's possession; that the carbon copy is a true and correct copy. He says Mr. Camp asked, "What do you think of Mr. Price withdrawing his guaranty?" to which he replied he thought it was a dirty trick, "when we were in trouble, when the real estate market all went to pieces," etc.; that Mr. Camp said he didn't care very much, that they had confidence in the judgment of the witness and he hoped that

the collateral would work; that Mr. Camp did not ask the witness to bring in any other guaranty in place of that one.

The carbon copy of the supposed letter was introduced in evidence and is as follows:

"October 1, 1930.

Albany Park National Bank & Trust Co.,
3424 Lawrence Avenue,
Chicago, Illinois.

Gentlemen: In connection with my written guarantee dated March 10th, 1930, delivered to your bank in connection with loan to be made by the Price Realty Securities Co., please be informed that I wish to terminate and cancel said guarantee.

I will not consent to the renewal or extension of any of the existing indebtedness owing by the Price Realty Securities Co., and insist that you demand payment on all obligations owing by said company.

Yours very truly,

JJP:RR"

Mr. Hurwith further said that thereafter he went to the bank and signed various notes for the Securities company and signed the two notes which were plaintiff's exhibits 2 and 3, on February 2, 1931, and March 30, 1931; that for three years he did not speak to Mr. Price.

The evidence shows that Mr. Camp died prior to the beginning of this suit.

Mr. Nagel, who was cashier and also vice-president of the bank, testified he had occasion to see Mr. Camp almost daily while he was in the bank and saw him daily in October, 1930, but that Mr. Camp never said anything to him about an attempted revocation of Mr. Price's guaranty; that he did not know anything about the letter of Price attempting to revoke the guaranty and did not remember that he ever saw any letter from Price to that effect; that he handled renewals of loans and lines of credit with the Price Realty Securities Co. but was not the only one in the bank who did so; that he had access to the file at any time he had anything to do with the account; that he had a conversation with Mr. Price in Mr. Price's office in the spring of 1931, with

reference to the indebtedness owed to the bank. Mr. Price at that time said he was unable to pay the notes and did not say anything about any revocation in the previous October.

The evidence also tends to show that April 14, 1931, Mr. Nagel, as cashier of the bank, wrote defendant telling him, in substance that he was a guarantor on notes of the Securities Co. to the amount of $2265.28; that the directors insisted that unless payment was made the matter would be turned over to attorneys for collection; that the writer had tried to avoid litigation and that it was up to defendant to make some sort of reduction and avoid further costs, which the writer trusted would be convenient for him to do in a day or two. No answer was received to this letter.

On cross examination Mr. Nagel said Mr. Camp and he did the same kind of work, at times consulted each other and at other times did things independently; that it was possible that when he was out ~~with~~ Mr. Hurwith saw Mr. Camp; that possibly he might have been mistaken when he testified that Mr. Camp had never told him about the letter of October 1st. He said he had always before found every paper around the bank he had to find and never missed any papers; that he had heard of papers being misfiled there but not lost. Mr. Nagel had no knowledge of any letter written by Mr. Price revoking his guaranty.

Dorothy Murphy testified that she was in charge of the files in the hands of the receiver of the Albany Park bank; that she had made a search for the letter from Mr. Price dated October 1, 1930, and had not found any such letter; that in searching for it she went through the regular receivership and the old bank files several times carefully but did not come across the letter. She said that prior to the receivership two girls did the filing in the bank; that in her experience letters may occasionally be misfiled but she did not recall any occasion of one being lost.

Letters were kept in the filing cabinets, which contained four drawers and were of standard steel. She could not say how many cabinets were in the bank. Letters were filed alphabetically except in some special cases. She said, "I have looked through every single file in an effort to find this supposed letter, both the receiver's files and the bank files. I have not found any trace of it." Further: "I made the search through these files almost a year ago, again last fall, and I believe last December I made a very thorough search. It was a search for this particular letter."

We find it quite difficult to accept the testimony of defendant and his two witnesses on this point. The burden of proof was on him to establish his affirmative defense. There is an atmosphere of improbability and unreality about this testimony which precludes its acceptance. In view of the financial situation and the ownership of the corporation it is extremely unlikely, in the first place, that Price would ask to be relieved of his liability under the guaranty; and, in the second place, that the bank would consent that he be relieved or would continue to extend credit after the guaranty was withdrawn. It is quite improbable that on October 1, 1930, defendant would drive to the bank, several miles away, having, as he says, no other business there, to deliver this letter and return immediately to his office, when the desired result could have been obtained much more effectively by use of the mails. Use of the registered mail would have given him absolute proof. His alleged conduct while at the bank is extremely improbable. He says that Mr. Nagel was out and he gave this important document to someone at the bank whose name he did not take and about whom he remembers little, if anything. Mr. Nagel's testimony is to the effect that he called upon defendant at his office downtown in the spring of 1931 and demanded payment under the guaranty and that at that time defendant made no claim to have given notice of revo-

cation. The evidence shows that a letter was sent to defendant on April 14, 1931, demanding that he meet his liability as a guarantor. He made no response. It is only fair to suppose that he would have done so if the notice of revocation had been in fact given. The discount teller, Mr. Masterson, also wrote him August 12, 1931, with reference to his liability, and again there was no response --- most improbable if he had revoked. It is singular indeed that the entire conversations of defendant's witnesses on this most important matter were with a man, who is now dead. It is impossible to believe that Mr. Nagel and Mr. Masterson, in view of all the circumstances, would have been ignorant of this revocation if it had in fact been given. Moreover, Mr. Nagel had handled practically all the other details in respect to the guaranty, and it is quite significant that this particular transaction should have been held with the man now dead, Mr. Camp. It is also quite improbable that if a notice of revocation was in fact served on October 1st the bank on the same day would have renewed note No. 27549 by note No. 28339 for $1314.48, extending the indebtedness for ninety days without further security.

A stenographer, who is said to have written the supposed letter, was still in the employ of Price but was not called as a witness. In view of the fact that the burden of proof was upon defendant, (notwithstanding the finding of the trial court, which is entitled to the same weight as the verdict of a jury) we find it quite impossible to exercise that degree of credulity that would lead us to accept this improbable testimony. The first point, namely, that the finding that the notice was served is against the manifest preponderance of the evidence, must be sustained.

If, however, we assume that the notice of revocation was in fact given, there would remain for consideration the question of its effect; in other words, whether the guaranty was in fact re-

vocable. Defendant says that this guaranty was a unilateral, continuing and revocable offer, which was withdrawn by the notice of October 1st; that it was prospective in its operation, indefinite in its duration and under its terms indicated an intention to provide the bank with security in its future transactions with the real estate corporation up to the limit of $4500 in principal. Defendant cites cases, such as Taussig v. Reid, 145 Ill. 488; Mamerow v. National Lead Co., 206 Ill. 626; National Eagle Bank v. Hunt, 16 R. I. 148; Lloyd's v. Harper, L. R. 16 Ch. Div. 290; American Chain Co. v. Arrow Grip Mfg. Co., 235 N.Y.S. 228, and numerous other cases, to these propositions.

It may be well to examine with some care the language of the guaranty and recall the consideration for its execution, for after all, in contracts of guaranty, as in other contracts, the purpose of construction is to ascertain the intention of the parties. Weger v. Robinson Nash Motor Co., 340 Ill. 81. The amount guaranteed is by the contract expressly limited to $4500. The guaranty is special, not general, in that it runs to the bank alone, and the obligation to pay is absolute in its nature, in that it is not made to rest upon any contingency. It is unique, in that it seems, in part, to create a temporary guaranty and, in part, a guaranty which is continuing in its nature. By its terms it includes sums of money which the bank "may at any time loan or advance to Price Realty Sec. Co." while in the same paragraph this obligation is expressly described as "including obligations now existing to the amount of Forty-Five Hundred dollars, together with interest on such loans and advances from the time the same are made, or have been made respectively." The evidence also shows that the obligations of the corporation to the bank at this particular time exceeded more than $4500, so that in effect the parties must have contemplated the guaranty of these existing obligations to that

amount. Not until such obligations were made would the guaranty by its terms become applicable as to other and future transactions. The consideration named was one dollar, which, so far as the evidence shows, was not paid. Other considerations were the advancements of moneys, which had already been made by the bank, and the extension of credit, which was executed and performed when the notes then about to mature were renewed by the bank. These notes, the evidence shows, were never in fact paid in full, although partial payments were made thereon from time to time, and there was an indefinite amount of collateral up with the bank to secure their payment. The guaranty being absolute in its nature, defendant remains liable for the balance of the indebtedness represented by these notes. In other words, the contingency upon which the guaranty would have become a continuing one did not at any time arise. The renewal notes did not represent new, but old, liabilities, and the consideration for the old indebtedness, namely, the extension of credit, had been fully executed and performed by the bank when the notes about to become due at the time the guaranty was signed were extended. The guaranty on the first of October was therefore absolute in form and temporary in its nature, and the notice of revocation was ineffectual to end it. Defendant is therefore liable.

While the cases are in many respects distinguishable, the conclusion at which we have arrived is consistent with the reasoning thereof. Estate of Rapp v. Phoenix Ins. Co., 113 Ill. 390; Lloyd's v. Harper, L. R. 16 Ch. Div. 290; Wise v. Miller, 45 Ohio St. 388; Zimetbaum v. Berenson, 267 Mass. 250, 166 N. E. 719; Nielsen v. Davidson, 226 Pac. 835. Defendant, therefore, as a matter of fact and law is liable for the principal amount of the notes sued on, namely, $1132.60 and $1132.68, with interest thereon at six per cent per annum from the maturity of the same, making a total sum of $2989.41 , for which judgment will be entered here.

REVERSED WITH JUDGMENT HERE AGAINST JACOB J. PRICE AND IN FAVOR OF GORDON A. RAMSAY, AS RECEIVER OF THE ALBANY PARK NATIONAL BANK AND TRUST COMPANY FOR $2989.41.

McSurely, P. J., and O'Connor, J., concur.

38770

SARAH GOLD,
Appellant,

vs.

RIVERVIEW PARK COMPANY,
a Corporation,
Appellee.

APPEAL FROM MUNICIPAL COURT OF CHICAGO.

29

286 I.A. 608²

MR. Presiding JUSTICE MATCHETT DELIVERED THE OPINION OF THE COURT.

This appeal is by plaintiff from an order entered October 11, 1935, vacating a judgment by default in favor of plaintiff for $1,000 entered September 5, 1935. The motion to set aside the judgment was first made by defendant before Judge Green of the Municipal court September 17th, twelve days after the judgment was entered. On the same day defendant filed a typewritten statement of reasons, for which it was claimed the judgment should be set aside, but this statement was not verified. The motion was continued from time to time until October 10th when it came up for hearing before Judge Green. The proceedings at that time have not been preserved, but it appears from the record that an order was entered on that day, as follows: "It is ordered by the court that the motion of the defendant heretofore entered herein to vacate judgment and default be and the same is hereby ordered withdrawn." On the same day defendant gave notice to plaintiff that on the following day a petition to vacate the judgment would be presented. On the next day, October 11th, the petition was presented to Judge O'Connell of the Municipal court and the order from which this appeal has been perfected, was entered. The order entered granted the prayer of the petition to vacate the judgment, denied a motion of plaintiff for leave to file counter affidavit to the petition, and ordered the petition to stand as an affidavit of merits.

Plaintiff contends, citing authorities such as Gilchrest Transportation Co. v. Northern Grain Co., 204 Ill. 510, that the

court erred in denying her motion for leave to file a counter affidavit, which, she says, was not to the merits but concerned the issue of diligence. There is no certificate of proceedings or bill of exceptions in the record, not does any counter affidavit appear therein. The proceedings have not been preserved by certificate, or otherwise; we are therefore unable to determine what were the circumstances under which leave to present the counter affidavit was denied. All the presumptions, however, are in favor of the order. It is for the party appealing to show error, which does not appear in this respect from the record presented to us.

The order appealed from was entered October 11th. The judgment set aside was entered September 5th, more than thirty days prior thereto. Plaintiff therefore contends that the proceeding was necessarily under Section 21 of the Municipal court act, and that the petition was insufficient when considered as a bill in equity, or its equivalent, under the rule stated in Imbrie v. Bear, 230 Ill. App. 155, and similar cases.

As already stated, the motion to vacate the judgment was first made September 17th, and was therefore within the thirty-day period, after which by virtue of the provisions of Section 21 of the Municipal court act, the judgment would become final. The order of October 10th by Judge Green directs the withdrawal of that motion. The proceedings before Judge Green are not preserved. Plaintiff argues that the motion was denied, but the record does not justify that inference. The language of the order does not seem to have been chosen with care. The court had no power to direct the withdrawal of the motion. That power was with the attorney for defendant alone. The court might have denied the motion, but the court was without power to cause an order withdrawing the motion to be entered. It seems altogether probable that the intention was to give defendant leave to withdraw its own unverified

petition. If we so regard this order, the motion to set aside the prior judgment was still pending and made in apt time, and the order granting it would not be an appealable order, and this appeal should be dismissed. As there is no report of proceedings or bill of exceptions, we do not know the reasons which moved the trial court to set aside the judgment. However, the petition filed October 11th was duly verified. It alleged facts which if true justified the inference that the judgment by default was procured under circumstances amounting to fraud. These allegations are not denied on this record, and the argument that the petition on its face shows negligence on the part of defendant and its attorney is not a sufficient reply to an averment charging fraud.

All presumptions are in favor of the order entered by the trial Judge, and it is affirmed.

AFFIRMED.

McSurely, P. J., and O'Connor, J., concur.

38780

R. G. LYDY, INC., a Corporation,
Appellee,

vs.

PAULINE PORTER WHITE,
Appellant.

APPEAL FROM SUPERIOR COURT OF COOK COUNTY.

286 I.A. 608[3]

30

MR. Presiding JUSTICE MATCHETT DELIVERED THE OPINION OF THE COURT.

June 21, 1929, plaintiff corporation entered into a writing whereby defendant, Pauline Porter White, demised to it for a term of five years beginning July 1, 1929, certain premises in Chicago known as 11 East Wacker drive, to be used for open air parking and an automobile filling and greasing station, with uses incident thereto. The lease was on form No. 42, "printed and for sale by the Chicago Legal News Co." and contained the usual provisions for what is known as a ground lease. To this printed form a typewritten rider was attached containing special matters agreed upon by the parties. The rent reserved was $325 per month. The lease was subject to cancellation upon conditions named. Plaintiff agreed to pay the expenses of wrecking an old building standing on the premises which had been condemned by the city. In the printed portion of the lease was a clause by which the lessee agreed to pay all taxes and assessments laid, charged or assessed pending the existence of the lease.

Plaintiff entered into possession and thereafter paid the monthly rental as agreed and complied with all other covenants except as to the payment of taxes and assessments. Defendant having demanded such taxes and assessments, amounting to between $6000 and $7000 annually, plaintiff filed its bill in equity in which it averred that the printed paragraph obligating it to pay taxes and assessments was left in the lease by mistake and that any such agreement was contrary to the actual intention of the

parties. The bill prayed that the lease might be reformed by the elimination from it of this paragraph; that an injunction might issue restraining interference with plaintiff's possession of the premises, and for other relief. Defendant answered denying that the paragraph became a part of the lease through mistake; averred that it was the intention of the parties that plaintiff should pay the taxes, and denied that plaintiff was entitled to relief. She also filed a cross bill averring facts similar to those set up in her answer, particularly with reference to the intention of the parties, and prayed that an accounting might be taken and a decree entered in her favor, requiring plaintiff to pay the amount found to be due under this paragraph of the lease. Plaintiff answered, denying the material allegations of the cross bill. Defendant filed a supplemental cross bill which plaintiff also answered, denying its material averments.

The cause was put at issue and referred to a master who reported in favor of plaintiff and recommended a decree as prayed in the bill. The cause was heard by the chancellor upon exceptions to the report of the master. The report was in all respects approved and a decree entered reforming the lease by the elimination of the paragraph in question, and from that decree defendant appeals to this court.

In the last analysis the case seems to turn on an issue of fact. The last lease by plaintiff of the premises made before the old building had been condemned by the City was for a term of three years at a rental of $750 a month. This prior lease by its terms ended April 30, 1927, and under its terms the lessor paid the taxes, special assessments, etc. If we assume the lease here to express the intention of the parties with regard to the payment of the taxes by the lessee, it would require the payment of rental exceeding $1000 a month, exclusive of the cost of the demolition

of the building. Negotiations for the leasing of this ground by plaintiff had been under way for some time, and the evidence shows without contradiction that at no time during such negotiations, either in the verbal conversations or in letters which passed between the parties, was anything said about the lessee paying taxes or special assessments. The monthly rental first suggested by plaintiff was $200 a month; later the offer was increased to $250 a month.

Mr. Templeton, who acted as attorney for both the lessor and the lessee in the preparation of the rider of the lease, says in substance that plaintiff had been much interested in getting a lease of this piece of ground and two similar adjoining pieces; that negotiations were begun by the owner to get a customer for a long-term lease of the same as early as 1926 and these were continued up to 1929. Each time the witness thought the negotiation would result in the execution of such lease, and he discouraged plaintiff for the reason that the execution of any such long-term lease (which the owner, of course, preferred) would necessarily result in the cancellation of any open-air-parking lease plaintiff might have obtained. However, each negotiation for a long-term lease fell through.

Mr. Templeton held conversations about the matter with Dr. White, husband of defendant, and she (anxious to have the property bring in some income) through her agents entered into negotiations with a man named Rosseau, looking toward the execution of a short-term lease of this kind; in fact, Rosseau made a verbal agreement through Mr. Rubloff of Robert White & Co., real estate agents for defendant, for a five-year lease of the premises for parking purposes. It was agreed that the rental should be $325 a month, and that the verbal agreement should be afterward reduced to writing.

of the building. Negotiations for the leasing of this ground by plaintiff had been under way for some time, and the evidence shows without contradiction that at no time during such negotiations, either in the verbal conversations or in letters which passed between the parties, was anything said about the lessee paying taxes or special assessments. The monthly rental first suggested by plaintiff was $200 a month; later the offer was increased to $250 a month.

Mr. Templeton, who acted as attorney for both the lessor and the lessee in the preparation of the rider of the lease, says in substance that plaintiff had been much interested in getting a lease of this piece of ground and two similar adjoining pieces; that negotiations were begun by the owner to get a customer for a long-term lease of the same as early as 1926 and these were continued up to 1929. Each time the witness thought the negotiation would result in the execution of such lease, and he discouraged plaintiff for the reason that the execution of any such long-term lease (which the owner, of course, preferred) would necessarily result in the cancellation of any open-air-parking lease plaintiff might have obtained. However, each negotiation for a long-term lease fell through.

Mr. Templeton held conversations about the matter with Dr. White, husband of defendant, and she (anxious to have the property bring in some income) through her agents entered into negotiations with a man named Rossean, looking toward the execution of a short-term lease of this kind; in fact, Rossean made a verbal agreement through Mr. Rubloff of Robert White & Co., real estate agents for defendant, for a five-year lease of the premises for parking purposes. It was agreed that the rental should be $325 a month, and that the verbal agreement should be afterward reduced to writing.

It is undisputed that in the arrangement between Mr. Rubloff and Mr. Rosseau no mention of taxes or assessments was made. Mr. Lydy of plaintiff company, having heard of this verbal arrangement with Russeau, took the matter up with Dr. Mark White, who told him he was interested only in the best offer and would be willing to lease to him instead of to Rosseau. Mr. Lydy thereafter paid Rosseau $600 for an assignment and withdrawal of his rights or any claim he might have on the lease.

The rider to the ground lease had already been prepared by Mr. Templeton, who, as before said, represented both parties. The rider was changed by inserting the name of plaintiff as lessee, instead of Rosseau, and it was taken by one of the real estate agents and affixed by him to the printed form of ground lease. Mr. Templeton did not see the printed portion of it until after this controversy arose. Plaintiff's real estate agent testified that the lease was made up in White's office, and the name "Robert White & Company, Real Estate and Renting, Chicago," appears thereon. Rubloff, who represented that firm in the execution of this lease, was not called as a witness in the case.

The lease was executed by the parties June 21, 1929. The transaction was closed without any prorating of the taxes, as would have been necessary had it been understood by the parties that the lessee was agreeing to pay the same. There is no provision in the lease requiring the lessee to deposit funds to meet assessments which were then behind schedule. Such provision is usual under such circumstances if the lessee is to pay the taxes. The real estate agents billed defendant for their commission and were paid by defendant. The bill was rendered on the basis of a "gross lease" as distinguished from a "net lease", terms which, the evidence shows, defendant understood perfectly. In a gross lease the lessor pays taxes and assessments; in a net lease taxes and

It is undisputed that in the arrangement between Mr. Rubloff and Mr. Rosseau no mention of taxes or assessments was made. Mr. Lydy of plaintiff company, having heard of this verbal arrangement with Rosseau, took the matter up with Dr. Mark White, who told him he was interested only in the best offer and would be willing to lease to him instead of to Rosseau. Mr. Lydy thereafter paid Rosseau $600 for an assignment and withdrawal of his rights or any claim he might have on the lease.

The rider to the ground lease had already been prepared by Mr. Templeton, who, as before said, represented both parties. The rider was changed by inserting the name of plaintiff as lessee, instead of Rosseau, and it was taken by one of the real estate agents and affixed by him to the printed form of ground lease. Mr. Templeton did not see the printed portion of it until after this controversy arose. Plaintiff's real estate agent testified that the lease was made up in White's office, and the name "Robert White & Company, Real Estate and Renting, Chicago," appears thereon. Rubloff, who represented that firm in the execution of this lease, was not called as a witness in the case.

The lease was executed by the parties June 21, 1929. The transaction was closed without any prorating of the taxes, as would have been necessary had it been understood by the parties that the lessee was agreeing to pay the same. There is no provision in the lease requiring the lessee to deposit funds to meet assessments which were then behind schedule. Such provision is usual under such circumstances if the lessee is to pay the taxes. The real estate agents billed defendant for their commission and were paid by defendant. The bill was rendered on the basis of a "gross lease" as distinguished from a "net lease", terms which, the evidence shows, defendant understood perfectly. In a gross lease the lessor pays taxes and assessments; in a net lease taxes and assessments are paid by the lessee. Dr. Mark White and his wife, defendant, made out a joint income tax return for the year 1929, on which appears as to another piece of real estate the term "net lease," and on cross examination Dr. White said he understood that phrase to mean "he paid the taxes, meaning that the lessee paid the taxes." Also on cross examination, when asked concerning another piece of property, in reply to the question, "Is that a net lease?" defendant answered, "They paid the taxes on it." The income tax returns of the Whites for 1929 and 1930 were made on an accrual basis, and showed income from this property of only $1950 and $3900 respectively. This was the amount of the rental without taxes or assessments. If it had been supposed that the lessee was to pay the taxes, the amount of such taxes would necessarily have been included in the income. It was not included. A revenue agent, Miss M. Austin, examined the lease and told Dr. White that the lessee was liable for the taxes. Up to that time neither defendant nor any of her agents had suggested that plaintiff was so liable. Thereafter, on June 13, 1931, Dr. White wrote plaintiff that the taxes for 1929 were $5016.31, with interest, and demanded payment of one-half thereof.

June 22, 1931, Robert White of Robert White & Co., sent plaintiff a bill for general taxes of 1929 amounting to $5117.16, and special assessments of $3241.38, making a total of $8358.54, and demanded that plaintiff should pay half. Upon receipt of these letters the secretary of plaintiff corporation, according to his testimony, called up Dr. White and told him he had received the letters, but did not understand them since nothing had ever been brought to his attention by anyone indicating that plaintiff was to pay taxes or assessments. Dr. White replied, "If you had read your lease through you would see that." The testimony of the secretary is further to the effect:

assessments are paid by the lessee. Dr. Mark White and his wife, defendant, made out a joint income tax return for the year 1929, on which appears as to another piece of real estate the term "net lease," and on cross examination Dr. White said he understood that phrase to mean "he paid the taxes, meaning that the lessee paid the taxes." Also on cross examination, when asked concerning another piece of property, in reply to the question, "Is that a net lease?" defendant answered, "They paid the taxes on it." The income tax returns of the Whites for 1929 and 1930 were made on an accrual basis, and showed income from this property of only $1950 and $3900 respectively. This was the amount of the rental without taxes or assessments. If it had been supposed that the lessee was to pay the taxes, the amount of such taxes would necessarily have been included in the income. It was not included. A revenue agent, Miss M. Austin, examined the lease and told Dr. White that the lessee was liable for the taxes. Up to that time neither defendant nor any of her agents had suggested that plaintiff was so liable. Thereafter, on June 15, 1931, Dr. White wrote plaintiff that the taxes for 1929 were $5016.31, with interest, and demanded payment of one-half thereof.

June 28, 1931, Robert White of Robert White & Co., sent plaintiff a bill for general taxes of 1929 amounting to $5117.16, and special assessments of $3841.38, making a total of $8958.54, and demanded that plaintiff should pay half. Upon receipt of these letters the secretary of plaintiff corporation, according to his testimony, called up Dr. White and told him he had received the letters, but did not understand them since nothing had ever been brought to his attention by anyone indicating that plaintiff was to pay taxes or assessments. Dr. White replied, "If you had read your lease through you would see that." The testimony of the secretary is further to the effect:

"I said, 'I don't know about that. Where do you find it in the lease?' He (Dr. White) said, 'Uncle Sam sent a pretty smart girl here to look over our income tax return. She showed it to me in the printed part of the lease. I had not known it myself, that it was there, and find that I had something now I did not know I had before. Mrs. White and I have considerable property. I am pretty hard up and having a hard time to pay our taxes, and here we find someone to pay our taxes for us.' I said, 'That is purely a technicality. Are you going ahead on a technicality?' He said, 'We have something here we did not know we had, and we need it very much. Perhaps if we had plenty of money to pay our taxes we would not take advantage of it, but I don't see anything for us to do but take advantage of it. I have deducted the amount of these taxes from our return, now we are going to have to pay income tax for the amount of these taxes, and I think we should have our taxes paid as we are going to have that additional expense,' and that was the sum and substance of it."

Dr. White admits the conversation by 'phone and that he said the government inspector had ruled that plaintiff should pay the 1929 taxes and led him to so understand, but denies having made other specific statements.

The evidence shows that later in the same year this lease was taken, plaintiff acquired three adjoining tracts of land for similar purposes; that the four leases contained similar riders attached to a similar printed form of ground lease, and that the ground lease in each case contained a printed covenant that the lessee should pay taxes and assessments. Prior to making those leases, Mr. Lydy handed to the lessors of these other tracts of land an original or copy of the lease entered into between plaintiff and defendant, and the lessors substantially copied the rider and attached it to this printed form of ground lease. Of the four lessors, defendant was the only one who made a demand for the payment of taxes or special assessments. Plaintiff conducts a number of these parking places in the city of Chicago and holds leases of the same but does not pay the taxes or assessments upon any of them.

Defendant says that there is no evidence in the record that any of the supposed agents for her ever agreed with plaintiff that the lessor, and not the lessee, should pay the taxes; that if any of them had so verbally agreed, such agent had no authority to bind

her for a term of five years, because such authority was not in writing, and, further, that there is no evidence that she gave any such authority, irrespective of the provisions of the statute which would require it to be in writing. She calls attention to the rule of law that in a case of this nature the proof must not be doubtful; that a mere preponderance of the evidence is not sufficient. It is so held in many cases, of which Lines v. Willey, 253 Ill. 440; Christ v. Rake, 287 Ill. 619; Mansell v. Lord Lumber & Fuel Co., 348 Ill. 140, are illustrative. The evidence in this case did not leave any doubt in the mind of the master, who saw and heard the witnesses, or in the mind of the chancellor, who gave consideration to the evidence. It leaves no doubt in our minds. The circumstances are such as to compel the conclusion that it was not the intention of the parties to this lease that the lessee should, in addition to the rental specified in the lease, pay the taxes and assessments, and that the insertion of this paragraph was the result of a mutual mistake. The evidence is uncontradicted to the effect that in negotiations leading up to the lease, no such matter was ever mentioned by any of the parties, and the conduct of defendant and her husband after the making of the lease is such as to demonstrate conclusively that they did not understand or believe that any such provision was in the lease. Whatever may have been the requirement of the statute, or the authority of defendant's agents, the contract was made when defendant, ratifying the actions of her husband and other agents, affixed her signature to the lease. It is perfectly clear that when she so signed it was with the understanding that she, not the lessee, would pay the taxes and special assessments.

The decree of the Superior court is right and is affirmed.

AFFIRMED.

McSurely, P. J., and O'Connor, J., concur.

38790

MABEL WINZENBURG,
Appellee,

vs.

GIRARD FIRE AND MARINE INSURANCE COMPANY, a Corporation,
Appellant.

APPEAL FROM SUPERIOR COURT OF COOK COUNTY.

286 I.A. 608[4]

MR. PRESIDING JUSTICE MATCHETT DELIVERED THE OPINION OF THE COURT.

In an action on a fire insurance policy covering a cottage and personal property therein, and upon trial by the court there was a finding for plaintiff and assessment of damages of $1250 for loss of the cottage and $350 for loss of personal property, with interest on both items amounting to $344.44, making a total of $1944.44, for which the court entered judgment.

The cottage in question was located on Lot 7 of Wy-Ho-Co's Shore Acres in Allegan County, Michigan. The insurance policy was issued by defendant through its agent, John W.Hardt Agency, Inc., of South Haven, Michigan, on September 1, 1930. Plaintiff was then and is now a resident of Chicago, Illinois, and the parties concede that the contract of insurance is an Illinois contract. The cottage and its contents were destroyed by fire April 22, 1931, while the policy was in force. The policy contained the following provision:

"This entire policy shall be void, unless otherwise provided by agreement in writing added hereto:
(a) if the interest of the insured be other than unconditional and sole ownership when loss or damage occurs."

Defendant contends that plaintiff was not the unconditional and sole owner within the meaning of this clause and that the policy is therefore void. The evidence shows that originally Frances M. Wyatt, the daughter of plaintiff, was the owner of the premises upon which the cottage was situated. On May 6, 1930, Frances M. and her husband, by warranty deed, conveyed these premises with other property to plaintiff, Mabel Winzenburg, mother of Frances M.

The deed delivered recited a consideration of $7000 and was duly executed and delivered. Two days later, May 8th, Mrs. Winzenburg executed and delivered a mortgage conveying the premises to her daughter, Mrs. Wyatt, to secure an indebtedness of $3500. The examination of plaintiff by defendant's attorney disclosed that Mrs. Wyatt had for ten years prior to this transaction been indebted to plaintiff in the amount of $3500, and that the daughter suggested to her mother that she, the mother, buy this cottage and take a deed therefor, giving back a mortgage for the difference between the amount of the consideration and the indebtedness of the daughter to her mother. The testimony of Mrs. Winzenburg upon the trial was clear and positive to that effect. Defendant, however, undertook to impeach her by statements made by her upon examination before a notary public on September 28, 1934, a year prior to the trial. This evidence was introduced by defendant for the purpose of impeaching plaintiff's testimony given on direct examination. The transaction was between mother and daughter and, more or less, a family affair. There are expressions made by plaintiff in her answers to leading and suggestive questions put to her by defendant's counsel to the effect that the deed was given to her as security. Her whole examination indicates, however, that while the attorney for defendant succeeded in confusing her, nothing was said by her which could overcome the deed and other written instruments, which disclose the intention of the parties that plaintiff should take title in fee simple to the premises.

It is next contended that plaintiff failed to comply with the condition precedent contained in the policy to the effect that she should within sixty days after any loss make a statement of proof thereof, signed and sworn to by her. Plaintiff made proofs of loss within sixty days, but these proofs were executed

by Mr. Wyatt, who acted as her agent in that matter. Defendant cites German Fire Ins. Co. v. Grunert, 112 Ill. 68, and Lumbermen's Mutual Ins. Co. v. Bell, 166 Ill. 400, to the point that proofs by an agent are not admissible under circumstances appearing herein, and that if the insured does not make proof, a valid reason therefor, as that the insured is dead, a non-resident, absent or insane at the time of the loss, must be shown.

Plaintiff gave evidence tending to show that Mr. Wyatt, as her agent, executed these proofs of loss at the request of defendant's representative, John W. Hardt. Defendant contends that evidence as to any conversations with Hardt was inadmissible, as he was deceased at the time of the trial; but irrespective of this testimony, it appears without contradiction that defendant received these proofs of loss as made by Mr. Wyatt without objection and retained them. We hold that upon the clearest principles, defendant is now estopped to urge that the proofs should have been executed by plaintiff personally. Mr. Wyatt was permitted to testify over objection made that John W. Hardt, deceased agent of defendant, requested him to execute the proofs in plaintiff's behalf. It is urged this evidence was not admissible by reason of section 4 of the Evidence act. Illinois State Bar Stats. 1935, chap. 51, p. 1616. Defendant cites Helbig v. Citizens Ins. Co., 234 Ill. 251, and Rouse v. Tomasek, 279 Ill. App. 557. Section 4, disqualifies a party to the cause from testifying to a conversation with the deceased agent of the other party. The question is whether this disqualification extends also to an agent of the party - a question raised but not decided in Buchanan v. Scottish Union & Nat'l Ins. Co., 210 Ill. App. 523. We held in Price Co. v. Ruggles & Rademaker Salt Co., 283 Ill. App. 447, that the disqualification did not extend to conversations by Mr. Wyatt, who acted as her agent in that matter. Defendant cites German Fire Ins. Co. v. Grunert, 112 Ill. 68, and Lumbermen's Mutual Ins. Co. v. Bell, 166 Ill. 400, to the point that proofs by an agent are not admissible under circumstances appearing herein, and that if the insured does not make proof, a valid reason therefor, as that the insured is dead, a nonresident, absent or insane at the time of the loss, must be shown.

Plaintiff gave evidence tending to show that Mr. Wyatt, as her agent, executed these proofs of loss at the request of defendant's representative, John W. Hardt. Defendant contends that evidence as to any conversations with Hardt was inadmissible, as he was deceased at the time of the trial; but irrespective of this testimony, it appears without contradiction that defendant received these proofs of loss as made by Mr. Wyatt without objection and retained them. We hold that upon the clearest principles, defendant is now estopped to urge that the proofs should have been executed by plaintiff personally. Mr. Wyatt was permitted to testify over objection made that John W. Hardt, deceased agent of defendant, requested him to execute the proofs in plaintiff's behalf. It is urged this evidence was not admissible by reason of section 4 of the Evidence act. Illinois State Bar Stats. 1935, chap. 51, p. 1616. Defendant cites Helbig v. Citizens Ins. Co., 234 Ill. 251, and Pigue v. Tomcsek, 279 Ill. App. 557. Section 4, disqualifies a party to the cause from testifying to a conversation with the deceased agent of the other party. The question is whether this disqualification extends also to an agent of the party - a question raised but not decided in Buchanan v. Scottish Union & Nat'l Ins. Co., 210 Ill. App. 523. We held in Price Co. v. Burgles & Hademaker Salt Co., 283 Ill. App. 447, that the disqualification did not extend to conversations of one agent with another. Wyatt had no financial interest in this controversy. In Feitl v. Chicago City Ry. Co., 211 Ill. 279, the Supreme court held that disqualification of a principal on the ground of interest did not extend to the agent of the principal, unless the agent himself had a legal interest in the outcome of the suit. To the same effect is 70 C. J. 266, par. 333. We hold the evidence was properly admitted.

Defendant argues that the damages are excessive and attacks two of plaintiff's witnesses, who testified as to the value of the premises, claiming that these witnesses were not qualified. The witnesses might have been better qualified, but their evidence was not incompetent. Plaintiff makes similar observations as to defendant's expert, and her observations are not without merit. The evidence affirmatively shows that defendant caused an appraisement of the cottage to be made prior to the issuance of the policy of insurance and agreed that the insurance upon it should be raised to the sum of $2500. Defendant had written a prior policy upon the same property for a lesser amount. After the fire plaintiff offered to let defendant replace the cottage, but the offer was not accepted. The court saw and heard the witnesses, and we think the amount allowed for the loss cannot be held so excessive as to require a reversal by this court.

There is a provision in the insurance policy to the effect that as to the personal property a chattel mortgage would render the policy void. The provision of the policy is:

"Unless otherwise provided by agreement in writing added hereto this company shall not be liable for loss or damage to any property insured hereunder while encumbered by a chattel mortgage, and during the time of such encumbrance this company shall be liable only for loss or damage to any other property insured hereunder."

The deed by which Mrs. Wyatt conveyed this and other property to her mother by its terms included "furniture and fittings on the premises." The real estate mortgage executed by plaintiff of one agent with another. Wyatt had no financial interest in this controversy. In Feitl v. Chicago City Ry. Co., 211 Ill. 279, the Supreme court held that disqualification of a principal on the ground of interest did not extend to the agent of the principal, unless the agent himself had a legal interest in the outcome of the suit. To the same effect is 70 C. J. 265, par. 355. We hold the evidence was properly admitted.

Defendant argues that the damages are excessive and attacks two of plaintiff's witnesses, who testified as to the value of the premises, claiming that these witnesses were not qualified. The witnesses might have been better qualified, but their evidence was not incompetent. Plaintiff makes similar observations as to defendant's expert, and her observations are not without merit. The evidence affirmatively shows that defendant caused an appraisement of the cottage to be made prior to the issuance of the policy of insurance and agreed that the insurance upon it should be raised to the sum of $3500. Defendant had written a prior policy upon the same property for a lesser amount. After the fire plaintiff offered to let defendant replace the cottage, but the offer was not accepted. The court saw and heard the witnesses, and we think the amount allowed for the loss cannot be held so excessive as to require a reversal by this court.

There is a provision in the insurance policy to the effect that as to the personal property a chattel mortgage would render the policy void. The provision of the policy is:

"Unless otherwise provided by agreement in writing added hereto this company shall not be liable for loss or damage to any property insured hereunder while encumbered by a chattel mortgage, and during the time of such encumbrance this company shall be liable only for loss or damage to any other property insured hereunder."

The deed by which Mrs. Wyatt conveyed this and other property to her mother by its terms included "furniture and fittings on the premises." The real estate mortgage executed by plaintiff reconveying to Mrs. Wyatt recites that it includes "furnishings on said lots". The court, as already stated, allowed plaintiff $350 for loss of chattels which were in the insured cottage. Does the word "furnishings" include furniture? Was the personal property conveyed by Mrs. Wyatt to Mrs. Winzenberg by the deed the chattels which were destroyed by fire, and for which proofs of loss were made and allowed by the court? There is an absence of proof on this point. The defense is an affirmative one. The burden of proof was on defendant. The insurance policy is to be construed most strongly against the insurance company. There was, strictly speaking, no chattel mortgage executed conveying this property. The mortgage was a real estate mortgage, and we think it doubtful whether, even as between the parties, it could be held to be a chattel mortgage upon these chattels. The description of the chattels is too indefinite. A chattel mortgage is not a real estate mortgage, and the provision of the insurance policy covering the chattels was not void for this reason. It follows the judgment of the trial court should be and it is affirmed.

AFFIRMED.

O'Connor and McSurely, JJ., concur.

reconveying to Mrs. Wyatt recites that it includes "furnishings on said lots". The court, as already stated, allowed plaintiff $350 for loss of chattels which were in the insured cottage. Does the word "furnishings" include furniture? Was the personal property conveyed by Mrs. Wyatt to Mrs. Winnenberg by the deed the chattels which were destroyed by fire, and for which proofs of loss were made and allowed by the court? There is an absence of proof on this point. The defense is an affirmative one. The burden of proof was on defendant. The insurance policy is to be construed most strongly against the insurance company. There was, strictly speaking, no chattel mortgage executed conveying this property. The mortgage was a real estate mortgage, and we think it doubtful whether, even as between the parties, it could be held to be a chattel mortgage upon these chattels. The description of the chattels is too indefinite. A chattel mortgage is not a real estate mortgage, and the provision of the insurance policy covering the chattels was not void for this reason. It follows the judgment of the trial court should be and it is affirmed.

AFFIRMED.

O'Connor and Donnelly, JJ., concur.

38808

SAMUEL H. GILBERT, Appellant,	)	APPEAL FROM CIRCUIT COURT OF COOK COUNTY.
vs.	)	
JAMES ZAJICEK and ALBIE ZAJICEK, Appellees.	)	286 I.A. 609[1]

MR. PRESIDING JUSTICE MATCHETT DELIVERED THE OPINION OF THE COURT.

This appeal is by plaintiff from a decree entered by the Circuit court of Cook county October 17, 1935, dismissing his bill for want of equity. Plaintiff is the assignee of a judgment entered October 20, 1933, in the Circuit court of Cook county against James Zajicek, in favor of Robert L. Floyd and Andrew Mitchell for $400 in an action begun June 7, 1932. The judgment not having been paid, execution issued to the Sheriff of Cook county, demand was made and the execution returned no part satisfied.

May 4, 1934, plaintiff filed his bill in equity, setting up the foregoing facts and alleging that James Zajicek and Tillie, his wife, on or about October 5, 1909, acquired title in fee simple and in joint tenancy to certain real estate situated in Cook County; that April 18, 1932, the owners conveyed this real estate by quitclaim deed to their daughter, Albie Zajicek; that the conveyance was made without consideration and with the intention to cheat the creditors of James Zajicek - Floyd and Mitchell - and was therefore void. The bill prayed the conveyance might be set aside and the interest of the judgment debtor sold to satisfy plaintiff's claim.

Defendants answered, admitting the rendition of the judgment, the acquisition of title to the real estate, the recording of same, and the conveyance of the premises to Albie Zajicek on April 18, 1932. The answer also stated defendants had no knowledge of the alleged assignment and demanded strict proof. It denied that the conveyance to Albie was made without consideration or with intention to defraud, but averredthat the conveyance was made for

good and valuable consideration moving from Albie Zajicek to James Zajicek and was in all respects valid. The cause was heard in open court. Exhibits showing the rendition and the assignment of the judgment were offered and received in evidence, and plaintiff also submitted depositions of defendants Albie and James Zajicek.

The testimony of Albie Zajicek was to the effect that in 1915 she lent to her father, James Zajicek, $3000 to finish paying for the building erected on the premises in which they lived; that he did not make any payments to her from that time to April 15, 1932; that the matter of her father giving her a deed was discussed a couple of months before the deed was given; that she collected rent ever after the building was erected; she has never paid a penny for rent of the flat she occupied; the tenants never paid rent to her father but always to her. She also testified that the fact that her father was in litigation or that suits were threatened did not enter her mind in connection with the deed, and that she was never told anything of the sort. She testified that besides the $3000 she gave her father everything she had after 1930: $3000 in 1915 and about $1000 after 1930. She said that the contractor's bill for constructing the building on the property was $5098; that she put about $4000 cash into the building in 1932; the taxes each year amounted to $143, $184, - "different amounts," and that she paid them; after she got the deed she kept the rents and she paid the expense of making the deed of the premises to her.

James Zajicek testified that he was engaged in fishing and hunting; that he lived with his daughter; that he turned the property over to his daughter in 1932 and owned no other property, except personalty in the way of a couple of tables, drawers, two stoves and a wardrobe; that he got $3000 from his daughter and with it paid the balance for the building, which cost $5098; that

the building was started in 1914 and finished in 1915; that his daughter lived on the property, took care of it, paid the taxes, and if there was anything left, turned it over to him; that he got some income from it every year; that his daughter had been supporting him since October, 1934; that prior to that time he supported himself, living on the lake. He said that the tenants never paid him any rent, his daughter did all the collecting, paid the taxes, water rent, repairs, etc. He said, "She lately was asking me for money. I said, 'I ain't got any more money.' She said, 'The only thing you can give me is the property,' and I said, 'All right.' That, I think, was in 1932; I ain't quite certain."

This is the material evidence submitted, and it tended to show the conveyance was made for a valuable consideration before the rendition of the judgment. While the effect of the conveyance of the premises by James Zajicek was to give to his daughter a preference over other creditors, this is not contrary to law, as a debtor has a right to prefer one creditor over others in the absence of fraud. Third National Bank v. Norris, 331 Ill. 230; Hurt v. Ohlman, 349 Ill. 163; Doty v. O'Neill, 272 Ill. App. 212. Plaintiff having called these adversaries as witnesses has vouched for their credibility. Luthy & Co. v. Paradis, 299 Ill. 380. No contrary evidence was offered.

The cases with practical unanimity show that a decree dismissing the bill for want of equity was the only one that could have been properly entered under the evidence. For this reason it is affirmed.

AFFIRMED.

McSurely, P. J., and O'Connor, J., concur.

38822

LIPPEL & FEIT, INC., a Corporation, Appellee,

vs.

ALBERT J. HORAN, Bailiff of the Municipal Court of Chicago, Appellant.

APPEAL FROM MUNICIPAL COURT OF CHICAGO.

33

286 I.A. 609[2]

MR. PRESIDING JUSTICE MATCHETT DELIVERED THE OPINION OF THE COURT.

This is an appeal by defendant from a judgment in the sum of $435.50 in favor of plaintiff entered upon the finding of the court. Defendant is bailiff of the Municipal court of Chicago. The action of plaintiff was for alleged negligence by which goods, upon which the bailiff had levied under an execution issued in favor of plaintiff against one Julius Siegel, were lost by burglary. The defense interposed was that defendant was not negligent.

The facts appear to be that Julius Siegel, the judgment debtor of plaintiff, owned a suit and dress store located at 3234 W. Roosevelt Road in Chicago. On December 18, 1934, plaintiff obtained a judgment against him for $409.24, execution thereon issued to the bailiff, and on December 28th plaintiff's attorney requested the bailiff to levy this execution on the fixtures and goods in the store. Plaintiff gave the usual bond of indemnity to the bailiff on that day. The arrangement for the levy was made with Mr. Orr, a deputy bailiff in defendant's office, in charge of such matters. Mr. Lipman, the attorney of record for plaintiff in the suit against Siegel, was in Florida at this time, and his associate, another attorney, Stephen T. Ronan, represented plaintiff. On the morning of the following day, December 29th, Deputy Froehlich of defendant's office, made the levy, taking with him Sam Simon, who was made custodian, Harry Hayman and Walter Krietzberg. An inventory of the property, consisting of fixtures and 207 dresses, was made. Siegel turned over the key to the front door of the building,

which was one story in height. The deputy obtained an additional lock, which was put on the front door. The back door was made of metal and had no lock but was barricaded with a 2 by 4 plank placed crosswise and fastened at the ends with iron hooks. Siegel, the owner, testified that the barricade of the back door was in very good condition. The custodian proceeded to make it more secure by another barricade made by using a ladder, one end of which he placed against the door and the other against a table. The owner had for some months been sleeping every night in the store, and he told the deputies that the place had been robbed during the previous year.

Froehlich testifies that he told the attorney for plaintiff that a day and night watchman would be needed. Mr. Orr, who was in charge of the levy, testifies that the deputy made a suggestion to him for a day and night custodian; that he took the matter up with attorney Ronan, then acting as plaintiff's attorney, who said that inasmuch as a day man was in possession and would lock up the store at night, he would not want a night custodian. Ronan denies that he used this precise language but says that he was told a custodian had to be appointed and the hours he had to be there, and he says, "I just authorized them to put in a custodian, night or day. I supposed they did their duty there."

Siegel had purchased the dresses, in part, from the firm of Jack Camac and, in part, from Bennett Munves. The goods and chattels had been advertised to be sold January 9, 1935, and on January 7th Camac took out a summons in a proceeding demanding the trial right of property as to the goods sold by him. The records of the bailiff's office show that this writ was filed in the office of the bailiff January 8, 1935, and was delivered to Mr. Lane, a deputy bailiff head of the assignment department,

whose duty it was to take care of service of writs in the trial right of property. He testified that he served that writ on the attorney representing defendant on January 8th, and the writ was returned to the clerk January 9th. In the case brought by Munves the writ was filed in the bailiff's office January 8, 1935, delivered to Lane for service on the same date and returned served to the clerk's office on January 9th. The return on the summons shows that it was served upon plaintiff by service on S. T. Ronan, attorney and agent. Lane testified that when a writ of this kind would first come to the office it was served on the bailiff by the clerk, and that the man in the filing department immediately telephoned the attorney representing the defendant in the case, telling of the notice for trial of right of property so that he could offer to accept service. The writs are not given to persons to take out and serve, but the bailiffs call up the attorneys representing the judgment creditors. Lane testified that Ronan was invited to the bailiff's office and that he came and stated he was attorney for plaintiff in the case in which judgment was obtained and asked to be served with summons. Lane is positive that Ronan presented himself on the 8th, and the return on the summons and files of the bailiff's office so indicate. Ronan denies Lane's testimony with respect to his acting as agent and attorney for plaintiff, and says he had nothing to do with trial right of property cases except as interested as being with Mr. Lipman. He was in court, however, with Mr. Lipman when the cases were tried.

Orr testified that January 8th Mr. Lipman, plaintiff's attorney, came to his office and stated that he wished to keep down the costs and expressed the wish that a custodian should not be kept longer in possession of the store. Orr then handed to Lipman a written request to that effect, which is in evidence. It is addressed to the bailiff, is dated Chicago, January 8, 1935, requests

that one Davey be appointed custodian without compensation and agrees to indemnify the bailiff and his deputies from all damages by reason of such appointment. This writing is signed, "David Lipman, attorney for Lippel & Feit, Inc."

On the morning of January 9th Simon, the custodian for the bailiff, telephoned to the office of the bailiff that the store had been robbed during the night. Orr went there immediately, found that the roof ventilator had been torn away, apparently with crowbars, and that the plaster fastened underneath the ventilator was ripped down, part of it lying on the floor, a ladder was hanging underneath the ventilator, and a rope across the ventilator was hanging down from the top. All but 10 of the 207 dresses shown by the inventory had been stolen. Under date of January 8, 1935, the bailiff wrote a letter to Lipman, giving formal notice of the suits begun by Jack Camac, Inc., and Bennett Kunves against the bailiff and Lippel & Feit, Inc., plaintiff. The writs were returnable in court on January 14, 1935. The letter asked Lipman to confer with the attorney for bailiff, Benjamin E. Cohen.

Lipman testified that he went to the bailiff's office not on January 8th but on January 9th, in response to this letter, between 11 and 12 o'clock and talked with Orr; that he asked him what could be done to stop custodian's costs in view of the proceedings for trial right of property; that Orr said they would settle the custodian costs for $40, although $44 was then due at the rate of $4 a day. He says that Mr. Orr said that this could be done by dating the written request back to January 8th, and that the costs would thereby appear to be only $40; that Orr agreed with him on the payment of $40 and that he signed the release in evidence there on January 9th, it being dated back to January 8th. The attorney was permitted to corroborate this testimony by reading into the record personal memoranda made by him to that effect. He also testified that he first heard that the goods had been stolen

when the attorney for plaintiff in the trial of the property right cases telephoned him on January 9th; that in company with Ronan he went over to see Orr about four o'clock and told him of the information given him, and he says that Orr said he had found it out only five minutes before, and told him, "Don't worry, I won't let you hold the bag."

Over objection of defendant, plaintiff was permitted to put in evidence a letter of January 9, 1935, giving further corroboration. The letter, written by Lipman to defendant bailiff, directed to the attention of Orr, states that Lipman had signed the release dated back to January 7th, as agreed, and that he had heard of the theft of the goods from Mr. Reeder, attorney for plaintiffs in the property right cases. It was clearly a self-serving document and should not have been admitted in evidence. Five other letters, also written by plaintiffs' attorney to the bailiff after the controversy arose and not in reply to any letter from the bailiff, were improperly admitted in evidence. They should have been excluded because self-serving documents.

Orr testifies positively that the request for the appointment of Davey as custodian was not predated and denies _in toto_ the evidence given by attorneys for plaintiff to that effect. The testimony of Orr is corroborated by that of Lane and by the records and files of the bailiff's office. The burden of proof so far as the predating of this document was concerned was upon plaintiff, and we are of the opinion that the contention of plaintiff with respect to it is contrary to the evidence.

There is some controversy between the parties as to the rule of law applicable to sheriffs and bailiffs and similar officials who come into the possession of goods as the result of levy by final process. The briefs would indicate a dearth of cases from the courts of Illinois on this subject. Both parties cite

Jones v. McGuirk, 51 Ill. 382, where the defendant, a United States marshal, levied upon a boat under a writ of attachment. The rule there stated is that "due diligence" must be exercised. In Moore v. Westervelt, 27 N. Y. 234, the court said that a sheriff in such case was obliged to use ordinary diligence in taking care of property seized. A few cases, such as Hartlieb v. McLane's Administrators, 44 Pa. 510, impose a much more stringent rule holding the officer liable for the loss of property in his custody unless due to the act of God, the public enemies or some irresistible accident. Freeman in his work on Executions, vol. 2, sec. 270, seems to approve of the same rule, although admitting that the tendency of modern decisions is to place levies under attachment upon the same footing with levies under execution and to exact of officers in both cases that degree of care "which an owner of ordinary prudence and sagacity would exercise in preserving like property." We think this to be the true rule. The bailiff having the custody of the property, proof of his failure to produce it made a prima facie case, but when the evidence was produced affirmatively showing that the property had been stolen without negligence by the bailiff or his deputies, it then was necessary for plaintiff to produce further proof tending to show that the sheriff was negligent and that his negligence caused the loss of the goods.

The evidence in this record comes short of establishing these necessary facts. This levy was made under the direction of plaintiff's attorney. There is no proof tending to show that any reasonable request made by him was disregarded by the bailiff, and the clear inference from all the evidence is that he requested only one custodian should be employed. Much was made upon the trial of the fact that no lock was obtained for the back door. The door was of metal, and it was practically impossible to use a

lock on it. Moreover, the evidence clearly shows that the robbers came through the roof and not by way of the back door, so that the absence of a lock on the back door did not in any way cause the loss of the goods. There was, of course, no reason why the bailiff should not have been entirely willing to appoint any number of custodians requested. There appears in the record a statement which purports to be by the trial Judge as to his reasons for his finding. The document was apparently drawn by attorneys in the case and partakes very much of the nature of findings formerly required to sustain a decree in equity. Such statement does not comply with either the rules of the Municipal court or the provisions of the Practice act. The controlling issue in this case - one of fact - must be determined by the credence given to the testimony of Orr and Lane as corroborated by the records and files of the court, and the testimony of attorneys for plaintiff, which is quite improbable and corroborated only by self-serving memoranda and letters. If issues of fact could be determined through the admission in evidence of letters written by the attorneys for one of the parties, it would not be difficult for a plaintiff to prove any kind of a case. Such evidence is by rule of law inadmissible. It, apparently, was permitted to determine the issue of fact in this case.

For this reason the judgment of the trial court is reversed with a finding of fact here that defendant bailiff was not negligent as alleged in the statement of claim, and that as a matter of law he is not liable to plaintiff.

REVERSED WITH FINDING OF FACT.

O'Connor and McSurely, JJ., concur.

38844

ROSE MANASTER, Appellant,

vs.

HARRY'S NEW YORK CABARET, Inc., a Corporation, Appellee.

APPEAL FROM MUNICIPAL COURT OF CHICAGO.

34

286 I.A. 609[3]

MR. PRESIDING JUSTICE MATCHETT DELIVERED THE OPINION OF THE COURT.

November 8, 1935, plaintiff filed in the Municipal court a statement of claim in which she averred that defendant Cabaret conducted a restaurant in Chicago; that on or about August 3, 1935, she purchased ice cream from defendant for immediate consumption in the restaurant; that the ice cream was not, in fact, wholesome as warranted but dangerous and unfit to be eaten, and without knowledge or notice as to the condition of the ice cream and relying on defendant's warranty that it was wholesome, she ate it, and that several fragments of glass in the ice cream became imbedded in her throat, causing her to become violently sick, etc. The statement of claim also averred that the ice cream served was manufactured by the Goodman-American Ice Cream Co., a corporation of Chicago, and said company was joined as defendant to the suit. A summons issued returnable November 21, 1935, and was served upon both defendants. Upon the return day the default of the Cabaret for want of an appearance was entered, and on the following day, November 22nd, the court, as the record shows, found from plaintiff's statement of claim that there was due plaintiff $1000 and entered judgment by default against the Cabaret Co. for that amount. December 2nd the Ice Cream Co. made a motion that the statement of claim be stricken, and December 27, 1935, plaintiff dismissed her suit as to the Ice Cream Co. January 3, 1936, which was more than 30 days after the judgment was rendered, the Cabaret company filed a motion to vacate the

default and judgment entered against it, and on January 8th filed its affidavit and petition in support of the motion.

In this petition the Cabaret company stated that it was served with summons November 12, 1935; that the Goodman-American Ice Cream Co. was impleaded with it, both defendants being sued jointly; that immediately thereafter it communicated with the Ice Cream Co. and imparted to it the information that defendant Cabaret Co. had been served with summons returnable November 21, 1935; that a representative of the Ice Cream Co. personally visited the premises of defendant and stated to Mr. Hepp of the Cabaret Co. that it would not be necessary for the Cabaret Co. to file any appearance or answer to the suit, but that the Ice Cream Co. would cause an appearance for both defendants to be filed; that the Ice Cream Co. had already employed competent attorneys to defend the action both for the Ice Cream Co. and the Cabaret Co., and that the action was baseless. The petition averred that the Cabaret Co. relied on these representations, took no further steps in the matter, fully believing that the representations and statements made to it by the representative of the Ice Cream corporation were true and the interests of the Cabaret Co. fully protected; that the Cabaret had no knowledge of any judgment entered against it in the case until December 31, 1935, when it was served with an execution and a levy upon its goods upon the judgment entered November 22, 1935; that as a matter of fact the attorneys for the Ice Cream Co. took no steps whatever in behalf of defendant Cabaret, failed and neglected to file an appearance or affidavit of merits, in disregard and violation of the promises of the Ice Cream Co.; that the Ice Cream Co. in its own behalf caused a motion to be entered on November 21st asking for ten days to file an affidavit of merits and at the same time allowed a default to be entered against defendant Cabaret; that on November 22nd damages were assessed by the court on the affidavit

of claim without hearing evidence, for $1000, when, as a matter of fact, the affidavit of claim was incomplete, in that it stated no amount of money to be due in the action, which was for the recovery of an unliquidated sum, and that on December 27, 1935, upon motion of plaintiff, the suit was dismissed as to the Ice Cream Co. and thereupon an execution was levied upon the Cabaret company. The petition avers that by these acts and doings of the parties fraud was perpetrated upon the court, and that the court would not have entered a judgment against the Cabaret company had it been advised of the facts, and further that it was a fraud upon the court to cause a judgment to be entered _pro confesso_ and damages to be assessed against defendant Cabaret company upon an incomplete and imperfect affidavit of claim in an action for unliquidated damages without the court hearing proof or evidence to sustain the judgment.

The affidavit goes on to state that the Cabaret company has a good and meritorious defense to the whole of the demand, in that the ice cream sold and delivered to plaintiff was good and wholesome, contained no dangerous foreign substances, and was safe for human consumption; specifically denies that defendant Cabaret by its agents and servants was careless or wrongfully served and sold the ice cream to plaintiff; denied that by reason of eating such ice cream, fragments of glass were imbedded in plaintiff's throat, and denies that she became violently sick, etc.; further avers that the ice cream served was a product manufactured by the other defendant, Goodman-American Ice Cream Co., a corporation.

Upon the filing of this petition, leave was given plaintiff to file an answer on the question of diligence within five days, and the hearing was set for January 10, 1936. No answer was filed, and on January 10th the court sustained the motion, vacated the

judgment, quashed the execution and levy, and released forthcoming bond which had been given. From that judgment plaintiff has appealed to this court.

Plaintiff contends that since more than thirty days had elapsed after the entry of the original judgment, the court was without jurisdiction to vacate the judgment, except by motion in the nature of a writ of error coram nobis, or by filing a petition which would be sufficient to cause the judgment to be vacated or set aside by a bill in equity. Such is the law as stated in section 21 of the Municipal Court act and construed in Imbrie v. Bear, 230 Ill. App. 155, upon which plaintiff relies. In the absence of denial, the averments of the petition must be taken to be true, and from these averments, taken together with other facts disclosed by the record, it clearly appears that an unjust judgment was rendered, and the circumstances of its entry amounted to the perpetration of a fraud upon the court. Whether we regard this petition as in the nature of a bill in equity, or as an affidavit in support of a motion in the nature of a writ of error coram nobis, it was sufficient. Liberman v. South Side Furniture House, etc., 281 Ill. App. 104; Heinsius v. Poehlmann, 282 Ill. App. 472; Cummer v. Cummer, 283 Ill. App. 220. The facts set up in the petition, which are undenied, render comment unnecessary.

The order vacating the judgment is just and it is affirmed.

AFFIRMED.

O'Connor and McSurely, JJ., concur.

38852

WILLIAM E. MAHER,
Appellee,

vs.

THE NEW YORK, CHICAGO & ST. LOUIS RAILROAD COMPANY, a Corporation,
Appellant.

APPEAL FROM SUPERIOR COURT OF COOK COUNTY.

35

236 I.A. 609

MR. PRESIDING JUSTICE MATCHETT DELIVERED THE OPINION OF THE COURT.

I. In an action on the case based upon the Employers Liability act and upon trial by jury, there was a verdict for plaintiff for $50,000. Upon a remittitur of $10,000 the court overruled motions for a new trial and in arrest of judgment and entered judgment in favor of plaintiff for the sum of $40,000. The same case was before this court on a former appeal, 280 Ill. App. 223, where a judgment in favor of plaintiff for $24,600, entered also upon a verdict of a jury, was reversed on account of procedural errors.

The facts are stated in the opinion rendered on the former appeal and need not be repeated here, further than to state that November 12, 1931, plaintiff (then 29 years of age) while employed by defendant in interstate commerce and while working as one of a switching crew engaged in moving cars, in the switch yards of defendant located at 87th street in Chicago, was injured when the car on which he was riding collided with other cars which had "fouled" the track. Plaintiff was thrown under the car, and the car passing over plaintiff's right arm crushed it, making necessary the amputation of it near the shoulder.

II. It is urged that the court committed reversible error in refusing an offer of defendant to contradict the evidence of plaintiff upon a material issue. On cross examination of plaintiff he was asked if it was not true that at the time of the accident he was leaning around the end of the car trying to lift the pin lifter,

and plaintiff answered, "No." On redirect examination plaintiff was asked by his counsel whether he had ever told anybody else that he was trying at this time to operate the pin lifter; he replied, "No, sir. I never operated it." He was then asked whether he had ever before been accused of operating the pin lifter and falling between the cars because of his effort to do so, and he replied, "No, sir."

At the close of the case (it having been stipulated by the parties that plaintiff was in the court room and listened to the entire argument of attorney for defendant on the former trial) attorney for defendant offered to show that at the time in his argument to the jury he used these words:

> "I submit the evidence in this case furnishes a fair basis for the inference that Maher was trying to throw the switches, or throw the levers around in front of that car, with his arm down, and he did not have hold, as he claims he did, and when the cars came together, he went under, with his right arm, just as he naturally would, through the natural law of momentum, as he was going along that spur."

An objection to this offer was sustained by the court. Defendant argues error, citing such authorities as Wigmore on Evidence, vol. 2, 2nd ed., sec. 1000, pp. 430, 431; Jones on Evidence, 2nd ed., vol. 6, sec. 2469, p. 4890; 70 C. J., sec. 1340, p. 1155; Bray v. Latham, 8 S. E. 64; Johnson v. Ebensen, 160 N. W. 847; Briggs-Weaver Machinery Co. v. Pratt, 184 S. W. 732, which hold that a party who is sued has the right to contradict the testimony of a witness against him by showing that at another time and place the witness made a contrary statement, or that the statement made by him is untrue. This is, of course, only elementary law. In the present case, no witness had given any direct testimony to the effect that plaintiff attempted any such use of the pin lifter. We think the question of plaintiff's attorney as to any former accusation obviously referred to testimony given by some witness in the case rather than to the argument of defendant's lawyer on the

former trial. The argument of a lawyer on the opposite side made to the jury on a former trial is not ordinarily admissible to impeach a party who is a witness. If defendant's attorney desired to use his own argument in that way, he should in fairness have specifically called the attention of plaintiff to the time, place and language of his accusation in order to lay the foundation for the subsequent impeachment. There was, however, no basis in the evidence for injecting the inference that plaintiff was injured while using the pin lifter in the manner indicated, and it was unfair for defendant to inject it into the case by cross examination. The court did not err in sustaining this objection.

III. It is argued that comments of the trial Judge in the presence of the jury with reference to the attitude of a witness for defendant, Mr. Vanderhye, who was in charge of the train at the time the accident occurred, were prejudicial and erroneous. The incident of which defendant strenuously complains occurred on cross examination. The evidence of the witness was important, and his cross examination severe. At the suggestion of counsel for both sides, we have read his testimony as it appears in the record. His answers as to material matters were often unresponsive and evasive, and he was admonished by the court several times on this account. The incident which is characterized in defendant's brief as "an assault by both court and counsel" is as follows:

"Q. Will you pardon me a minute. Did you understand that question? A. Yes.
Q. You understood it perfectly, didn't you? A. Yes.
Q. All right, suppose you are finding these two cars, after they were impacted together with violence, fifteen or twenty feet apart?
A. I don't see how they could.
Q. What did you say?
The Court: 'I don't see how they could' he said. Will you listen to the man's question. Your demeanor on the stand---
The Witness: I am trying to answer him. He don't know the nature of railroading, I don't think.
The Court: Listen to the question.

* * * *

Q. Does that indicate to you how far the engine and cars

moved that hit these cars?

A. The slack would not permit them to move that far.

The Court: Does it indicate or doesn't it?

Mr. Ryan: I guess I won't waste time pursuing this.

The Court: You are not answering the question.

Mr. Smith: If your Honor please, I take exception to the remark of Mr. Ryan in the presence of the jury.

Mr. Ryan: What was that remark?

(Remark read.)

Mr. Smith: I take exception to that remark.

The Court: There is nothing wrong about that remark.

Mr. Smith: I take an exception to the remark of the court that he is wasting time.

The Court: There is nothing about that.

Mr. Smith: In confirming the statement of Mr. Ryan.

Mr. Ryan: This gentleman is drawing on his imagination.

The Court: He has asked me-- let the record show that the witness' demeanor on the stand is continually to evade the questions."

Defendant cites E. J. & E. Ry. Co. v. Lawlor, 229 Ill. 621, where it was held error for the trial judge to say that the evidence of a witness was not credible; Kane v. Kinnare, 69 Ill. App. 81, where Judge Gary made the classic statement - "One of the greatest difficulties of a nisi prius judge is to keep his mouth shut," and similar cases.

The remark of the trial Judge, while not directed to the weight of the evidence, had a tendency to discredit the witness's testimony to a certain extent. However, what the Judge said must have been obvious to the jury. It would have been better left unsaid, but the error is not, we think, reversible. We shall speak of it in a later paragraph of the opinion. Several other alleged errors need only brief attention.

IV. It is urged that the court abused its discretion in permitting leading questions by plaintiff's attorney; but that is a matter very much in the discretion of the trial judge, and error in that respect is reversible only when there is an abuse of discretion with prejudice. Jones on Evidence, vol. 5, 2nd ed., sec. 2332, p. 4562; People v. Schladweiler, 315 Ill. 553; C. & A. R. R. Co. v. Eaton, 96 Ill. App. 570. Introductory

matters, and matters not in controversy, may properly be the subject of leading questions. Greenup v. Stoker, 3 Gilm. 202; Chambers v. The People, 4 Scam. 351. Indeed, it often happens that the trial of cases may be much expedited by the use of such questions. We find no reversible error in this respect.

Defendant also objects that the court permitted impeaching testimony of defendant's witnesses as given to the jury on the former trial to be read to the trial Judge after these witnesses had admitted that they so testified on the former trial. That this is erroneous, he cites Jones on Evidence, vol. 6, 2nd ed., sec. 2405; Swift & Co. v. Madden, 165 Ill. 41, and similar authorities. Defendant specifies Vanderhye and Bonta as witnesses concerning whose testimony the court erred in this respect. In each of these cases the witnesses gave evasive answers, and we think the court did not err in permitting their former evidence to be read.

It is urged that the court erred in permitting witnesses to be interrogated as to the custom of lighting the yards because counsel did not in any count of his declaration charge negligence against defendant on account of its failure to light the yard with flood lights which were stationed at the north end of the yard. These flood lights were out at the time of the accident, but there was no charge of negligence against defendant in this respect, probably for the reason that as to such alleged negligence it would be held plaintiff assumed the risk. While this evidence would have been inadmissible as tending to support an independent cause of action, it was nevertheless admissible in the absence of such charge because of its bearing on other issues and because plaintiff was entitled to show in their entirety the conditions under which plaintiff usually performed his work and the conditions under which his work was performed at the time he

was injured. Evidence is not rendered inadmissible by the fact that it tends to support a charge of negligence not made in the declaration, if, in fact, is is material in its bearing on other charges of negligence which are averred. South Chicago City Ry. Co. v. Purvis, 193 Ill. 454. Moreover, this evidence was properly limited by an instruction given to the jury, and the attorney for defendant explained in his address to the jury that liability could not be predicated on the fact that the lights were out when the accident occurred, and the jury was, at his request, specifically instructed to that effect.

It is urged that defendant was deprived of a fair trial through the repeated use by plaintiff's attorney of highly prejudicial and inflammatory language in the presence of the jury. The particular misconduct complained of is that throughout the trial the attorney for plaintiff from time to time injected remarks intended to prejudice the jury. On the former trial we criticized both counsel in this respect. While this record is not entirely free from conduct of the same kind, we are glad to note some improvement by both of them. We are not disposed to enforce with harshness a rule which would tend to discourage the manifestation of zeal by attorneys for their clients or to discourage eloquence on the part of advocates.

Again defendant argues, as on the former trial, that the verdict is against the manifest weight of the evidence. The evidence on this trial is not materially different from that given on the former trial, although it slightly differs in some respects. We adhere to our holding on the former appeal.

V. We reserved for final consideration the first and second points made in defendant's brief. It is urged that the damages allowed were so excessive as to indicate such passion and

prejudice on the part of the jury as could not be cured by a remittitur. The verdict was unusual in that plaintiff was allowed the full amount of damages he claimed, - $50,000. From that verdict the court required a remittitur of $10,000 and a judgment for $40,000 was entered in favor of plaintiff and against defendant. Measured by all the cases in which damages have been allowed for a similar injury in this jurisdiction, the judgment is yet excessive. It is not easy to determine the amount of damages which should be allowed for a mutilation of the body such as plaintiff sustained, with the pain and suffering which followed and which will follow. In a sense of course, no amount of money can give adequate compensation for such an injury. Nevertheless, the courts, for obvious reasons, have found it necessary to give protection from excessive verdicts and judgments. The amount of this judgment, wisely invested, would yield more than the yearly earnings of plaintiff at the time of his injury. Unfortunate and severe as the injury was, his earning capacity has not been entirely destroyed. This accident occurred November 12, 1931. The defenses interposed are largely technical. This case has been twice tried and twice appealed. It is a rule of law that in such case the reviewing court will not order a third trial because the verdict is contrary to the weight of the evidence (Greer v. Shell Petroleum Corp., 281 Ill. App. 238) and that the court will not interfere except to prevent manifest injustice (Barnes v. Means, 82 Ill. 379.) To the same effect is Calvert v. Carpenter, 96 Ill. 63. We have no doubt that any number of successive juries to which this case might be submitted would return verdicts for amounts as much or more than was returned at the first trial. The judgment for $40,000 is, however, still excessive from the viewpoint of the law, and we think a further remittitur of $5000 should be required. If plaintiff will, within

ten days of the filing of this opinion, remit from the judgment entered the sum of $5000, the judgment will be affirmed; otherwise it will be reversed and the cause remanded.

AFFIRMED UPON REMITTITUR;
OTHERWISE REVERSED AND REMANDED.

O'Connor and McSurely, JJ., concur.

38763

ROBERT HIMMEL, Appellant,

vs.

EDWARD SAGER, Appellee,

APPEAL FROM MUNICIPAL COURT OF CHICAGO.

36

286 I.A. 610[1]

MR. JUSTICE McSURELY DELIVERED THE OPINION OF THE COURT.

Plaintiff by this action sought to recover damages alleged to be sustained by him on account of defendant's failure to perform a certain agreement. Defendant filed a counterclaim. After trial before a jury, and the entry of a number of orders hereinafter noted, the court ordered plaintiff's cause of action dismissed and he appeals.

The jury returned a verdict for plaintiff, assessing his damages at $7500, and against the defendant's counterclaim; subsequently, on motion, the court on November 15, 1935, denied defendant's motion for a new trial but sustained defendant's motion for judgment for defendant notwithstanding the verdict, overruled defendant's motion for a new trial on his counterclaim and entered final judgment that the plaintiff take nothing by the suit; afterward plaintiff filed a petition seeking to set aside these orders, and on December 10, 1935, the court allowed the motion of plaintiff to vacate the order of November 15th, also allowed defendant's motion for a new trial, and at the same time entered an order dismissing the case "for want of jurisdiction" and ordered that defendant have judgment "as in case of nonsuit," the defendant to recover his costs from plaintiff. The record shows that the court based the order of dismissal upon its opinion that plaintiff should have proceeded by a bill in equity instead of by an action in law. This was a misapprehension of the character of plaintiff's claim, which was a simple action at law alleging a breach of contract by defendant

with ensuing damages to the plaintiff. This seems to be conceded by respective counsel.

Plaintiff appealed from the judgment entered November 15, and from the order entered December 10, 1935, dismissing plaintiff's cause of action.

We do not think it necessary to reconcile these orders or to agree with the reasons given by the trial court for dismissing the cause. Defendant made a motion to instruct the jury to find against the plaintiff, which was overruled. Had the court allowed defendant's motion on the ground that on the undisputed evidence defendant was entitled to a directed verdict, we would not reverse although erroneous orders may have been entered. In Estate of Grossman, 175 Ill. 425, the court held that the only question was whether the judgment of the trial court was correct, and in Launtz v. Kinloch Telephone Co., 239 Ill. App. 204, it was held that where the record showed that plaintiff was not entitled to recover the Appellate court would not reverse a judgment "because of erroneous processes in reaching it." Erroneously granting a nonsuit is harmless where a defendant is entitled to a directed verdict. People's Bank of Greenville v. Aetna Ins. Co., 74 Fed. 507, and Zittle v. Schlesinger, 46 Nebr. 844. In Welch v. Northern Pacific Ry. Co., 96 Minn. 211, orders like those in the instant case were entered; defendant moved for a directed verdict, which was denied, there was a verdict for plaintiffs; on motion the court entered judgment for the defendant notwithstanding the verdict, and at the same time ordered that the action be dismissed with costs against plaintiffs; it was held that these irregularities in the orders were not ground for reversal.

The decisive question is whether, on the undisputed evidence, there could be any recovery by plaintiff. The contract

between the parties arose in the following manner: One W. Dumke was the nominal owner and holder of all the capital stock of the Radio Products Corporation. May 1, 1933, Dumke gave to the defendant a written option to purchase this stock for $10,000, payable at the rate of 50 cents on each radio manufactured by the corporation; under the contract defendant took full control of the corporation, but Dumke, the seller, retained possession of the stock as a pledge to secure the payments and as a protection against any breach of any of the covenants of the contract, which required that the necessary working capital be provided by Sager, the defendant, that a financial statement of the condition of the company be issued each month showing the number of radios manufactured, and that no radios be manufactured except upon bona fide orders; the contract also provided that Sager's rights under the contract would cease and Dumke would be at liberty to deal with the stock certificates as he chose in the event Sager violated any of these previous obligations or permitted the corporation to incur obligations in excess of the reasonable and fair value of its assets, exclusive of the value of its R. C. A. (Radio Corporation of America) license. A breach of any of these provisions gave Dumke the right to terminate the contract. Sager accepted the contract and operated the business until October, 1933; at the time this contract was signed the Radio Products Corporation owned the R.C.A. license, a small amount of equipment, less than $500 in value, and it owed no debts.

October 4th this contract was amended in writing, changing the rate of payment on the purchase price of the stock from 50¢ on each radio to 25¢, extending the time of payment to May 1, 1935, and incorporating a provision that no radio be manufactured by the corporation except when it "shall be in receipt of actual orders from a bona fide customer."

Plaintiff and defendant had a verbal agreement looking to plaintiff obtaining a half interest in the stock of the corporation. This was later reduced to writing and executed by both parties. The main features of this contract, which is the subject matter of this suit, were that plaintiff would be placed in full charge of the management of the business, manufacturing on a cash basis, and was not to incur any indebtedness for merchandise until the purchase price of the stock was paid and unless there was cash on hand equal to the amount of any indebtedness incurred. Defendant, an attorney at law, knew nothing about the manufacturing of radios. Plaintiff was experienced in the radio business and at one time conducted a large business in this line; he also owned a majority of the stock of the Hudson-Ross Company, a distributor of radios. The Hudson-Ross company did not have an R.C.A. license to manufacture radios and apparently it was to plaintiff's advantage to secure an interest in the Radio Products Corporation which owned such a license.

It is admitted that plaintiff, as president and general manager of the Radio Products Corporation, sold to his company, the Hudson-Ross Company, on credit to the extent of many thousands of dollars. It is also not denied that plaintiff incurred debts against the Radio Products Corporation for merchandise to the extent of at least $8000.

Defendant on learning that plaintiff was selling on credit and running up large merchandise bills, in violation of the terms of the contract, after several verbal complaints, on February 18, 1935, called attention in writing to these violations of the conditions of the contract, charged plaintiff with using the Radio Products Corporation to finance his private interests, and served notice that he terminated the agreement between them.

The contract contemplated that no debts should be incurred

by the corporation until the full balance of the $10,000 purchase price of the stock was paid. This payment was to be made out of the current income, not out of capital assets. By incurring a large debt the stock would, by so much, be reduced in value.

Counsel for plaintiff concede breaches of the contract by plaintiff, but argue that the breach of these conditions had been waived by a subsequent oral understanding of the parties. The statement of claim did not claim any waiver of these conditions but predicated plaintiff's claim upon the full performance by him of all the provisions of the contract.

We find no evidence in the record that defendant waived these conditions. Plaintiff testified that he had several conversations with defendant about the manner of conducting the business but did not testify as to what was said in these conversations. He does testify that he had numerous disputes with defendant. There was undisputed evidence that the Products Corporation lost money on the Hudson-Ross account because plaintiff fixed the price at which the Products Corporation would sell radios to the Hudson-Ross company, of which plaintiff was manager and in control, at less than the cost of manufacture.

At the time defendant terminated the contract there had been paid on the Dumke contract some $8000; no part of this was paid by plaintiff; it was paid by the Products Corporation. There is force in the claim that plaintiff, by violating the contract, supplied his own company with radios at a price less than the cost of manufacturing to the Products Corporation, and that by purchasing merchandise for the Products Corporation on credit the Corporation was forced to the verge of bankruptcy.

It is undisputed that the officials of the Utah Radio Company, the real owner of the stock and the Dumke contract, learning of the financial distress of the Products Corporation,

demanded that defendant assign his interest in the contract to his daughter Grace on pain of a forfeiture of the contract. The daughter apparently was a business woman, about twenty-five years of age, and owned almost all the shares of stock in the Grace Radip Corporation. This assignment was made and Grace Sager paid the unpaid balance on the contract. Grace sold this stock for $25,000, from which was deducted $8000 in debts due creditors of the Radio Products Corporation, and the balance of the purchase price was to be paid, $5000 in cash and $12,000 in monthly installments over a period of about two years. There is nothing to justify any attack on the bona fides of this transaction. The evidence shows that these payments were made not to defendant but to Grace Sager, who was already in the radio distributing business. There is no evidence that defendant profited by this sale.

Moreover, in view of the admitted failure of plaintiff to observe the conditions of his contract, which justified the action of defendant in terminating it, it is no concern of plaintiff what disposition was made of the assets of the Products Corporation after the contract was terminated.

Upon the evidence shown by the record plaintiff cannot recover in this action. The order of November 15, 1935, entering judgment for the defendant non obstante veredicto on plaintiff's statement of claim was proper and the final judgment that plaintiff take nothing by this suit should be affirmed. Chap. 110 (Practice Act) Sec. 92, sub-par. (f) gives the reviewing court power to enter such judgment as ought to have been rendered in the lower court.

The judgment entered November 15, 1935, is affirmed, but in order to clear the record, judgment will also be entered in this court that plaintiff take nothing. No points are made or arguments presented upon the counterclaim of defendant.

JUDGMENT AFFIRMED AND JUDGMENT FOR DEFENDANT UPON PLAINTIFF'S STATEMENT OF CLAIM ENTERED IN THIS COURT.

Matchett, P. J. and O'Connor, J., concur.

38778

ANNE HENSON,
Appellee,

vs.

ALMA NEUMANN et al.,
Appellants.

LOUISE REGEL,
(Intervening Petitioner),
Appellant.

37

APPEAL FROM CIRCUIT COURT OF COOK COUNTY.

286 I.A. 610[2]

MR. JUSTICE McSURELY DELIVERED THE OPINION OF THE COURT.

This is an appeal from an order entered in the case of Henson v. Neumann, No. 38774, opinion filed this day, striking the intervening petition of Louise Regel, one of the daughters of Anna Neumann, and also the answer of the defendants Alma Neumann and Anna Neumann to her intervening petition.

In her petition Louise Regel purported to adopt all of the allegations of the plaintiff in Henson v. Neumann. The petition alleged that on about December 1, 1935, the intervenor made a demand upon Anna Neumann that she give to this intervenor her share of the estate and was told by Anna Neumann that there was nothing coming to her. The petition to intervene was filed after the master in chancery had made his report in Henson v. Neumann. The facts alleged in the intervening petition as a reason for her intervention are different from the facts set forth in plaintiff's complaint and relied upon in her suit. The chancellor was of this opinion and granted the motion to strike.

However, we have already held in the opinion filed in No. 38774 that the defendant is bound under her agreement to devise her property equally among her three children, and also that no proceedings can be sustained to enforce this contract while the defendant is still alive. This disposes of the contentions of Louise Regel in her petition, and the order striking it is therefore affirmed.

ORDER AFFIRMED.

Matchett, P. J., and O'Connor, J., concur.

38752

FRANK WODECKI, Appellee,

vs.

HAROLD M. PITMAN COMPANY, a Corporation, Appellant.

APPEAL FROM CIRCUIT COURT OF COOK COUNTY.

38

286 I.A. 610[3]

MR. JUSTICE O'CONNOR DELIVERED THE OPINION OF THE COURT.

Plaintiff brought an action before a justice of the peace against Harold M. Pitman Company, a corporation, and Adolph Mlyniec, to recover for damages to his Plymouth automobile which was struck by an Oldsmobile automobile belonging to the Pitman company and driven by defendant Mlyniec. The defendants were defaulted and judgment was entered against them in favor of plaintiff for $332.20. Afterward the Pitman company, hereinafter called the defendant, appealed to the Circuit court of Cook county where there was a trial before the court without a jury and a finding and judgment in plaintiff's favor for $332.20. Defendant appeals.

The record discloses that on June 20, 1934, and for some time prior thereto, Adolph Mlyniec conducted a gasoline station and also did greasing and simonizing of automobiles, and during the forenoon of that day defendant Pitman company delivered an automobile to Mlyniec for the purpose of having it simonized. The charge was to be five dollars and the car was to be ready about five o'clock in the afternoon. About 5:45 o'clock in the evening of that day Mlyniec, having completed the simonizing of the car, was driving the Oldsmobile from his place of business to the Pitman company. The car was being driven south in 51st avenue, Cicero, and at the time plaintiff was driving his automobile east in West 29th Place. The cars collided in the southeast part of the street intersection, plaintiff's car being struck on its north side

by defendant's automobile. Plaintiff's car was damaged to the extent of $332.20.

Defendant contends (1) that plaintiff was guilty of contributory negligence as a matter of law, and (2) that Mlyniec, who had just completed simonizing the defendant's car and who was returning it to defendant at the time of the collision, was not acting as defendant's agent but was driving defendant's car as part of the service he was to render defendant.

The day was bright and clear and the pavement dry. Plaintiff testified he lived a short distance from the place of the accident and was familiar with the neighborhood, having passed the street intersection for the past fifteen years; that he was driving east on the south or righthand side of 29th Place at about twenty-five miles an hour, and as he entered the street intersection of 51st avenue, he "released the gas, blew his horn and shifted his gears;" that as he looked to the north or to his left, defendant's car crashed into him; that the collision occurred near the center of the street intersection. "I didn't see him at all when I approached the corner. *** When I got hit - that is when I saw him." The Court: "You didn't see him until you were struck?" Answer: "I say I did not see him until I got struck;" that plaintiff skidded into him.

Marie Cech, called by plaintiff, testified that at the time of the accident she was standing at the northwest corner of the street intersection; that she saw the cars collide; that she saw both cars approaching the intersection as she was standing at the corner; that Mlyniec who was driving defendant's car, was going "pretty fast, about fifty miles an hour;" that plaintiff was going east at about twenty-five miles an hour; that the cars collided near the southeast corner of the intersection; that plaintiff's car was tipped over by the impact. There is other evidence that

Mlyniec was traveling at about 35 miles an hour and plaintiff at about the same speed.

Adolph Mlyniec, called by plaintiff, testified that a Mr. Driscoll, an employee of defendant, brought the car to the witness's place of business about twelve o'clock of the day in question to have it simonized, leaving the car for that purpose; the charge was to be five dollars and the job was to be finished about five o'clock; that shortly before that time he received a telephone call from defendant asking whether the car was ready; that he advised the job was not quite finished but would be completed shortly after five o'clock; that he was then asked by defendant's representative whether the witness would drive the car to defendant's place of business and he agreed to do so; that when the car was left in the morning there was nothing said about the witness returning the car to defendant.

Charles Driscoll testified he was employed by defendant and delivered the automobile to Mlyniec between nine and nine thirty o'clock of the morning in question for the purpose of having it simonized, which Mlyniec agreed to do for five dollars, and at that time Mlyniec agreed to return the car when the simonizing was completed.

Sec. 33, chap. 95a, Cahill's 1933 Statutes, which was in force at the time of the collision, provided: "motor vehicles traveling upon public highways shall give the right-of-way to vehicles approaching along intersecting highways from the right and shall have the right-of-way over those approaching from the left." This statute, of course, is applicable only to automobiles approaching the intersection at about the same time. Heidler Co. v. Wilson & Bennett Co., 243 Ill. App. 89; Ward v. Clark, 232 N.Y. 195; Fitts v. Marquis, 127 Maine, 75 (140 Atl. 909.) It is also the law that in such a situation as is disclosed by the evidence, plaintiff cannot recover unless he is in the exercise of due care

for his own safety. It was the duty of both drivers, as stated in Hilton v. Iseman, 212 Ill. App. 255, to "proceed with due circumspection so as not to come into collision with other vehicles. Rupp v. Keebler, 175 Ill. 619," and that where both drivers fail in this respect and there is a collision resulting in damage, neither can recover.

In Crowe Name Plate & Mfg. Co. v. Dammerich, 279 Ill. App. 103, the court, in discussing the duty of drivers of motor vehicles when approaching an intersection, said (p. 107): "It is the duty of the operator of a motor vehicle approaching a crossing or intersection to keep a lookout ahead of him, and also to look for approaching vehicles on the intersecting street or highway; and although the latter duty is particularly imperative with respect to the direction from which vehiclew having the right of way over him would approach, full performance of the driver's duty requires that he shall look in both directions," and that failure to so look is negligence per se.

In Specht v. Chicago City Railway Company, 233 Ill. App. 384, it is said (p. 385): "The controlling question presented by this record is whether, in an action to recover damages resulting from a collision between plaintiff's truck and defendant's street car, the court properly directed a verdict at the close of plaintiff's ease." The evidence disclosed that a truck was being driven south in Wabash avenue at about eight or ten miles an hour and a street car east on 39th street at about twenty-five to thirty-five miles an hour. There was nothing to divert the attention of plaintiff, who sat beside the driver of his truck, to prevent their seeing the street car after the truck reached 39th street. When the truck was about twenty-five feet north of 39th street they looked to the west, from which the street car was coming, and which was then about 200 feet away, but at that time they did not see the street car because of a building on the

corner. They did not look to the west again until they were about six to eight feet from the eastbound street car track which was too late to avoid the collision, as the heavy truck was loaded with merchandise and could not be stopped within that distance. The court further said (p. 386): "The bare statement of these facts as disclosed by plaintiff's own evidence shows not only failure to sustain the burden of proof with respect to the exercise of ordinary care on the part of plaintiff or his driver, but affirmatively establishes contributory negligence on their part, conceding the evidence tends to show negligence in the operation of the car." The court affirmed the judgment, holding that the verdict was properly directed for the defendant.

In the instant case, plaintiff's testimony (and there is none to the contrary) is that upon entering the intersection he looked to his right or to the south, but did not look toward the north until he was near the middle of the intersection, when defendant's automobile was just colliding with plaintiff's car. He testified, "I say I did not see him until I got struck." We think this shows that plaintiff was not in the exercise of due care for his own safety, but on the contrary affirmatively shows that he was guilty of negligence which contributed to ~~the~~ injury. The court should have found in favor of defendant, and since no recovery can be had, it is unnecessary to discuss the question of whether Mlyniec was at the time of the collision the agent of defendant company.

Since all the evidence shows that plaintiff was guilty of contributory negligence, the judgment of the Circuit court of Cook county is reversed.

JUDGMENT REVERSED.

Matchett, P. J., and McSurely, J., concur.

corner. They did not look to the west again until they were about six to eight feet from the eastbound street car track which was too late to avoid the collision, as the heavy truck was loaded with merchandise and could not be stopped within that distance. The court further said (p. 366): "The bare statement of these facts as disclosed by plaintiff's own evidence shows not only failure to sustain the burden of proof with respect to the exercise of ordinary care on the part of plaintiff or his driver, but affirmatively establishes contributory negligence on their part, conceding the evidence tends to show negligence in the operation of the car." The court affirmed the judgment, holding that the verdict was properly directed for the defendant.

In the instant case, plaintiff's testimony (and there is none to the contrary) is that upon entering the intersection he looked to his right or to the south, but did not look toward the north until he was near the middle of the intersection, when defendant's automobile was just colliding with plaintiff's car. He testified, "I say I did not see him until I got struck." We think this shows that plaintiff was not in the exercise of due care for his own safety, but on the contrary affirmatively shows that he was guilty of negligence which contributed to the injury. The court should have found in favor of defendant, and since no recovery can be had, it is unnecessary to discuss the question of whether Klynlee was at the time of the collision the agent of defendant company.

Since all the evidence shows that plaintiff was guilty of contributory negligence, the judgment of the Circuit court of Cook county is reversed.

JUDGMENT REVERSED.

Matchett, P. J., and McSurely, J., concur.

38766

PETER QUARACINO, Administrator of Estate of TOMASINA QUARACINO, Deceased, Appellee,

vs.

SOCIETA AGRICOLA OPERAIA S. CRISTOFORO E. MARIA VERGINE INCORONATA DI RICIGLIANO, Appellant.

) APPEAL FROM MUNICIPAL COURT OF CHICAGO.

39

286 I.A. 610[4]

MR. JUSTICE O'CONNOR DELIVERED THE OPINION OF THE COURT.

Plaintiff brought suit against defendant to recover $330 and interest amounting to $33 claimed to be due from defendant as a death benefit under an agreement entered into between the parties. There was a trial before the court without a jury, a finding and judgment in plaintiff's favor for $363, and defendant appeals.

Plaintiff's position is that his wife, Tomasina Quaracino, was a member of defendant society in good standing, having paid dues and assessments up until the time of her death May 23, 1933, and that under Article 29 of the by-laws of defendant society he was entitled upon the death of his wife to $500, of which he had been paid but $170, leaving a balance of $330, and that he was further entitled to interest of $33 on this sum because of unreasonable and vexatious delay on the part of defendant in refusing to pay the balance claimed.

On the other hand, defendant's position is that Article 29 of the by-laws, which was in force and effect at the time Tomasina Quaracine joined the society, provided for the payment to her family of $500 upon her death, but that this article was amended December 4, 1932, so that the family of a deceased member of the society should thereafter receive a sum made up by the payment of $1 per member as a mortuary benefit; that there were but 170 members in the society when plaintiff's wife died, and therefore he was entitled to but $170, which had been paid to him.

The facts were stipulated, and from them it appears that there was no written contract or certificate issued by defendant to plaintiff's wife, who had been a member of defendant society for many years and continued to be a member in good standing until the time of her death May 23, 1933. Article 28 provided that from October 4, 1918, "The Society will pay $500.00 to the family for funeral expenses," and that in certain cases the society would conduct the funeral of the deceased member, paying all necessary expenses and that "the rest (of the $500) will be sent to the beneficiary, the Society must respect any testamentary disposition of the deceased and of his will." Article 29 provided that the mortuary tax per capita would be fixed each year at the first meeting in December for the following year; that "This quota may vary annually, according to the number of members, due to the fact that the family should receive Five Hundred Dollars." And by Section 30 it was provided, "Whoever is in arrears in funeral payments, oven though currently paid up with monthly dues, shall not have any right to a mortuary benefit. The society shall pay the funeral benefit (meaning mortuary benefit) not later than sixty (60) days, however, in case of misfortune, which may cause more than one death, and any other exceptional cases, the society reserves to itself the right to adopt those provisions necessary for the protection and existence of the society."

The stipulation of facts further shows that after due notice a meeting of the society was held November 6, 1932, and of its council November 20, 1932, and a new by-law was proposed and recommended to the society for its adoption at a regular and special meeting to be held December 4, 1932, pursuant to notice to its members, including Tomasina Quaracino; that on December 4, 1932, the society adopted the recommended change of the by-laws and the members present voted unanimously for the amendment to Article 29, to read as follows: "Effective December 4, 1932,

monthly dues fifty cents; mortuary dues $1.00 per death. ***

"Mortuary Benefits: $1.00 per member for the number of members current."

In addition to the facts, as above stipulated, witnesses testified. Peter Quaracino, the surviving husband, called by the defendant, testified that he received a check from defendant for $170, dated October 1, 1933, payable to his order, and that he cashed the check; that at the time of delivery the check bore the following endorsement: "Received as full & complete settlement of Benefit Mortuary a/c Death of Mrs. Tomasina Quaracino" - signed Pietro Quaracino; that before this date he received another check for apparently the same amount but returned it; that his wife did not attend the meetings of the society regularly and was not present at the meetings in November and December, 1932.

The financial secretary of defendant's society testified that he kept the records of the society; that Mrs. Quaracino paid her monthly dues of fifty cents regularly and after the change of the by-laws in December, 1932, she made four payments of one dollar each for mortuary benefits or funeral assessments; that the payments were made to him by Frank Taglia, a relative of the deceased.

Taglia was then called by defendant and testified that he was a member of the society and a cousin of deceased; that he was in the habit of paying her dues to the society, and that he explained to her the doings of the society; that he was not familiar with the changes made in the by-laws in December, 1932; that he was present at that meeting but that he left before the question of amending the by-laws was taken up; that he did not tell Mrs. Quaracino about the reduction in the amount of mortuary benefits the members would be required to pay thereafter; that he had been paying the dues for Mrs. Quaracino for many years and transacted

all her business with the society.

Defendant also offered in evidence letters sent by the society to its members, dated June 1, November 30, and December 28, 1932. The letter of June 1 stated that the next regular meeting would be held June 5th, at a certain time and place; that the meeting was of importance, requiring the attendance of the members, and it then gave a list of the deceased members. In the letter of November 30th it was stated that the last and most important meeting of the year would be on December 4th, specifying the time and place, and requesting the members to attend; that at that meeting the program for 1933 would be arranged, the nomination and election of officers would take place, and other matters, not important here, were mentioned. In the letter of December 28th it was stated the next regular meeting would be held January 1st. The letter referred to a number of matters, such as the minutes of the previous meeting, the disposition of pending items, the installation of new officers, amendment to the bylaws for payments and benefits, "Effective Dec 4th 1932, Monthly dues Fifty Cents; Mortuary dues $1.00 per death;" sick benefit five dollars per week during illness not to exceed thirteen weeks. Mortuary benefits, "1.00 per member for the number of members current." A great many other matters are mentioned in the letter. Neither in the letter of June 1st nor that of November 30th was any mention made that it was proposed to change the by-laws so that the mortuary benefit of $500 would be reduced to $1 per member. And a consideration of all the evidence shows, we think, that the member, Mrs. Quaracino, did not consent to such reduction.

The by-laws from which we have above quoted, provide that upon the death of a member the defendant society will pay $500 to "the family" of the deceased member. And defendant contends that any amount due from it was payable to Mrs. Quaracino's surviving

husband, Peter Quaracino, that he alone could maintain the suit, and therefore the suit brought by the surviving husband as administrator of his wife's estate will not lie. The argument in support of this is that if the money is paid by defendant to plaintiff, it would become a part of the assets of the estate of Mrs. Quaracino, and counsel cites the case of People v. Petrie, 191 Ill. 497, which was an action of debt on a bond brought by the People for the use of the widow and children of Benjamin Brooks, deceased, against Petrie and others, sureties on the bond. It was held that the sureties were not liable because the money paid did not belong to the estate of Benjamin Brooks, deceased. In a case brought under the statute for the wrongful death, the suit to recover is by the administrator and the money recovered does not belong to the estate but to the heirs.

In the instant case, upon the death of Mrs. Quaracino the mortuary benefit was payable to her "family" and it seems to be agreed that Peter Quaracino was the family. Obviously, if the judgment is paid, no one can maintain another suit on the same claim.

Defendant further contends that the court erred in striking its additional defense in which it set up that it was incorporated under the laws of 1872 as amended in 1927, and the latter act provided that after it became effective no such societies should engage in business other than that they may retain their corporate existence for six months for the sole purpose of winding up their business or re-incorporating under some other act; that defendant did not wind up its business after June, 1927, when the act became effective, and did not re-incorporate under any other act, therefore all acts performed by it after the act of June 1927 became effective were ultra vires the corporation. We think this contention cannot be sustained. This same act was before our

Supreme court in Jones v. Lealeen Mut. Benefit Assoc., 337 Ill. 431, where it was held (p. 438) that "Neither the old association nor the legislature could take any action which would impair the contract of the certificate holder unless such certificate holder consented to such change, and there is nothing in this record to indicate that the certificate holder consented to a modification of his rights or the reduction of the amount due under the certificate of membership." See also York v. Cent. Ill. Relief Assoc., 340 Ill. 595.

In the instant case we hold that since the member, Mrs. Quaracino, did not consent to the change in the by-laws whereby the mortuary benefit of $600 was reduced to $1 per member, such change was ineffective as to her or her family.

Nor do we think it can be said that she acquiesced in such change because she, after the amendment was adopted, paid four mortuary benefits of one dollar each. There is no evidence in the record that would warrant the court in holding that she knew the assessment of one dollar reduced the mortuary benefit which would be payable to her family upon her decease.

Defendant further contends there was an accord and satisfaction because plaintiff, the surviving husband, demanded $600 from defendant after the death of his wife and refused to accept its tendered check for $170; that he afterward did accept a check for this amount, endorsed as above quoted. And counsel says: "It is apparent that the check was offered to him on the condition that his acceptance would be in full satisfaction of the demand." Where there is a bona fide dispute between parties as to the amount due, the acceptance of the check will be a satisfaction of the demand, although the acceptor protests at the time. Canton Union Coal Co. v. Parlin, 215 Ill. 244.

Plaintiff testified that a couple of months after the death of his wife, officers of the company called at his home with a

check. "I did not take the check. I wanted more money. They did not give me any more; they told me to go to court. They held the check;" that some time afterward the officers sent for him and then tendered to him the check which is in evidence; that the president then said, "Take the check. If Taglia win the case, you get the balance;" that thereupon he took the check. Defendant's president denied that he had made this statement. At the time Taglia had a case pending against the society where many of the facts were substantially the same as in the case before us. Afterward that case was decided by another Division of this court, where the judgment in the Taglia case against the defendant was affirmed. Taglia, Admr. v. Societa Agricola Operaia S.Cristoforo E. Maria Vergine Incoronata Di Ricigliano, No. 37637 (opinion filed March 29, 1935, not reported.) About two months afterward the instant suit was brought. Moreover, the evidence does not show what was said by the parties on the two occasions when the check was presented by defendant's officials to plaintiff. This appears only by inference. The witnesses were not asked what was said at the time in order that it might be determined whether there was a bona fide dispute between the parties. But in any event, the amount ($500) due under the law from defendant to plaintiff, was liquidated.

Defendant further contends that the court erred in allowing interest of $33 on the ground that its delay in payment was unreasonable and vexatious; that it defended the action in good faith. The record discloses that in May, 1933, shortly after Mrs. Quaracino died, defendant tendered to plaintiff $170, which he refused to accept, claiming he was entitled to $500; and plaintiff testified that at the time defendant's officials told him if he wanted more he would have to go to court; that in October following defendant's officers sent for plaintiff, and he further testified that they told him to take the check for $170, and that

if Taglia won his case then pending against defendant, it would pay plaintiff the balance of $330. The record discloses that the opinion of this court, affirming the judgment in favor of Taglia and against defendant, was filed March 29, 1935, and plaintiff brought this suit about two months thereafter, May 27, 1935. Defendant's president denied that he had made the statement testified to by plaintiff, but the trial Judge apparently took plaintiff's view of the case, and we are of opinion we would not be warranted in disturbing the finding of the court on this question. In these circumstances, we think the court was warranted in allowing the interest.

The judgment of the Municipal court of Chicago is affirmed.

JUDGMENT AFFIRMED.

McSurely, P. J., and Matchett, J., concur.

40 H

38596

THREE BEST CLEANERS, INC., a corporation, Appellee, v. WILLIAM D. MEYERING, sheriff of Cook County, Appellant.	)	APPEAL FROM CIRCUIT COURT, COOK COUNTY. 236 I.A. 611

MR. PRESIDING JUSTICE SULLIVAN DELIVERED THE OPINION OF THE COURT.

This is an action in replevin instituted in the Circuit court by plaintiff, Three Best Cleaners, to repossess itself of certain chattels consisting of motor trucks and machinery levied upon by the sheriff of Cook county under an execution on a judgment in favor of Leo Oslan against the New Drexel Cleaners, Inc. The cause was tried by the court without a jury and judgment entered finding the right of property in plaintiff. This appeal followed.

As cause for reversal defendant's major contentions are: (1) That no demand was made upon the sheriff for the return of the property before filing this action; and (2) that plaintiff failed to prove its title or right of possession to said chattels.

It is sufficient answer to defendant's first contention to state that this question not having been raised in the trial court cannot be raised for the first time on appeal.

As to defendant's second contention the evidence shows that in March, 1933, all the stockholders of three corporations known as Klever Shampay Karpet Kleaners, the Circle Cleaners, and the New Drexel Cleaners, decided to consolidate the business of the three companies and a new corporation known as Three Best Cleaners was

organized. All the stockholders delivered their stock of the aforesaid three corporations to the Three Best Cleaners and received in return stock of the latter corporation. The New Drexel Cleaners dismantled its plant and moved all its business, together with its machinery and equipment, into the plant of the Klever Shampay Karpet Kleaners, which became the officer and headquarters of the Three Best Cleaners.

The judgment pursuant to which the execution issued on which the sheriff levied upon the property in question was procured by Leo Oslan on a judgment note ostensibly executed by the New Drexel Cleaners and it is insisted that the property seized by the sheriff still belonged to the New Drexel Cleaners and is liable for the obligation of that corporation. The difficulty with this position is that the New Drexel Cleaners have long since gone out of business, all of its corporate stock, machinery and equipment having been transferred to the Three Best Cleaners and its business taken over by that company. The business of the Three Best Cleaners was conducted principally in the plant and in the name of the Klever Shampay Kleaners and it was natural that the property in question should be delivered to that plant and used in plaintiff's business under that name. The possession of the property by the Klever Shampay Karpet Kleaners was the possession of plaintiff. The ownership of all the stock of the New Drexel Cleaners by the Three Best Cleaners and the outright delivery of the chattels of the former company to the latter vested it at least with the right to possession of the property as against defendant's levy on the aforesaid execution; and whether under the doctrine that a consolidated corporation having received all the assets of a consolidating corporation must also assume its liabilities, a creditor of the New Drexel Cleaners might recover from the Three Best Cleaners in a proper proceeding against it, is an entirely different question.

Other points are urged, but they have either been covered by what has been said, or in the view we take of this cause we deem it unnecessary to discuss them.

The motions of plaintiff heretofore made and reserved to hearing to strike the report of proceedings, to strike defendant's notice of appeal, to strike the proof of service of notice of appeal and to assess damages against defendant upon dismissal of his appeal are at this time denied.

In our opinion the judgment entered by the Circuit court on its finding of right of property in plaintiff was proper.

JUDGMENT AFFIRMED.

Friend and Scanlan, JJ., concur.

Other points are urged, but they have either been covered by what has been said, or in the view we take of this cause we deem it unnecessary to discuss them.

The motions of plaintiff heretofore made and reserved to hearing to strike the report of proceedings, to strike defendant's notice of appeal, to strike the proof of service of notice of appeal and to assess damages against defendant upon dismissal of his appeal are at this time denied.

In our opinion the judgment entered by the Circuit court on its finding of right of property in plaintiff was proper.

JUDGMENT AFFIRMED.

Friend and Scanlan, JJ., concur.

4/A

38728

WALTER HACKETT, Appellant,	)	APPEAL FROM CIRCUIT COURT,
v.	)	COOK COUNTY.
RIVERVIEW PARK COMPANY, a corporation, Appellee.	)	

286 I.A. 611²

MR. PRESIDING JUSTICE SULLIVAN DELIVERED THE OPINION OF THE COURT.

By this appeal plaintiff, Walter Hackett, seeks to reverse a judgment rendered against him July 13, 1935, in an action for personal injuries brought by him against defendant, Riverview Park Company. The only question presented for review is whether the verdict upon which the judgment was entered was manifestly against the weight of the evidence.

Plaintiff's amended declaration alleged that defendant owned and operated a roller coaster ride called the "Bobs" in Riverview Park; that on July 29, 1933, he became a passenger for hire on such ride; that thereupon it became defendant's duty to exercise the highest degree of care and caution for plaintiff's safety consistent with the practical operation of the ride; that he at all times exercised due care for his own safety; that defendant so carelessly and negligently operated said roller coaster ride as to cause plaintiff's foot to become wedged and caught in the car in which he was a passenger on said ride, resulting in painful, serious and permanent injuries to him. No evidence was offered to support the second count of the declaration, which alleged the failure of defendant to keep the ride properly equipped and in a good state of repair. Defendant filed a plea of the general issue. No question is raised

on the pleadings.

Hackett, who was fifty-one years of age, six feet three and a half inches tall and weighed about one hundred and ninety-nine pounds, visited Riverview Park with a party of six young friends on the evening of July 29, 1933. Tickets were purchased and all the members of the party were admitted to the crowded platform from which the passengers were loaded into the cars of the trains which carried them on the roller coaster ride called the "Bobs," which was owned and operated by defendant. The "Bobs" was a circular railway upon which trains started from the loading platform and traveled up and down over various inclines and declines and around curves until they returned to the starting point. From the platform or starting point, the trains proceeded slowly of their own momentum down a mild grade for a distance of sixty to seventy feet until they reached the first incline, up which they were hauled by an endless chain operated electrically, gravity furnishing the momentum for the rest of the ride. Each train consisted of eleven cars coupled together and each car contained a single seat capable of seating two persons. Each car was equipped with a handlebar extending the width of the car and supported by upright bars on both sides, by which said handlebar was moved forward or backward through slots in the floor. While passengers were entering the cars and until they were properly seated, the usual and regular position of the handlebars was toward the front end of the car and away from the seat. When the passengers were seated facing forward, the handlebar was pulled backward and downward toward them, and when it was pulled backward as far as it would go it was above their knees and forward of and about opposite their waistlines. Each handlebar was equipped with a lock below the footboard of the car and when pulled backward and downward toward the passenger as far as it would go, it locked automatically. When thus locked the handlebar could not be unlocked or moved until the ride was about completed

and the train approached the loading platform, when it passed over a "block," which automatically unlocked the handlebars on all the cars of the train. If the train was not in motion the handlebar of any particular car could have been unlocked by operating a "trip" underneath that car. The equipment did not include a device for locking the handlebars on all the cars of a train with one operation, it being necessary that the bar on each car be moved backward toward the seat as far as it would go until it was locked, either by the passenger or one of defendant's attendants. About four or five inches back from the front board of the car and about six inches above the floor, there was a three quarter inch iron rod attached to the floor of the car as a footbrace. This rod was stationary as to location but revolved about a half inch turn in its place when the handlebar was pulled back and locked.

Plaintiff's theory of fact is that he, not having theretofore taken this "ride," in following Johnny Monahan, one of his young friends, in boarding the car from the platform to its right, stepped down into the car with both feet, his right foot landing on that portion of the floor of the car between the footbrace rod and the front board of the car; that before he was afforded an opportunity to become safely and properly seated, the train started while his right foot was still between the footbrace rod and the front board of the car, and the handlebar was pulled backward and locked either by himself, one of the guards or in some other manner, pinioning his right leg and foot at an angle between the locked handlebar on one side of his leg and the footbrace rod on the other side of his leg and foot; that he was forced to a position half standing and half leaning back over the seat and was unable to extricate his foot; that he immediately exclaimed "My God, you have my foot caught here - stop the car, you have my foot caught;" that attendants or guards of the defendant heard his outcry, and although the train could have been stopped

when it reached the endless chain at the foot of the first incline, no effort was made by defendant's servants to stop it; that he continued to hold on to the handlebar as best he could as the car ascended the incline; that, when the car almost reached the top of same, his young friend Monahan, fifteen years old at that time, crawled under the handlebar and succeeded in unlacing Hackett's shoe and releasing his foot just as the train reached the top of the incline; and that when the ride ended he was assisted from the car, given first aid on the grounds, taken to a hospital and then home, at which time his family physician was called.

It is undisputed that plaintiff's foot was "caught" and injured while he was on defendant's train as a passenger, and his testimony as to the manner in which his injury occurred was corroborated by the testimony of four other witnesses. Defendant called as witnesses the builder of the ride and a city elevator inspector, who were not present at the time of the occurrence, but who, testified concerning the mechanism of the cars and the ride and their operation, and that same were in good condition. Another witness for defendant, a loading attendant, testified substantially that it was his duty to see that the handlebars were locked on all cars before the trains started; that, if the passengers did not pull the handlebars so that they locked, he did; that he could not identify Hackett, but recalled that on the night of July 29, 1933, after a train had started down the grade from the loading platform "one lad said, 'stop the train;'" that he had locked the bars on all the cars on that train; that he was about twelve feet from the moving train when he heard the call to stop the car; that he saw no one on the train in a standing or reclining position; that from the starting point the trains moved very slowly to the point where they connected with the endless chain to be hauled up the first incline, and that they could not be stopped between the starting point and the chain; that as loading attendant it was not up to him to do anything

after the ride started, and that he could not do anything when the man shouted that his foot was caught; that he saw "a fellow stoop over there and unlace his shoe, - he was in a stooping position;" that when the car got onto the chain, "he raised up and said it was O.K.;" and that nothing was done to stop the ride at any time.

The only other witness to the occurrence for the defendant was the manager of the ride, who testified that on the occasion in question, while he was unloading passengers on the rear platform, one of the attendants reported to him that a man "had his foot caught in the bar" of one of the cars; that "I followed the cars as best I could with my eyes and saw somebody was seated in a bending over position;" that he saw no one in that car "standing up or leaning or half leaning;" that "after the car got up the incline a ways the party that was bent over raised up and waved O.K.;" that he did not see plaintiff get on the train; that he did nothing to stop the ride when the train reached the incline, although he could have stopped it there by simply pressing a button to shut off the electrical power; and that "after the train came back in a man got out of the car and that he had one shoe off and I asked him what was the matter with him and he said that he had his foot caught in the bar."

Defendant contends that plaintiff's conduct in voluntarily placing his right foot forward of the footrail and between it and the front board when stepping into the car was an act of contributory negligence in itself. This position is untenable. The space between the footrail and the front board was as open as the balance of the floor of the car, and while it is true that passengers properly seated and in position for the ride would not ordinarily use that space for their feet, the undisputed evidence shows that the loading platform was so crowded that the members of plaintiff's party became separated and that those on the platform waiting to get on the trains for the rides

were "pushing and shoving" when Hackett and his friends boarded the cars. It appears almost conclusively from the evidence that in the rush for seats Hackett was not afforded an opportunity for deliberation in boarding the car or a reasonable time to scrutinize the floor to ascertain where his feet should be placed thereon. Hackett was a big man and from the pictures of one of the cars in evidence, the opening on its side between the front end of the side armrail and the front board of the car, even under the most favorable circumstances, offered scant room for entrance and scanter opportunity to examine the floor of the car.

It was uncontradicted that Hackett's foot and leg were wedged and caught in the manner testified to by him and that the train was started before he was properly seated. It was admitted by defendant that plaintiff's outcry to stop the car because his foot was caught was heard by at least one of its attendants immediately after the car was started, that this attendant so advised the manager of the ride and that neither the manager nor the attendant did anything to stop the car, although either of them could have done so by simply touching a button when the train reached the endless chain at the bottom of the first incline.

Defendant sought to avoid the effect of this evidence by the testimony of the manager and attendant, neither of whom saw plaintiff enter the car nor his position when the car started. The attendant testified that it was his duty to see that before the trains started the handlebars of all the cars were locked. He also testified that they were all locked on the train in which Hackett rode and that the first time he noticed plaintiff was immediately after the train had started, when he made the outcry, and at that time "he was sitting down * * * looking around toward me * * * and he was hollering."

The manager testified that when the attendant reported to him

that the foot of a passenger was caught, he followed the particular train with his eyes and saw no one in that train "standing up or leaning or half leaning" over the seat.

Although not stated, defendant's theory of fact seems to be that, its attendant having testified that it was his duty to see that the handlebars on all cars were locked before the trains were started and that all the bars on the train in which Hackett rode were locked, and its evidence being to the effect that no one, including Hackett, in that particular train was standing or leaning over his seat after the train started down the grade toward the first incline, Hackett must have been properly seated before the train in which he was riding started. In our opinion this theory cannot possibly be reconciled with the admitted facts and the uncontradicted testimony. It is admitted that plaintiff's foot was caught some place below the seat of the car. It is not denied that in stepping into the car his right foot was placed between the footrail and the front board, with its toe toward the left side of the car and the heel toward the right side, and that the foot was pinioned while in that position. If defendant's theory is correct, while plaintiff's foot was still in the position indicated, plaintiff seated himself, bending his foot and leg over the footrail lmost at a right angle, and drew back and locked the handlebar or ermitted the attendant to do so without either pain or outcry before he train started from the platform. That such a theory is fallacious s readily apparent.

It is, of course, the settled rule that in actions for personal njuries the questions of negligence and contributory negligence are rimarily for the jury, but it is also the established rule that where he verdict of a jury is clearly and manifestly against the weight of he evidence, the failure of the trial court to grant a new trial upon proper motion constitutes reversible error.

The case of Olsen, Admr. v. Riverview Park Co., No. 33270

(not reported), decided by this court and cited by defendant in support of its theory, is readily distinguishable on the facts from the instant case in that there was evidence in that case that the handlebar of the car in which plaintiff was riding was locked and that she was thrown out of the car on one of the inclines or curves because she did not maintain a secure hold of the bar.

On both the questionsof plaintiff's exercise of due car and defendant's negligence, it is our opinion that the verdict was clearly against the manifest weight of the evidence and that the trial court erred in failing and refusing to grant plaintiff's motion for a new trial.

For the reasons indicated the judgment of the Circuit court is reversed and the cause is remanded.

REVERSED AND REMANDED.

Friend and Scanlan, JJ., concur.

38108

CITY OF CHICAGO,

v.

CHICAGO & NORTHWESTERN R. R. CO. et al.

IN RE PETITION OF DANIEL L. MADDEN and EDWARD J. KELLEY, Appellees

v.

SARAH L. JOHNSON et al. Respondents.

ON APPEAL OF SARAH L. JOHNSON, Appellant.

APPEAL FROM COUNTY COURT, COOK COUNTY.

286 I.A. 611[3]

MR. JUSTICE FRIEND DELIVERED THE OPINION OF THE COURT.

By this appeal, which was transferred here from the Supreme court and consolidated with case No. 38109, Sarah L. Johnson seeks to reverse an order of the county court directing the county treasurer to pay Daniel L. Madden and Edward J. Kelley $5,811.45 theretofore deposited by the City of Chicago in a condemnation proceeding, entitled "City of Chicago v. Chicago & Northwestern R. R. Co. et al.," then pending in the county court. The facts necessary to an understanding of the issues involved are sufficiently stated in the opinion filed this day in No. 38109. In that case Sarah L. Johnson had filed an answer to the petition of Madden and Kelley in the county court averring that all her right, title and interest in and to the fund deposited by the City of Chicago with the county treasurer and to the real estate involved in the condemnation pro-

9

ceeding, had been assigned and quitclaimed to Elaine Johnson Burgess and Isabelle C. Johnson, plaintiffs in error. If that were true, it is difficult to understand why Sarah L. Johnson, having parted with all her interest in the real estate and fund, should have prosecuted an appeal from the judgment of the court, holding in effect that she was still the owner of the property and the fund, subject only to petitioners' lien. Nevertheless she has filed a comprehensive brief and sets forth eight separate grounds for reversal.

It is first urged that the county court had no general equity jurisdiction to enter the judgment sought to be reversed. While it may be conceded that county courts have no general equity jurisdiction, it has been held that where the power of eminent domain is exercised the fund paid stands in the place of the land condemned, and the lien attaches to the fund, and if there is money in the hands of the court or its officers belonging to a litigant, anybody having an interest therein may file an intervening petition to have it paid over, and the court has jurisdiction to entertain a petition for that purpose. (Illinois Trust & Savings Bank v. Robbins, 38 Ill. App. 575; Keller et al. v. Baldwin, 169 Ill. 152; C. & N. W. R. R. Co. v. Garrett, 239 Ill. 297.)

It is next urged that the decree of the superior court of June 7, 1933, does not grant petitioners a lien on the condemned land, which is now represented by the fund on deposit with the county treasurer, and that the decree is void in so far as it affects to deal with the real estate, since the superior court had no jurisdiction over the real estate. These contentions were disposed of by the appellate court in Madden et al. v. Johnson, 274 Ill. App. 661, wherein Sarah L. Johnson contended, among other things, that the final decree was erroneous in granting a lien on the property described in the bill because it was not supported by allegations of fact; that at common law an attorney's lien does not arise under the attorneys' lien act

without the service of the notice therein prescribed; that the contract did not create a specific lien; that the final decree is erroneous in finding that petitioners are entitled to an interest in the property described in the bill of complaint; and that the alleged contract does not belong to the class of agreements which are specifically enforced in equity. As to these contentions, we then said:

"All these points are argued at length with numerous citations of authorities, but none of them was presented for consideration upon the former appeal, and all of them might have been presented at that time. This court and the Supreme Court have many times held in substance that upon the second appeal of a case, either to this court or to the Supreme Court, the judgment of the court rendered on the first appeal is res adjudicata as to all persons who were parties to the proceeding, not only as to questions actually decided but as to all questions which might have been decided, if properly presented." (Citing Davis v. Muncie, Admr., 140 Ill. App. 171.)

What was said in the foregoing decision is alike applicable to the other points urged for reversal. Sarah L. Johnson seeks by this proceeding to contest the rights of petitioners which have been passed upon twice by the appellate court, and twice reviewed by the Supreme Court. Grounds urged for reversal were available to her when the second appeal from the superior court was prosecuted. Notwithstanding that fact she failed to raise some of them and seeks now to make this appeal the basis for urging additional errors, and to still further postpone the rights of petitioners which they have been seeking to enforce through some fifteen years of litigation. This cannot be done. The superior court, this court on two occasions, and the Supreme Court, by twice denying certiorari, have finally adjudicated the rights of petitioners to the sum awarded them for legal services rendered under a written agreement which was held to be valid and binding upon her, and substantially all the additional grounds now urged for reversal hark back to the superior court decree, the validity of which can no longer be questioned.

We find among the points advanced by counsel for Sarah L. Johnson no convincing reason for reversal. The rights of petitioners

in the money decree awarded them and to the enforcement of the lien which the superior court and the reviewing courts have held to be valid, should no longer be the subject of controversy. The judgment of the county court is therefore affirmed.

AFFIRMED.

Sullivan, P. J., and Scanlan, J., concur.

38109

CITY OF CHICAGO,

v.

CHICAGO & NORTHWESTERN R. R. CO. et al.

IN RE PETITION OF DANIEL L. MADDEN and EDWARD J. KELLEY, Petitioners,

v.

SARAH L. JOHNSON et al., Respondents.

ELAINE JOHNSON BURGESS and ISABELLE C. JOHNSON, Plaintiffs in Error,

v.

DANIEL L. MADDEN, EDWARD J. KELLEY, ROBERT M. SWEITZER, successor in office to THOMAS D. NASH, county treasurer of Cook county, Illinois, and SARAH L. JOHNSON, Defendants in Error.

ERROR TO COUNTY COURT, COOK COUNTY.

286 I.A. 611

MR. JUSTICE FRIEND DELIVERED THE OPINION OF THE COURT.

Elaine Johnson Burgess and Isabelle C. Johnson, who were not parties to the proceedings below but claim to have been adversely affected thereby, sued out a writ of error in the Supreme court to reverse a judgment of the County court directing the treasurer of Cook county to pay Daniel L. Madden and Edward J. Kelley, petitioners in that proceeding, $5,811.45 theretofore deposited by the City of Chicago for the owner or owners of certain property taken for public use by the city in a condemnation proceeding then pending in the county court. Prior thereto Sarah L. Johnson, who was made

principal defendant under the petition filed in the County court, appealed to the Supreme court of Illinois from the judgment there entered against her. The Supreme court found that both the appeal and the writ of error were wrongfully taken and transferred the causes to this court for determination. January 7, 1936, by order of the appellate court, cases 38108 and 38109 were consolidated for hearing.

The claim of Madden and Kelley, hereinafter referred to as petitioners, grows out of litigation dating back to 1923. Sarah L. Johnson and petitioners have twice been before the Superior court of Cook county, twice before this court (Madden et al. v. Johnson, 257 Ill. App. 635; same, 274 Ill. App. 661), and two petitions for certiorari filed in the Supreme court to review the appellate court decisions have been denied. Petitioners' claim is predicated upon a certain decree entered in the Superior court June 7, 1933, allowing them $15,600 for legal services theretofore rendered to Sarah L. Johnson under an agreement between the parties, and petitioners claim that by virtue of the decree thus entered they were awarded a lien on the real estate belonging to Sarah L. Johnson, including that part taken for public use.

November 15, 1934, following the entry of the decree by the Superior court, Madden and Kelley filed a petition in the County court, in a case then pending, entitled "City of Chicago v. Chicago & Northwestern R. R. Co. et al.," joining as defendants to the petition Sarah L. Johnson, City of Chicago and Thomas D. Nash as county treasurer, praying for an order directing Nash, as treasurer, to pay petitioners $5,811.45 which had been deposited by the City of Chicago for the owner or owners of, and parties interested in, certain property taken for public use, and that upon payment of this sum to petitioners Sarah L. Johnson have credit for that amount on the decree of the Superior court awarding

petitioners $15,600 from Sarah L. Johnson.

The petition of Madden and Kelley, filed in the County court, is rather voluminous and traces the claim of petitioners through various proceedings, culminating in a decree of the Superior court ordering that Sarah L. Johnson pay petitioners $15,600 for legal services rendered, and directing that said sum be paid to petitioners by Sarah L. Johnson within five days and that upon her failure so to do, the property be sold by a master in chancery. The petition alleges that under the terms of the Superior court decree petitioners were given a lien on the property of Sarah L. Johnson, including the part taken by the city in the condemnation proceedings then pending in the County court, and that petitioners were entitled to have the sum of $5,811.45, theretofore deposited by the City of Chicago with the County treasurer, turned over to them as a credit upon the amount due under the decree of the Superior court, and they prayed for judgment accordingly.

November 26, 1934, Sarah L. Johnson filed her answer to the foregoing petition, admitting most of the essential averments of fact relating to the proceedings theretofore had in the Superior court and the review of the decree of the Superior court and other proceedings by the Appellate and Supreme courts. She denied, however, that the bill filed in the Superior court sought to impress a lien upon her real estate for fees due petitioners, and averred that it was merely a bill to pay petitioners compensation for services rendered as her attorneys. It was further averred by her answer that Madden and Kelley were not made parties to the suit of the City of Chicago v. C. & Northwestern R. R. Co., and that they never served notice in writing, as provided in par. 13, sec. 1, chap. 13, Cahill's Ill. Rev. Stats., 1931, and that no notice of service of attorney's statutory lien is alleged in the bill of complaint filed in the Superior court.

It is further averred that on September 26, 1931, Sarah L. Johnson, for a good and valuable consideration, sold, assigned, transferred, set over and delivered to Elaine Johnson Burgess and Isabelle C. Johnson all sums of money due and owing to her or to become due and owing, and all claims, demands and causes of action of every kind that she had against the City of Chicago by reason of two certain condemnation proceedings, one pending in the Superior court and the other in the County court, and that notice of said assignment was given to the then county treasurer on May 20, 1933, a copy of which is attached to her answer as exhibit "A"; that any rights which petitioners may have under the decree of the Superior court date from the time the decree was entered on June 7, 1933, and that the decree does not by its terms have any retroactive affect upon the rights, properties or moneys of defendant, Sarah L. Johnson, and that the County court has no jurisdiction to subject the condemnation money on deposit with the County treasurer to the payment of a claim or lien which did not exist at the time of the entry of the order of the County court requiring the deposit of the condemnation moneys to be made.

November 28, 1934, the County court entered the judgment order which is sought to be reversed by this writ of error, reciting the petition, the answer of Sarah L. Johnson, the default of the City of Chicago and of Thomas D. Nash as county treasurer, finding that the court had jurisdiction of the parties and of the subject matter; that Madden and Kelley had a right and interest in, and a lien upon, the real estate of Sarah L. Johnson which is described in the order; that petitioners were entitled to receive as compensation for their services, in conformity with the agreement between the parties as established by the decree of the Superior court, one-third of said real estate or the equivalent of its value in money, less $3,200; that pursuant to the statute the City

of Chicago, on May 16, 1930, deposited with the county treasurer the compensation fixed by the court for the property taken, at $5,811.45, and that the rights and interests of petitioners had attached to said fund. It was ordered that Nash, as county treasurer, pay petitioners the said sum, and upon payment thereof, that Sarah L. Johnson shall take and receive credit upon the decree of the Superior court.

Edward J. Kelley, one of the petitioners, died during the pendency of this cause, and on September 25, 1935, Elaine Johnson Burgess and Isabella Johnson, plaintiffs in error, suggested his death and moved the court that Nora G. Hand, administratrix of the estate of Edward J. Kelley, deceased, be substituted as a party in lieu of Edward J. Kelley. The motion was allowed and summons issued to the administratrix. Prior thereto, during the lifetime of Edward J. Kelley, he and Madden, as defendants in error, filed a motion to dismiss the appeal, which was reserved to the hearing. Briefly stated, the motion is predicated on the fact that neither Elaine Johnson Burgess nor Isabella C. Johnson were parties to the proceedings below, and, being strangers to the record, they have no appealable interest in the cause and therefore cannot maintain the writ of error. The order of the County court directing the county treasurer to pay petitioners $5,811.45 theretofore deposited by the City of Chicago as damages awarded to Sarah L. Johnson, recites that witnesses were sworn and examined in open court on the hearing and exhibits offered and received in evidence. Notwithstanding this recital, no report of the proceedings was filed herein, and the only basis for this writ of error on the part of Elaine Johnson Burgess and Isabelle C. Johnson is an affidavit by Edward J. Padden, filed in the County court after the entry of the judgment order, stating that he is the duly authorized agent of Sarah L. Johnson, Elaine Johnson Burgess and Isabelle C. Johnson, that he has personal knowledge

of the matters and things stated therein, and makes the affidavit on behalf of all three persons; that Sarah L. Johnson assigned her interest in the fund in question and also quitclaimed her interest in the real estate of which the condemned property was a part, to Elaine Johnson Burgess and Isabelle C. Johnson, who were not made parties to the proceeding. There also appears the affidavit of Edward J. Kelley, likewise stating that plaintiffs in error were not parties to any proceeding in the controversy between Sarah L. Johnson and petitioners; and that Edward J. Padden, who filed the affidavit on behalf of Sarah L. Johnson and plaintiffs in error, is an attorney at law, practicing at the Chicago bar; that he took an active part in this proceeding from the time of its commencement to the present; that he was in court at various hearings held in the Superior court and a witness in the chancery proceeding; that on appeal of the decree of the Superior court to the Appellate court Padden appears as "of counsel," and that he filed a petition for certiorari in the Supreme court of Illinois and when the matter was remanded to the Superior court Padden participated in the hearing and was also present and participated in the argument at the close of the hearing in the County court; that during all this time Padden never informed the chancellor in the Superior court or anyone connected with the said cause that Sarah L. Johnson had quitclaimed her interest in the real estate to plaintiffs in error.

In support of their motion to dismiss the writ of error petitioners have filed voluminous typewritten suggestions, with authorities, to sustain their position, and counsel for plaintiffs in error has filed counter-suggestions thereto. After carefully examining these decisions we have reached the conclusion that the writ of error should be dismissed, for the following reason: Neither Elaine Johnson Burgess nor Isabelle C. Johnson were parties to the proceedings below, and, having no appealable interest, cannot bring

a writ of error to reverse a judgment by which they were not directly affected. Neither can the fact that they became interested in the subject matter of the suit, as they contend, since the entry of the decree of the Superior court, be shown by affidavit. Wuerzburger v. Wuerzberger, 221 Ill. 277, is precisely in point. In that case Mary Madison and Leona Colburn, who were not parties to the suit in the court below either as complainants or defendants, sued out a writ of error, claiming to have an interest in the subject matter of the decree by inheritance through their deceased father, Richard Colburn. In discussing the subject under consideration the Supreme court said (pp. 280-282):

"It was, however, sought to be shown by affidavit, at the time the writ of error was sued out, that said Mary E. Madison and Leona Colburn have, by inheritance * * * an interest in the subject matter of the decree entered in the court below. Their interest could not thus be shown. In Hauger v. Gage, 168 Ill. 365, on page 367, the court said: 'The general rule is that writs of error must be sued out in the name of parties to the action below. "No person can bring a writ of error to reverse a judgment who was not a party or privy to the record or prejudiced by the judgment, and therefore to receive advantage by the reversal of it." (Tidd's Prac. title "Error," 1189.) "Whether the plaintiff in error be a party or privy or is aggrieved by the judgment must appear by the record. A court for the correction of errors cannot, at common law, hear evidence to determine whether a party seeking a reversal is aggrieved by the judgment. Its mission is to examine the record upon which judgment was given, and upon such examination to reverse or affirm."' * * * 'The record certified to this court speaks for itself, and we cannot hear extrinsic evidence to determine whether a party seeking a reversal is aggrieved by the judgment.' * * *

"For the reasons hereinbefore suggested, we are of the opinion the writ of error was improvidently sued out and that the motion to dismiss the writ must be sustained."

In McIntyre v. Sholty et al., 139 Ill. 171, it was laid down as a general rule "that no person can sue out a writ of error who is not a party, or privy to the record, or who is not shown by the record to be prejudiced by the judgment." Numerous cases from various jurisdictions are cited therein to sustain the conclusion. Counsel for plaintiffs in error argues that he could not seek reversal of the judgment of the county court by appeal, since, as he states, the condemnation statute is expressly exempted from the civil practice act. We do not pass upon this question. There is before us a writ of

error, and under the clear weight of authority in this state Elaine Johnson Burgess and Isabelle C. Johnson, who were not parties to the proceeding below and whose interest is not disclosed by the record in the writ of error, but merely by affidavit, cannot prosecute or maintain a writ of error.

Moreover, it appears from the affidavits of Kelley and Padden that Padden, as attorney for plaintiffs in error as well as for Sarah L. Johnson, was thoroughly familiar with all the proceedings below, not only in the Superior court but in the County court as well, and participated in some of them. It must therefore be presumed that his knowledge was imputed to his clients, and we think they are estopped, after silently sitting by and allowing both the Superior and the County courts to enter judgments and decrees without asserting their rights, to claim at this late date, on writ of error, that the interest of Sarah L. Johnson, in the property and the fund, was assigned to them back in 1931.

For the reasons stated the motion of petitioners to dismiss the writ of error must be allowed, and it is so ordered.

WRIT OF ERROR DISMISSED.

Sullivan, P. J., and Scanlan, J., concur.

44 A

38383

JAMES D. HUESTIS, Trustee in Bankruptcy of NICHOLAS J. DOBEL, doing business as Dobel Manufacturing and Plating Company, Appellee,	)	APPEAL FROM MUNICIPAL
v.	)	COURT OF CHICAGO.
NEO-GRAVURE COMPANY OF CHICAGO, a corporation, Appellant.	)	

286 I.A. 612[1]

MR. JUSTICE FRIEND DELIVERED THE OPINION OF THE COURT.

James D. Huestis, trustee in bankruptcy of Nicholas J. Dobel, doing business as Dobel Manufacturing and Plating Company, filed a first class contract action in the municipal court to recover $1,884 alleged to be due for gravure cylinders sold to the defendant by the bankrupt. A summary or partial judgment of $596 was entered in favor of plaintiff upon the pleadings, from which this appeal is prosecuted.

Plaintiff's statement of claim alleges that Dobel manufactured and delivered to defendant at its special instance and request twelve gravure cylinders at a purchase price of $3,576, for which defendant paid on account $1,692, leaving a balance of $1,884, as well as interest thereon amounting to $56.52, aggregating $1,940.52.

The amended affidavit of merits admits the delivery of the twelve cylinders, denies that the purchase price was $3,576, and refers the court to a written agreement between the parties for the terms of sale. The written contract recites that Dobel had previously delivered eighteen cylinders to defendant, all of

which were defective and were returned to Dobel for rebuilding in accordance with the specifications upon which they were originally ordered. It states that in view of the fact that these cylinders were not built in accordance with defendant's specifications, ten of them having again been delivered, the parties agreed that the remaining eight cylinders should be eliminated from the order and that Dobel would release defendant from any and all costs incurred in connection with these eight cylinders. The agreement further states that Dobel has rebuilt the ten cylinders with three bearings each, instead of two as required by the specifications; that defendant agrees to place these ten cylinders in service and test them through one season's work; that if proven satisfactory, defendant agrees to pay $2,980 for the ten cylinders, less $1,692 which had already been paid on account, plus further deductions representing freight charges paid by defendant. The contract further provides that if the ten rebuilt cylinders prove unsatisfactory after one season's run, Dobel will, at defendant's option, rebuild them with five bearings instead of three before payment of the balance is made. It is further agreed that Dobel may rebuild two of the remaining eight cylinders according to defendant's specifications, copy of which was attached to the agreement, each cylinder to contain five bearings instead of three, and that if after thorough test the two cylinders prove satisfactory to defendant it would pay $596 therefor.

The amended affidavit of merits further avers that defendant made known to Dobel that it relied upon Dobel's skill with a resulting implied warranty that the goods should be of merchantable quality, and alleges that only the last two cylinders were used through a season's run and that they were not of merchantable quality, but were defective in the following respects: (1) the copper coatings were defective; (2) the welding holding the shaft mandrel was

defective; that six of the cylinders were used for a part of the season, but proved defective in all these respects, and in addition thereto were defective in that they ceased to be approximately perfect cylinders, but "were out of round" due to insufficient bearings; that the remaining four of said cylinders were so defective in the respects enumerated that they could not be used at all; that prompt notice was given to Dobel of the defects in the cylinders, and requests made that they should be rebuilt to conform to specifications; that Dobel offered to rebuild eight of the cylinders with five bearings and deliver them to defendant, but this was never done; that defendant again suggested that Dobel rebuild three of the cylinders with five bearings, to which no reply was made, all of which was brought to plaintiff's attention by letters and telegrams. The amended affidavit further avers that none of the ten cylinders rebuilt proved satisfactory during the season's run, that none was used throughout the season, due to their defective manufacture, and offers return thereof upon the return of payments already made. It was also averred that the twelve cylinders as delivered were not worth more than $250 because of the defects stated in the affidavit, and defendant denies that it is indebted to plaintiff in any sum whatsoever.

Defendant also filed a statement of claim by way of recoupment, incorporating by reference the amended affidavit of merits and averring that cylinders of proper quality and construction would reasonably have been worth $3,576, but that the cylinders as delivered were not worth to exceed $250, by reason whereof defendant has sustained damages of $1,530, being the excess of the amount already paid by defendant over the value of the cylinders delivered.

Plaintiff advances the theory that the contract for the purchase of the cylinders was a severable contract, and that since no legal defense was raised in the pleadings as to the purchase price

of two of the cylinders, plaintiff was entitled to a partial judgment therefor. The court evidently adopted this theory and entered a summary partial judgment as heretofore stated of $596. Two principal grounds are urged for reversal: (1) that the amended affidavit of merits states a defense upon the merits to the whole of plaintiff's demand, and (2) that defendant's counterclaim should be a bar to any summary judgment on the pleadings.

From a careful examination of the pleadings, including the written agreement incorporated in the amended affidavit of merits, we are satisfied that plaintiff's demand is based upon a single, indivisible contract. The amended affidavit of merits avers that the two cylinders were not of merchantable quality but were defective in the following respects: The copper coatings were defective, and the welding holding the shaft mandrel was defective. It also avers that defendant advised Dobel on August 4, 1934, that the cylinders were not satisfactory. Inasmuch as the agreement provides that as to these two cylinders payment is to be made only "if, after thorough tests, cylinders prove satisfactory to us," the averment specifically claiming defects would, if established by competent evidence, constitute a defense. The affidavit of merits certainly raises a controversy of fact between the parties which cannot be determined without a hearing. Such controversies are not the subject of summary or partial judgment. We think this statement is sustained by a plain reading of the statute and the rules of the municipal court, and requires no citation of authorities.

Moreover, by its counterclaim defendant set up a good affirmative cause of action against Dobel for $1,580 in excess of the value of the cylinders delivered by him. A recoupment is not a cross demand, but a defense or counterclaim arising out of the same transaction upon which suit is based. Rights of a trustee in bankruptcy arise out of and are governed by the Bankruptcy Act, of two of the cylinders, plaintiff was entitled to a partial judgment therefor. The court evidently adopted this theory and entered a summary partial judgment as heretofore stated of $[illegible]. Two principal grounds are urged for reversal: (1) that the amended affidavit of merits states a defense upon the merits to the whole of plaintiff's demand, and (2) that defendant's counterclaim should be a bar to any summary judgment on the pleadings.

From a careful examination of the pleadings, including the written agreement incorporated in the amended affidavit of merits, we are satisfied that plaintiff's demand is based upon a single, indivisible contract. The amended affidavit of merits avers that the two cylinders were not of merchantable quality but were defective in the following respects: The copper coatings were defective, and the welding holding the shaft mandrel was defective. It also avers that defendant advised Nebel on August 4, 19[illegible], that the cylinders were not satisfactory. Inasmuch as the agreement provides that as to these two cylinders payment is to be made only "if, after thorough tests, cylinders prove satisfactory to us," the averment specifically claiming defects would, if established by competent evidence, constitute a defense. The affidavit of merits certainly raises a controversy of fact between the parties which cannot be determined without a hearing. Such controversies are not the subject of summary or partial judgment. We think this statement is sustained by a plain reading of the statute and the rules of the municipal court, and requires no citation of authorities.

Moreover, by its counterclaim defendant set up a good affirmative cause of action against Nebel for $1,380 in excess of the value of the cylinders delivered by him. A recoupment is not a cross demand, but a defense or counterclaim arising out of the same transaction upon which suit is based. Rights of a trustee in bankruptcy arise out of and are governed by the Bankruptcy Act.

sec. 108a of which provides as follows:

> "In all cases of mutual debts or mutual credits between the estate of a bankrupt and a creditor the account shall be stated and one debt shall be set off against the other, and the balance only shall be allowed or paid." (U. S. Code, Title 11, sec. 108a.)

Plaintiff seeks to avoid the effect of defendant's recoupment by contending that it should be limited to the purchase price of ten cylinders, and not against the two cylinders specially provided for in the agreement. This contention is untenable, however, since by his own statement of claim plaintiff claims that the bankrupt manufactured and delivered to defendant "12 gravure cylinders at a price of $3,576; that the defendant paid on account the sum of $1,692, leaving a balance due of $1,884." Thus the entire transaction is treated as a single, indivisible agreement, and defendant's recoupment goes to the whole transaction. Under the circumstances the counterclaim, if established by competent evidence and to the satisfaction of the court, would defeat plaintiff's claim and should, as defendant contends, be a bar to any summary judgment on the pleadings.

It is conceded by the pleadings that defendant paid $1,692 toward the purchase of ten cylinders, which, according to defendant's contention, proved to be defective and useless. Defendant should, therefore, not be summarily compelled to pay $596 additional for two other cylinders included in the same contract which are averred to have been of unmerchantable quality and found upon a season's test to be defective in coating and welding. If plaintiff believed that the amended affidavit of merits was not sufficiently specific it was incumbent upon him to secure a more specific affidavit of merits by motion to strike, made in apt time, or other procedure employed under the municipal court practice.

The controversy between the parties should be tried upon issues made up by the pleadings and determined only after a hearing

of the controverted issues of facts and law made by the pleadings. Therefore the judgment of the municipal court is reversed and the cause is remanded with directions to proceed with the trial of the entire cause.

JUDGMENT REVERSED AND CAUSE REMANDED
WITH DIRECTIONS.

Sullivan, P. J., and Scanlan, J., concur.

45 A

38491

VICTOR WIECZOREK, administrator of the estate of Ida Wieczorek, deceased,
Appellee,

v.

THE PRUDENTIAL INSURANCE COMPANY OF AMERICA, a corporation,
Appellant.

APPEAL FROM MUNICIPAL COURT OF CHICAGO.

286 I.A. 612[2]

MR. JUSTICE FRIEND DELIVERED THE OPINION OF THE COURT.

Plaintiff, as beneficiary, brought an action on the double indemnity provisions of two life insurance policies issued by defendant. Trial was had by jury resulting in a verdict and judgment for plaintiff in the sum of $404, from which this appeal is taken.

Plaintiff's statement of claim alleged that $472 was due under the terms of policies on the life of Ida Wieczorek, which provided that upon receipt of due proof that the insured had sustained bodily injury, solely through external, violent and accidental means, resulting in the death of the insured within ninety days from the date of such bodily injury, the company will pay in addition to the other sums due under the policies a benefit equal to the face amount of the insurance. It was further alleged that deceased came to her death by reason of a fracture of the right femur, occasioned by a fall in the bathroom of her home, occurring June 27, 1934, and that the insured died August 13, 1934. Plaintiff was paid the face amount of the policies, and this action is brought to recover double indemnity, which defendant refused to pay.

By way of defense defendant averred that the death of insured was not the result of injuries sustained through external, violent and accidental means, but that said injury which preceded her death was caused by physical weakness, disease, stroke and general debility, and also that defendant never received due proof as required by the policy and is therefore not liable for the sum claimed.

Briefly stated, the facts disclose that defendant issued two policies on the life of Ida Wieczorek, one for $184, dated October 15, 1923, and the other for $220, dated December 29, 1924. She gave her age as 58 when the latter policy was issued, and was approximately 68 years of age at the time of her death. Deceased resided with her daughter. About five years prior to her death she had suffered a paralytic stroke affecting her right leg, which caused her some difficulty in walking. June 27, 1934, she was assisted to the bathroom by her daughter. Shortly thereafter both her daughter and grandson heard a thump in the bathroom, where the insured had fallen. She was found lying over the threshold and carried back to her room. There appears to be some conflict in the evidence as to when Dr. Fowler, the attending physician, was called. However, upon examination he found that her left hip was broken. She was taken to a hospital for a day, where a cast was placed upon both legs from the waist down below her knees and she was then removed to her daughter's home, where she remained in bed. She appeared to be getting along fairly well but developed a bed sore on the left hip resulting in an infection, producing fever and high blood pressure. The physician testified that she had rales in the chest and that her heart became decompensated. Death resulted on August 13, 1934. Dr. Fowler testified that some time after the injury she became incontinent and was unable to control her bowel movements. Ultimately bronchial pneumonia set in and d eath ensued.

As ground for reversal it is urged that plaintiff failed to prove that insured sustained bodily injury solely through external, violent and accidental means which resulted in her death within ninety days from the date of such injury. It is undisputed that decedent's death ensued within ninety days after the accident occurred, but defendant insists that plaintiff was not entitled to recover because her death was the result of pneumonia, which is a disease, and that proof was lacking to sustain the allegation that death resulted from bodily injuries sustained solely through external, violent and accidental means. The gravamen of the defense is best set forth in the following excerpt from defendant's brief:

"The insured had a stroke of paralysis about five years prior to the date when she broke her leg. The stroke of paralysis rendered her right leg practically helpless. Her fall, which occurred in June, 1934, caused a fracture of her left hip. If the insured were not partially paralyzed, she would not have fallen and broken her leg. * * * It is our contention that the death of the insured was the result of her disease and bodily infirmity. If the paralyzed right leg, with which it is admitted the insured was afflicted, contributed to her fall or if bronchial pneumonia caused her death, the plaintiff is not entitled to recover."

To sustain its contention defendant cites Kerns v. Aetna Life Ins. Co., 291 Fed. 289, where an action was brought on a life insurance policy containing similar provisions. The insured was a physician and while eating he swallowed a small piece of metal which lodged in his esophagus. He suffered some pain and was ill about two weeks, but seemingly recovered and resumed his practice. He stated that some four months later, while attending a professional call, his automobile became stalled in the snow and in assisting the chauffeur to push the car he slipped and felt a pain. His death a month later was attributed to abscesses, superinduced by the breaking down of the incapsulation surrounding the piece of metal which he had swallowed. It was the theory of medical experts who testified that the metal had become quiescent and harmless, but that the shock of slipping had dislodged

it and brought out a reinfection causing abscess and hemorrhages, which produced death. Plaintiff was precluded from recovering on the policies in that case, on the principal ground, however, that death did not occur as provided in the policy until more than ninety days subsequent to the initial accident, and in the course of its opinion the court said that the initial injury was such as came within the category of injuries insured against and that if the insured's death had ensued within ninety days, or if the initial injury had induced a continuing total disability of 200 weeks and at the end thereof death had ensued, a recovery could have been had.

Another case which defendant says is very similar to the case at bar is O'Meara v. Columbian National Life Ins. Co., 119 Conn. 641, 178 Atl. 357, decided in April, 1935, and there also suit was brought under the double indemnity portion of the policy containing similar provisions to those here involved. The insured was a butcher, 47 years of age, who appeared to be in good health. On the date of his death he had eaten a hearty meal in the afternoon and thereafter played cards with a companion until early the next morning. Later he was seen by a police officer entering the laneway south of his home, and about an hour later was found unconscious near the steps of his house with an abrasion over his left eye. Taken to a hospital, a diabetic condition was discovered, and an examination disclosed that he was suffering from bronchitis, nephritis and chronic gout. He contracted lobar pneumonia from which he died two days later. No recovery was permitted in that case. However, we think this decision does not help defendant, because the court said that there was an entire absence of any testimony to show that the unconscious condition of insured was due to the injury received in falling or that the injury was of such a character as would tend to produce unconsciousness. His attending physician declined to express an opinion as to how the unconsciousness was produced, and an expert it and brought out a reinfection causing abscess and hemorrhages, which produced death. Plaintiff was precluded from recovering on the policies in that case, on the principal ground, however, that death did not occur as provided in the policy until more than ninety days subsequent to the initial accident, and in the course of its opinion the court said that the initial injury was such as came within the category of injuries insured against and that if the insured's death had ensued within ninety days, or if the initial injury had induced a continuing total disability of 200 weeks and at the end thereof death had ensued, a recovery could have been had.

Another case which defendant says is very similar to the case at bar is O'Meara v. Columbian National Life Ins. Co., 119 Conn. 641, 178 Atl. 387, decided in April, 1935, and there also suit was brought under the double indemnity portion of the policy containing similar provisions to those here involved. The insured was a butcher, 47 years of age, who appeared to be in good health. On the date of his death he had eaten a hearty meal in the afternoon and thereafter played cards with a companion until early the next morning. Later he was seen by a police officer entering the laneway south of his home, and about an hour later was found unconscious near the steps of his house with an abrasion over his left eye. Taken to a hospital, a diabetic condition was discovered, and an examination disclosed that he was suffering from bronchitis, nephritis and chronic gout. He contracted lobar pneumonia from which he died two days later. No recovery was permitted in that case. However, we think this decision does not help defendant, because the court said that there was an entire absence of any testimony to show that the unconscious condition of insured was due to the injury received in falling or that the injury was of such a character as would tend to produce unconsciousness. His attending physician declined to express an opinion as to how the unconsciousness was produced, and an expert diagnostician stated that the unconscious condition was a diabetic coma, in no way attributable to the injury to the head. Other medical testimony tended to show that a contributing cause of the death was diabetes, and of course there was no recovery under the circumstances.

In Globe Accident Ins. Co. v. Gerisch, 163 Ill. 625, also cited by defendant, suit was predicated upon an accident alleged to have resulted from a strain produced by lifting a box of cinders and ashes. From an examination of the opinion it appears that there was no proof whatever that deceased had strained and injured his body in this manner, and the court, in discussing the facts, said that "one essential fact - indeed, the all-important fact, - is therefore wanting in order to make out a case."

In support of the judgment plaintiff cites Prehn v. Metropolitan Life Ins. Co., 267 Ill. App. 190, where defendant made the same contention as is here urged under a policy containing similar provisions. Prehn, the deceased, had fallen from a scaffold on June 14, 1930, apparently sustaining a slight injury to his spleen, and the following September, while at work, he arose suddenly from a chair, complained of a pain in his back, and was taken to a hospital, where he died shortly thereafter. A post-mortem examination disclosed a ruptured spleen with evidence of prior injury. Judgment for plaintiff on the policy was affirmed, although defendant's edical expert testified that the rising from a chair in the manner iescribed would not be sufficient to rupture a healthy spleen. The court held, however, that the evidence sufficiently showed Prehn's eath was traceable to the original injury and "did result from uch violent and accidental means and independent of other causes s rendered the defendant liable under the certificate or policy ued on."

In Christ v. Pacific Mutual Life Ins. Co., 312 Ill. 525, it

was held that blood poisoning caused by an accident was the direct or proximate result of the accident and plaintiff was therefore permitted to recover on the policy.

In Bohaker v. Travelers Ins. Co., 215 Mass. 32, plaintiff was allowed to recover under a policy of insurance "against bodily injuries effected directly and independent of all other causes through external, violent and accidental means." The deceased, while ill with typhoid fever, in an effort to reach fresh air, went to a balcony outside his window, and, as stated by the court, "without premeditation or purpose or delirium, but only through weakness lost his balance and went over the low railing and received mortal harm." In commenting on the question under consideration, the court said:

> "The point of difficulty in this condition is whether the disease did not contribute to the injuries, or at least was it not a cause co-operating with the fall in inducing the result, but the disease may have been found to have been simply a condition and not a moving cause of the fatal injuries. A sick man may be the subject of an accident which but for his sickness would not have befallen him. One may meet his death by falling into imminent danger in a faint or in an attack of epilepsy. But such an event commonly has been held to be the result of accident rather than of disease." (Italics ours.)

In Miner v. New Amsterdam Casualty Co., 220 Ill. App. 74, suit was brought on a policy containing provisions similar to those contained in the policies involved herein. The evidence showed that the insured became sick to his stomach from eating peanuts on a train and went to the rear platform and sat down. He was found under the train with his legs severed, from which accident he died. There was no evidence to disclose how he had fallen. A judgment in the beneficiary's favor was sustained. In the course of its opinion the court said:

> "Even if it could legitimately be found to be a fact that Roberts was nauseated and that, because of his nausea, he went out on the platform and that he then became dizzy, either from nausea or the motion of the train, and fell off from the platform and under the car and there received the injuries in question, Roberts would not thereby be precluded from recovering * * * because the sickness or disease mentioned in the limitation clause of the

policy above referred to does not mean every momentary indisposition that is suffered by the insured. * * * It means a sickness of some seriousness and permanency which, in itself, directly contributes to the loss suffered and but for which the loss would not have been sustained." (Italics ours.)

It is plaintiff's contention that the death of the insured in the case at bar may be traced to the bronchial pneumonia resulting from the infection from bed sores which arose out of the condition created by the plaster cast and the post traumatic incontinency of the insured, and that her death therefore resulted directly as a result of the accident. We think plaintiff made out a prima facie case of death of the insured within the provisions of the policy, and thereafter it became the burden of defendant to show that the death resulted from a cause excepted in the policy. (Rogers v. Prudential Ins. Co., 270 Ill. App. 515; Nalty v. Federal Casualty Co., 245 Ill. App. 180.) Defendant's counsel argue that Dr. Fowler, the attending physician who testified at the trial, failed to express an opinion that the broken leg was the sole cause of death, and it is urged that without such evidence plaintiff cannot recover. Defendant's abstract of record does not accurately show the proceedings had when Dr. Fowler was on the witness stand, but from an examination of the record the following appears:

"Q. Doctor, have you an opinion based upon a reasonable medical certainty as to whether the death that occurred in August is traceable to the accident and the subsequent causes coming through it?

A. The line of events --

Mr. Welsh (counsel for defendant): Just a minute, it calls for an answer yes or no.

The Court: Yes, or no.

Mr. Harris (attorney for plaintiff): Q. And what is your opinion?

Mr. Welsh: I object, he has already told us the facts.

The Court: Well, he is the attending physician. Why couldn't he express an opinion?

Mr. Welsh: Why, he has told us, your Honor please, all the facts. Now, this jury is here for the purpose of solving that. What he says doesn't make any difference, any more than anybody else.

The Court: He is a medical expert.

Mr. Welsh: If he hadn't given us the facts, if it was a hypothetical question of some other doctor's testimony it would be different, but here he has given us the facts.

Mr. Harris: I think I will withdraw the question, your Honor.

The Court: All right."

It appears from another part of the record that plaintiff's counsel asked Dr. Fowler whether he had an opinion, based upon a reasonable medical certainty, as to whether or not the bronchial pneumonia could have resulted from bed sores, about which Dr. Fowler had testified, and the following ensued:

> "Mr. Welsh: He said they could come from infection. He has already testified there was an infection in these bed sores.
> The Court: I guess that objection he makes is a good one. I am going to sustain it, because the doctor stated all his findings here.
> Mr. Harris: Not to argue with the court, of course, I was just covering this question of infection, your Honor.
> The Court: He has testified it came from an infection."

Defendant's counsel say, on page 8 of their brief, that "it should be noted that not even Dr. Fowler stated at any place in his testimony that the bronchial pneumonia and decompensated heart of the insured were caused by the broken leg." In view of the proceedings hereinbefore quoted, indicating that defendant objected to the testimony proferred, it is not in a position to claim that plaintiff failed to make the requisite proof. The record clearly shows that the bed sores caused an infection, and plaintiff tried to elicit from Dr. Fowler an opinion whether the infection could have produced the bronchial pneumonia from which plaintiff died. Since defendant objected to the evidence it cannot now complain that plaintiff failed to assume the burden of showing the connection between infections resulting from the injury and the post traumatic pneumonia which evidently caused insured's death.

Defendant's argument that if the insured were not partially paralyzed she would not have fallen and broken her leg is untenable. Well people may stumble and fall. The deceased had moved about for more than two years following her paralytic stroke, and we cannot presume that but for her illness she would not have fallen and suffered the injury to her hip. There is nothing in the record touching upon the cause which produced the fall, and under the authorities hereinbefore cited we think it may clearly be

characterized as an accident within the provisions of the policies. It clearly appears from the evidence that the chain of circumstances resulting from the injury proximately led to infection, pneumonia and death, and in such cases courts will not distinguish between the accident itself and the means whereby it was brought about. We so held in the recent case of Burns v. Metropolitan Life Ins. Co., 283 Ill. App. 431, where an action for double indemnity for accidental death was brought under the policy, death having resulted from a fall from the second story window to the sidewalk. There was evidence that the insured, who was sixty-three years of age, suffered from arteriosclerosis which caused dizziness and headaches, but this illness was held insufficient to establish that insured's disease or bodily or mental infirmity was either an immediate or co-operative cause of her death. To the same effect were Burns v. Prudential Ins. Co. of America, 283 Ill. App. 442, and Illinois Commercial Men's Ass'n v. Parks, 179 Fed. 794.

Finding no convincing reason for reversal, the judgment of the Municipal court is affirmed.

AFFIRMED.

Sullivan, P. J., and Scanlan, J., concur.

46 H

38499

WALTER C. ERIKSON,
Appellee,

v.

CHICAGO PARK DISTRICT,
a body politic and corporate,
Appellant,

and

HARRY BAIRSTOW,
Intervener and Appellee,

v.

CHICAGO PARK DISTRICT,
a body politic and corporate,
Appellant.

APPEAL FROM
MUNICIPAL COURT
OF CHICAGO.

286 I.A. 612[3]

MR. JUSTICE FRIEND DELIVERED THE OPINION OF THE COURT.

Walter C. Erikson, hereinafter called plaintiff, brought an action in assumpsit against the Chicago Park District, hereinafter called defendant, for damages of $20,500 growing out of a contract between plaintiff and the North Shore Park District, hereinafter called Park District, which was superseded by Chicago Park District by operation of law. Harry Bairstow, defendant intervener and appellee, hereinafter called the intervener, claims an interest in the proceeds of the suit by virtue of an assignment by plaintiff to him of $12,269.38. Defendant filed an amended affidavit of defense to plaintiff's amended statement of claim and to the statement and affidavit of claim filed by the intervener. The court sustained plaintiff's motion to strike the amended affidavit of defense, and defendant elected to stand thereby. Accordingly a draft order was entered finding that the amended affidavit of defense was insufficient in law, and adjudging defendant in default

for want of a sufficient affidavit of merits. Thereupon judgment was entered in favor of plaintiff for $19,765, $12,269.38 of which is for the use of the intervener. Defendant appeals.

It appears from the pleadings that March 22, 1934, North Shore Park District, a body corporate, entered into a written agreement with plaintiff pursuant to a prior Park District resolution whereby the latter agreed to purchase, accept as and when it desired to, and pay for, not to exceed 30,000 cubic yards of dirt fill to be deposited in an area under the control of the Park District. The price stipulated in the agreement was $1.05 per cubic yard, payable 85% on engineer's certificates and 15% on completion and acceptance by the Park District engineers, payable at the Park District's option in its bonds at full face value. All except 700 cubic yards of fill were delivered, leveled off to grade and accepted by the Park District. Certificates of acceptance were issued therefor, and as part payment the Park District delivered to plaintiff its tax anticipation warrants in the amount of $10,500. Plaintiff sublet a part of his contract to intervener, Harry Bairstow, who furnished and delivered 27,361 cubic yards of fill in accordance with the specifications. Defendant admits that there was furnished by plaintiff 30,000 cubic yards of fill, for which the court permitted his recovery of $19,765. The amount of the judgment was arrived at by giving defendant a credit of $735 for the 700 cubic yards claimed by defendant as not having been delivered. It further appears from the pleadings that by consolidation the Chicago Park District became successor to North Shore Park District, and as such refused the demands of plaintiff and intervener for payment of the balances respectively due them.

Defendant interposed several defenses, the first of which is that a contract for the delivery of dirt fill at a specified price, which provides that payment should be made in bonds of the

North Shore Park District, is a contract promising to deliver so many dollars numerically of the securities described, and that upon a breach of this contract by failure to deliver bonds, the measure of damages is the market value in specie of the bonds. In making provision for the payments to become due plaintiff the written contract employed the following language: "May make all payments provided for in bonds." We have carefully examined the authorities cited by both parties and have reached the conclusion that the current weight of authority is clearly to the effect that an agreement to pay a certain sum in specified articles of personal property at a fixed time, and a failure to deliver the articles in accordance with the agreement, converts the transaction into a money obligation. It was so held in the early case of Borah v. Curry and Owen, 12 Ill. 65, where suit was brought upon a note for $40 which provided that payment may be discharged in sound corn at twenty cents a bushel. In discussing the effect of this provision, the court said (p. 68):

"It is not a note for the payment of personal property other than money, but a note for the payment of money, with a privilege to makers to discharge it in corn at a certain price.

The right to have the note paid in money or corn, was not left to the payee, but the makers reserved that privilege to themselves.

Had corn at the time the note fell due, been worth fifty cents to the bushel, the payee could not have compelled its delivery, while he would have been compelled to take it, if tendered, though its value should fall to ten cents."

In Bilderback v. Burlingame, 27 Ill. 337, suit was brought upon a note which read: "Due Wm. B. Goddard four hundred and fifty dollars, to be paid in lumber when called for, in good lumber, at one dollar and twenty-five cents." After citing Borah v. Curry and Owen, supra, the court in discussing the question under consideration said (p. 342):

"It was a money demand from which the acceptor could have discharged himself only by proving the delivery, or offer to deliver, the proper quantity of lumber, or by the payment of the money. It was not a bill for the delivery of lumber in any sense, nor like a

covenant to deliver lumber, for a breach of which the party could recover damages. It was a privilege to the maker to discharge his acceptance in lumber, and on his failure so to do, the money could be demanded."

It appears from the pleadings that defendant failed to make payment when due in bonds, as it had the option to do under the written agreement, and thereupon plaintiff had the right to demand payment in legal tender. It was so held in McKinnie v. Lane, 230 Ill. 544, where the court held that upon the failure of defendant to pay a certain sum in specified articles or personal property on a day certain day converted the transaction into a money obligation. Snyder Co. v. Sisson, 233 Ill. App. 248, is to the same effect. There a building contract was involved in which defendant agreed to pay 10% of the net cost of the building, and was given the option of making payment in stock of the corporation, but failed so to do. In holding that the option was no longer available, after default, the court said (p. 252):

"We think that by a fair construction of the contract, the defendant agreed to pay complainant 10 per cent of the net cost of the building; that the defendant was given the option to make this payment in stock of the hotel company, and that since the defendant failed and was unable to avail itself of this option on account of its encumbering the property for about $400,000 more than the contract provided it should be encumbered, and on account of the law making that part of the contract ultra vires, it must pay complainant in money."

In County of Jackson v. Hall, 53 Ill. 440, plaintiff contracted to build a county jail and to receive in payment bonds of the county. Upon completion of the building he received the bonds specified but they were afterward repudiated by the county as invalid, and it was held that the county having denied the validity of the bonds, plaintiff could recover the price agreed to be paid therefor in money and that the county would be estopped to assert their invalidity so as to defeat the action. See also the County of Coles v. Goehring, 209 Ill. 142.

Defendant argues that because the specifications attached to the contract provided that payments would be made in bonds,

that thus was the only way that payment could be made, and that since the Park District was unable to issue such bonds, plaintiff is limited in his recovery to the market value of the bonds at the time payment should have been made. This argument is based on the false premise that the contract provides that payment would be made in bonds, whereas in fact it provides that payment may be so made. The clear contents of the agreement, as shown by the pleadings, indicate that defendant had an option which it failed to exercise, and thereupon, under the great weight of authority, the transaction became converted into a money obligation. Defendant relies on Smith v. Dunlap, 12 Ill. 184, and Danville Brick Co. v. Yeager, 271 Ill. App. 86, but upon examination of these decisions we find neither of them in point.

It is next urged that the park commissioners had no authority to issue bonds without first authorizing the same by enactment through ordinance. The record discloses that in the instant case the bonds were not issued, and defendant's argument is therefore tantamount to saying that the bonds were illegal notwithstanding the fact that they were never issued. This presents a purely imaginary issue. People v. Chicago Heights Ry. Co., 319 Ill. 389, is cited by defendant to support the second defense, but that case merely holds that the power to issue bonds is strictly statutory and throws no light upon the question under discussion. Any lack of power to issue bonds, or even a valid exercise of that power, would simply result in defendant's inability to make its optional payment, and the bonds for which there was no ordinance and which were never issued merely emphasize defendant's inability to avail itself of its optional privilege to make payment in valid bonds. Since defendant admitted of record its inability to pay in bonds, the argument advanced and the case cited in support of the proposition are not convincing.

It is next urged that an ordinance is a condition precedent

to the validity of a contract for a local improvement, and defendant argues that the failure of the Park District to pass an ordinance is fatal to the contract and constitutes a complete bar to plaintiff's claim and that of the intervener. In arguing this point, however, defendant's counsel say that if we should hold the failure to enact an ordinance as merely an irregular exercise of the power of the park commissioners to contract, the measure of damages upon breach of such a contract would be the fair cash market value of the materials furnished and the labor performed. The rule, as we understand it, is laid down in Badger v. The Inlet Drainage District, 141 Ill. 540, wherein it was held that when a park district is empowered to do a particular thing but is not authorized to proceed in the manner employed, if after it is done and the benefits are accepted and enjoyed by the municipality, the latter should pay for what it accepted and enjoyed such amount as it would have had to pay had it secured the benefits in the rightful way. In Hitchcock v. Galveston, 96 U. S. 341, a city council had contracted for certain construction work to be paid for by issue of city bonds. The council stopped work after part performance, whereupon suit was filed for breach of contract. The city contended that the contract was void because it had no authority to issue the bonds, but the United States Supreme Court, in discussing the contention, stated what we believe to be the correct rule, as follows (p. 350):

"If it were conceded that the city had no lawful authority to issue the bonds, described in the ordinance and mentioned in the contract, it does not follow that the contract was wholly illegal and void, or that the plaintiffs have no rights under it. They are not suing upon the bonds, and it is not necessary to their success that they should assert the validity of those instruments. It is enough for them that the city council have power to enter into a contract for the improvement of the sidewalks; that such a contract was made with them; that under it they have proceeded to furnish materials and do work, as well as to assume liabilities; that the city has received and now enjoys the benefit of what they have done and furnished; that for these things the city promised to pay; and that after having received the benefit of the contract the city has broken it. It matters not that the promise was to pay

in a manner not authorized by law. If payments cannot be made in bonds because their issue is ultra vires, it would be sanctioning rank injustice to hold that payment need not be made at all. Such is not the law. The contract between the parties is in force, so far as it is lawful."

It is next argued that where a municipality has power to enter into a contract but exercises that power irregularly it is estopped to set up a defense of ultra vires to the extent of what it has received, and recovery can only be had on a quantum meruit. We think defendant is estopped from taking this position because the North Shore Park District fully ratified and approved the work done under the contract with plaintiff and issued its acceptance through its president as provided in the agreement. Subsequently it repudiated the theory of recovery on quantum meruit by electing to pay one-third of the sum due, namely $10,500, in its own tax anticipation warrants of a face value of one hundred cents on the dollar, thus indicating its intention to stand by the agreement. The defense in this case is not made by the North Shore Park District, nor by a taxpayer litigating the legality of a proceeding, but by a body corporate which came into existence after the ordinance which culminated in the instant agreement was adopted and after the work was fully performed by plaintiff and accepted by the North Shore Park District.

Lastly it is urged that a contract expressly prohibited by a valid statute is void. In support of this contention it is argued that the provisions of sec. 18, par. 76, chap. 19, Cahill's Ill. Rev. Stats., 1933, prohibit the deposit of fill or the construction of a bulkhead and make it unlawful so to do without first obtaining a permit, and prescribes a penalty for violation of the act. Counsel for defendant say that it necessarily follows that any contract made in violation of the act is null and void and of no force and effect, and cite Duck Island Hunting & Fishing Club v. Gillen Co., 330 Ill. 121, to support their position. Unlike the circumstances

in the Gillen case, plaintiff's contract was for the delivery of dirt fill to be dumped and spread upon the land and property of the North Shore Park District, and not, as defendant contends, for the erection of a bulkhead. The statute itself does not make any agreement for construction of a bulkhead or breakwater void, and it certainly does not contemplate that when such work is done and accepted by a municipality, that payment shall be unlawful. Moreover, plaintiff's contract did not cover work "in any of the public bodies of water within the State of Illinois," within the meaning of the statute, or the building of any bulkhead by Erikson. If a permit were required to do the work provided for in the contract it was the duty of the commissioners to obtain the permit. Considerable time has elapsed since the dirt fill was delivered and leveled off, and the public has enjoyed the benefits of the improvement during all this time. Therefore, in harmony with Badger v. The Inlet Drainage District, 141 Ill. 540, supra, the municipality should pay for "what it would have had to pay had it got it in the right way."

From what has been said it follows that none of the contentions made by defendant constitutes a valid defense to plaintiff's claim for damages for breach of an express contract, which is set out with great particularity in its amended statement of claim. Since by consolidation the North Shore Park District no longer exists, and the optional payment by bonds could not be made, the effect of defendant's position, if sustained, would be to deprive plaintiff and intervener of payment for the labor and material furnished and unjustly give the municipality the benefit of the executed contract at plaintiff's expense. The authorities do not sanction such inequitable results.

The judgment of the Municipal court is affirmed.

AFFIRMED.

Sullivan, P. J., and Scanlan, J., concur.

47 A

38519

TAUBER MOTORS, Inc., Appellant, v. HENRY S. TAUBER, for use of Maurice E. Zuker et al., Appellees.	)	APPEAL FROM CIRCUIT COURT, COOK COUNTY.

286 I.A. 613

MR. JUSTICE FRIEND DELIVERED THE OPINION OF THE COURT.

This is an appeal from an order of the Circuit court refusing to vacate and set aside a judgment in garnishment entered against Tauber Motors, Inc., as garnishee, and also refusing leave to file answer as such garnishee.

The history of the proceeding is rather involved. It was initiated by complaint of Maurice E. Zuker, also known as James Zuker, by Charles E. Zuker, his next friend, against Henry S. Tauber, doing business as Broadway Auburn Company, and Motor Acceptance Company, a corporation, to rescind a certain contract entered into May 12, 1930. Maurice E. Zuker had purchased from Tauber, doing business as Broadway Auburn Company, a Lincoln automobile, for the stipulated sum of $1,800, and delivered in trade his Chrysler car for which he was given credit in the sum of $1,100. The balance of $700 was evidenced by certain promissory notes, secured by chattel mortgage. The notes and mortgage were negotiated by Tauber to the Motor Acceptance Company, which was joined as defendant in the original proceeding. The complaint was predicated upon the infancy of Maurice E. Zuker, who sought to rescind the contract and secure the cancellation of the notes and mortgage.

The Motor Acceptance Company appeared and filed its answer

to the complaint, and answer was also filed by Tauber, doing business as Broadway Auburn Company, both denying that Zuker was a minor and that any advantage was taken of him in the transaction. The cause was heard by the chancellor, resulting in a decree in favor of complainant, finding that Tauber was indebted to complainant in the sum of $700, that Zuker was under the age of twenty-one years, and ordering Tauber to pay Zuker the sum of $700, and also decreeing that the notes and mortgage be cancelled and held for naught.

December 16, 1932, the court entered an order giving Tauber leave to appeal from the decree thus entered upon filing an appeal bond in the sum of $1,500 within thirty days. January 18, 1933, some eleven months later, complainant's solicitor filed his petition asking that Tauber be adjudged guilty of contempt of court for failure to file his appeal bond, and asking that an order be entered in accordance with the prayer of the petition. An order was entered, not however in accordance with the prayer of the petition, but modifying the decree so as to provide that judgment be entered against Tauber and that execution issue thereon. In accordance with this decree execution issued January 19, 1933, and was on April 19, 1933, returned "no property found."

No further action was taken until March 11, 1935, when a garnishment summons was issued to the Tauber Motor Sales, Inc., garnishee, and a certain affidavit in garnishment and interrogatories were filed. April 24, 1935, another judge of the Circuit court entered an order reciting that summons had been served on Tauber Motors, Inc., that it had failed to file an answer or appearance and was in default, and giving conditional judgment against Tauber Motors, Inc. May 7, 1935, a scire facias was filed in the clerk's office, same having been served on Tauber Motors, Inc., on May 2, 1935, ruling it to show cause on May 3, 1935, why judgment should

not be entered against it, and on June 12, 1935, final judgment was entered against Tauber Motors, Inc., for the sum of $700 and costs.

July 24, 1935, Henry S. Tauber filed an affidavit with the clerk of the Circuit court setting forth that he had never been served with or received any wage demand, prior to institution of this proceeding, as required by law; that at the time judgment was rendered against him in favor of Zuker, Tauber was a married man and the head of a family; that he was not served with execution on the judgment and that the return of "No property found" was without his knowledge; that Tauber Motors, Inc., the garnishee, was not indebted to him as of March 11, 1935, and had no property of any kind, nature or description belonging to him as judgment debtor then or at the date of garnishment. Another affidavit was filed by Max P. Tauber, setting forth that Tauber Motors, Inc., as garnishee, had never been served with a wage demand as required by law, prior to the institution of the garnishment suit; that Henry S. Tauber was, at the time judgment was entered against him, a married man and head of a family and that Tauber Motors, Inc., was not indebted to Henry S. Tauber on March 11, 1935, and had no effects or estate of his in its hands on that date; that any notice or summons served on Tauber Motors, Inc., as garnishee, by leaving copies with Ed Meyer or L. H. Hurt as agents, were without authority inasmuch as the latter were not officers or agents of the corporation; that the first knowledge that Tauber Motors, Inc., had of these proceedings was at the date of levy; and it was averred that garnishee was willing to answer any interrogatories and asked that the conditional judgment be vacated and leave granted to file its answer as garnishee.

July 23, 1935, counsel for Tauber Motors, Inc., served notice on complainant's attorney and also on the sheriff of Cook county stating that they would on July 24, 1935, appear before the

court and move to set aside the judgment in garnishment, and ask leave to file answer as garnishee. The motion was continued until July 26, 1935, and on that date denied. Thereafter, July 29, 1935, Tauber Motors, Inc., by its counsel, served notice of appeal to this court, specifying as ground the refusal of the trial court to vacate and set aside the judgment against Tauber Motors, Inc.

Tauber Motors, Inc., appellant, assigns six separate grounds for reversal, but upon oral argument its counsel stated that it relied only upon the two following: (1) That the court had no power to modify the original decree after the close of the term at which it was rendered, and (2) that no wage demand having been served upon defendant, Henry S. Tauber, or Tauber Motors, Inc., the issuance of garnishment summons against Tauber Motors, Inc., was unlawful.

As to the first ground, it is argued that the chancellor on January 18, 1933, modified the decree of December 16, 1932, by permitting execution to issue on the judgment after the expiration of the term, when the court had lost jurisdiction to so modify the decree. Under the original decree the complainant was awarded $700, and the subsequent modification merely provided that execution issue to enforce payment thereof. As a general rule, courts have no power to modify, alter, change or interfere with their decrees or judgments after expiration of the term at which they were rendered, but it has been generally held that a court of chancery has power to enforce its decrees by lawful methods and that an execution is a lawful method of enforcing the payment of decrees. (Durbin v. Durbin, 71 Ill. App. 51.) In the latter case the court modified its original decree, entered some thirteen months prior thereto, so as to provide for the issuance of an execution, and in sustaining the action of the chancellor the appellate court said that the

modification of the decree complained of consisted only in providing an ordinary method for collecting judgments and enforcing decrees, namely, the issuance of an execution against the property of the delinquent debtor, and approved the modification. In Totten v. Totten, 299 Ill. 43, the court in commenting on Fulton Investment Co. v. Dorsey, 220 Fed. 298, stated:

"It was there held that while the court may not, after the term, amend the principles of a final decree, it has the inherent right to modify by a subsequent order the time of its enforcement or the manner in which it shall be enforced - citing numerous cases of the Federal court. This we believe to be the true rule. * * *"

In Sterling National Bank v. Martin et al., 213 Ill. App. 566, the court pointed out that it was not within the power of the chancellor to amend or correct a decree in any manner affecting the merits after the adjournment of the term, "but the limitation of the court's control to the term at which the decree was rendered does not apply to provisions inserted for the purpose of carrying the decree into effect." To the same effect is The People v. Lyons, 168 Ill. App. 396. Litigants have the right to the same remedies to enforce the collection of a decree in chancery for a specific sum of money as they have to enforce a judgment at law (Weightman v. Hatch, 17 Ill. 281) and in modifying the decree in the instant case the court did not in anywise alter the decree affecting the merits thereof but merely provided a means for enabling complainant to collect the same. This it had jurisdiction to do, even after the expiration of the term.

The second contention is that no wage demand was served upon Henry S. Tauber within the provisions of section 14 of the Garnishment act. This contention is predicated upon the affidavits of Henry S. Tauber and Max R. Tauber. We find from the record, however, that complainant filed counter affidavits from which it appears that Ellis Byman had personally served the wage demand on Henry S. Tauber

by delivering a true copy of the original wage demand on him at the address of the Tauber Motors, Inc., on March 8, 1935, and also served a copy of the original wage demand upon a brother of Henry S. Tauber at the same address, as an officer or agent of Tauber Motors, Inc., as garnishee. Byman's affidavit was supported by that of Clara Louise Crosby, who stated that she acknowledged the wage demand signed by Byman and caused the original thereof to be attached to the affidavit for garnishment, or the summons, in the garnishment suit. It is pointed out by Zuker's counsel that both of the Tauber affidavits are insufficient in law because they fail to state that Henry S. Tauber was an employee of the garnishee, and that this omission was made advisedly because, as Zuker contends, Tauber was in fact an officer of the garnishee corporation instead of an employee, and it is argued that this defect is fatal since it is the clear intent of the garnishment act to enable only employees who are heads of families residing with the same to reserve from garnishment part of the wages necessary to support their families. Harris v. Montague, 247 Ill. App. 89, is cited to support this contention. That case holds that the burden of proof is on the plaintiff in garnishment to establish a garnishable debt, and having done so it then becomes the burden of the garnishee to show, as against proof of the garnishable debt, the right to any reduction therefrom for exemptions of salary of an employee under the statute. In the instant case Zuker in instituting the garnishment proceedings, and not knowing whether an employment relation existed between the garnishee and the principal defendant, took the precaution of proceeding under both section 5 and section 14 of chap. 62, Ill. State Bar. Stats., 1935. He assumed the burden of establishing a garnishable debt, and it then became the duty of the garnishee defendant to show that the principal debtor was entitled to exemptions under the statute. By failing to include in the

affidavits of the two Taubers the necessary showing that Henry S. Tauber was an employee of the garnishee, we think the garnishee failed to meet the burden thus placed upon it, and it cannot now assert that he was an employee and entitled to any exemption.

The four affidavits appearing of record presented to the court for determination the credibility of the Taubers on the one hand, and Ellis Byman and Clara Louise Crosby on the other hand, and in judging their credibility the court evidently took into account the fact that Tauber also denied service of the execution upon him, although the return of the sheriff showed that service was had. In serving wage demand on the principal defendant and garnishee, Zuker cannot be said to have acknowledged that an employment relationship existed between defendant and garnishee, especially in view of the fact that interrogatories were filed under section 5 with the garnishment summons. The relationship of Henry S. Tauber to the Tauber Motors, Inc., in the absence of any showing to the contrary, must be held to have been not one of employer and employee but that of an officer of the corporation. Under the circumstances of this case we have reached the conclusion that the chancellor properly denied the motion of Tauber Motors, Inc., to vacate and set aside the judgment entered against it in the garnishment proceedings and for leave to file an answer as garnishee.

The order of the Circuit court is affirmed.

AFFIRMED.

~~Scanlan, P. J., and Sullivan, J., concur.~~

Sullivan, P. J., and Scanlan, J., concur.

48 A

38602

WILLARD WESTMAN,
Appellee,

v.

TIRES INCORPORATED,
a corporation,
Appellant.

APPEAL FROM SUPERIOR COURT,
COOK COUNTY.

286 I.A. 613[2]

MR. JUSTICE FRIEND DELIVERED THE OPINION OF THE COURT.

Willard Westman, plaintiff, while crossing an intersection in the City of Chicago, was struck by an automobile owned by Tires Incorporated and operated by William Hoferle, its servant or agent. Suit was instituted in the Superior court to recover for injuries sustained by plaintiff, naming both the corporation and Hoferle as defendants. During the trial before a jury, Hoferle was dismissed and a verdict was returned against Tires Incorporated for $5,000, upon which judgment was entered. This appeal followed.

The accident occurred December 9, 1933, at about 8:30 or 9:00 p.m. Western avenue runs north and south, while Belmont avenue runs east and west. Both streets are traversed by street car tracks. It is a busy intersection, and there are stop and go lights to regulate traffic. Plaintiff had been employed as a chauffeur for many years. On the evening in question he alighted from a westbound Belmont avenue street car at the northeast corner of the intersection, crossed Belmont avenue to the southeast corner, and then proceeded to cross to the west side of Western avenue, a street approximately 75 feet wide. There is a safety island in the center of the street. In approaching the

safety island plaintiff looked to his left for northbound traffic, and, there being none, walked west and reached the center of the street in safety. He then observed that the green lights were still in his favor and proceeded toward the west side of the street at a rather rapid pace. Defendant's automobile was standing along the west curb of Western avenue north of Belmont, waiting for a change of signals. To the east of its car, also southbound, were one or two other automobiles. A street car, going west on Belmont avenue, enabled the cars standing to the east of defendant to start in motion slightly in advance of defendant's car, and it is defendant's contention that these cars obstructed Hoferle's view to the left. After plaintiff had proceeded part of the way from the center of Western avenue, his attention was attracted to the north, and he saw defendant's car about twenty feet away, coming directly toward him. He hesitated momentarily and then made a dash toward the west curb, but was struck by defendant's car just before reaching the curb and severely injured.

The principal question for determination is whether plaintiff was in the exercise of due care for his own safety, and also whether defendant was guilty of any negligence. The complaint specifically alleged defendant's negligence in operating the automobile, in failing to keep a proper lookout, and in failing to sound a warning. There was in effect at the time of the occurrence an ordinance of the City of Chicago (sec. 16, art. 4 of Traffic Code, Uniform Traffic Code for the City of Chicago, July 30, 1931) which provides:

> "At intersections where traffic is controlled by official traffic signals or by police officers, operators of vehicles shall yield the right of way to pedestrians crossing or those who have started to cross the roadway on a Green or 'Go' signal, and in all other cases pedestrians shall yield the right of way to vehicles lawfully proceeding directly ahead on a Green or 'Go' signal."

Under the plain implication of this ordinance, defendant's automobile was bound to yield "the right of way" to defendant. Evidently the traffic signals changed while plaintiff was crossing from the center

of Western avenue to the west curb. It is undisputed that when he left the safety island in the center of the street he still had the green, or "go" lights in his favor and was walking rapidly to reach the other side of the street. In that situation he was suddenly confronted with danger. It is conceded that the two cars to the left of defendant were proceeding south, just behind plaintiff. Therefore, it would not have been safe for him to turn around and try to reach the safety island in the center of Western avenue. Defendant's counsel stated on oral argument, in response to the court's question, that "plaintiff should have stood still." This, however, might have been fatal to plaintiff. Under the circumstances, he pursued the only course left open to him and made a dash for the west curb, hoping to reach there in safety. These facts do not indicate a lack of due care and caution on the part of plaintiff for his own safety. Under the ordinance it was defendant's duty to "yield the right of way" and proceed in a cautious manner until its car had cleared the path of pedestrian traffic between the safety island the west curb. Defendant's driver had a clear vision before him, his headlights were turned on, and if he had been in the exercise of care, he would undoubtedly have observed plaintiff rushing across the street in time to have avoided the collision. We think the accident resulted from defendant's negligence, and that plaintiff, when suddenly confronted with danger under the circumstances hereinbefore narrated, did nothing to contribute to the accident. At that moment the law of self-preservation prompted him to escape injury, and he was not governed by the rules ordinarily relating to the care and caution required of persons in other situations. (Stack v. East St. Louis & Sub. Ry. Co., 245 Ill. 308. See, also, Mahan v. Richardson et al., 284 Ill. App. 493.) Pedestrians crossing the street at busy intersections are entitled to the protection which traffic signals are intended to afford them, and

automobiles crossing the path of pedestrian travel at such intersections should proceed cautiously. Traffic lights are likely to change while pedestrians are enroute across the street, and cautious drivers should foresee the possible danger of relying entirely upon a change of lights. It is their duty under the law to drive carefully until they have passed the line of pedestrian travel and allow pedestrians to cross.

It is urged that the court erred in instructing the jury at plaintiff's request that on the day of the occurrence in question, there was in effect the ordinance hereinbefore set forth. It is argued that this instruction is mandatory in its language and that its effect was to charge the jury in positive language that if plaintiff started to cross the intersection with the green lights in his favor, it then became the duty of defendant to yield to him the right of way, thus disregarding the element of due care on the part of plaintiff as well as defendant's negligence, and gave plaintiff an absolute right to cross the intersection, regardless of the surrounding circumstances or conditions. We do not regard the instruction as objectionable. It was simply a statement of the law in the language of the statute, and apprised the jury of the fact that if plaintiff was crossing with the green lights in his favor, it became defendant's duty to yield the right of way to him.

Defendant also complains of the following instruction, given at plaintiff's request:

"If, after fairly and impartially considering the testimony of all the witnesses in this case and the evidence and the facts and circumstances in evidence before you in this case, you believe from the evidence that the plaintiff at the time of and prior to the accident in question exercised that degree of care for his own safety that an ordinarily prudent person would have exercised under the same circumstances and conditions as shown by the evidence in this case, then you are instructed that the plaintiff was at and before the time of the accident in question in the exercise of ordinary care for his own safety."

This instruction was nothing more than a definition of ordinary care, and since the care exercised by plaintiff was one of the

issues in the case the jury were entitled to know the effect or meaning of that term. The instruction has been given and approved in other cases, and, in our opinion, is not subject to the objections urged by defendant. (Wilcke v. Henrotin, 241 Ill. 169.)

No point is raised as to the measure of damages, the conduct of the trial or the admissibility of evidence. We find no convincing reason for reversal, and therefore the judgment of the Superior court is affirmed.

JUDGMENT AFFIRMED.

Sullivan, P. J., and Scanlan, J., concur.

issues in the case the jury were entitled to know the effect or meaning of that term. The instruction has been given and approved in other cases, and, in our opinion, is not subject to the objections urged by defendant. (Wilcke v. Henrotin, 241 Ill. 169.)

No point is raised as to the measure of damages, the conduct of the trial or the admissibility of evidence. We find no convincing reason for reversal, and therefore the judgment of the Superior court is affirmed.

JUDGMENT AFFIRMED.

Sullivan, P. J., and Scanlan, J., concur.

49 A

38615

JOHN STRYZEWSKI, also known as John Strewe, and ANTHONY POPPERT, for use of Howard Larsen, a minor, by Ignatius Larsen, his guardian, Appellees,	APPEAL FROM SUPERIOR COURT, COOK COUNTY.
v.	
AMERICAN MOTORISTS INSURANCE COMPANY, a corporation, Appellant.	286 I.A. 613[3]

MR. JUSTICE FRIEND DELIVERED THE OPINION OF THE COURT.

John Stryzewski, also known as John Strewe, and Anthony Poppert, filed a garnishment proceeding in the Superior court as nominal plaintiffs for the use of Howard Larsen, a minor, by Ignatius Larsen, his father and next friend, the beneficial plaintiff. The court found that there was due under the garnishment writ from American Motorists Insurance Company, the garnishee defendant, to the nominal plaintiffs for use of the beneficial plaintiff $4,500. Judgment was entered accordingly, from which defendant appeals.

It appears from the record that John M. Strewe and Anthony Poppert, as copartners, applied for the issuance of an insurance policy for the copartnership, whose address was given as 6248 Warwick avenue. Henry Carson, an insurance solicitor for the Assureds Service Corporation, took the application. The premium amounted to $59.85, on which there was paid $10 on account. Two policies were issued, one by the American Motorists Insurance Co., covering insured against liability or injury to the person, or death, and against property damage, and one by the National Retailers Co., covering fire and

theft. The liability policy was No. 3,537,060, and was issued for a term of one year commencing August 22, 1931. By the terms of the policy the insurance company agreed to pay on behalf of the assureds all sums which the latter should become obligated to pay by reason of the liability imposed upon them by law for damages, and contained a provision that the policy might be cancelled "at any time by either the Named Assured or the Company by giving not less than ten (10) days' written notice to the other party of said cancellation, which shall be effective at 12:01 a.m. on the date specified for cancellation in said notice. * * * If cancelled by the company at any time, the Company shall be entitled to the earned pro rata premium. Notice of cancellation in writing mailed to or delivered at the address of the assured as herein given shall be a sufficient notice on the part of the Company." On the back of the policy, printed in bold type, was the name of "Assureds Service Corporation," which was a recording agency and made up the policies on blanks furnished by the insurance company. Between August 22, 1931, when the policy was issued, and November 14, 1931, the assured paid only $10 on account of the premium of $59.85. November 14, 1931, the following notice of cancellation was sent by letter to John M. Strewe et al., 6248 Warwick avenue, Chicago:

"November 14th, 1931.

Mr. John M. Strewe et al.,
6248 Warwick Avenue,
Chicago, Illinois.

Re: Policy No. 3537060.

Dear Mr. Strewe:

We hereby give you notice of the cancellation of policy #3537060, issued to you by the American Motorists Insurance Company and that said company will not be liable for any loss on property described in said policy after the expiration of ten days from the receipt of this notice, as provided by its conditions.

If payment of $49.85, due on your premium, or a substantial part is made to us before the expiration of ten days from the above date, this notice may be regarded as void, otherwise, it will be necessary to charge you for the number of days the policy has been in force.

We regret the necessity for this action and trust you will avail yourself of the opportunity to pay before cancellation theft. The liability policy was No. 5,537,060, and was issued for a term of one year commencing August 22, 1931. By the terms of the policy the insurance company agreed to pay on behalf of the assureds all sums which the latter should become obligated to pay by reason of the liability imposed upon them by law for damages, and contained a provision that the policy might be cancelled "at any time by either the Named Assured or the Company by giving not less than ten (10) days' written notice to the other party of said cancellation, which shall be effective at 12:01 a.m. on the date specified for cancellation in said notice. * * * If cancelled by the company at any time, the Company shall be entitled to the earned pro rata premium. Notice of cancellation in writing mailed to or delivered at the address of the assured as herein given shall be a sufficient notice on the part of the Company." On the back of the policy, printed in bold type, was the name of "Assureds Service Corporation," which was a recording agency and made up the policies on blanks furnished by the insurance company. Between August 22, 1931, when the policy was issued, and November 14, 1931, the assured paid only $10 on account of the premium of $69.85. November 14, 1931, the following notice of cancellation was sent by letter to John M. Strewe et al., 6248 Warwick Avenue, Chicago:

"November 14th, 1931.

Mr. John M. Strewe et al.,
6248 Warwick Avenue,
Chicago, Illinois.

Re: Policy No. 5537060.

Dear Mr. Strewe:

We hereby give you notice of the cancellation of policy #5537060, issued to you by the American Motorists Insurance Company and that said company will not be liable for any loss on property described in said policy after the expiration of ten days from the receipt of this notice, as provided by its conditions.

If payment of $49.85, due on your premium, or a substantial part is made to us before the expiration of ten days from the above date, this notice may be regarded as void, otherwise, it will be necessary to charge you for the number of days the policy has been in force.

We regret the necessity for this action and trust you will avail yourself of the opportunity to pay before cancellation date.

Yours very truly,
ASSURED'S SERVICE CORPORATION,
F. W. Lobingier,
Asst. Manager
Department of Insurance."

The trial judge held that this notice was not a cancellation and that it amounted "simply to a threat." Plaintiff's counsel, in justification of the court's conclusion and finding, argues that the foregoing letter purported to give notice of cancellation only of the policy issued by the American Motorists Insurance Company, whereas the insurance in question was provided by two companies issued together for a joint premium; that the letter does not even amount to a cancellation of the policy of the American Motorists Insurance Company in its entirety, but only as to "loss on property described in said policy," and did not purport to cancel the company's liability for injury to the person, as involved in the present case; that the notice did not say that the policy had been cancelled, or that it would be cancelled, except as may be implied from the statement contained in the letter "that said company will not be liable for any loss on property described in said policy after the expiration of ten (10) days from the receipt of this notice." It is also urged that the notice was never actually received by the assured, and therefore the company failed strictly to comply with the cancellation provisions in the policies, and that the notice of cancellation was signed by the Assured's Service Corporation, without any showing that the latter acted as agent of either of the companies.

With reference to the last two contentions, we have examined the record carefully and find abundant evidence to sustain the conclusion that F. W. Lobingier, as assistant manager of the department of insurance of Assured's Service Corporation, dictated and signed the letter dated November 14, 1931, directed to John M.

Strewe et al., 6248 Warwick avenue, and sent the same by registered mail, with a request for a return receipt; that a receipt, signed by "A. Poppert" was delivered to him by the postman in the regular mail, and that the registered letter was never returned. It further appears from the evidence that one Fred Meyer, a letter carrier, who had been delivering mail to the residence at 6248 Warwick avenue for some eight years, returned to the registry clerk in the post office a return receipt signed by the addressee or someone at the house, and he testified that he believed he had delivered the letter to John Strewe at the address designated. While both Strewe and Poppert denied that they had received the cancellation letter, Poppert admitted that he had always lived at 6248 Warwick avenue, and there was sufficient evidence, including that of a handwriting expert, to show that the registered letter was delivered at Poppert's address. Since notice to one partner is notice to all partners (Lurya Lumber Co. v. Bernstein, 168 Ill. App. 85), we think the letter of November 14, 1931, sufficiently apprised the assured of the cancellation of the policy. As to the other contention, the record shows that the Assured's Service Corporation was authorized to cancel the policy on behalf of the insurance company, and there is no provision in the policy to the contrary. Moreover, plaintiffs', by their own testimony, developed the fact that the Assured's Service Corporation was the agent of the insurance company.

The objections urged to the sufficiency of the cancellation are highly technical and in our opinion are untenable. The contention that the notice was ineffective because it purported to cancel only one of the policies is sufficiently answered by the fact that the parties expressly agreed in the policies that cancellation could be made separately. The argument that the notice of cancellation covered only loss on property described in the policy, and did not purport to cancel the company's liability for

Throne et al., 6850 Warwick avenue, [illegible] the same by registered mail, with a request for a return receipt; that a receipt,
signed by "R. Roppert" was delivered to him by the postman in the
regular mail, and that the registered letter was never returned.
It further appears from the evidence that one Emer Hagen, a letter
carrier, who had been delivering mail at the residence at 6850
Warwick avenue for some eight years, returned to the registry clerk
in the post office a return receipt signed by the addressee or someone at the house, and he testified that he delivered [illegible]
the letter to John Throne at the address designated. While both
Throne and Roppert denied that they had received the cancellation
letter, Roppert admitted that he had always lived at 6850 Warwick
avenue, and there was sufficient evidence, including that of a
handwriting expert, to show that the registered letter was delivered
at Roppert's address. Since notice to one partner is notice to all
partners (Wayne Lumber Co. v. Bernstein, 161 Ill. App. 415), we think
the letter of November 14, 1941, sufficiently apprised the insured
of the cancellation of the policy. As to the other contention, the
record shows that the Hammond's Service Corporation was authorized
to cancel the policy on behalf of the insurance company, and there
is no provision in the policy to the contrary. Moreover, plaintiffs, by their own testimony, developed the fact that the Hammond's
Service Corporation was the agent of the insurance company.

The objections urged to the sufficiency of the cancellation
are highly technical and in our opinion are untenable. The contention that the notice was ineffective because it purported to
cancel only one of the policies is sufficiently answered by the
fact that the parties expressly agreed in the policies that cancellation could be made separately. The argument that the notice
of cancellation covered only loss on property described in the
policy, and did not purport to cancel the company's liability for

injury to the person, is rebutted by that portion of the letter which gives "notice of the cancellation of policy No. 3,537,060, issued to you by the American Motorists Insurance Company." This amounted to a cancellation of the policy and all the provisions contained therein, including the company's liability for injury to the person. As pointed out by defendant, the language employed in the letter may be regarded as mere surplusage, and could not have misled or prejudiced the policy holder as to the effect of the notice. (Commercial Standard Insurance Co. v. Garrett, 70 Fed. (2d) 969.)

Plaintiffs' principal criticism of the notice of cancellation, and the view that the court evidently adopted, is that "it is not in effect a cancellation, but merely a threat," and that in order to have made the cancellation valid it should have been followed by another letter after the ten days, notifying defendants that, having failed to comply with the requirements of the first letter, the policy was cancelled. We think the notice was a cancellation of the policy and required no further communication. It stated "We hereby give you notice of the cancellation of Policy #3,537,060 * * * after the expiration of ten (10) days from the receipt of this notice, as provided by its conditions." The letter then stated that if payment of $49.85, due on the premium or a substantial part thereof, "is made to us before the expiration of ten days * * * this notice may be regarded as void, otherwise it will be necessary to charge you for the number of days the policy had been in force." The plain implication of this letter, and the only construction that a reasonable person could place upon it, is that the company was availing itself of the provisions of the policy and serving notice of cancellation thereof on the assured, by reason of their failure to pay the balance of the premium; but that the notice would be regarded as void if the assured, within the ten

days, paid $49.85 then due on the premium. The accident which plaintiffs claimed was covered by this policy did not occur until April 8, 1932, so that the assured seek to take the benefits of a policy upon which they claimed the defendant became liable many months after they were notified that the balance of the premium was due. They made no effort to pay the balance of the premium, and could not expect the insurance company to continue the policy in force under an agreement which assured had failed to fulfill.

The contract of the parties expressly provided that cancellation in writing should be sufficient notice, and the courts have generally held that no particular form of notice is required for the cancellation of a policy. It was so held in Colonial Assurance Co. v. Nat. Fire Ins. Co., 110 Ill. App. 471, where the court said: (p. 474)

> "Appellee was thus informed of the instructions given by appellant to its Chicago agents to 'take up' or cancel these policies; and while it may be true, as argued by appellee, that this letter was not in form a cancellation of the certificates, it was a distinct notice to appellee that appellant had ordered the cancellation; and served upon appellee as it was constituted, we think, a 'notice of such cancellation,' sufficient to meet the requirements of the policies in that respect, and terminate the liability five days thereafter. * * *"

In Sill v. Burgess, 134 Ill. App. 373, it was said:

> "No particular form of notice of election to rescind a contract is necessary. Any act which clearly indicates an intention by the party to rescind a contract is sufficient and constitutes notice. Chrisman v. Miller, 21 Ill. 226; Murray v. Schlosser, 44 Ill. 14; Anderson v. McCarty, 61 Ill. 64."

We have no doubt that the letter addressed to the assured sufficiently complied with the requirements of the policy and fully apprised them of the cancellation of the liability unless within ten days the assured paid the balance of the premium. This the assured failed to do, and the policy was therefore effectually cancelled upon the expiration of ten days after November 14, 1931.

One of the major contentions raised by defendant is that the court had no jurisdiction to enter the garnishment judgment, because the authority of Ignatius Larsen to represent the minor

had ceased when the original proceeding had terminated in a judgment. In view of our conclusion as to the sufficiency of the notice of cancellation, it will be unnecessary to discuss the legal aspects of this jurisdictional question.

We think the court erred in entering the judgment in favor of plaintiffs, and in view of what we have said it would serve no purpose to remand the cause. Therefore, the judgment of the Superior court is reversed and judgment entered here for the garnishee defendant and against plaintiffs for costs.

REVERSED AND JUDGMENT HERE FOR DEFENDANT AND AGAINST PLAINTIFFS FOR COSTS.

Sullivan, P. J., and Scanlan, J., concur.

50 A

38635

MARY DAUBNER,
Appellee,

v.

JOHN STENBERG,
Appellant.

FRANK GEBHARDT,
Appellee,

v.

JOHN STENBERG,
Appellant.

APPEAL FROM SUPERIOR COURT, COOK COUNTY.

286 I.A. 613[4]

MR. JUSTICE FRIEND DELIVERED THE OPINION OF THE COURT.

By this appeal defendant, John Stenberg, seeks to reverse two judgments entered by the Superior court upon two jury verdicts returned after a single trial of two causes which had been consolidated by the trial court. The actions were for personal injuries arising out of the same accident, a collision between two automobiles. The plaintiff in one case was Mary Daubner, in whose favor judgment was entered for $4,000; the other plaintiff was Frank Gebhardt, who was awarded $6,000.

The collision occurred at noon, December 24, 1930, at the intersection of Diversey and Cicero avenues, in Chicago. Plaintiffs were standing at the northwest corner of the intersection, waiting for a street car. A Buick automobile, owned by Stenberg, collided with a Chrysler car and then struck plaintiffs, causing injuries. The Chrysler car was driven by Emmett J. Duffy, a codefendant, against whom no judgment was rendered. The driver of the Buick automobile stepped out and ran from the scene of the

accident immediately after the occurrence. It was alleged by plaintiffs and denied by defendant that the driver of the Buick car was John Stenberg. The determination of this question of fact adversely to defendant, together with the amounts of the verdicts and the charge that plaintiffs' counsel made improper and prejudicial statements and arguments in the presence of the jury, are urged as grounds for reversal.

It appears from the evidence that for seven or eight years prior to the accident Stenberg owned his own home at 6959 Ridge avenue, in Chicago, where he resided with his wife and family. He was forty-nine years of age and was the owner and operator of a garage at Ridge avenue and Peterson road, Chicago, which he built in 1924. He was also an officer of Acacia Park Cemetery Association of Buffalo, N. Y.

On the day of the accident Stenberg left home in his Buick car at about 8:30 a.m. and drove to his garage, where he was in conference with his partner, Fitzgerald, until about ten o'clock. He then drove the Buick to the Builders & Merchants Bank, located on the northeast corner of Clark street and Rascher avenue, parked along the curb where other cars were also parked, and went into the bank, where he talked at length with O. A. Christensen, one of the vice presidents who was also treasurer of the cemetery company. According to Stenberg's testimony, he and Christensen were expecting the arrival of some mail from Buffalo, and Stenberg decided to wait for the second delivery, at about 12:00 o'clock. While in the bank Christensen had conferences with other persons, but returned at intervals to talk to Stenberg. Stenberg also conversed with Martin Catte, the cashier, and stated that he remained in the bank constantly for about two hours, and left about noon. According to the evidence the accident occurred between 12:00 and 12:15 p.m., and it was stipulated that the Builders & Merchants Bank was located some seven miles from the scene of the accident.

Stenberg testified that when he left the bank he looked for his car. It was gone. He returned to the bank and told Christensen, who suggested that he look for it again. Stenberg then left the bank and resumed the search, but could not find his automobile. He went back to the bank, told Christensen his car was not there and that he was going to the Summerdale police station to report the loss. The station was located on Foster avenue, about a mile and a half from the bank. Stenberg walked to the station, and on the way over met an acquaintance named Walter Conroy at Clark street and Foster avenue. He told Conroy that his car had been stolen. Conroy, who was engaged in the automobile business, testified to the conversation and fixed the time of the meeting at a little past noon. At the station Stenberg reported the loss to sergeant William H. Kelly and officer Adolph Meyer. Because Stenberg did not know his license number and did not have his automobile identification card with him, no written report was made of the theft at that time. Kelly and Meyer both testified that Stenberg arrived at the station between 12:30 and 1:15 p.m. After remaining at the station about ten minutes, Stenberg returned to his home for the license card, taking the Clark street car. Gus Newberg, a carpenter who had been working at Stenberg's home preparing a Christmas tree, took him back to the police station in Newberg's automobile, where Stenberg again reported the loss and furnished the necessary license information. The written report, dated December 24, 1930, 2:00 p.m. was prepared.

According to Stenberg's testimony, he did not know his automobile had been in an accident until December 26, 1930, two days after the accident, when police officers came to his home and notified him. It was thus Stenberg's contention that his car had been stolen on the day of the accident, that he was not the driver thereof when the collision occurred, and that he did not know of the accident until

December 26th.

On behalf of plaintiffs, Duffy testified that he had known Stenberg for twenty years, had frequently seen him in a saloon on West Madison street, but not within three to five years before the accident; that he saw the driver of the Buick car step out and run north immediately after the collision, and that he recognized him as the defendant, Stenberg. He stated that the driver of the Buick got out of the car on the side opposite from him, and he could see him only partially through the windows of the car, - a distance of some fifty feet. He saw his back and shoulders and got a side and back view of the man as he left. Duffy immediately took the license number of the Buick and then went to the police station for the purpose of finding out in whose name the license was issued. The police, after consulting the records, informed him that Stenberg was the owner of the car, and two days' later Duffy swore out a warrant.

The other identifying witness was Nellie Peterson, who was also injured as a result of the accident and subsequently brought suit against Duffy and Stenberg. She was ill at the time of the trial, and the hearing was delayed while her depositions were taken. She did not identify Stenberg as the driver of the Buick, but stated that she remained at the scene of the accident and about twenty minutes after it occurred a checker cab, driven by Vane Jaudon, arrived. A passenger alighted and removed from the Buick three 5 gallon cans of alcohol and a basket of bottles, put them in the cab and drove away. She did not know who this man was at the time, but later saw him in the police court and found out that his name was Stenberg. She testified that no one tried to stop the man who removed the cans from the Buick, no one spoke to him, and although she was close enough to speak to him, she did not ask his name or make any other inquiry.

To support Stenberg's testimony that he was not the driver of the Buick nor present at the time of the accident and that his car had been stolen, O. A. Christensen, vice president of the Builders & Merchants Bank, and Martin Catte, the cashier, both testified to Stenberg's presence in the bank at or about the time of the accident and for approximately two hours prior thereto and of his report to them shortly after 12:00 o'clock that his car had been stolen. Walter Conroy also corroborated Stenberg's testimony as to the conversation had on Clark and Foster streets, which was approximately seven miles from the scene of the accident, shortly after twelve noon, wherein Stenberg told him that his car had been stolen. Officer Meyer and sergeant Kelly stated that Stenberg was actually present at the police station at about 12:30 to report his loss, and again at about 2:00 o'clock. Gus Newberg testified that he drove Stenberg to the station to report the theft. Vane Jaudon, also confined to a hospital at the time of the hearing and testified by deposition, stated that he was at the intersection shortly after the accident, stopped his car and walked over to the automobiles involved; that he was alone and then drove his cab back to the cab station at Cicero and Milwaukee avenues. He stated that he did not see any cans of alcohol in or around the Buick, and denied that any were taken from the Buick and put in his cab. He never knew Stenberg. He testified that he had no passengers when he arrived at the scene of the accident, and took none away. This is substantially all the evidence as to the identification of Stenberg and the question whether or not he was the driver of the Buick when the accident occurred.

It is urged as one of the grounds for reversal that plaintiffs' counsel made improper and prejudicial statements and arguments in the presence of the jury, which resulted in the verdicts against defendant and in the award of excessive damages. The statements complained of were that Stenberg was in the liquor

To support Stenberg's testimony that he was not the driver of the Buick nor present at the time of the accident and that his car had been stolen, O. A. Christensen, vice president of the Builders & Merchants Bank, and Martin Catte, the cashier, both testified to Stenberg's presence in the bank at or about the time of the accident and for approximately two hours prior thereto and of his report to them shortly after 12:30 o'clock that his car had been stolen. Walter Conroy also corroborated Stenberg's testimony as to the conversation had on Clark and Foster streets, which was approximately seven miles from the scene of the accident, shortly after twelve noon, wherein Stenberg told him that his car had been stolen. Officer Meyer and sergeant Kelly stated that Stenberg was actually present at the police station at about 12:30 to report his loss, and again at about 2:00 o'clock. Gus Newberg testified that he drove Stenberg to the station to report the theft. Vern Jensen, also confined to a hospital at the time of the hearing and testified by deposition, stated that he was at the intersection shortly after the accident, stopped his car and walked over to the automobiles involved; that he was alone and then drove his cab back to the cab station at Cicero and Milwaukee avenues. He stated that he did not see any cans of alcohol in or around the Buick, and denied that any were taken from the Buick and put in his cab. He never knew Stenberg. He testified that he had no passengers when he arrived at the scene of the accident, and took none away. This is substantially all the evidence as to the identification of Stenberg and the question whether or not he was the driver of the Buick when the accident occurred.

It is urged as one of the grounds for reversal that plaintiffs' counsel made improper and prejudicial statements and arguments in the presence of the jury, which resulted in the verdicts against defendant and in the award of excessive damages. The statements complained of were that Stenberg was in the liquor bootlegging business and operated a saloon. In his opening statement to the jury when plaintiffs' counsel outlined the evidence that he expected to introduce, he stated:

"At that time, the defendant, Stenberg, owned three cars, as I understand it. Among his various occupations, he had a garage. * * * Mr. Stenberg at one time, years ago, I think, operated a saloon. Later on, he operated this garage, and I presume operated somewhat on the side in spirituous liquors.

Mr. Montgomery (of counsel for defense): I object to that. I don't know that it has any bearing here. I think it is inflammatory.

The court: I do not think that it is hardly material in this case.

Mr. Irwin (counsel for plaintiffs): I think it will be important in this particular way. It is material. I will show in a very few moments why it is material.

The Court: You might as well tell the jury now.

Mr. Irwin: I am going to."

Later, in his opening statement counsel for plaintiffs further said:

"Now, the reason I said this about this man's business, after the accident, or at the time of the accident, there were two empty cans thrown out of this coupe, Mr. Stenberg's car, these big five-gallon cans that are used for alcohol, and inside of the car was at least one can of alcohol, and bottles of beer; and after the accident, about twenty minutes after the accident, or a half hour, a man drove up in a Checker taxicab - I got the number of the cab and the driver - whom we believe was Stenberg, and loaded from this taxicab - loaded from this Buick car into the taxicab, this liquor, and drove away with it."

And in his closing argument to the jury, plaintiffs' counsel stated:

"Then another thing. The man who was driving that car at the time of this accident was evidently conveying liquor contrary to the prohibition act. Now you know sometimes we don't admit that we know all that we do know, but some of us know a little about the bootleggers' system that were in business. In those days the man who conveyed liquor was not conveying it in stolen cars, and there was a good reason why. The man who was conveying liquor in those days wascovering up. He was not taking any chances of being caught."

It is argued that whether or not Stenberg was engaged in the illicit sale of liquor or the owner of a saloon was immaterial and was brought into the case for the sole purpose of prejudicing the jury against defendant and to support the conclusion that if Stenberg was a bootlegger or a saloon keeper, the presence of alcohol in the car showed that he was using the car in and about his regular business of bootlegging at the time of the accident.

bootlegging business and operated a saloon. In his opening statement to the jury when plaintiffs' counsel outlined the evidence that he expected to introduce, he stated:

"At that time, the defendant, Stenberg, owned three cars, as I understand it. Among his various occupations, he had a garage. * * * Mr. Stenberg at one time, years ago, I think, operated a saloon. Later on, he operated this garage, and I presume operated somewhat on the side in spirituous liquors.

Mr. Montgomery (of counsel for defense): I object to that. I don't know that it has any bearing here. I think it is inflammatory.

The Court: I do not think that it is hardly material in this case.

Mr. Irwin (counsel for plaintiffs): I think it will be important in this particular way. It is material. I will show in a very few moments why it is material.

The Court: You might as well tell the jury now.

Mr. Irwin: I am going to."

Later, in his opening statement counsel for plaintiffs further said:

"Now, the reason I said this about this man's business, after the accident, or at the time of the accident, there were two empty cans thrown out of this coupe, Mr. Stenberg's car, these big five-gallon cans that are used for alcohol, and inside of the car was at least one can of alcohol, and bottles of beer; and after the accident, about twenty minutes after the accident, or a half hour, a man drove up in a Checker taxicab - I got the number of the cab and the driver - whom we believe was Stenberg, and loaded from this taxicab - loaded from this Buick car into the taxicab, this liquor, and drove away with it."

And in his closing argument to the jury, plaintiffs' counsel stated:

"Then another thing. The man who was driving that car at the time of this accident was evidently conveying liquor contrary to the prohibition act. Now you know sometimes we don't admit that we know all that we do know, but some of us know a little about the bootleggers' system that were in business. In those days the man who conveyed liquor was not conveying it in stolen cars, and there was a good reason why. The man who was conveying liquor in those days was covering up. He was not taking any chances of being caught."

It is argued that whether or not Stenberg was engaged in the illicit sale of liquor or the owner of a saloon was immaterial and was brought into the case for the sole purpose of prejudicing the jury against defendant and to support the conclusion that if Stenberg was a bootlegger or a saloon keeper, the presence of alcohol in the car showed that he was using the car in and about his regular business of bootlegging at the time of the accident.

Moreover, defendant's counsel insists that there is no evidence in the record to support either of these conclusions, and therefore under the close questions of fact pertaining to the identification of Stenberg, the opening statements and concluding arguments upon these subjects were especially damaging. We find no evidence to support the statement that Stenberg operated a saloon. Duffy testified that years before he had frequently seen Stenberg in a saloon, sometimes standing "at the bar" and on other occasions "in the rear of the saloon, sitting down." We have searched the record in vain for any evidence to sustain the statement that Stenberg was in the liquor bootlegging business, or that he "operated somewhat on the side in spirituous liquors." It is conceded that the question of Stenberg's identity presented a sharp conflict of fact, and the assertion that he operated a saloon and was engaged in the illicit sale of liquor, without any evidence to support it, undoubtedly produced a prejudicial effect on the minds of the jurors. Plaintiffs' counsel not only made the opening statements heretofore referred to but after the court had sustained objections thereto, repeated similar statements in his concluding argument. Although the court finally told the jury to "disregard it and consider it as though you had never heard it," the damage had been done and the effect of the statements had undoubtedly operated upon the jurors' minds. As was said in Chicago Union Traction Co. v. Lauth, 216 Ill. 176, at p. 183:

> "But a ruling does not always remove the ill effects of misconduct of counsel. The rule is, that although the trial court may have done its full duty in its supervision of the trial and in sustaining objections, a new trial should be granted where it appears that the abuse of argument has worked an injustice to one of the parties."

To the same effect are the following cases: Bale v. Chicago Junction Ry. Co., 259 Ill. 476; Appel v. Chicago Ry. Co., 259 Ill. 561; Mattice v. Klawans, 312 Ill. 299.

Moreover, defendant's counsel insists that there is no evidence in the record to support either of these conclusions, and therefore under the close questions of fact pertaining to the identification of Stenberg, the opening statements and concluding arguments upon these subjects were especially damaging. We find no evidence to support the statement that Stenberg operated a saloon. Duffy testified that years before he had frequently seen Stenberg in a saloon, sometimes standing "at the bar" and on other occasions "in the rear of the saloon, sitting down." We have searched the record in vain for any evidence to sustain the statement that Stenberg was in the liquor bootlegging business, or that he "operated somewhat on the side in spirituous liquors." It is conceded that the question of Stenberg's identity presented a sharp conflict of fact, and the assertion that he operated a saloon and was engaged in the illicit sale of liquor, without any evidence to support it, undoubtedly produced a prejudicial effect on the minds of the jurors. Plaintiffs' counsel not only made the opening statements heretofore referred to but after the court had sustained objections thereto, repeated similar statements in his concluding argument. Although the court finally told the jury to "disregard it and consider it as though you had never heard it," the damage had been done and the effect of the statements had undoubtedly operated upon the jurors' minds. As was said in Chicago Union Traction Co. v. Lauth, 216 Ill. 176, at p. 183:

"But a ruling does not always remove the ill effects of misconduct of counsel. The rule is, that although the trial court may have done its full duty in its supervision of the trial and in sustaining objections, a new trial should be granted where it appears that the abuse of argument has worked an injustice to one of the parties."

To the same effect are the following cases: Hale v. Chicago Junction Ry. Co., 255 Ill. 476; Appel v. Chicago Ry. Co., 259 Ill. 561; Mattice v. Klawans, 312 Ill. 299.

Since there was a sharp conflict in the evidence as to the identity of the driver of the Buick automobile, the injection of prejudicial statements, unsupported by evidence, was unfair to defendant and might well have been the deciding factor in producing the verdicts against him.

It is also urged that the verdicts and judgments are against the manifest weight of the evidence, and that the damages awarded plaintiffs are excessive. In view of the fact that the causes will have to be retried, we refrain from commenting on the weight of the evidence or as to the damages.

For the reasons stated the judgments of the Superior court will be reversed, and the causes remanded for a new trial.

REVERSED AND REMANDED.

Sullivan, P. J., and Scanlan, J., concur.

5 / A

38411

UNITED STATES FIDELITY AND GUARANTY COMPANY, a corporation, Appellant,

v.

ALBERT SABATH, Appellee.

APPEAL FROM CIRCUIT COURT OF COOK COUNTY.

286 I.A. 613[5]

MR. JUSTICE SCANLAN DELIVERED THE OPINION OF THE COURT.

Plaintiff appeals from a judgment sustaining defendant's general demurrer to the second amended first count of its declaration. The declaration also contained the common counts, which were withdrawn before the court entered judgment, so as to permit an appeal on the ruling sustaining the demurrer to the second amended first count. After the demurrer had been sustained, but before judgment, plaintiff's motion for leave to further amend the count was denied.

The second amended first count alleges, in substance, that on July 16, 1928, an attachment suit was pending in the Circuit Court of the City of St. Louis, Missouri, wherein Pollock Clothing Company was plaintiff and Millard's, Inc., was defendant; that certain goods of Millard's, Inc. of the value of $3,150 had been seized by the sheriff under the writ in the case; that Millard's, Inc. desired to regain possession of the goods and it became necessary that it should give bond with surety in the penal sum of $6,300, conditioned upon delivery of the property to Pollock Clothing Company, if delivery should be adjudged, and that in default of the delivery Millard's, Inc. should pay to Pollock Clothing Company the assessed value of the property, together with damages

for injuries thereto, etc.; that on July 16, 1928, Millard's, Inc. applied to plaintiff in writing to execute as surety a bond as aforesaid; that on the same date defendant, to induce plaintiff to execute a bond as aforesaid, executed and delivered to plaintiff his indemnifying agreement whereby he agreed to keep plaintiff indemnified and to hold it harmless from and against all demands, liabilities, charges and expenses, of whatever kind or nature, which it at any time might sustain or incur by reason of or in consequence of its having executed such bond as surety; that the application and indemnity agreement are in words and figures as follows:

"UNITED STATES FIDELITY AND GUARANTY COMPANY
Baltimore, Maryland

1. Name of Applicant . . . Millard's, Inc.
2. Occupation
3. Address
4. Nature of Bond applied for . . . Release of Attachment
5. Penalty $6300.00
6. Title of case . . . Applicant vs Pollock Clothing Co.
7. Court in which filed . . . Circuit Court, City of St. Louis, Missouri.

* * *

SIGNED, SEALED AND DELIVERED this 16th day of July, 1928.

WITNESS: Victor E. Krajci — MILLARD'S INC. (SEAL)
By Lawrence Neumann (SEAL)

INDEMNITY AGREEMENT

THE UNDERSIGNED HEREBY AGREES TO INDEMNIFY and keep the UNITED STATES FIDELITY AND GUARANTY COMPANY indemnified and to hold and save it harmless from and against any and all demands, liabilities, charges and expenses of whatever kind or nature, which it may at any time sustain or incur by reason or in consequence of its having executed the above described bond. And thereto he agrees to waive, and does hereby waive, any right to claim any property, including homestead, as exempt, under the constitution or law of any state or states, from levy, execution, sale or other legal process.

AND, FURTHER, HE GUARANTEES that the premium on the bond will be paid as above agreed.

SIGNED, SEALED and DELIVERED this 16th day of July, 1928.

WITNESS ....

Albert Sabath (SEAL)
Lawrence Neumann
Julius Heldman (SEAL)"

The count further alleges that because of the application, the indemnity agreement, and a premium of $63, it executed, as surety, a Release of Attachment bond in the sum of $6,300, by which bond plaintiff jointly, with the said Millard's, Inc., and severally, became bound unto Pollock Clothing Company in the penal sum aforesaid, conditioned for the delivery of the property to said company if delivery should be adjudged, and in default of such delivery for the payment to the said company of the assessed value of the property, for the payment to said company of all damages for injuries to said property and for its taking and detention, and all costs that might accrue in said suit, which said bond was dated July 16, 1928. (The bond is set up verbatim.) The count further alleges that on July 16, 1928, the said bond was delivered to and accepted by the sheriff, and the property that had been seized by the latter under the writ was returned to Millard's, Inc.; that thereafter proceedings were had in the suit, and on November 10, 1930, judgment was entered in the cause against Millard's, Inc. for $3,139.50 and the property that had been released to Millard's, Inc. under the bond was ordered delivered to the sheriff to answer the judgment in favor of Pollock Clothing Company; that on December 8, 1930, an execution issued upon the judgment for the amount thereof with interest and costs, and for the return of the property; that the writ was delivered to the sheriff to execute; that Millard's, Inc. did not pay the judgment and did not return the property to Pollock Clothing Company nor to the sheriff, and on December 13, 1930, the sheriff returned the writ, "No property found, and no part satisfied;" that sections 1297 and 1327 of the Missouri statutes were in force and effect at the time. (Said sections are set up verbatim.) The count further alleges that the judgment remained unsatisfied; that the value of the property was greater than the amount of the judgment and costs; that plaintiff, as surety on the

bond, became liable to pay the amount due upon the execution; that under section 1327 of the Missouri statutes Pollock Clothing Company, on December 29, 1930, filed its motion for judgment against plaintiff as surety on the bond and that judgment was entered against plaintiff, on the motion, on January 3, 1931, for $3,767.40 and costs, and execution was ordered issued thereon; that thereafter, on January 31, 1931, execution was issued on the judgment and plaintiff, on said date, with the knowledge and consent of defendant, satisfied the judgment by paying to Pollock Clothing Company the sum of $2,622.35. The count further alleges that Millard's, Inc. was then insolvent and bankrupt and that defendant, under his indemnity agreement, became liable to pay plaintiff $2,622.35, and being so liable promised to pay to plaintiff said sum; that plaintiff in the defense, settlement and satisfaction of the proceedings incurred additional liabilities, charges and expenses in the sum of $750, and that defendant, under the terms of the indemnity agreement, became liable therefor, and being so liable promised to pay the same, etc.

The decision of the trial court was based upon the theory, advanced by defendant, that the bond given by plaintiff was not the kind of bond that was applied for by Millard's, Inc.; that the application contemplated only a bond which would dissolve the attachment, - in other words, a "dissolution" bond; that the bond given was a "forthcoming" bond, and, therefore, defendant was not liable under his indemnity agreement. Plaintiff contends that the court erred in so holding. A like theory, advanced by the same defendant, was considered by us in United States Fidelity and Guaranty Company v. Albert Sabath, Gen. No. 38410, wherein an opinion has been filed this day. In that case we considered the question at length, and held that an application practically the same as the one in the instant proceeding contemplated a forthcoming bond. What we there said fully answers the question now before us

and need not be here repeated.

Defendant also urges, in support of the ruling of the trial court, that the bond furnished by plaintiff was not a "Release of Attachment" bond, but that it was in the nature of a "Counter Replevin" bond that is furnished in a replevin suit. The demurrer admitted all of the allegations of the declaration well pleaded. The declaration alleges that an attachment suit was pending; that goods of Millard's, Inc. had been seized on an attachment writ; that to effect their restoration to Millard's, Inc. the bond was applied for and given; that it was given to the sheriff, and accepted by him, as a forthcoming bond. That the St. Louis court so treated it is evident from the judgment entered. The Missouri courts have held that a rigid compliance with the statute is not indispensable to the validity of a bond and that to hold otherwise would be sacrificing undoubted justice to a mere technicality. (See Hoshaw v. Gullett, 53 Mo. 208, 210; Henry County v. Salmon, 201 Mo. 136, 152-3; State v. O'Gorman, 75 Mo. 370; Newton v. Cox, 76 Mo. 352; Wimpey v. Evans, 84 Mo. 144.) There is also merit in plaintiff's argument that even if the bond given was not in rigid compliance with the statute, nevertheless, it was a good common-law bond and accomplished the same purposes that would have been accomplished under a bond drafted in strict accordance with the statute, and that it was, therefore, valid and enforceable. In Drake on Attachment (7th Ed., sec. 327-a), in speaking of forthcoming bonds, the auther says:

> "A bond of this description, given where not authorized by statute, or in terms variant from those prescribed, though not enforceable as a statutory obligation, is not necessarily invalid; it will be good as a common-law bond, where it does not contravene public policy, nor violate a statute. And so, where it is given to the officer who levied the attachment, when the law required it to be given to the attaching plaintiff."

In State v. O'Gorman, supra, the Missouri court said (p. 378):

> "Conceding the bond not to be good as a statutory bond, the conclusion drawn from this fact by counsel by no means follows. If not good as a statutory bond, being voluntary, it is nevertheless

good as a common law bond, and the parties executing it are bound by all the conditions it contains, and to the full extent of such conditions."

Defendant further urges, in support of the judgment, that when plaintiff asked leave to amend the court had already sustained the demurrer, and it thereby confessed the insufficiency of the count. We find no merit in that contention, and the cases cited do not support defendant's position. The judgment of the trial court was not entered until after plaintiff's motion for leave to amend had been denied, and it recites that "the plaintiff, in accordance with agreement heretofore made in open Court, withdraws and dismisses the Second Count of the plaintiff's Declaration, being the consolidated Common Counts." This recital evidences clearly that plaintiff withdrew the common counts so that there might be an appeal from the judgment on the demurrer.

We do not approve the action of the trial court in denying plaintiff's motion for leave to amend the second amended first count. In our opinion in the case of Schatzkis v. Rosenwald & Weil, 267 Ill. App. 169, we said (p. 176):

> "Under our statute, Chapter 7, Cahill's Ill. Rev. Stats. 1931 (Amendments and Jeofails), it is hardly ever too late to amend pleadings, whether before or after verdict on such terms as justice may seem to demand. The trial court should have granted the motion. (Tomlinson v. Earnshaw, 112 Ill. 311; Thompson v. Sornberger, 78 Ill. 353; Goldstein v. Chicago City Ry. Co., 286 Ill. 297; Delfosse v. Kendall, 283 Ill. 301.)"

The new Practice act has not changed the above rule. The amended first count set up a good claim, which defendant was attacking on technical grounds, and the court should have allowed plaintiff every reasonable opportunity to cure any technical defects in the count, if any existed.

The judgment of the Circuit court of Cook county is reversed and the cause is remanded with directions to the trial court to overrule the general demurrer filed by defendant and for further proceedings not inconsistent with this opinion.

JUDGMENT REVERSED AND CAUSE REMANDED WITH DIRECTIONS.

Sullivan, P. J., and Friend, J., concur.

527 A

38442

ROBERT OSBORN BLAIR, SELLAR BULLARD and THE FIRST NATIONAL BANK OF CHICAGO, a corporation, etc., as Trustees under the Last Will and Testament of Sidney O. Blair, Deceased,
Appellants,

v.

BETTER REAL ESTATE IMPROVEMENT CORPORATION et al.,
Defendants.

CHARLES P. SCHWARTZ and LAVINIA S. SCHWARTZ, (Defendants)
Appellees.

APPEAL FROM SUPERIOR COURT OF COOK COUNTY.

286 I.A. 614[1]

MR. JUSTICE SCANLAN DELIVERED THE OPINION OF THE COURT.

An appeal by plaintiffs from a part of a foreclosure decree wherein the trial court sustained exceptions of defendant Charles P. Schwartz to findings in a master's report that Schwartz had assumed and was personally liable for the mortgage indebtedness and decreed that the contract, upon which plaintiffs based their claim of assumption, had been cancelled.

Plaintiffs made Howard W. Hayes and wife, the original makers of the note secured by the mortgage, Schwartz, who is alleged to have assumed and agreed to pay the indebtedness, and others, defendants.

The following findings by the master, to which there were no exceptions filed, are incorporated in the decree: On July 26, 1926, Howard W. Hayes and Harriet Hayes, his wife, made and delivered their note of that date, for $22,000, payable to bearer five years

after date with interest at six per cent per annum, payable semi-annually, the interest payments being evidenced by ten interest notes of $660 each; that to secure the payment of the said notes they executed their trust deed, bearing the same date, conveying the premises in question; that the trust deed was duly acknowledged and recorded; that nine of the interest notes were paid; that plaintiffs are the owners of the principal note and interest note No. 10, both of which matured July 26, 1931, and are unpaid; that certain taxes against the premises for the years 1928, 1929 and 1930, aggregating $4,525.95 were unpaid; that the total amount due under the mortgage and notes, including attorneys' fees, etc., is $31,220.24; "that complainants have a valid and subsisting lien upon the premises involved herein, and the rents, issues and profits thereof for said sum, together with interest on $29,791.49 thereof at five per cent from the date of this report and all taxable costs, and complainants are entitled to the foreclosure of said trust deed." The master further found:

"That on September 20, 1926, Howard W. Hayes and Harriet Hayes, his wife, by Warranty Deed dated that date, conveyed and warranted unto Charles P. Schwartz and Lavinia S. Schwartz, his wife, the premises herein involved and herein sought to be foreclosed. That prior to the execution and issuance of the aforesaid Warranty Deed on August 20, 1926, a contract was made and entered into between Charles P. Schwartz and Howard W. Hayes and Harriet Hayes, dated August 20, 1926, for the purchase of said premises, and the Master finds from all the evidence that Charles P. Schwartz did purchase said premises sought to be foreclosed herein from Howard W. Hayes and Harriet Hayes, and that the amount of the indebtedness secured by the Trust Deed herein sought to be foreclosed, was a part of the consideration which Charles P. Schwartz promised to pay for said premises, and that Charles P. Schwartz did retain that part of the purchase price; that said contract provided, among other things, that Charles P. Schwartz assumed and agreed to pay the indebtedness evidenced by the notes described in and secured by the Trust Deed being foreclosed herein, and the Master finds that in and by said contract, Charles P. Schwartz assumed and agreed to pay the indebtedness secured by the Trust Deed being foreclosed herein; that the aforesaid contract bearing date August 20, 1926 and a certified copy of the Warranty Deed aforesaid, were introduced in evidence.

"That Howard W. Hayes and Harriet Hayes were duly served with process and are the makers of the principal and interest notes

and the Trust Deed, and that Charles P. Schwartz was personally served with process in this cause, and is the maker of the aforesaid contract for the purchase of the premises involved herein, and that Howard W. Hayes and Harriet Hayes and Charles P. Schwartz are personally liable to the complainants herein for the sum of $31,220.24 with interest thereon as aforesaid, and all taxable costs herein found to be due."

To these findings defendant Schwartz filed the following exceptions:

"1. For that said Master has in and by his report certified that the defendant, Charles P. Schwartz, assumed and agreed to pay the indebtedness evidenced by the notes described in and secured by the trust deed being foreclosed herein, as part of the consideration for the purchase of the premises involved herein.

"2. For that the Master has failed to show in his report that said contract referred to was marked on its face cancelled, and there was no evidence introduced to overcome the cancellation.

"3. For that the said Master found that part of the consideration for the sale of said premises was the assumption of the mortgage debt being foreclosed herein, whereas the warranty deed introduced in evidence dated September 20, 1926, expressly states that the property was being sold subject to said mortgage indebtedness.

"4. For that the Master made many rulings concerning the admissibility and exclusion of certain evidence, that the rulings were and are in all respects erroneous, and the proof introduced in said cause in all respects insufficient to warrant the findings of said Master."

The trial court sustained the exceptions and the decree provides:

"That on September 20, 1926, Howard W. Hayes and Harriet Hayes in and by a Warranty Deed bearing that date, conveyed and warranted unto Charles P. Schwartz and Lavinia S. Schwartz, his wife, the premises involved herein, subject to the mortgage herein foreclosed; that prior to the execution and issuance of the aforesaid Warranty Deed, bearing date September 20, 1926, on August 20, 1926, a contract was made and entered into between Charles P. Schwartz and Howard W. Hayes and Harriet Hayes, his wife, bearing date August 20, 1926, for the purchase of said premises, and the court finds that said contract was cancelled and that Charles P. Schwartz did purchase said premises foreclosed herein from Howard W. Hayes and Harriet Hayes, his wife.

"That the defendants herein, Howard W. Hayes and Harriet Hayes, were personally served with summons and are the makers of said principal note and interest coupons and trust deed; that Charles P. Schwartz was personally served and is the maker of the aforesaid contract for the purchase of the premises involved herein, and therefore the court finds that Howard W. Hayes and Harriet W. Hayes are personally liable to the complainants herein for the sum of $31,220.24 with interest as aforesaid, and all taxable costs."

The following are the relevant provisions of the written contract of August 20, 1926:

"Charles P. Schwartz hereinafter called the purchaser,

hereby agrees to purchase at the price of Thirty-Eight Thousand and no/100 Dollars the following described real estate (here follows the legal description of the premises in question), and Howard W. Hayes and Harriet Hayes hereinafter called the seller, agrees to sell said premises at said price, and to convey or cause to be conveyed to the purchaser a good title thereto by general warranty deed, * * * subject to: * * * (5) General taxes for the year 1926 and subsequent years; * * * (10) Principal indebtedness aggregating $22,000.00 secured by mortgage, trust deed of record, which indebtedness the purchaser does agree to assume * * *.

"The purchaser has paid Two Thousand and no/100 Dollars as earnest money to be applied on said purchase when consummated, and agrees to pay, within five days after the title is shown to be good or is accepted by him, the further sum of Fourteen Thousand and no/100 Dollars, provided a deed as aforesaid shall then be ready for delivery. The above described mortgage of Twenty-Two Thousand Dollars ($22,000) is dated July 26, 1926 and recorded as Document #9353753 and due on or before five (5) years after date with interest at the rate of six per cent (6%) per annum payable semi-annually. * * *"

The contract also provides that "Buyer is to have possession of the within described premises immediately." It was signed, "Charles P. Schwartz Howard W. Hayes per T. C. Ernest Harriet H. Hayes." Written across the face of the contract is the following: "Cancelled by Delivery of Deed & Commission paid in Full 9/20/26 Alvin H. Reed & Co. by T. C. Ernest."

The warranty deed from defendants Hayes and wife conveyed the premises in question to defendants Charles P. Schwartz and Lavinia S. Schwartz, his wife, in joint tenancy, "for and in consideration of the sum of Ten Dollars and other good and valuable considerations," "Subject to trust deed dated July 26th, 1926 and recorded," etc.

The original bill alleges that Schwartz and his wife occupied the premises and claimed to be the owners thereof, and asks that it be determined who is liable for a deficiency and that a deficiency decree be entered against such person. The answer of the Schwartzes neither admits nor denies the allegations in the bill, alleges that Lavinia Schwartz was the owner of the mortgaged premises, and denies that any good purpose would be served by the appointment

of a receiver. The answer of the Hayeses alleges that some time prior to September 20, 1926, they made and entered into a contract with Charles P. Schwartz and Lavinia S. Schwartz, his wife, wherein, for a good and valuable consideration, they agreed to convey and sell the premises to the Schwartzes, and the latter expressly promised and agreed to pay the note and trust deed described in the bill, and thereby they became principally liable on the said note and trust deed; that the amount due, owing and secured by the said trust deed was deducted from the purchase price of the property at the time the same was sold to the Schwartzes, who thereby impliedly promised and agreed to pay all sums due under and by virtue of the trust deed; that by reason of the express assumption and implied assumption of the Schwartzes they became primarily liable for the debt sought to be foreclosed by the bill; that defendants Hayeses are not personally liable on the note and trust deed for the reason that when the note and trust deed became due, on July 26, 1931, certain extensions were given to the Schwartzes without the knowledge and consent of defendants Hayeses.

On March 27, 1933, plaintiffs closed their proof under the original bill. On May 5, 1933, defendant Howard W. Hayes testified in his own behalf as follows: "My name is Howard W. Hayes. I am a Justice of the Municipal Court. * * * I was at one time the owner of the premises being foreclosed herein. I entered into a contract with Mr. Schwartz for the sale of those premises on or about the middle of September, 1926. That was a written contract. I have not got that contract with me. * * * I made a search through my safe deposit box, through pigeonholes, drawers and desks and everywhere that I worked in the different courts where I kept my private papers, and entirely through my home and through every law office I have been associated with, but I have never been able to find it. It was just the stereotyped form of agreement to buy and sell, and as I recall,

one of the Chicago Real Estate Board forms, mostly typewritten in the usual language that is contained in such documents;" that the consideration named in the contract to sell was $40,000; that the mortgage was made a part of the purchase price; that at the time of the closing of the deal Schwartz stated to witness that he wanted to buy the premises and would take over the mortgage and pay the notes and the mortgage as they became due; that Schwartz prepared the deed and submitted it to the witness and his wife for signature; that after the property was sold the witness did not receive any notices from the holder of the mortgage when interest became due; that such notices were never sent to him; that he knows that they were sent to defendant Schwartz; that it was the middle of June or the first of July, 1932, when he first learned that there was a default in any of the payments; that he then asked defendant Schwartz why he had not paid these notes, why he had not paid the back taxes, and why he was in default on the principal note, to which questions Schwartz replied that he did not think that he would be able to handle it; that he told Schwartz that he and his wife would join with Schwartz in getting an extension of the loan for five years; that the bank would be willing to make the extension if the witness and his wife would join in the execution of the note for extension, that all that the bank required was the payment of the taxes that were past due and the payment of the past due interest on the loan; that Schwartz said he would try to work it out with the bank, that he "had a good deal of money stuck in that house;" that he had put in $2,000.00 for some improvements and had made alterations that were completed after he took possession; that he had spent considerable money in putting an oil burning system in the house; that witness said to him: "You fell down upon your payments, but you recognized your responsibility on this inasmuch as I am advised by the bank you did make some payments after the first and second year

that you went into possession of the house on the notes. * * * Why don't you and I get together and work this out, because I will do anything in the worldto assist you by signing new paper, if you will;" that Schwartz "said he would try to work it out himself at the bank, and that is the last I heard of it. He said he would be able to live in the house he thought, during the foreclosure period, but he did not think the property was worth over half what he paid for it, and he did not think they would foreclose on him, and if they did foreclose, he would remain there probably during the period of foreclosure;" that Schwartz also said that he could not pay the mortgage as he did not have any funds with which to pay it. The witness further testified that Mr. Thies, of plaintiff bank, told him that he had not considered it necessary to notify the witness that Schwartz was in default in payments for two or three years, as the latter had "promised a dozen times to pay" the amounts due. While this testimony as to what Mr. Thies said is hearsay in its nature, nevertheless, defendant Schwartz made no objection to its introduction upon that ground, and therefore it must be considered and given its natural probative effect as if it were in law admissible. (See Diaz v. United States, 223 U. S. 442, 450, and cases cited therein; Sawyer v. French, 235 S. W. 126, 130, and cases cited therein; Sutkus v. Walter, 268 Ill. App. 624 (Abst.); Harding v. Dodson, 259 Ill. App. 655 (Abst.); Hoover v. Empire Coal Co., 149 Ill. App. 258, 263; Percival v. Schneider, 255 Ill. App. 428, 435.) Defendant Schwartz made no attempt to answer any of the testimony relating to the payment by him of interest notes.

On August 7, 1933, defendant Charles P. Schwartz testified in his own behalf. Upon direct he testified as follows: That he was a lawyer; that on September 20, 1926, he purchased the property in question from Howard W. Hayes and received a deed from him at that time. "Q. (By Mr. Adelman, attorney for defendants Schwartz

and wife) Were there any other agreements between you and Howard Hayes and Harriet Hayes, his wife, at the time you took the deed? A. I bought the property for $16,000.00 subject to the mortgage. I paid them $16,000.00 and took the deed. Q. Was any agreement executed by you under which you assumed to pay that mortgage? A. I never assumed to pay that mortgage. We closed the deal on the basis of $16,000.00 cash and I took the deed subject to the mortgage. The mortgage was executed by Mr. Hayes at the time he bought the property from Mr. Blair as part of the purchase price. Q. At no time did you agree to pay that mortgage, you took that property subject only to the mortgage? A. That is the way I bought it, the way the deed talks." Upon cross-examination the following occurred: "Q. Before you purchased, you executed a contract to purchase, is that right? A. I looked for the papers, I couldn't find them. I presume there was a contract to purchase. Q. You are not positive? A. No. Q. Isn't it a fact that a contract was executed about thirty days prior to the time the deed was given? A. There might have been. Q. You have had enough experience in purchasing real estate to know that there was a contract? A. You can close a deal with a contract or without. Q. In this case? A. I don't know. Q. How much did you agree to pay for this property? A. $16,000.00. Q. Are you positive of that? A. Yes. Q. Was the mortgage deducted from the purchase price? A. We never talked about the mortgage. They said the mortgage was a purchase money mortgage for $22,000.00. I was to pay $16,000.00. Q. You are positive that is what took place? A. It is seven years ago. I have not got the papers. Mr. Rosenberg (representing defendants Hayes and wife): Let me refresh your recollection. Mark this defendant Howard Hayes' Exhibit No. 1 for identification. Q. Does your signature appear upon that document? (Howard W. Hayes' exhibit No. 1 for identification, shown the witness, was afterward introduced in evidence as complain-

ants' exhibit No. 8, and is the contract of August 20, 1926.) A. Yes, that is my signature. Q. Do you recollect signing this document now? A. As I say, my signature is on there. I don't recollect the transaction except as I recalled it - Q. You recall it now? Isn't it a fact that you agreed to pay $38,000.00 for the property? A. I have told you about the transaction as I recollect. Q. Are you willing to change your testimony? A. No, I am willing to stand by my testimony. Q. Your signature appearing on this contract does not mean anything? A. That is my signature. Q. Isn't it a fact that this contract to purchase property was executed August 20, 1926? A. I don't know. Q. Isn't it a fact that you agreed to pay $38,000.00? A. I told you what the facts were as I recollect them. Q. Isn't it a fact that you assumed to pay the mortgage? A. I don't recollect. The contract speaks for itself, whatever it says. Q. What other signatures appear thereon? A. Howard Hayes and Harriet Hayes. That apparently was signed by their agent. It must be a real estate agent. Q. You signed it? A. I don't recollect. Q. Do you deny the signature? A. No. Q. Do you admit it is your signature? A. Certainly. Q. How much did you pay, $16,000.00? A. In rough figures, it is seven years ago, I don't recollect the deal." Redirect by Mr. Adelman: "Q. At the time this deed was- A. Apparently this was cancelled at the time of the delivery of the deed. * * * Q. At the time that deed was delivered for that property, was this agreement cancelled by the parties? * * * A. I don't recollect what happened to the- * * * I don't recollect what happened to the agreement except that we got a deed. That closed the transaction, and that was the basis we closed it on. * * * Q. At the time the deed was delivered, the total agreement between the parties was contained in that deed? A. Yes. * * * Q. Now were there any other agreements in existence between Howard Hayes and Harriet Hayes, his wife, and yourself and wife at the time that

deed was executed and delivered which is not contained in this deed? A. That is all. * * * Q. When was the last time you saw that document? A. I don't have an independent recollection of the document. I see my signature there and notice here the notation of cancellation by delivery of deed, and commission paid in full 9/20/26 signed by Alvin H. Reed & Company, per somebody, which is the same date the deed bears. I don't know if I saw this instrument on that date."

After defendants Hayes and Schwartz had testified before the master plaintiffs filed an amended and supplemental bill, which alleges the making of the Hayes-Schwartz written contract and that defendant Schwartz thereby assumed and agreed to pay the debt and is personally liable therefor. Still later, the bill as so amended and supplemented, with the issues thereon, was referred to the same master "without prejudice to the order of reference and the evidence heard and taken in pursuance thereof."

Plaintiffs contend:

"1. The Court erred in sustaining the exceptions and each of them of the defendant, Schwartz.

"2. The Court erred in not confirming the Master's report in its entirety.

"3. The Court erred in not decreeing Schwartz assumed and agreed to pay the indebtedness evidenced by the note and mortgage and is personally liable for the deficiency, if any, herein."

In support of their position plaintiffs cite the following principles of law, none of which is disputed by defendant:

"I. A person who purchases land and agrees to pay off an incumbrance on the same as a part of the purchase price of the land, is liable to the holder of the lien for the sum due him. (Citing cases.)

"II. To impose a personal liability for a mortgage debt on a grantee in a deed there must be (1) an express agreement to that effect or (2) a retention by him of a part of the purchase price for the purpose of paying the debt. (Citing cases.)

"III. It is not necessary that the assumption of a mortgage indebtedness be in the deed. It may be by a separate written contract or by a parol contract, and a grantee in a deed who agrees, either in writing outside of the deed or by parol,

to assume and pay an incumbrance to which the premises conveyed to him are subject, will be held upon the agreement, not only by his grantor, but by the owners of the notes, the payment of which he assumes, although his deed contains an express covenant that the premises are free from incumbrance. (Citing cases.)

"IV. It is well settled that, where one person enters into a simple contract with another for the benefit of a third person, such third person may maintain an action for the breach, and such a contract is not within the Statute of Frauds. (Citing cases.)

"V. The intention of a grantee to assume the debt is a question of fact. It may be derived from a contract which recites what liens the property is subject to, in connection with the closing statement showing to whom charged although that statement does not expressly mention the mortgage except as to interest thereon. (Citing cases.)

"VI. Where in purchasing premises which are incumbered, the amount of the incumbrance is taken into account in fixing the consideration and becomes part of the consideration, the purchaser thereby becomes liable for the amount of the incumbrance." (Citing cases.)

The theory of plaintiff is "that by express provisions of the contract of sale of said premises, the defendant expressly assumed and agreed to pay the debt and became liable for the deficiency herein and, second, even though the debt were not expressly assumed by the defendant, Schwartz, having purchased the property at the price of $38,000 and paid but $16,000 cash and the mortgage indebtedness of $22,000 making the balance of the $38,000 consideration, it was included in and forms a part of the consideration of the conveyance. Schwartz thereby assumed the debt by operation of law."

In his brief defendant Schwartz states his position as follows: We find no occasion to dispute the general propositions of law and the cases cited by counsel in their brief. It can be admitted that grantees in a deed may become personally liable to pay a mortgage note either by an express contract or an implied contract resulting either from a recital in the deed to that effect or proof of the fact that, at the time of the conveyance, the amount of the mortgage was part and parcel of the purchase price. It can also be admitted that the holder of the mortgage debt may sue the grantees in his own name as third party beneficiary. <u>The only issue in</u>

this case is one of fact: Whether plaintiffs alleged and proved an express or implied contract of assumption by Charles P. Schwartz." (Italics ours.) Schwartz contends that "plaintiffs failed to allege or prove a contract of assumption by Charles P. Schwartz of the Hayes note, either express or implied at the time of the transfer of the property."

"All of the testimony taken in this case was taken before the master in chancery. None of it was taken in open court. The master had some advantage in being able to see and hear practically all the witnesses, but the chancellor was in no better position to weigh the evidence than we are. Inasmuch, therefore, as the chancellor has not seen and heard the witnesses we are not bound by the rule that the finding of the chancellor will not be disturbed unless it is clearly and manifestly against the weight of the evidence. (Larson v. Glos, 235 Ill. 584.)" (Oliver v. Ross, 289 Ill. 624, 637.)

If it were necessary subsequent decisions of our Supreme court to the same effect might be cited.

At the conclusion of the testimony of Judge Hayes it seemed probable that the written agreement about which he had testified would not be found. In the direct examination of Schwartz he stated that he "never assumed to pay that mortgage;" that at no time did he agree to pay the mortgage; that he took the property subject only to the mortgage. Upon cross-examination, after he was shown the written contract, he stated that he had no independent recollection of the document, did not recollect signing it and did not recollect the transaction save as he had stated it upon direct. During the cross-examination the following occurred: "Q. Isn't it a fact that you assumed to pay the mortgage? A. I don't recollect. The contract speaks for itself, whatever it says." The written contract fixes the purchase price at $38,000, and provides that $16,000 shall be paid in cash and that Schwartz assumes the $22,000 mortgage debt. In other words, Schwartz assumed the payment of the mortgage as a part of the purchase money and agreed that the amount of the mortgage indebtedness should be included in and form a part of the consideration for the conveyance. Schwartz, in his testimony, did not claim that

between the time of the execution of the written contract and the execution of the warranty deed there was any new agreement that changed or modified the written contract. He testified, upon redirect examination, as follows: "Q. At the time that deed was delivered for that property, was this agreement cancelled by the parties? The Witness: I don't recollect what happened to the agreement except that we got a deed. That closed the transaction, and that was the basis we closed it on." In considering the equivocal testimony of Schwartz it must be borne in mind that the written contract gave him immediate possession of the property - a somewhat unusual concession. Yet, before it appeared that the contract had been found, he was willing to claim that no such contract was ever executed. From certain parts of Judge Hayes' testimony, not disputed by Schwartz, it appears that at the time of the execution of the warranty deed Schwartz stated that he would take over the mortgage and pay the notes and mortgage as they became due; that for a number of years after the sale Schwartz paid the interest notes as they became due. But the great depression came on, real estate values tumbled, and Schwartz no longer met his obligations. Even then he did not deny that he had assumed to pay the mortgage indebtedness. His attitude, as stated to Judge Hayes, was that he did not think the property was worth "over half what he paid for it;" that he could not pay the mortgage, as he did not have "any funds with which to pay it;" that if the bank foreclosed he could probably remain in the premises during the period of foreclosure. As a defense Schwartz now relies upon the words written upon the face of the contract by an assistant of the real estate firm, although the first knowledge he had of the superscription upon the contract was when the document was shown him during his cross-examination. The contract provides that it shall be held in escrow by the real estate firm. Under what circumstances the words were written does not appear.

Neither Hayes nor Schwartz knew that the real estate firm's employee had written the words across the face of the contract. The words in question were used by a layman and were intended by him, apparently, as a memorandum that the written contract was closed by the delivery of the deed. The written contract provided that the seller agrees to pay a broker's commission to Alvin H. Reed & Company, and the superscription contains the statement that that commission had been paid. In our judgment the defense was clearly an afterthought.

In support of his claim that the written contract was cancelled defendant Schwartz relies upon Rapp v. Stoner, 104 Ill. 618. We find that case entirely different from the instant one upon the facts. There the Supreme court held (p. 623):

"There is much evidence in the record tending to prove that this written proposition was abandoned, and a new and different contract agreed upon before the contract between the parties was closed. * * * Indeed, there was no dispute in regard to the fact that upon the consummation of the trade there was a material departure from the terms of the original written proposition. By the original proposition 800 acres of Kansas lands were to be given in exchange for the block, but by the terms of the trade, as consummated, 400 acres were given for the block, and 160 acres for a tenement house, which was not mentioned in the original proposition. The fact that there was such a clear departure from the written proposition when the trade was finally closed, in connection with the evidence that the written proposition was rescinded, when considered in connection with the further fact that the deed conveying the lots did not bind Reiss to pay off the incumbrances, was enough, in our judgment, to justify the circuit court in holding that the written proposition was canceled by the parties, and a new agreement made."

In the instant case, as we have heretofore stated, Schwartz did not claim that between the time of the execution of the written contract and the execution of the warranty deed there was any new agreement that changed or modified the written contract.

Plaintiffs contend that even if it were possible to find from all the facts and circumstances that the written contract was cancelled by Schwartz and Hayes, such cancellation would be ineffectual as against plaintiffs, the mortgagees.

"Where the conveyance is absolute to the grantee, his assumption of an existing mortgage creates against him an absolute obligation for its payment, and a release of this obligation can not be made by the grantor without the assent of the mortgagee.

The acceptance on the part of the mortgagee of the benefit of the assumption is a legal presumption, in the absence of proof, of his actual dissent." (2 Jones on Mortgages (8th ed.) 344, sec. 960.)

A purchaser of mortgaged premises from the mortgagor, who assumes payment of the mortgage debt, or who accepts a conveyance reciting his assumption of the same with a knowledge of such recital, will at once become personally liable to the mortgagee for the mortgage indebtedness, and he can not defeat the mortgagee's right to hold him responsible by procuring a release from the mortgagor. (Bay v. Williams, 112 Ill. 91.)

"While it is true that the recital in the deed itself was not sufficient to render appellant liable for this indebtedness and to authorize a deficiency judgment against him, yet it is true that where a grantee in a deed in fact assumes the mortgage and as part of the consideration of the purchase price agrees to pay the same, he is liable therefor and a deficiency judgment against him is proper, even though there is no express provision in the deed to this effect. Lobdell v. Ray, 110 Ill. App. 230; Drury v. Holden, 121 Ill. 130; Bay v. Williams, 112 Ill. 91, and Eggleston v. Morrison, 83 Ill. App. 625." (West Frankfort Bldg. & Loan Assn. v. Muir, 237 Ill. App. 122, 128-9.)

While the contention seems to have merit, we do not deem it necessary to pass upon it.

Defendant Schwartz has raised several technical points, none of which possesses any merit, and it would unduly lengthen this opinion to specifically refer to the same. As he conceded in his brief: "The only issue in this case is one of fact: Whether plaintiffs alleged and proved an express or implied contract of assumption by Charles P. Schwartz." We may say, however, that plaintiffs do not claim that Schwartz is liable by reason of any provision in the deed. Their cause of action, as alleged in the amended and supplemental bill, is that by the terms of the written contract Schwartz assumed and agreed to pay the mortgage deed and that the deed was given pursuant to the terms of the written contract. Plaintiffs concede that as Lavinia S. Schwartz did not sign the written contract she is not personally liable for the mortgage debt, and they are asking for a personal deficiency decree against Charles P. Schwartz only.

The decree of the **Superior** court of Cook county in so far as it denies the right of plaintiffs to a conditional personal deficiency decree against Schwartz, is reversed, and the cause is remanded with directions to modify the decree by providing therein for such conditional personal deficiency decree against Schwartz.

DECREE REVERSED IN PART AND CAUSE REMANDED WITH DIRECTIONS.

Sullivan, P. J., and Friend, J., concur.

533 H

38515

LESTER JANKOWSKI,
Appellant,

v.

JOHN P. KOBRZYNSKI,
Appellee.

APPEAL FROM CIRCUIT COURT OF COOK COUNTY.

286 I.A. 614[2]

MR. JUSTICE SCANLAN DELIVERED THE OPINION OF THE COURT.

This is an appeal from a judgment in an action in trover, tried by the court without a jury. The court found defendant not guilty and plaintiff has appealed from a judgment entered upon the finding.

The first count of the complaint alleges, in substance, that on December 6, 1929, plaintiff was the owner and possessed of a certain note and trust deed of the value of $32,500 and that defendant at that time wrongfully took, carried away, and unlawfully converted the same to his own use. The second count is the same as the first save that it further alleges that defendant wilfully, maliciously, tortiously and fraudulently took and carried away the property and converted the same to his own use. The third count is the same as the first save that it further alleges that defendant unlawfully pledged the property as collateral security for his loan of $4,800 and that plaintiff was compelled to pay the loan to recover his property. The fourth count is the same as the second count save that it further alleges that defendant wilfully, maliciously, tortiously and fraudulently pledged the property as collateral security in the payment of his loan of $4,800 with the intent to cheat and defraud plaintiff. The fifth count consists of the common counts.

The instant suit was started a few days before the running of the statute of limitations. Defendant's wife is a sister of plaintiff. Defendant and his wife had been separated for some time prior to the trial, the wife living in Europe with her parents. Until 1928 the note and trust deed undoubtedly belonged to the father and mother of plaintiff, who resided in Europe. Plaintiff, a lawyer, claims that while he was in Europe, in 1928, his father made him a present of the mortgage. At that time the note and trust deed were in plaintiff's safety deposit box in Chicago. Plaintiff's mother, while in this country in the early part of 1928, had turned over the note and trust deed to plaintiff to keep for her, and plaintiff placed the note and trust deed in his safety deposit box and they were there when he left for Europe in September, 1928. Prior to his departure he executed a power of attorney to his sister. Thereafter no one but plaintiff and his sister had access to the box. Plaintiff testified that when he returned to Chicago, in the latter part of August, 1929, he went to his deposit box and found that the note and trust deed were not in the box; that he then spoke to his sister and defendant about the matter and defendant told him he had pledged the note and trust deed at a bank to secure a loan and that he was then unable to pay the loan; that plaintiff paid the loan to obtain the security, pledging the note and trust deed to his own bank to secure the money to pay for defendant's loan; that the wife of defendant thereafter paid $1,000 of her own money on account of plaintiff's loan. Plaintiff further testified that on November 15, 1930, defendant needed some money and asked plaintiff if he would place the note and mortgage as collateral security for a loan to defendant, that plaintiff agreed to the request and defendant and plaintiff signed a note to the Noel State Bank for the amount of the loan, plaintiff giving the note and trust deed as collateral security

to the bank for the loan; that subsequently, by arrangement of the parties, Edward S. Scheffler paid the Noel State Bank the amount of the loan and now holds the note which plaintiff and defendant signed, also the collateral.

Plaintiff contends that he established every essential element of his case by a preponderance of the evidence and that this court should enter a judgment for him, "or in the alternative that the cause be remanded to the Circuit court for a new trial." The trial court found for defendant on the ground that the evidence was "vague" and unsatisfactory. After a careful consideration of the entire evidence we have reached the conclusion that justice will be best served by a retrial of this cause.

The judgment of the Circuit court of Cook county is reversed and the cause is remanded for a new trial.

JUDGMENT REVERSED AND CAUSE
REMANDED FOR A NEW TRIAL.

Sullivan, P. J., and Friend, J., concur.

38535

OLGA M. JANELUNAS, as Executrix of the Estate of KAZIMIR MULIOLIS, Deceased,
Appellee,

v.

METROPOLITAN LIFE INSURANCE COMPANY, a corporation,
Appellant.

APPEAL FROM MUNICIPAL COURT OF CHICAGO.

286 I.A. 614[3]

MR. JUSTICE SCANLAN DELIVERED THE OPINION OF THE COURT.

This is an action on an insurance policy issued by defendant on the life of Kazimir Muliolis. A jury returned a verdict against defendant and assessed plaintiff's damages in the sum of $626.18. This appeal is from a judgment entered upon the verdict.

The policy was issued May 11, 1931, and the insured died June 13, 1931. No medical examination is required under the type of policy issued. The policy provides:

> "If, (1) the Insured is not alive or is not in sound health on the date hereof; or if (2) * * * the Insured * * * has, within two years before the date hereof, been attended by a physician for any serious disease or complaint, or, before said date, has had any pulmonary disease, or chronic bronchitis or cancer, or disease of the heart, liver or kidneys, * * * then, in any such case, the Company may declare this Policy void and the liability of the Company in the case of any such declaration or in the case of any claim under this Policy, shall be limited to the return of premiums paid on the Policy, except in the case of fraud, in which case all premiums will be forfeited to the Company."

Defendant contends that the great weight of the evidence shows that the insured on the date of the application, also on the date of the policy, was not in sound health, but that on the said dates he was suffering from tuberculosis and cancer, which diseases had existed for a considerable period of time. After a careful consideration of all the facts and circumstances in the case we

have reached the conclusion that the contention of defendant must be sustained. Defendant also contends that the evidence shows that the deceased was aware of his physical condition at the time that he made the application for insurance, and that in obtaining the insurance he was guilty of a fraud upon defendant. We do not deem it necessary to pass upon this contention. As the case may be tried again we purposely refrain from commenting upon the evidence.

The judgment of the Municipal court of Chicago is reversed and the cause is remanded for a new trial.

JUDGMENT REVERSED AND CAUSE REMANDED FOR A NEW TRIAL.

Sullivan, P. J., and Friend, J., concur.

38580

CENTRAL STATES FINANCE COMPANY, a corporation, (Plaintiff) Appellee,

v.

ADOLPH SCHULTZ et al., Defendants.

LONDON & LANCASHIRE INDEMNITY COMPANY OF AMERICA, a corporation, (Defendant) Appellant.

APPEAL FROM MUNICIPAL COURT OF CHICAGO.

577

286 I.A. 614[4]

MR. JUSTICE SCANLAN DELIVERED THE OPINION OF THE COURT.

This is an appeal from a judgment in an action in debt brought upon an injunction bond. The suit was brought against Adolph Schultz as principal and the London & Lancashire Indemnity Company of America as surety but no service of summons was had on Schultz. After a trial by the court without a jury, judgment was entered for $500, in debt, and plaintiff's damages were assessed at $350.

Schultz filed a bill in equity against the Central States Finance Corporation, in which he alleged that the Central States Finance Corporation secured a judgment by confession against him on a note; that to satisfy the judgment certain premises were sold by the bailiff of the Municipal court of Chicago, without the complainant's knowledge; that on June 6, 1929, a deed was issued to the said corporation by the said bailiff, purporting to convey the property in question to said corporation; that complainant has a good defense to the action in question (the nature of the defense is set forth in detail); that the said judgment was obtained by fraud (described in detail); that the sale of the property was made by fraudulently concealing the facts from the complainant with the intention of depriving him of his legal rights; that the Central States Finance Corporation

had instituted a forcible detainer action against the complainant to secure possession of the premises. The bill prayed that the judgment rendered against the complainant be set aside, that the judgment note be delivered up and cancelled, that the deed of conveyance issued by the bailiff to defendant be set aside and declared void as against the complainant as a cloud upon his title, and that in the meantime the court restrain and enjoin defendant from proceeding in the forcible detainer suit or in any other action to oust complainant from the premises. Schultz filed an injunction bond in the penal sum of $500, signed by himself as principal and the defendant (appellant here) London & Lancashire Indemnity Company of America as surety, and when the equity cause came on for trial it was dismissed without costs for want of prosecution upon motion of the court.

In the trial of the instant cause plaintiff's damages were assessed at $350, $25 of which represents a sum paid for a real estate expert and the balance for attorney's fees incurred and paid by plaintiff for all legal services involved in its defense of the equity suit in which the injunction bond was filed. Upon the oral argument in this court it was conceded that the trial court erred in assessing damages for attorney's fees and other expenses incurred in the general defense of the suit in equity, and counsel for appellant, while contending that the amount allowed was grossly excessive, stated that it was willing that judgment be entered here in favor of the plaintiff in such sum as this court deemed proper. Counsel for plaintiff stated that a judgment for plaintiff for $100 damages would be satisfactory to plaintiff, and counsel for appellant stated that appellant was willing to have a judgment entered against it for that amount. It was also agreed that each party should bear its own costs.

The judgment of the Municipal court of Chicago is reversed and judgment is entered here in favor of plaintiff and against defendant London & Lancashire Indemnity Company of America for $500 debt and damages are assessed in the sum of $100, each party to bear its own costs.

JUDGMENT REVERSED AND JUDGMENT HERE IN FAVOR OF PLAINTIFF AND AGAINST DEFENDANT LONDON & LANCASHIRE INDEMNITY COMPANY OF AMERICA FOR $500 DEBT AND DAMAGES ARE ASSESSED IN THE SUM OF $100, EACH PARTY TO BEAR ITS OWN COSTS.

Sullivan, P. J. and Friend, J., concur.

56 A

38590

ROGERS PARK POST, NO. 108, DEPARTMENT OF ILLINOIS, THE AMERICAN LEGION, a Corporation, Appellee,	)	APPEAL FROM MUNICIPAL
v.	)	COURT OF CHICAGO.
CHICAGO PARK DISTRICT, a Body Politic and Corporate, Appellant.	)	286 I.A. 615[1]

MR. JUSTICE SCANLAN DELIVERED THE OPINION OF THE COURT.

This is an action in forcible detainer in which the trial court found the defendant guilty of unlawfully withholding from plaintiff the possession of the premises in question. Defendant has appealed from a judgment entered upon the finding.

Plaintiff's statement of claim (filed July 5, 1935) alleges that it is entitled to the possession of the premises described as Canteen No. 1, situated on the property formerly controlled by the North Shore Park District at Lake Michigan between Farwell avenue and Greenleaf avenue, in the city of Chicago; that the defendant unlawfully withholds the possession of the premises from plaintiff.

Defendant contends that plaintiff failed to prove, (1) that the defendant was in possession of the property at the time of the commencement of the suit, and (2) that the defendant unlawfully withholds possession from the plaintiff. Under the facts of this case these contentions must be sustained.

It is the law that in forcible detainer actions it is incumbent on plaintiff to prove that defendant was in possession and withheld possession at the time of the commencement of the

action. The right to possession is all that is involved, or that can be determined. (See Shulman v. Moser, 284 Ill. 134; West Side Trust & Savings Bank v. Lopoten, 358 Ill. 631, 637-8.) Plaintiff, in its evidence in chief, introduced a lease, dated February 28, 1934, between North Shore Park District, a municipal corporation, and plaintiff, for the property known as Canteens Nos. 1, 2 and 3, for a period commencing June 1, 1934, and ending May 30, 1939, for a consideration of $50, payable in five annual installments of $10 each, upon the first day of June of each year of the term. The trial court held that the introduction of the lease made out a prima facie case for plaintiff, that he was not concerned with the question of possession, and that it devolved upon the defendant to make a defense to the lease. No evidence was introduced by plaintiff that had any bearing upon the question of possession. However, upon rebuttal the plaintiff introduced evidence tending to show the following state of facts: That George Kayworth, acting for plaintiff, had charge of Canteen No. 1; that he had during the time in question and still had at the time of the trial the keys to the canteen; that when he left the canteen on July 5, he locked the two doors of the same; that he has not attempted to enter the canteen since he left it on July 5. It further appears from the testimony of this witness that in June, 1935, a police officer asked him if he had a permit to operate the place, to which the witness answered that he was operating the place under the lease and that that "acted as our permit;" that the police officer said to him, "If you make a sale, I will have to lock you up;" that the witness thereafter made a sale and that he was then arrested by the officer; that on a later day in June he made a sale and was again arrested; that on July 5, after he had made a sale, he "was locked up again." There was no evidence introduced to prove that the defendant was in the actual possession of the canteen at any time. At the conclusion of action. The right to possession is all that is involved, so that can be determined. (See [illegible] v. [illegible], [illegible] Ill. App. [illegible]; Trust & Savings Bank v. [illegible], [illegible] Ill. [illegible], [illegible].) Plaintiff, in the evidence in chief, introduced a lease, dated February 24, 1956, between North Shore Park District, a municipal corporation, and plaintiff, for the property known as concessions Nos. 1, 2 and 3, for a period commencing June 1, 1956, and ending May 31, 1959, for a consideration of $[illegible], payable in five annual installments of $[illegible] each, upon the first day of June of each year of the term. The trial court held that the introduction of the lease made out a prima facie case for plaintiff, that he was not concerned with the question of possession, and that it devolved upon the defendant to make a defense to the lease. No evidence was introduced by plaintiff that had any bearing upon the question of possession. However, upon rebuttal the plaintiff introduced evidence tending to show the following state of facts: That George Gregory, acting for plaintiff, had charge of Concession No. 1; that he was during the times in question and still had at the time of the trial the keys to the canteen; that when he left the canteen on July 5, he locked all the doors of the canteen; that he was not compelled to enter the canteen since he left it on July 5. It further appears from the testimony of this witness that in June, 1956, a police officer asked him if he had a permit to operate the place, to which the witness answered that he was operating the place under the lease and that that was our permit; that the police officer said to him, "If you make a sale, I will have to lock you up"; that the witness thereafter made a sale and that he was then arrested by the officer; that on a later day in June he made a sale and was again arrested; that on July 5, after he had made a sale, he "was locked up again." There was no evidence introduced to prove that the defendant was in the actual possession of the canteen at any time. At the conclusion of the evidence the trial court adhered to his ruling, heretofore referred to, and held that the lease was a good and binding one and therefore plaintiff was entitled to judgment. His action in that regard constitutes error. If the defendant is illegally preventing plaintiff from selling articles under the lease a forcible detainer suit is not the proper action in which plaintiff may obtain relief.

The defendant contends that the evidence shows that the lease, upon which plaintiff bases its right to possession of the premises, is a fraudulent and void lease. It also contends that plaintiff had not the power to enter into such a lease. In our view of this appeal we do not deem it necessary to pass upon either of these contentions.

The judgment of the Municipal court of Chicago is reversed.

REVERSED.

Sullivan, P. J., and Friend, J., concur.

57A

38620

MABEL ISSLEB, Appellee,

v.

JOSEPH WOLEK, Appellant.

APPEAL FROM SUPERIOR COURT, COOK COUNTY.

286 I.A. 615[2]

MR. JUSTICE SCANLAN DELIVERED THE OPINION OF THE COURT.

Defendant appeals from a judgment in the sum of $5,500, entered upon a jury verdict.

Plaintiff was injured in an automobile accident that occurred about 7 P.M. on December 14, 1933, on Diversey avenue at its intersection with Major avenue. At the time of the accident she was a passenger in an automobile that was being driven by her husband in an easterly direction on Diversey avenue, which is a four-lane street, forty-two feet wide. At the time of the collision the car in which plaintiff was riding was in the outer, or most southerly, lane, "about four feet from the south curb." Just before defendant's automobile collided with the automobile in which plaintiff was riding he was driving in a westerly direction on Diversey avenue.

Three points are urged by defendant in support of his contention that the judgment should be reversed: "I. The Court erred in refusing proper instructions suggested by the defendant. II. The Court erred in admitting improper evidence offered by the plaintiff over the objection of the defendant. III. The verdict is excessive."

As to point I, defendant contends that the court erred in/ refusing

38620

MABEL ISSLER,
Appellee,

v.

JOSEPH WOLEK,
Appellant.

APPEAL FROM SUPERIOR COURT,

COOK COUNTY.

286 I.A. 615

MR. JUSTICE SCANLAN DELIVERED THE OPINION OF THE COURT.

Defendant appeals from a judgment in the sum of $5,500, entered upon a jury verdict.

Plaintiff was injured in an automobile accident that occurred about 7 P.M. on December 14, 1933, on Diversey avenue at its intersection with Major avenue. At the time of the accident she was a passenger in an automobile that was being driven by her husband in an easterly direction on Diversey avenue, which is a four-lane street, forty-two feet wide. At the time of the collision the car in which plaintiff was riding was in the outer, or most southerly, lane, "about four feet from the south curb." Just before defendant's automobile collided with the automobile in which plaintiff was riding he was driving in a westerly direction on Diversey avenue.

Three points are urged by defendant in support of his contention that the judgment should be reversed: "I. The Court erred in refusing proper instructions suggested by the defendant. II. The Court erred in admitting improper evidence offered by the plaintiff over the objection of the defendant. III. The verdict is excessive."

As to point I, defendant contends that the court erred in refusing the following instructions:

"The jury are instructed that the marring of personal appearance and humiliation resulting from the contemplation thereof are not elements entering into computation of pecuniary damages for personal injury sustained by reason of alleged negligence, if any."

"The jury are instructed that if they believe from the evidence under the instructions of the court that the injury to the plaintiff was caused by a mere accident occurring without the negligence of either the plaintiff or the defendant, or if they believe it was caused by the negligence of the plaintiff, or if they believe it was caused by the combined negligence of the plaintiff and the defendant, then in either of such cases the jury should find the defendant Joseph Wolek not guilty."

As to the first instruction: In the case of Nosko v. O'Donnell, 260 Ill. App. 544, 554, the court, in sustaining the action of the trial court in refusing to give a like instruction, said:

"Defendant also contends that the court erred in refusing to give as requested by defendant an instruction that the marring of personal appearance and humiliation resulting from the contemplation of bodily disfigurement are not elements entering into computation of pecuniary damages for personal injuries sustained by reason of alleged negligence, and it is asserted that the question of law raised by the refusal of the court to give the instruction 'has never been put squarely to the Supreme Court.' Defendant says the question was not before the court at all in Chicago City Ry. Co. v. Smith, 226 Ill. 178. We do not so construe that case. Moreover, the question was passed on in Fitzgerald v. Davis, 237 Ill. App. 488, and we adhere to that decision."

We are in entire accord with that ruling. Moreover, a jury might well understand from the instruction that if injuries marred the personal appearance of plaintiff such injuries could not enter into their computation of pecuniary damages to be awarded plaintiff. It would be a strange doctrine if such were the law.

As to the second instruction refused it is sufficient to state that we can find no evidence upon which a jury could reasonably find that the injuries to plaintiff were due to a mere accident alone, not coupled with neglect. Defendant was the sole witness in his behalf, and it is plain from his evidence that the accident was due to the fact that he was determined to pass cars that were ahead of him even if he had to travel westward in the eastbound lanes to do so.

the following instructions:

"The jury are instructed that the marring of personal appearance and humiliation resulting from the contemplation thereof are not elements entering into computation of pecuniary damages for personal injury sustained by reason of alleged negligence, if any."

"The jury are instructed that if they believe from the evidence under the instructions of the court that the injury to the plaintiff was caused by a mere accident occurring without the negligence of either the plaintiff or the defendant, or if they believe it was caused by the negligence of the plaintiff, or if they believe it was caused by the combined negligence of the plaintiff and the defendant, then in either of such cases the jury should find the defendant Joseph Wolek not guilty."

As to the first instruction: In the case of Mosko v. O'Donnell, 260 Ill. App. 544, 554, the court, in sustaining the action of the trial court in refusing to give a like instruction, said:

"Defendant also contends that the court erred in refusing to give as requested by defendant an instruction that the marring of personal appearance and humiliation resulting from the contemplation of bodily disfigurement are not elements entering into computation of pecuniary damages for personal injuries sustained by reason of alleged negligence, and it is asserted that the question of law raised by the refusal of the court to give the instruction 'has never been put squarely to the Supreme Court.' Defendant says the question was not before the court at all in Chicago City Ry. Co. v. Smith, 226 Ill. 178. We do not so construe that case. Moreover, the question was passed on in Fitzgerald v. Davis, 237 Ill. App. 488, and we adhere to that decision."

We are in entire accord with that ruling. Moreover, a jury might well understand from the instruction that if injuries marred the personal appearance of plaintiff such injuries could not enter into their computation of pecuniary damages to be awarded plaintiff. It would be a strange doctrine if such were the law.

As to the second instruction refused it is sufficient to state that we can find no evidence upon which a jury could reasonably find that the injuries to plaintiff were due to a mere accident alone, not coupled with neglect. Defendant was the sole witness in his behalf, and it is plain from his evidence that the accident was due to the fact that he was determined to pass cars that were ahead of him even if he had to travel westward in the eastbound lanes to do so.

It is idle to argue that the accident occurred without any fault on the part of defendant. In none of the three points urged why the judgment should be reversed is it specifically contended that defendant was not guilty of negligence. In our opinion it would have been error to give the instruction in question. (See Streeter v. Humrichouse, 357 Ill. 234, 244; Peters v. Madigan, 262 Ill. App. 417; Mississippi Lime & Material Co. v. Smith, 282 Ill. App. 361, 369.)

As to point II, that the court erred in admitting improper evidence offered by plaintiff over his objection, defendant's counsel states in his brief:

> "On the evening of July 2, 1935, at the close of the court day, the plaintiff rested her case, and on the morning of July 3rd, the Court called counsel into his chambers, and on his own motion said: 'I am going to allow him to call the plaintiff for the purpose of exhibiting to the jury the scar on her head, and following that you put down, the plaintiff rests.' Whereupon the plaintiff was recalled, and over defendant's counsel's objection was told and allowed to step over and walk along the jury box, and exhibit the scars on her head. No motion or request was ever made by the plaintiff or her counsel to exhibit the scars on the forehead to the jury at any time. * * * Nevertheless after the plaintiff had rested, the Court took it upon himself to reopen the case and to suggest, and allow the prejudicial exhibition despite the objection. The effect of this, in view of the Court's previous ruling, would call to the jury's particular attention that the scars on the forehead must have meant something. Sympathy, passion and prejudice was the logical result of this error. * * * There can be no question, we believe, but that the jury were influenced by the conduct of the Judge in reopening the matter on his own motion and suggesting that the plaintiff be placed upon the witness stand for the purpose of demonstrating her scars. That such a demonstration, emphasized by the reopening of the case to stage it, would affect the verdict seems to be self-evident. * * * The Court by his action in staging a show for the benefit of the jurors in allowing the display of the scars, on his own motion, forcibly brought to the juror's attention and consideration these scars."

In support of this attack upon Judge Gridley counsel refers to page 139 of the record. By a reference to that page we find the following:

"July 3, 1935.
10 o'clock A. M.

Court met pursuant to adjournment.

Present: Counsel same as before.

(The following took place in the court's chambers)

It is idle to argue that the accident occurred without any fault on the part of defendant. In none of the three points urged why the judgment should be reversed is it specifically contended that defendant was not guilty of negligence. In our opinion it would have been error to give the instruction in question. (See Streeter v. Humrichouse, 357 Ill. 234, 244; Peters v. Madigan, 262 Ill. App. 417; Mississippi Lime & Material Co. v. Smith, 282 Ill. App. 361, 369.)

As to point II, that the court erred in admitting improper evidence offered by plaintiff over his objection, defendant's counsel states in his brief:

"On the evening of July 2, 1935, at the close of the court day, the plaintiff rested her case, and on the morning of July 3rd, the Court called counsel into his chambers, and on his own motion said: 'I am going to allow him to call the plaintiff for the purpose of exhibiting to the jury the scar on her head, and following that you put down, the plaintiff rests.' Whereupon the plaintiff was recalled, and over defendant's counsel's objection was told and allowed to step over and walk along the jury box, and exhibit the scars on her head. No motion or request was ever made by the plaintiff or her counsel to exhibit the scars on the forehead to the jury at any time. * * * Nevertheless after the plaintiff had rested, the Court took it upon himself to reopen the case and to suggest, and allow the prejudicial exhibition despite the objection. The effect of this, in view of the Court's previous ruling, would call to the jury's particular attention that the scars on the forehead must have meant something. Sympathy, passion and prejudice was the logical result of this error. * * * There can be no question, we believe, but that the jury were influenced by the conduct of the judge in reopening the matter on his own motion and suggesting that the plaintiff be placed upon the witness stand for the purpose of demonstrating her scars. That such a demonstration, emphasized by the reopening of the case to stage it, would affect the verdict seems to be self-evident. * * * The Court by his action in staging a show for the benefit of the jurors in allowing the display of the scars, on his own motion, forcibly brought to the juror's attention and consideration these scars."

In support of this attack upon Judge Gridley counsel refers to page 139 of the record. By a reference to that page we find the following:

"July 3, 1935.
10 o'clock A. M.

Court met pursuant to adjournment.

Present: Counsel same as before.

(The following took place in the court's chambers)

"THE COURT: I am going to allow him to call the plaintiff for the purpose of exhibiting to the jury the scar on her head and following that you put down the plaintiff rests.

Defendant's motion for a directed is denied and an exception. Plaintiff dismisses the second or wilful and wanton count from the consideration of the jury."

After the filing of defendant's brief in this court, Judge Gridley, upon motion of plaintiff's attorney, signed the following amendment to the report of proceedings:

"This cause coming on to be heard upon motion of the attorneys for the plaintiff for an amendment to the report of proceedings, and counsel for the defendant having been given due notice thereof, and it appearing to the court from files, records, notes and memoranda in its possession that the report of proceedings heretofore filed in this cause does not fully and accurately set out said proceedings as they occurred, the said report of proceedings heretofore signed and certified in this proceeding is amended at page 139 to read as follows, to-wit:

Wednesday, July 3rd, 1935
10 o'clock, A.M.

Court convened pursuant to adjournment
Counsel present, as heretofore.

Court and counsel retired to the court's chambers whereupon Mr. Sinnott, attorney for the plaintiff, asked the court for leave to recall the plaintiff to the stand for the purpose of exhibiting to the jury the scars upon her forehead. The plaintiff's attorney also then and there stated to the court that he would dismiss the second or wilful and wanton count of the plaintiff's complaint from the consideration of the jury.

- - - - - - - - - - - - -

(Proceedings in Chambers at which the Reporter was not present, pursuant to which the following proceedings, among others, were had in Open Court):

'THE COURT: We will go on with the plaintiff's case. I am going to allow him to recall the plaintiff just for the purpose of exhibiting to the jury the scar on her head.

Now, (addressing the reporters) you put down 'Plaintiff rests.' Then you put down, 'Defendant's motion for a directed verdict in his favor is denied,' and 'Exception.' 'Plaintiff dismisses the second or wilful and wanton count from the consideration of the jury.'

(Mrs. Mabel Issleb recalled.)

The foregoing amendment to the said report of proceedings is approved, signed, sealed and filed in accordance with the statute this 6th day of January, A. D. 1936.

Enter:

(Signed) M. M. Gridley
Judge."

That the charge made was without foundation in fact also clearly appears from the written motion for a new trial, wherein no complaint was made as to the conduct of the trial judge. The original report of proceedings, insufficient and unfair as it was, failed entirely to justify any attack upon Judge Gridley. Since the filing in this court of the amendment to the original report, counsel has not seen fit to retract the unwarranted and unjust charge, nor to apologize to this court for making it. Judge Gridley has had a long and honorable career upon the trial bench and in this court, and the bench and bar know and appreciate his absolute fairness in the performance of his judicial duties. A judge who fearlessly performs his duty, however unpleasant it may be, sometimes incurs a spirit of animosity which may, at times, manifest itself. The case of Watson v. Trinz, 274 Ill. App. 379, was decided when Judge Gridley was a member of this division of the court.

Defendant contends that it was error for the court to allow plaintiff to exhibit to the jury the scar on her forehead. We find no merit in this contention. In Minnis v. Friend, 360 Ill. 328, the court said (p. 336):

> "The contention is made that it was error to permit the appellee to display his injured leg to the jury when, as here, there was no dispute as to the fact and nature of the injury. It is claimed that the purpose of such an exhibition was to excite feelings of sympathy and passion rather than to enlighten the jury. The question whether injuries to the person shall be shown to the jury rests within the sound discretion of the trial court. When the question is as to the extent of the wound or injury it is the common and correct practice to exhibit the wound or injury to the jury so that they may see for themselves. (Walsh v. Chicago Railways Co., 303 Ill. 339, 346.) In arriving at an amount to be paid as damages, if damages were to be allowed, the jury would have to determine the nature and extent of the appellee's injuries even though the fact and nature of the injury were conceded. The trial court did not commit error when it permitted the appellee to display his injuries to the jury."

In our opinion, if the scar upon the forehead were eliminated entirely in considering the damages sustained by plaintiff, still the amount allowed by the jury would be a very reasonable compensation for

the other injuries sustained by plaintiff.

We find no merit in the third, and last, point urged by defendant, that the verdict is excessive. Plaintiff was thrown through the windshield by the force of the collision. She was immediately taken to a doctor's office, where glass was removed from a large cut in her forehead and first aid treatment was given her right knee and ankle. The police then took her, in an ambulance, to Belmont hospital, where her family physician was called. X-rays were taken of her right knee and ankle. The X-ray of the ankle "shows no bony pathology," but her physician testified that in his opinion the ankle ligaments were undoubtedly torn. The X-ray picture of the knee showed a compound, comminuted fracture of the patella, "showing one large and three small fragments of the bone." The following day the plaintiff was given an anesthetic and an attempt was made to bring the fragments of the patella together and to sew them to a lower small fragment which was badly damaged. The attempt proved unsuccessful, and the smaller fragments were then removed and the ligament was sewed to the upper portion of the patella with kangaroo tendon and wire. The ligament had been crushed and almost entirely severed. As a result the limb was shortened an inch and a quarter, which lessened the ability of plaintiff to move the knee joint either backward or forward. After the operation a plaster of Paris cast was applied, which extended from just below the hip to the ankle, with an opening to permit dressing of the wound and to allow drainage of the pus, which continued to discharge for about three months. Plaintiff remained in the hospital for three weeks, after which time she was taken home, where she remained in bed for four months. On April 19 she was able to move around on crutches. Subsequently she discarded them and used a cane, which she was still obliged to use at the time of the trial, eighteen months after the accident. At that time she had "about a 50 per cent mobility of

extension and about 30 to 35 of flexion," which condition is permanent. She was still under a doctor's care, and heat treatments and forcible manipulation of the knee joint were being resorted to in an effort to improve her condition. She experiences great difficulty in climbing and descending stairs, and when she rides upon a street car she has to allow her foot "to stick out in the aisle." Her doctor's bill was $549 and her hospital bill was $147.10. In our judgment a larger verdict would have been justified.

Defendant has had a fair trial and the judgment of the Superior court of Cook count should be and it is affirmed.

JUDGMENT AFFIRMED.

Sullivan, P. J., and Friend, J., concur.

38 A

38643

PEOPLE OF THE STATE OF ILLINOIS, Defendant in Error, v. HARRY B. KAUNG, Plaintiff in Error.	)	ERROR TO MUNICIPAL COURT OF CHICAGO.

286 I.A. 615[3]

MR. JUSTICE SCANLAN DELIVERED THE OPINION OF THE COURT.

In a trial by the court, without a jury, defendant was found guilty of obtaining money by false pretenses. Defendant has sued out this writ of error from a judgment entered upon the finding.

The information filed and the affidavit attached thereto are as follows:

"STATE OF ILLINOIS,)
COUNTY OF COOK,) ss. IN THE MUNICIPAL COURT OF CHICAGO.
CITY OF CHICAGO.)

"Miss Julia De Jay, a resident of the City of Chicago in the State aforesaid, in his own proper person, comes now here into court, and in the name and by the authority of the People of the State of Illinois, gives the Court to be informed and understand that Harry B. Kaung heretofore, to wit: on the 7 day of April A. D. 1935, at the City of Chicago, aforesaid Did then and there willfully and unlawfully obtain from this affiant the sum of One Thousand dollars in United States currency by means of False Pretenses and Misrepresentation. VS 253 ch 38 S-Hds R S 1931 contrary to the form of the Statute in such case made and provided, and against the peace and dignity of the People of the State of Illinois.

"X J DeJay

"STATE OF ILLINOIS,)
COUNTY OF COOK,) ss.
CITY OF CHICAGO.)

"Miss Julia DeJay Atlantic 2862
being first duly sworn, on her oath, deposes and says that she resides at 4433 University Av., that she has read the foregoing

information by her subscribed and that the same is true.

"X J DeJay

"Subscribed and sworn to before me
this 5 day of Oct. A. D. 1935.

"Joseph L. Gill
Clerk of The Municipal
Court of Chicago."

The major contention of defendant is that the information is fatally defective because it fails to aver essential elements of the offense of obtaining money by false pretenses. This contention is clearly a meritorious one. The information does not allege that defendant obtained the money with intent to cheat or defraud the prosecuting witness. It makes no attempt to allege the false statements or misrepresentations made by defendant in order to obtain the money. It does not allege that the money was the property of the prosecuting witness, nor that she was induced to part with it because of the false statements and misrepresentations. The state's attorney admits that the information does not charge the offense with the particularity required by the statute, but he argues that because the sufficiency of the information was not raised in the trial court defendant is now barred from raising the instant contention. It is undoubtedly true that a defendant, by his conduct in the trial court, may waive formal defects in an indictment or an information, but if an indictment or an information is fatally defective a defendant may take advantage of that fact in this court even though he did not raise the question in the trial court. A fatally defective indictment or information is not cured by verdict and judgment.

The judgment of the Municipal court of Chicago is reversed and as the information may be amended the cause is remanded.

JUDGMENT REVERSED AND CAUSE REMANDED.

Sullivan, P. J., and Friend, J., concur.

38551

PEOPLE OF THE STATE OF ILLINOIS ex rel. JOHN S. RUSCH, Defendant in Error,

vs.

LOUIS MATTHIESEN, PATRICK FOLEY, JOSEPH E. WOLF, Plaintiffs in Error.

ERROR TO COUNTY COURT OF COOK COUNTY.

5917

286 I.A. 615[4]

MR. JUSTICE O'CONNOR DELIVERED THE OPINION OF THE COURT.

August 3, 1935, John S. Rusch, chief clerk of the Board of Election Commissioners of Chicago, filed a verified petition against the judges and clerks of election of the 22nd Precinct of the 4th Ward of Chicago, charging that at the general election held April 2, 1935, he was advised and believed that the judges and clerks were guilty of misconduct and misbehavior in the performance of their duties, (1) in that while acting as such judges and clerks they did "fraudulently and unlawfully make a false canvass and return of the votes cast," and (2) "were guilty of corrupt and fraudulent conduct and practice" in the performance of their duties, and prayed that a rule be entered against them commanding them to appear and show cause why they should not be adjudged guilty of contempt of court. The defendants denied any wrongdoing. Afterward the court heard the evidence, found the two persons who acted as clerks not guilty, found the three judges guilty and sentenced them to imprisonment in the county jail for six months.

Respondents contend that their motion for a bill of particulars should have been allowed because the petition filed by Rusch was insufficient to inform them of the nature of the charges made against them. It is unnecessary to pass upon this contention because the record discloses that the case went to trial September 5, 1935, and was continued from time to time,

when the hearings were resumed and opposing counsel examined the records of the Election Commissioners' office, so that it appears defendants were sufficiently advised of the specific charges made against them. In these circumstances, it is obvious that respondents were in no way prejudiced in presenting their defense. Nor was there any substantial error in overruling respondent Matthiesen's motion to quash the service of the writ of attachment upon him because of his contention that it was not served by the sheriff. As a judge of election he was an officer of the court, and since he appeared and presented his defense he has no ground for complaint.

In the judgment order the court found (1) that the respondents knowingly and fraudulently permitted David Wagner, Mrs. Marie Wagner, Charles H. Graham, Todd O. Maynard, Paul Henrhan, Miss Mary Walsh, Gerald Peterson and Hiram Shaw, to vote twice; (2) that respondents knowingly and fraudulently permitted Stewart L. Rice, Chris Michalson, Lewis Levy, William Nelson and Mildred Schenk to vote when their names had been erased from the register, and (3) that the respondents unlawfully and fraudulently permitted Samuel Lewis, Charles E. Allen and Margaret Sloan to vote from a different address in the precinct from the address appearing in the register, without requiring them to make affidavits as required by the statute.

The evidence shows that at six o'clock on the morning of the election, when the polls opened, the only member of the board that appeared was respondent Foley; one of the other judges had been disqualified the day before by the Election Commissioners because he did not live in the precinct. Thereupon Foley swore in two persons to act as clerks of election, and respondents Matthiesen and Wolf to act as judges, all of whom were then at the polling place for the purpose of voting; a number of other

persons were also there to vote. Wolf was a Democrat and Matthiesen a Republican. Margaret J. Dahlman was there as a challenger.

Clifford G. Fordan, called by petitioner, testified that he was an investigator of the Fraud Department of the Election Commissioners; that about thirty days after the election he investigated the register and poll books of the precinct. The two poll books and the two registers were offered in evidence. The witness further testified as to certain names appearing in the register under which a line had been drawn indicating that the persons were not entitled to vote, but who had voted, as appeared from the poll books. The witness gave further testimony, some of which will be hereinafter referred to.

Margaret J. Dahlman, called by petitioner, testified that she lived in the vicinity but not in the precinct in question; that she went to the polling place in question about 5:30 in the morning and remained all day; that she had made a partial canvass of the precinct Saturday before the election, accompanied by one of the clerks, Mrs. Rissi, who did not serve on the Board on the day in question; the extent of such canvass does not appear except that she testified concerning the canvass made in a few buildings in the precinct; that in making the canvass she marked down the information she received as to whether the voters lived in the buildings which she canvassed; that she was in the polling place all day except for about ten minutes when she went to her own precinct to vote; the judges and clerks of election were in the precinct during the entire day; that "it was a hectic day, there was a great deal of confusion;" that she challenged a great many voters and made notes at the time, which she produced in court; that she thought she challenged more than 50 people; but that the judges did not pay any attention to the challenges; that "There was so much confusion;" that she challenged some of the

persons because she was told by the owners of the buildings she canvassed that they did not live there; she specified a number of the persons whom she challenged; that she challenged Stewart Rice but he was given a ballot; that she did not know where he lived; "I was doing about seven people's work there." Later she testified as to a number of persons whom she challenged but apparently they were permitted to vote; that "the board seemed to be quite new"; that sometimes when the voters came in to receive their ballots, respondent Matthirsen, who was handing out the ballots, did not announce the names of the voters, and she was unable to learn their names; that she had some argument with him and that he made insulting remarks; that "I was only one and had seven jobs to do."

On cross examination she testified that she made the canvass on Friday or Saturday before the election; she put in one afternoon and went to the hotels and apartments and spent four or five hours making the canvass. The court erroneously refused to permit her to answer the question as to how many buildings she had canvassed in the precinct. She further testified as to the names of a number of persons she challenged and that some of them "wouldn't make an affidavit;" that Mr. Wuffum from the Election Commissioners' office said it was done by the wish of the majority of the judges; "It is O. K. for this man to vote." She further testified that about 6:30 in the morning she telephoned the Election Commissioners' office and stated that there was trouble in the precinct and about seven o'clock Mr. Wuffum came to the polling place and stayed there all day; that when she challenged a voter respondents Foley and Wolf would examine the registers and would tell respondent Matthiesen that the voter was qualified, and the latter would then give the voter a ballot; that she ran for alderman in the primaries before the election

and told the voters at that time she belonged to the Voters Information League.

Respondent Foley testified that he was a colortype pressman and had done such work since 1889; that he served on the Board as an election judge in November, 1934, and at the primary election in February, 1935, and on April 2 (the election in question) he served the third time as judge of election; that he arrived at the polling place a few minutes before six o'clock; that Mrs. Dahlman was there at the time but none of the old Board was there; then he picked out the first four men and swore them in as clerks and judges; that when persons came in to vote they announced their names to Matthiesen; that the witness and Wolf then examined the two registers and if the person was registered they advised Matthiesen, who gave the voter a ballot; that Mrs. Dahlman challenged about 90 persons during the entire day, which was about 25% of the persons who appeared; that when she challenged a person the two registers were consulted and if he was properly registered he was permitted to vote; that witness had charge of one register and Mr. Wolf of the other; that on account of the challenging there was much confusion; that he did not understand what was meant by underscoring a person's name in the register; that after the election, when he was taken to the detective bureau, he found out this meant that the person was disqualified and not entitled to vote; that he did not apply to the Election Commissioners to be appointed judge of election but was called there some time before and qualified; that Mr. Hahn, who was a member of the old Board, did not appear on the morning in question, but witness did not know why; that he studied some of the instructions sent to him by the Election Commissioners. He was then asked how he would explain the fact that some names appeared on the poll book twice, indicating that they had voted twice at the election, and his

reply was, "The only way I can account for that would be the stupidity of the board," including himself. He was then asked by the court what experience would be necessary to find out whether a person had voted once and then came in later in the day and voted again, and his answer was, "Well, the turmoil was so great -- when a man came in to vote whose name appeared as having been voted the judges refused to let him vote."

The court then asked counsel, who, during one of the continuances of the hearing had examined the records in the Election Commissioners' office, "How many names do you have in this case that voted more than once?" to which counsel for two of the respondents replied, "There are six, your Honor, and there is one name, Thomas Maynard, that appears as Todd Maynard in one book and the witness said he couldn't tell whether it was Thomas or not in another book." Mr. Johnson (counsel for petitioner): "Yes, six of them." Foley then continuing testified that when a person came to vote who gave a different address from that shown on the register, he was not allowed to vote but that in the confusion, "persons might have been permitted to vote from a different address;" that he knew affidavits were required where, since the registration, people had moved to a different address in the precinct; that no affidavits were taken in four instances where people had moved within the precinct; that he held no political office and had received no promise or inducement and had only received his daily wage for the work he did; that he had never been arrested before and was never in trouble; that when a person whose qualifications were questioned came to vote, the registers were consulted and then the three judges decided whether he was qualified to vote; that respondent Matthiesen had nothing to do with the registers during the entire day; that Mr. Grace, one of the judges of election, did not appear when the polls opened, and

that he first learned that Grace was not to appear when he arrived at the polling place on the morning of the election; that he did not know Matthiesen until he met him at the polling place on the morning of the election.

There is also in evidence a letter dated March 27, 1935, from Judge Jarecki, addressed to all the judges and clerks of election, in which it is stated that it is the duty of the judges and clerks of election to see that all votes are counted in accordance with the way they were cast. "For your own protection you should read and become familiar with all of the law and the rules and regulations prepared for your guidance. No excuse for your failure to observe the law will be accepted." That in the past the court had found it necessary to discipline election officials and to commit some of them to jail for misconduct and misbehavior in office and that the law requires and the Court expected them to perform their duties free from partisanship and in strict compliance with the law; that a police officer who was under the judges' control and direction would be detailed to the polling place and would carry out their orders.

Respondent Wolf testified that he was a waiter employed at a tavern and that he had never served as a judge of election before; that he got through work at one o'clock on the morning of April 2nd, "went over to see a party and stayed out all night, so he figured he would go over to vote." When he got to the polling place he was asked by Foley to serve as judge of election; that Mrs. Dahlman was there at the time and some other persons; that Foley told him if he acted he would receive eight dollars and his duties were to check off names of persons voting who were on the registers; that he told Foley he was a Democrat; that he was given one of the registers; that when a person came in to vote, if his name appeared on the register it was checked off by himself

and Foley, who had the other register, but nothing was told him that lines appearing under names indicated they were scratched and the persons not entitled to vote; that Foley told him if a line was drawn through the name, such person could not vote. The respondent was then asked, "Is there any way that you can account for a person's name appearing twice in the poll books?" Answer: "No, sir, I did not remember. There was nothing said to me about affidavits;" that he did not receive any instructions regarding his duties except to be told to check off the names when persons were given ballots to vote.

Sarah Rissi, called by the Court, testified that she was was a Republican clerk qualified to act in the precinct on the day of election but that she did not serve; that she canvassed two rooming houses on the Saturday afternoon with Mrs. Dahlman at her request; that "I got my feet and ankles wet and got laryngitis very badly and was in bed all day Sunday and Monday;" that she notified Mr. Jones, the Republican precinct captain, Monday afternoon about 6:30 o'clock that she would not be able to serve at the election; that she did not notify the Board of Election Commissioners because it was always the custom to notify the precinct captain, and that Mr. Jones stated he would take care of calling the Election Commissioners' office; that nobody asked her not to serve; that the reason she did not serve was that she had laryngitis and could not speak; that the polling place was "cold and draughty"; that there were some 500 registered voters in the precinct and some transients in rooming houses.

Counsel for petitioner then stated to the Court that Mrs. Brown, who was one of the qualified clerks of election but who did not appear, failed to do so because she was ill, and the Court when so informed said he was satisfied that the reason given was a valid one.

Mr. Grace, one of the other qualified judges, as above stated, was removed by the Election Commissioners at about 4:30 in the afternoon on the day before the election because he did not live in the precinct.

William L. Hahn, called by the Court, testified that he was a qualified Republican clerk of the precinct in question but did not serve on April 2nd "because of my job, the election coming at the busy time of the month. I am an accountant. *** The only reason I did not serve was that I might jeopardize my job;" that he notified the precinct captain Sunday afternoon prior to the election, as he understood this was the customary method; that no one approached him and told him not to serve; that he had served at one prior election; that William R. Hahn was his son and lived at the same address with his father, - "There should be three Hahns in the register;" that he did not vote at the election in question; that he knew respondents Foley and Sloan, the latter being one of the clerks, but that he did not know whether Sloan knew witness.

Jack Clifford, called by respondents, testified that he was a police officer assigned to the precinct on the day of election; that he arrived there a few minutes before six o'clock and stayed until the polling place closed in the evening; that when he arrived at the polling place Mrs. Dahlman was there; that during the day there was lots of challenging; that he did not see anything wrong; at times people were lined up seeking to vote; that Mrs. Dahlman did a great deal of challenging, and that the Board, after satisfying itself that the persons were qualified, allowed them to vote; that Mrs. Dahlman told him a lot of people who were voting were not qualified; that he told her to find out who they were and he would look them up; that he did not notice anything unusual or illegal; that he did not know any members of the Board, nor any

voters; that neither Mrs. Dahlman nor anyone else complained to him about anyone in particular attempting to vote who was not entitled to; that respondent Matthiesen's duty was to pass out the ballots; that when a person came to vote Matthiesen would call out the name and the other judges would look at the register and that the person would then vote; sometimes when the voter was challenged by Mrs. Dahlman the judges would then decide whether to permit the person to vote.

Otto A. Wuffum, called by the petitioners, gave his address on the North side of Chicago, and testified he was sent to the precinct in question, as a watcher, by the Board of Election Commissioners, arriving there about seven o'clock in the morning; that when he arrived there was a lady challenging some of the voters, and he asked the judges if the challengers and watchers had credentials, "and they didn't seem to know what it was all about"; that Matthiesen and Foley were handling the registers and the clerks were writing in the poll books; "There was some question as to whether or not the judges were required to have the challenged person make out an affidavit, and the judges requested information from me. I referred them to the section in the 'blue book' that covers the point. I believe it is section 5, article 4. The Board asked no other questions except as to challenging;" that during his stay of all day he did not observe anything that in his opinion was illegal or unusual, except that there was much confusion on account of Mrs. Dahlman challenging; that when a voter came in who was challenged by Mrs. Dahlman, Matthiesen would wait until the other two judges checked the registers, and on several occasions asked the voter where he registered the last time; that "I submitted a report to the Election Commissioners."

Morris Frank, called by respondents, testified that his place of business was at 1353 East 47th street; that the election

in question was held in his shoe store; that he was present nearly all day; that he knew a man named Glenn Parks who was one of his customers and lived on Lake Park avenue; that he did shoe repairing and hat cleaning work for him; that he did not see Glenn Parks at the polling place on election day.

At the conclusion of the witnesses' testimony the Court found the respondents Sloan and Stephens not guilty. Sloan was then called by respondents and testified he was a brother of Margaret Sloan, whose name appeared on the poll book, and that she and witness lived for more than two years at 4723 Kenwood avenue; that he wrote this address down; that when she appeared to vote she said her address was 1357 East 47th street and that he wrote both addresses and struck out the wrong one; that he did not know Matthiesen before election day and that Matthiesen made no entries in any of the books.

Two witnesses were called and testified, one that he had known respondent Wolf for 25 years and that his reputation for honesty and integrity was good; the other testified he had known respondent Foley for about 25 years and that his reputation for honesty and integrity was good.

Respondent Matthiesen testified that he went to the polling place about five minutes to six o'clock of the morning of election to vote and was asked by Foley to act as a judge of election; there were some 15 or 20 people then waiting to vote; that Mrs. Dahlman caused a good deal of commotion by challenging persons who came to vote; that after about half an hour he called up the Election Commissioners' office and asked for advice and about a half hour thereafter Mr. Wuffum came and said he was from the Election Commissioners' office; that the latter stayed there all day; that nobody asked him to act as judge until he appeared at the polling place to vote and that he gave out the ballots

when the other two judges stated the person was registered; that on April 30th, after the election, he went to the Election Commissioners' office and signed a written statement as to what had taken place on election day.

Counsel for respondents then introduced two exhibits showing the names of 41 persons as they appeared in the registers and which were erased by drawing lines through the names instead of under them. These exhibits show the names of the persons and the line on the register on which they appear. This is substantially all the evidence in the record.

Respondents contend that to warrant the Court in finding them guilty, the law requires "most convincing evidence of the truth of the charge" and that the evidence not only is not convincing but, on the contrary, the finding of the Court is against the manifest weight of the evidence; that the evidence all shows there was no intent on the part of the respondents to act fraudulently or dishonestly in performing their duties as election officials, but the most that can be said against them is that they made some excusable mistakes.

In People ex rel. Rusch v. Kotwas, 275 Ill. App. 406, which was a case where charges were made against election officials similar to the charge in the instant case, we said (p. 412): "In a contempt case of this kind, we think the petitioner is not required to prove the guilt of respondents beyond a reasonable doubt, but is required to produce 'most convincing evidence of the truth of the charge' before the respondents could be found guilty, the proceeding being quasi criminal. Oehler v. Levy, 168 Ill. App. 41."

The trial Judge, in deciding the case, said, among other things: "This was not an attempt to steal votes. This was what we would call an attempt to stuff the ballot box, if anything at

all. The significant thing about this particular precinct was the absence of duly appointed officials on the day of the election. The presence of the two men available, one who left his place of employment at one o'clock that night to be available at six in the morning without sleep, and the other one who had appeared at the polling place five minutes before six; things occurred in that polling place that should not have happened there. No doubt some of it was provoked by the actions of the challenger. No official can assume the position that he does not know the law because every opportunity is given him, and they testified themselves, we sent a man down from the election commissioners' office to assist them, to help them out, and we have written books of instructions, we have written letters of instructions and warnings to the officials, and what else can we do for them, try to help every one who is called to serve, give him instructions so that he may know his position when he is serving. If he is in need of help we will do everything in our power to assist him."

We have above set forth in considerable detail the evidence, and while some unfavorable inferences might legitimately be drawn from the fact that none of the old Board except Foley was present at the opening of the polls, and from the circumstances under which some of the new persons appeared and were sworn in, yet we are of opinion that the explanation given by the new officials, and by some of the old ones called by the Court, ought not to be ignored.

Donald Grace, one of the clerks, had been removed about 4:30 o'clock on the afternoon before the election by the Election Commissioners because he was not then living in the precinct; Mrs. Rissi, the Republican clerk, testified that she got her feet wet in assisting Mrs. Dahlman canvass part of the precinct on

Saturday afternoon before the election and was confined to her bed with laryngitis Sunday and Monday, and that she notified the Republican precinct captain Monday afternoon that she would not be able to serve; that this was the custom on former occasions.

It was conceded that Mrs. Brown, another judge of the old Board, was unable to serve on account of her physical condition. Hahn, the other clerk, testified that he was employed as an accountant, and the only reason he did not work was that he was afraid he might jeopardize his job and that he notified the precinct captain on Sunday afternoon before the election that he would be unable to serve. And the evidence also is that respondent Foley and the persons sworn in by him were unacquainted prior to that time.

We think the evidence that five persons whose names had been erased were allowed to vote, shows that the judges permitted them to vote through an excusable mistake. Respondent Wolf had never before acted as judge of election. He did not know what the lines under the names meant but understood that the names appearing on the register through which lines were drawn (and there were 41 of such names) were the names of persons who were not entitled to vote, and there is no contention that any of such 41 persons voted. Matthiesen had never before acted as a judge of election. He had nothing to do with the registers. His work was at the ballot box giving ballots to persons when Foley and Wolf advised him they were properly registered. The testimony shows the judges consulted together to see that a person presenting himself was qualified before he was given the ballot by Matthiesen; obviously, Matthiesen had to do this; this was the proper way for him to act. Foley had acted as a judge of election on two prior occasions - one in the fall election of 1934, and in the primary election in February, 1935. He testified that he understood a person's name was scratched from

the register when a line was drawn through it and not under it, and, as stated, there are 41 names scratched from the register by drawing a line through them and not under them. All the witnesses agree that there was considerable confusion on account of the great number of challenges made by Mrs. Dahlman. No witness was asked how the 41 names came to be scratched by drawing the line through instead of under the names.

The three persons who were permitted to vote and who were registered in the precinct, but who had moved after their registration to a new address within the precinct, were permitted to vote without requiring affidavits. Matthiesen and Mrs. Dahlman each testified that shortly after the polls opened and Mrs. Dahlman had challenged a number of persons, they called up the Election Commissioners' office for instructions and they sent Mr. Wuffum to the polling place, where he arrived at about seven o'clock in the morning. He testified the judges asked him for information concerning making affidavits where voters were challenged. But instead of telling them that affidavits were required in such cases, all he did, as he himself testified, was to refer them to a section in the "blue book" which he said covered the point. Obviously, this was of little or no assistance. The three persons were duly qualified to cast their votes and there was but a mere technical violation of the law in not requiring them to make affidavits, which did not affect the result. Blattner v. Dietz, 311 Ill. 445; Siedschlag v. May, 363 Ill., 538.

The order also finds that there were eight persons who voted twice (their names appearing twice on the poll books) whose names appeared but once on the register. One of these names is Todd O. Maynard, but Mr. Fordhan, who was connected with the Election Commissioners' office, as above stated, testified: "Both Todd O. Maynard and Thomas Maynard appear in the register as eligible to vote and that the registers show that they both voted

at the election." Moreover, the evidence shows that counsel for both parties, during an adjournment of the hearing (the case having been on hearing a number of times) examined the records and in response to a question by the court it was agreed by counsel that it appeared from the poll books that six persons had been permitted to vote twice, one of whom was probably Maynard. Foley testified, "When a man came in to vote whose name appeared as having been voted, the judges refused to let him vote." There were about 500 registered voters, and although Mrs. Dahlman challenged about 25% of the persons who appeared, nowhere does she testify that she challenged a voter on account of his having previously voted.

When counsel for respondents announced that he would call character witnesses, counsel for petitioner said he would stipulate as to the good character of the respondents, but counsel for respondents then called two character witnesses and the testimony was that Wolf and Foley, whom witnesses had known for 25 years, were men of good reputation for honesty and integrity. Foley testified he had never been in trouble before and had never been arrested, and there is no evidence to the contrary.

From a careful consideration of all the evidence, we are of opinion that the evidence is not of that convincing character required by the law before one can be found guilty of a charge of contempt, as in the instant case. But in any view of the case, we are clear that Matthiesen should have been discharged, and that the six months imprisonment as against Foley and Wolf is greatly excessive.

In People ex rel. Rusch v. Greenzeit, 277 Ill. App. 479-487, it is said: "Under section 13 [par. 267, chapter 46, Illinois State Bar Stats. 1935] the court undoubtedly has the power, in a proper case, to punish an election official for carelessness in the performance of his duties." In view of this holding, we

think the facts warrant a small fine against Wolf, such as a day's pay he received, which would be sufficient punishment, and a slightly larger fine is all that the law warrants as against Foley. We would enter such a judgment against Wolf and Foley in this court, but probably have not that power. O'Brien v. Int. Ladies' Garment Workers' Union, 214 Ill. App. 46; same case reported as Ash-Madden-Rae Co. v. Internat. Union, 290 Ill. 301.

The judgment of the County court of Cook county as to respondent Matthiesen is reversed; and as to respondents Wolf and Foley the judgment is reversed and the cause remanded.

JUDGMENT REVERSED AS TO MATTHIESEN;

REVERSED AND REMANDED AS TO WOLF AND FOLEY.

Matchett, P. J. dissents. (See next page).

McSurely, J., concurs.

38551 MR. PRESIDING JUSTICE MATCHETT DISSENTING.

I have not been able to agree with my brethren that this record shows only unintentional wrongdoing. Foley, in particular, had experience, and his cross examination disclosed that he knew a line drawn under the name appearing on the register indicated that such name was eliminated and that the person did not have a right to vote. Such persons were permitted to vote, notwithstanding. At least six persons were permitted to vote twice. The oath and affidavit envelope of this precinct returned to the election commissioners, when opened in court, was found to contain no affidavits, although three persons who voted had, since last registration, moved within the precinct. The absence of the duly chosen officials at the opening of the polls placed upon Foley the duty of obtaining and swearing in helpers. He chose Matthiesen and Wolf, and they were subservient. These respondents were not so stupid as they pretend. I think the punishment to be inflicted ought to be left to the trial Judge who saw and heard the witnesses.

38818

THE PEOPLE OF STATE OF ILLINOIS, ex rel. Alice Hoffman, Appellee,

vs.

JOHN JOSEPH COURTS, Appellant.

APPEAL FROM MUNICIPAL COURT OF CHICAGO.

607

286 I.A. 616[1]

MR. JUSTICE O'CONNOR DELIVERED THE OPINION OF THE COURT.

May 29, 1935, Alice Hoffman, an unmarried woman, filed a complaint against defendant, Dr. Joseph Courts, charging that on May 8, 1935, she was delivered of a male child and that Courts was its father. November 6, 1935, there was a trial before the court without ajury; the court found that defendant was the father of the child and he was adjudged to pay $1100 in installments for its support, maintenance and education, in accordance with the statute. To reverse the judgment defendant, Courts, appeals.

Pursuant to an order of court, a bill of particulars was filed in which it was stated the conception of the child took place between July 20, 1934, and August 20, 1934.

The record discloses that defendant is a dentist and had been practicing his profession in Chicago for a little over three years. In January, 1934, Alice Hoffman, an unmarried woman about 19 years of age, became a patient of defendant and the dental work continued over a number of months. The doctor was unmarried. She testified that she had been introduced to him in 1933; that in January, 1934, she was at defendant's office for some dental work and he then gave her a glass of water which made her drowsy, and thereafter defendant had sexual relations with her; that after this time she called two or three times a week at his office for dental work and on these occasions the sexual relations were repeated; that after July 20, 1934, she "missed her regular menstrual period and was scared about it," and told defendant she thought she was

pregnant; that he told her not to worry, that he would give her some pills, and asked her to go and see Dr. Redman, and while she was in defendant's office he called a telephone number, talked to Dr. Redman and made an appointment for her to call and see the doctor; that some time afterward, the first part of September, defendant gave her some brown pills and told her to take them and she would get rid of the baby; that she took the pills but they had no effect and she told defendant of this; that thereafter she often talked about her condition to defendant during September, November, December, January and February, and he asked her why she didn't go to see the two doctors he had named; that one of the doctors called her on the telephone in April, 1935, and asked her to come down, stating that "John (defendant) called me about your condition;" that she went to the doctor's office and while there the doctor called defendant on the telephone, and the doctor told her that defendant said he would not do anything about the matter; that May 8, 1935, the baby was born; that she talked to defendant about it and he told her to keep quiet and he would marry her. The bottle of pills which she said she had received from defendant was offered and received in evidence.

The evidence further shows that Alice Hoffman lived at home with her parents, not far from defendant's dental office. The appointments made with defendant by relatrix were usually at about 11 o'clock at his office, and the evidence shows that on a number of occasions after relatrix had been to defendant's office he walked with her on her way back home. Relatrix testified she had never had any relations with any other man.

Martha Hoffman, mother of relatrix, testified she had known defendant for some time before January, 1934, and that he had done dental work for her, starting in December, 1933; that May 8, 1935, a baby was born to her daughter while on the way to the hospital;

that she afterward went to see defendant at his office and wanted him to go to the hospital to see the baby and he said he did not have any time - "So he pulled out the marriage license, he is now married;" that he said, "What are you going to do about it?" and he further said that if Alice had listened to him and had gone to Dr. Redman for an abortion neither of them would be in difficulty; that about five days later she again went to his office and asked him to go to see the mother of the baby, that her lungs were infected; that he refused to go, and said that relatrix had called him up from the hospital and that there was nothing wrong with her lungs.

Dr. Poborsky testified that he was a physician and surgeon, practicing in Chicago for 10½ years; that he knew Alice for three or four years and had treated her family; that the latter part of April, 1935, when he was in his office his telephone rang and he answered the call; that the person talking said he was Dr. Courts, that he was calling "in return of a conversation he had with a friend of his by the name of Dr. Redman whom I had spoken to concerning Alice Hoffman;" that in that conversation the witness told the person who said he was Dr. Courts that Alice Hoffman was pregnant - about ready to have a baby - and that she claimed Courts was the father; that Courts asked him when he thought the baby would be born and he replied in two or three weeks; that he further asked the witness what could be done, and witness replied that he could marry the girl, send her to a hospital, or have the baby sent for adoption out of town; that Courts said he would call back in a day or two when he had decided what to do. The witness further testified that two or three days later his office telephone rang, he answered the call, and the voice again said he was Dr. Courts; that he had thought over the matter seriously and had decided to forget about it; that he recognized the voice as that of the same person to whom he had

talked a few days before; that he took care of Alice Hoffman when the baby was born on May 8th.

On cross examination Dr. Poborsky testified that he had never met Dr. Courts prior to the telephone conversation and had never seen him; that he had been a physician for the Hoffman family for two or three years; that he was not paid any money for delivering the baby; that he did not examine Alice Hoffman prior to the telephone conversation; that he saw her in person "at my doorstep about two weeks before I delivered her." On motion of counsel for defendant the court struck out the two telephone conversations above mentioned. Counsel for the People objected to this and said he would bring in some authorities at a later date, and it seems to be conceded that no authorities were subsequently submitted and nothing further was done in reference to the matter.

Defendant testified, denying any improper relations with the relatrix. He further testified that he met her about December of 1933; that she came to his office for dental work in January or February, 1934, and that he continued to do work for her for a number of months thereafter. He then identified a book which he kept, showing the appointments with his patients, and it was offered and received in evidence, but is not in the abstract or the record. He further testified that on occasions he gave her pills for the purpose of relieving pain which was the result of the dental work; that he did not give her pills for any other purpose; that he never saw the pills which relatrix produced and had not given them to her; that she never talked to him of being pregnant; that he did not tell her to go to see Dr. Redman or Dr. Poborsky; that he did not call Dr. Redman on the telephone in her presence; that he never called Dr. Poborsky; that he was married June 1,1935; that he had one or more conversations with Mrs. Hoffman, mother of Alice, in May, 1935; that he talked to her out in the hall adjoining

his office; that the mother then asked him what he had done to her daughter and he asked her what she was talking about; that the mother replied that Alice had a baby and accused him of being the father, and that he denied it; that the mother than wanted him to go to the haspital and he refused, saying he was too busy; that about five or six days afterward he had another conversation with the mother, and she asked him what he intended to do, and why he did not marry the girl, "and I says, 'Why should I marry the girl?' and she started laughing and says, 'The baby looks like you;'" that she then said they had a rich aunt and were going to employ a good lawyer and ruin him; that the mother then said the daughter was "pretty sick" and they were liable to lose her; that defendant then said, "Well, she can't be very sick because she just called from the hospital and asked me to come down and see her;" that thereupon the mother left; that at the time in question he lived about a block from the Hoffmans and that during the time he was treating Alice he walked home with her about ten times.

Dr. Redman, called by defendant, testified and denied that defendant had called him on the telephone and asked him to perform an abortion on Alice Hoffman. He further testified that he did give defendant some pills but they "were not exactly like these." (Being the pills produced by relatrix, as above mentioned.)

There is other evidence in the record, but we think it would serve no useful purpose to discuss it further. The question whether the defendant was the father of the child was one of fact for the court. He found against the defendant, and upon a consideration of all the evidence in the record, we are unable to say that the finding is against the manifest weight of the evidence.

Defendant further contends that the court erred in admitting evidence over his objection, (1) that the pills which the relatrix testified defendant gave her "to get rid of the baby" should have

been excluded because there was no analysis of their contents. We think there is no merit in this contention. There is evidence to the effect that defendant had been intimate with relatrix on a number of occasions; that she told him she was pregnant; that he told her he would see a doctor and give her some pills, and that later he did give her the pills which were offered in evidence. This would render them clearly admissible regardless of what the pills contained. The weight to be given was, of course, for the court to determine. (2) it is said that the court erred in permitting the two telephone conversations between Dr. Poborsky and the person who had called, because Dr. Poborsky did not know the voice of the person calling. Whether this testimony, taken in connection with all the evidence in the case, was admissible we do not pass upon because the court struck out the two conversations. (3) That the court erred in admitting receipts given by defendant to relatrix for payments made between "February 17, 1934, May 31, 1934, and other irrelevant dates." And the contention seems to be that these receipts should have been excluded because the bill of particulars, filed by the relatrix, specified that the "conception of the child took place between July 20, 1934, and August 20, 1934." And that no receipts were admissible nor testimony as to acts of intimacy between the parties that did not occur between these two last mentioned dates. There is no merit in this contention. The evidence was admissible to show the relation of the parties from January, 1934. The trial Judge should have been apprized of all the facts and not limited to the period between July 20 and August 20, 1934, because evidence of such prior relationship might or might not throw light on the question whether there had been illegitimate relations between the two dates.

The judgment of the Municipal court of Chicago is affirmed.

JUDGMENT AFFIRMED.

Matchett, P. J., and McSurely, J., concur.

38839

RICHARD NEWTON, Administrator of the Estate of Josephine Newton, Deceased,
Appellee,

vs.

METROPOLITAN LIFE INSURANCE COMPANY, a Corporation,
Appellant.

APPEAL FROM MUNICIPAL COURT OF CHICAGO.

286 I.A. 616[2]

MR. JUSTICE O'CONNOR DELIVERED THE OPINION OF THE COURT.

Richard Newton, as administrator of the estate of Josephine Newton, deceased, brought two suits against the Metropolitan Life Insurance Company on two policies, one for $800 and the other for $468, issued to Josephine Newton, who had been his wife but was divorced from him about a year before the policies were issued. The cases were tried separately and plaintiff had a verdict and judgment in each case. The defendant appealed to this court where the judgments were reversed and the causes remanded. The cases are numbered 37044 and 37045. Pursuant to our suggestion, the cases were consolidated, again tried, and there was a verdict and judgment in plaintiff's favor for the amount of the two policies, $1592.47, and defendant appeals.

The facts are set forth in the two opinions filed by this court, and the evidence being substantially the same except as will be hereinafter noted, we will not analyze the facts in detail.

The policy for $468 is dated January 9, 1928, and the one for $800 is dated December 1, 1928. The premium on the latter policy was payable monthly and on the former weekly. All premiums were paid to and including March, 1930, and it is admitted that both policies had lapsed for non-payment of dues.

The evidence shows that the parties were divorced in Chicago in 1927, and thereupon Josephine Newton took up her residence in Toledo, Ohio, living with several of her sisters. Her former

husband remained in Chicago. The two policies were issued in Toledo to her, payable to her estate. September 17, 1930, Josephine Newton was taken to a hospital in Toledo and operated on the next day for gallstones. She died September 29, 1930. September 19th Newton, with Mrs. Ross, Josephine Newton's sister, who lived with her in Toledo, called to see Josephine at the hospital, he having driven from Chicago the day before. The next day about noon Newton and Mrs. Ross called to see William Davis, an agent of the defendant in Toledo, who had formerly collected premiums from Josephine Newton on the two policies, but some months prior to this date the territory in which Josephine and her sister lived in Toledo had been turned over to another agent of defendant. Davis was not at home and they called again at about six o'clock that evening.

Davis testified that Mrs. Ross represented herself to be Mrs. Newton and told him she wanted to reinstate the two policies, which had lapsed, by paying all back premiums; that thereupon he figured out the amount of back premiums which was about $22, and that amount was paid, apparently by ~~Newman,~~ Newton, Davis giving them a receipt, which is in evidence. In the receipt it was stated that the money was tendered to revive the policies which had lapsed, "No obligation under such POLICY is incurred by said Company by reason of such tender. If such application is approved by said Company, said POLICY will be reinstated and placed in full force, otherwise the sum so tendered will be returned." At the time Mrs. Ross signed an application for the revival of the policies by writing the name Josephine Newton. This document states that the policies, having lapsed for non-payment of premium, the undersigned applied for revival of the policies, "and to induce the Metropolitan Life Insurance Company to revive same, *** represents and declares" that Josephine Newton, the husband remained in Chicago. The two policies were issued to Toledo to her, payable to her estate, September 17, 1930. Josephine Newton was taken to a hospital in Toledo and operated on the next day for gallstones. She died September 29, 1930. September 19th Newton, with Mrs. Ross, Josephine Newton's sister, who lived with her in Toledo, called to see Josephine at the hospital, he having driven from Chicago the day before. The next day about noon Newton and Mrs. Ross called to see William Davis, an agent of the defendant in Toledo, who had formerly collected premiums from Josephine Newton on the two policies, but some months prior to this date the territory in which Josephine and her sister lived in Toledo had been turned over to another agent of defendant. Davis was not at home and they called again at about six o'clock that evening.

Davis testified that Mrs. Ross represented herself to be Mrs. Newton and told him she wanted to reinstate the two policies, which had lapsed, by paying all back premiums; that thereupon he figured out the amount of back premiums which was about $22, and that amount was paid, apparently by ~~Newton~~ Ross, Davis giving them a receipt, which is in evidence. In the receipt it was stated that the money was tendered to revive the policies which had lapsed, "No obligation under such POLICY is incurred by said Company by reason of such tender. If such application is approved by said Company, said POLICY will be reinstated and placed in full force; otherwise the sum so tendered will be returned." At the time Mrs. Ross signed an application for the revival of the policies by writing the name Josephine Newton. This document states that the policies, having lapsed for non-payment of premium, the undersigned applied for revival of the policies, "and to induce the Metropolitan Life Insurance Company to revive same, *** represents and declares" that Josephine Newton, the insured, had not been afflicted with any disease, met with accident or consulted any physician since the policy was issued "and the undersigned expressly agrees that said Company, because of this application, incurs no liability until said Company shall have approved this application for revival."

Davis further testified that neither Mrs. Ross nor Newton told him at that time Josephine was in the hospital, and that he did not know anything about it until some few days later; that after they left he became suspicious and on Monday morning following he called on Mrs. Ross at her home and had a conversation with her. Objection was made by plaintiff's counsel to witness stating the conversation because plaintiff was not present, which objection the court erroneously sustained. Obviously, the conversation was entirely proper and should have been admitted. Afterward, in rebuttal, defendant again called Davis, who testified he had a conversation with Mrs. Ross at her home September 22, in Toledo (the same conversation.) Thereupon counsel for plaintiff objecting, said, "He testified he had a conversation. It is not in rebuttal." What was said should have been admitted. Thereupon, out of the presence of the jury, counsel for defendant offered to prove that Mrs. Ross admitted she had impersonated her sister Josephine at Davis's home the Saturday evening before; that Davis then said she should not have done that, and he offered to return the premium ($21.87), but Mrs. Ross said that Newton had returned to Chicago.

Mrs. Ross and Newton testified, contradicting Davis's testimony as to what took place on the evening in question. He testified that he lived in Chicago; that he and his wife were divorced in 1927; that there were three children aged 9, 11 and 16, and apparently they lived with their mother in Toledo; that he arrived in Toledo on September 18th; at that time his former wife, Mrs.

insured, had not been afflicted with any disease, met with accident or consulted any physician since the policy was issued "and the undersigned expressly agrees that said Company, because of this application, incurs no liability until said Company shall have approved this application for revival."

Davis further testified that neither Mrs. Ross nor Newton told him at that time Josephine was in the hospital, and that he did not know anything about it until some few days later; that after they left he became suspicious and on Monday morning following he called on Mrs. Ross at her home and had a conversation with her. Objection was made by plaintiff's counsel to witness stating the conversation because plaintiff was not present, which objection the court erroneously sustained. Obviously, the conversation was entirely proper and should have been admitted. Afterward, in rebuttal, defendant again called Davis, who testified he had a conversation with Mrs. Ross at her home September 22, in Toledo (the same conversation.) Thereupon counsel for plaintiff objecting, said, "He testified he had a conversation. It is not in rebuttal." What was said should have been admitted. Thereupon, out of the presence of the jury, counsel for defendant offered to prove that Mrs. Ross admitted she had impersonated her sister Josephine at Davis's home the Saturday evening before; that Davis then said she should not have done that, and he offered to return the premium ($21.97), but Mrs. Ross said that Newton had returned to Chicago.

Mrs. Ross and Newton testified, contradicting Davis's testimony as to what took place on the evening in question. He testified that he lived in Chicago; that he and his wife were divorced in 1927; that there were three children aged 9, 11 and 16, and apparently they lived with their mother in Toledo; that he arrived in Toledo on September 13th; at that time his former wife, Mrs.

Newton, was in the hospital; that he saw her the next day at the hospital; that he and Mrs. Ross went to see Davis at the latter's home; that Mrs. Ross introduced him as her brother-in-law and stated she wanted to reinstate her sister's policies. "Mr. Davis asked where Mrs. Newton was and I said that she was in the hospital, sick. He says, 'Well, I hope she will get all right in a few days;'" that he then asked how much the back premiums amounted to and was told one was $9.45 and the other $12.42; that he paid the amount; that he gave Mr. Davis his Chicago address and left the next day, September 20th, which was Sunday, for Chicago; that on October 8th following he went to defendant's insurance office at 47th street and Wabash avenue, in Chicago, and talked with a Mr. Harrington, and told him he wanted to make proof of the death of Josephine Newton; that proof of death was made out on the blank form, filled out by the agent, and signed by Newton; that it was dated October 3, 1930, states that the cause of death was "Operation, Gallstone;" that at that time Harrington told him to come back in about 10 days or two weeks; that he later went back and on October 28th he again saw Harrington at defendant's Chicago office, who advised him that the company refused to pay.

Mrs. Ross, who was called in rebuttal (she was not called by plaintiff when putting in its case in chief), denied that she had impersonated her sister; she testified, "I told him (Davis) Mr. Newton was Josephine's husband, my brother-in-law from Chicago;" that he had collected insurance premiums from her for 4 or 5 years; that he also collected from her sister, Josephine Newton; that Davis had not been at her home for some time before Josephine went to the hospital; that she had never been to Davis's home before; that she did not impersonate her sister.

Mrs. Davis, wife of defendant's agent in Toledo, testified, corroborating her husband's testimony as to what took place at their home when Mrs. Ross and Newton called.

Newton, was in the hospital; that he saw her the next day at the hospital; that he and Mrs. Ross went to see Davis at the latter's home; that Mrs. Ross introduced him as her brother-in-law and stated she wanted to reinstate her sister's policies. "Mr. Davis asked where Mrs. Newton was and I said that she was in the hospital, sick. He says, 'Well, I hope she will get all right in a few days;'" that he then asked how much the back premiums amounted to and was told one was $9.45 and the other $12.42; that he paid the amount; that he gave Mr. Davis his Chicago address and left the next day, September 20th, which was Sunday, for Chicago; that on October 8th following he went to defendant's insurance office at 47th street and Wabash avenue, in Chicago, and talked with a Mr. Harrington, and told him he wanted to make proof of the death of Josephine Newton; that proof of death was made out on the blank form, filled out by the agent, and signed by Newton; that it was dated October 3, 1930, states that the cause of death was "Operation, Gallstone;" that at that time Harrington told him to come back in about 10 days or two weeks; that he later went back and on October 28th he again saw Harrington at defendant's Chicago office, who advised him that the company refused to pay.

Mrs. Ross, who was called in rebuttal (she was not called by plaintiff when putting in its case in chief), denied that she had impersonated her sister; she testified, "I told him [Davis] Mr. Newton was Josephine's husband, my brother-in-law from Chicago;" that he had collected insurance premiums from her for 4 or 5 years; that he also collected from her sister, Josephine Newton; that Davis had not been at her home for some time before Josephine went to the hospital; that she had never been to Davis's home before; that she did not impersonate her sister.

Mrs. Davis, wife of defendant's agent in Toledo, testified, corroborating her husband's testimony as to what took place at their home when Mrs. Ross and Newton called.

Defendant also called William H. Bell, who did not testify on the former trial. He was agent for defendant company with offices in Toledo, but was not connected with defendant at the time he testified. He testified he knew Josephine Newton and Mrs. Ross, her sister; that Saturday morning, September 20th, Mrs. Ross and Newton called at his office and there was a conversation at that time; that Mrs. Ross stated they wanted to reinstate her sister Josephine's two policies; that he asked Mrs. Ross how Josephine was and she replied, "She is all right." I says, "Well, before I can accept any money I have got to see her;" that they then left and never came back. This was denied by Newton and Mrs. Ross who said they did not call upon Bell.

There is other evidence in the record, but we think it obvious that no recovery can be had. On the former appeal to this court we said: "If Davis' testimony was true there was obviously a fraud attempted by the posing of Mrs. Ross as the insured, Josephine Newton. In such a case plaintiff could not recover. ***

"Plaintiff in his brief repeatedly asserts that Davis and defendant knew all the facts as to the insured's physical condition. The record before us does not support this. At the time Mrs. Ross interviewed Davis, Josephine Newton had undergone a major operation threatening her life, which, with a failing heart, resulted in her death within a few days. Mrs. Ross, according to her testimony, told Davis only that 'Mrs. Newton is sick in bed.' This is far from imparting to Davis all the facts as to the condition of the insured. It is inconceivable that if defendant had known that the insured was in fact on her death bed that the request for revival of the policy would have been approved." On the record before us, Newton, in response to a question asked by Davis as to where Mrs. Newton was, replied "that she was in the hospital, sick." As stated in our former

Defendant also called William H. Bell, who did not testify on the former trial. He was agent for defendant company with offices in Toledo, but was not connected with defendant at the time he testified. He testified he knew Josephine Newton and Mrs. Ross, her sister; that Saturday morning, September 30th, Mrs. Ross and Newton called at his office and there was a conversation at that time; that Mrs. Ross stated they wanted to reinstate her sister Josephine's two policies; that he asked Mrs. Ross how Josephine was and she replied, "She is all right." I says, "Well, before I can accept any money I have got to see her;" that they then left and never came back. This was denied by Newton and Mrs. Ross who said they did not call upon Bell.

There is other evidence in the record, but we think it obvious that no recovery can be had. On the former appeal to this court we said: "If Davis' testimony was true there was obviously a fraud attempted by the posing of Mrs. Ross as the insured, Josephine Newton. In such a case plaintiff could not recover. ***

"Plaintiff in his brief repeatedly asserts that Davis and defendant knew all the facts as to the insured's physical condition. The record before us does not support this. At the time Mrs. Ross interviewed Davis, Josephine Newton had undergone a major operation threatening her life, which, with a failing heart, resulted in her death within a few days. Mrs. Ross, according to her testimony, told Davis only that 'Mrs. Newton is sick in bed.' This is far from imparting to Davis all the facts as to the condition of the insured. It is inconceivable that if defendant had known that the insured was in fact on her death bed that the request for revival of the policy would have been approved." On the record before us, Newton, in response to a question asked by Davis as to where Mrs. Newton was, replied "that she was in the hospital, sick." As stated in our former opinion, "This is far from imparting to Davis all the facts as to the condition of the insured."

But counsel for plaintiff contends that there was a waiver and that the policies were revived because all of the facts as to the condition of Josephine, the insured, were disclosed to the agent Davis, and the premium having been paid on September 20th and retained by defendant until October 28th, defendant is estopped to contend that the policies were not revived and that in any event, the question was for the jury. And further, since three juries found in favor of plaintiff, the judgment ought not to be disturbed. If the trials had been without serious error, there would be much force in this contention. But we held in our former opinions that there was not a proper trial, and in the instant case a great deal of competent evidence was erroneously excluded. And the jury was erroneously instructed on the theory that Davis was authorized to reinstate the policies, which is contrary to the evidence.

We think it obvious that no fair man could say that Davis, defendant's agent, knew at the time Newton and Mrs. Ross called at his home on the evening of September 20th, that Josephine Newton had, two days before, undergone a major operation and was confined in the hospital, and that if he did so know, he would be perpetrating a fraud on the Insurance company in reviving the policies. In any view of the evidence, we think it clear that no judgment could stand except a judgment in favor of the defendant.

Moreover, we are of opinion that the court should have directed a verdict in defendant's favor as requested. The written documents, the receipt and the revival application above mentioned, which are not, and cannot be, the subject matter of dispute, expressly show that Mrs. Ross and Newton were applying to defendant Insurance company to have the two policies revived, and that the policies would not be revived until the application was approved opinion, "This is far from imparting to Davis all the facts as to the condition of the insured."

But counsel for plaintiff contends that there was a waiver and that the policies were revived because all of the facts as to the condition of Josephine, the insured, were disclosed to the agent Davis, and the premium having been paid on September 20th and retained by defendant until October 28th, defendant is estopped to contend that the policies were not revived and that in any event, the question was for the jury. And further, since three juries found in favor of plaintiff, the judgment ought not to be disturbed. If the trials had been without serious error, there would be much force in this contention. But we held in our former opinions that there was not a proper trial, and in the instant case a great deal of competent evidence was erroneously excluded. And the jury was erroneously instructed on the theory that Davis was authorized to reinstate the policies, which is contrary to the evidence.

We think it obvious that no fair man could say that Davis, defendant's agent, knew at the time Newton and Mrs. Ross called at his home on the evening of September 20th, that Josephine Newton had, two days before, undergone a major operation and was confined in the hospital, and that if he did so know, he would be perpetrating a fraud on the insurance company in reviving the policies. In any view of the evidence, we think it clear that no judgment could stand except a judgment in favor of the defendant.

Moreover, we are of opinion that the court should have directed a verdict in defendant's favor as requested. The written documents, the receipt and the revival application above mentioned, which are not, and cannot be, the subject matter of dispute, expressly show that Mrs. Ross and Newton were applying to defendant insurance company to have the two policies revived, and that the policies would not be revived until the application was approved by the company. Miller v. Met. Life Ins. Co., 286 N. Y. Supp. 126. In that case, the court said (p. 127): "Action upon an accident policy for double indemnity based on the theory that an expired policy had been reinstated by the company's acceptance of the premium after the expiration of the period of grace. The documentary evidence disclosed that the payment was made in connection with an application for reinstatement, signed by the deceased, which expressly provided that the policy was not to be deemed reinstated until the application had been favorably acted upon by the home office, and there was no proof of such favorable action." The court there held that a summary judgment should have been entered in favor of the insurance company.

The judgment of the Municipal court of Chicago is reversed, but since no recovery can be had, the cause will not be remanded.

JUDGMENT REVERSED.

Matchett, P. J., dissents. (See next page.)

McSurely, J., concurs.

by the company. Miller v. Met. Life Ins. Co., 236 N. Y. Supp. 126. In that case, the court said (p. 127): "Action upon an accident policy for double indemnity based on the theory that an expired policy had been reinstated by the company's acceptance of the premium after the expiration of the period of grace. The documentary evidence disclosed that the payment was made in connection with an application for reinstatement, signed by the deceased, which expressly provided that the policy was not to be deemed reinstated until the application had been favorably acted upon by the home office, and there was no proof of such favorable action." The court there held that a summary judgment should have been entered in favor of the insurance company.

The judgment of the Municipal court of Chicago is reversed, but since no recovery can be had, the cause will not be remanded.

JUDGMENT REVERSED.

Matchett, P. J., dissents. (See next page.)

McSurely, J., concurs.

38839 MR. PRESIDING JUSTICE MATCHETT DISSENTING.

This consolidated cause was before this court upon former appeals, Nos. 37044 and 37045, 274 Ill. App. 662. In each of these appeals a judgment was entered upon the verdict of a jury, which was approved by the trial Judge. The defense interposed in each case was the same as was presented upon the trial of the consolidated cause from which this appeal is taken. In this case, therefore, a third jury has returned a verdict in favor of plaintiff, and for the third time a trial Judge has entered judgment in favor of plaintiff upon such verdict. The opinions of this court upon the former appeals said:

"For the reasons that the verdict is against the manifest weight of the evidence, that the verdict should have been for the defendant, and that the instructions tended to mislead the jury, the judgment is reversed and the cause remanded."

Now, on substantially similar evidence, the court, reversing the judgment, says, "Since no recovery can be had, the cause will not be remanded." As the prevailing opinion now shows, there was an issue of fact upon the former trials, and these issues were submitted to the juries. There was an issue of fact on this trial, which was also submitted to the jury. The judgment of this court now entered reversing without remanding, in my opinion is erroneous in that it denies to plaintiff his right of trial by jury. (Mirich v. Forschner Contracting Co., 312 Ill. 343) and also disregards the rule laid down in Norkevich v. Atchison, T. & St. F. Ry. Co., 263 Ill. App. 1; In re Estate of Swift, 267 Ill. App. 224.

38914

WILLIAM E. WILSON, Administrator of the Estate of Alexander Krauchunis, Deceased,
Appellant,

vs.

CHICAGO & WESTERN INDIANA RAILROAD COMPANY,
Appellee.

APPEAL FROM SUPERIOR COURT OF COOK COUNTY.

62 A

286 I.A. 316[3]

MR. JUSTICE O'CONNOR DELIVERED THE OPINION OF THE COURT.

Plaintiff brought an action against defendant to recover damages for the wrongful death of Alexander Krauchunis. There was a trial before a judge and a jury, a verdict and judgment in defendant's favor, and plaintiff appealed to the Supreme court on the ground that constitutional questions were involved. But upon consideration by that court it was held that no such questions were presented and the cause was transferred to this court. Wilson v. C. & W. I. R. R. Co., 363 Ill. 81.

Plaintiff's contention is, and his evidence tends to show, that about six-thirty o'clock the evening of September 29, 1930, Alexander Krauchunis was walking west on the north sidewalk of 113th street in Chicago, and as he was crossing defendant's northbound track he was struck by one of its trains and fatally injured. Three tracks crossed the street in question in a general north and south direction, and a short distance south of 113th street they curved rather sharply toward the east. It was dark at the time. There was a tower at the street crossing in which defendant's employee was engaged in raising and lowering ordinary railroad gates, but plaintiff contends that the gates were up at the time Krauchunis entered the railroad right-of-way and were not lowered by the tower man until just about the time defendant's northbound train struck Krauchunis; that no whistle was sounded nor bell rung as the train approached the crossing; that the locomotive engine was backing

north, pulling three passenger cars which were unlighted at the time except the south end of the last car, where a part of the train crew was riding; that there was a box car attached to the north or front end of the tank or tender; that there was no light on the north end of this car; that the train was running at about 30 miles an hour. It was charged in counts of the declaration that ordinances of the City of Chicago required defendant to maintain and operate gates at the place in question and to have a light on the front end of the foremost car, to ring a bell, sound a whistle, and not exceed a speed of ten miles an hour across street intersections unless gates were operated.

On the other side, defendant's evidence tended to show that the man in the tower properly operated the gates at the time in question, having lowered them before the train reached the crossing; that the bell on the locomotive was being continually rung and the whistle was sounded; that there was no box car at the north, or front end, of the train and that there was a light on the north end of the tank or tender, and that there was other evidence tending to show there was no violation of any law or ordinance.

Defendant also offered evidence to the effect that Krauchunis was not struck at the crossing by the train, but that he was about 150 feet north of the crossing, sitting on the east rail of the northbound track; that he was under the influence of liquor; that he was struck by the tender, which threw him to the east and north; that he was picked up in his injured condition two or three feet east of the east rail of the northbound track.

Plaintiff also offered in evidence ordinances of the City of Chicago which required defendant railroad to operate gates, ring bells, sound a whistle, etc., at crossings such as the one at 113th street. He also offered in evidence orders passed by the Illinois Commerce Commission which tended to reinstate such ordi-

nances, the Supreme court having prior thereto handed down opinions which would invalidate such ordinances because the authority to regulate railroads, in such a situation as the one in question was taken from the City Council and given to the Commerce Commission by the passage of the Public Utility act of 1913.

Counsel for defendant objected to the ordinances and orders on the ground that the orders of the Commerce Commission were void because they had been entered without notice to defendant. The court sustained this objection and the ordinances and orders were excluded.

Plaintiff contends that this ruling was erroneous and prejudicial. On the other side, counsel for defendant contends that plaintiff is in no position to complain of the ruling of the trial Judge in refusing to admit the orders and ordinances in evidence, for the reason that at the close of the evidence the court refused to exclude the counts of the declaration which charged a violation of the ordinances, but on the contrary gave instructions at plaintiff's request based on those counts. And that since plaintiff offered evidence tending to show a violation of the ordinances, as alleged in certain of the counts, the exclusion of the ordinances and orders did not in any way prejudice plaintiff. And in support of this, the cases of The Lake Shore and Mich. So. R. R. Co. v. Bodemer, 139 Ill. 596, and Klonowski v. Crescent Paper Box Co., 217 Ill. App. 150, are cited.

The Bodemer case was a suit by the administrator of the estate of the deceased to recover for the wrongful death of deceased, struck and fatally injured at a street crossing. One of the counts charged defendant with negligence in running its train at a greater speed than that limited by an ordinance of the city where the injury occurred. Another charged neglect of the railroad company to ring a bell as required by another ordinance. The

ordinances were admitted in evidence but afterward the court withdrew such counts from the jury and the case proceeded under other counts. No motion was made to exclude the ordinances and it was held that since they were properly admitted at the time they were given, no complaint could be made.

In the Klenowski case, (217 Ill. App. 150), which was also a suit brought by the administrator to recover for the wrongful death of the deceased, in which the declaration charged the defendant negligently violated a certain ordinance of the City of Chicago, which was set up in the declaration but of which no proof was made, we said (p. 159): "But appellant urges very strenuously that although the ordinance is set forth in the declaration, no proof was made of it, and that since the Circuit court does not take judicial notice of city ordinances, and since the declaration was based solely on the violation of the ordinance, the case must fall for the reason that the allegations were not proven." We there held that the Circuit court did not take judicial notice of city ordinances but on the trial witnesses were interrogated as to whether the provisions of the ordinance had been complied with, and both parties offered evidence on this question. We said it was error to exclude the ordinance, but refused to disturb the judgment because the merits of the case had been tried. On this point we said (p.160): "In these circumstances we think appellant is in no position to urge that the ordinance was not offered in evidence. The jury were supposed to be familiar with the declaration and they were instructed that the plaintiff was required to prove his case as laid in the declaration. We think that since both parties assumed that the ordinance declared on was in force and effect, by the manner in which the case was tried, and since plaintiff offered proof tending to show a violation of the terms of the ordinance and appellant offered proof tending to show the contrary, there is no substantial ordinances were admitted in evidence but afterward the court withdrew such counts from the jury and the case proceeded under other counts. No motion was made to exclude the ordinances and it was held that since they were properly admitted at the time they were given, no complaint could be made.

In the Klonowski case, (217 Ill. App. 150), which was also a suit brought by the administrator to recover for the wrongful death of the deceased, in which the declaration charged the defendant negligently violated a certain ordinance of the City of Chicago, which was set up in the declaration but of which no proof was made, we said (p. 159): "But appellant urges very strenuously that although the ordinance is set forth in the declaration, no proof was made of it, and that since the circuit court does not take judicial notice of city ordinances, and since the declaration was based solely on the violation of the ordinance, the case must fail for the reason that the allegations were not proven." We there held that the Circuit court did not take judicial notice of city ordinances but on the trial witnesses were interrogated as to whether the provisions of the ordinance had been complied with, and both parties offered evidence on this question. We said it was error to exclude the ordinance, but refused to disturb the judgment because the merits of the case had been tried. On this point we said (p.160): "In those circumstances we think appellant is in no position to urge that the ordinance was not offered in evidence. The jury were supposed to be familiar with the declaration and they were instructed that the plaintiff was required to prove his case as laid in the declaration. We think that since both parties assumed that the ordinance declared on was in force and effect, by the manner in which the case was tried, and since plaintiff offered proof tending to show a violation of the terms of the ordinance and appellant offered proof tending to show the contrary, there is no substantial error in this regard." That opinion was handed down by this court in 1920, and *certiorari* denied by the Supreme court. Since that time the legislature, in 1929, changed the law so that now trial courts and courts of review are required to take judicial notice of "All general ordinances of every municipal corporation within the city, county, judicial circuit or other territory for which such court has been established, or within the city, county, or judicial circuit from which a case has been brought to such court by change of venue or otherwise." Par. 57, sec. 1, chap. 51, Ill. State Bar Stats. 1935. Since the passage of that act in 1929, it is not necessary or proper in the trial of a case to introduce general ordinances of a city, the violation of which is the basis of such a case as the one at bar, any more than it is necessary or proper to introduce a statute of this State where the basis of a suit is the violation of such statute.

In the instant case, the court at the request of plaintiff, instructed the jury that if it found from a preponderance of the evidence that Krauchunis was walking over and across the tracks of defendant on 113th street and was injured, "as alleged in the declaration," then the deceased was required to exercise only such care and caution for his own safety as a reasonably prudent and cautious person would exercise under the same conditions in approaching and passing over railroad tracks. The jury was also instructed that if it found from a preponderance of the evidence that defendant railroad had erected gates at 113th street and was operating them in the customary manner on the approach of trains, as a warning to persons approaching the track; and if it further found from a preponderance of the evidence that Krauchunis was walking over the track at 113th street in the exercise of ordinary care for his own safety, and the defendant failed to lower the gates or to give reasonable warning of the approach of the train, as the result of which deceased error in this regard." That opinion was handed down by this court in 1920, and certiorari denied by the Supreme court. Since that time the legislature, in 1929, changed the law so that now trial courts and courts of review are required to take judicial notice of "All general ordinances of every municipal corporation within the city, county, judicial circuit or other territory for which such court has been established, or within the city, county, or judicial circuit from which a case has been brought to such court by change of venue or otherwise." Par. 57, sec. 1, chap. 51, Ill. State Bar Stats. 1935. Since the passage of that act in 1929, it is not necessary or proper in the trial of a case to introduce general ordinances of a city, the violation of which is the basis of such a case as the one at bar, any more than it is necessary or proper to introduce a statute of this State where the basis of a suit is the violation of such statute.

In the instant case, the court at the request of plaintiff, instructed the jury that if it found from a preponderance of the evidence that Kreuchunis was walking over and across the tracks of defendant on 115th street and was injured, "as alleged in the declaration," then the deceased was required to exercise only such care and caution for his own safety as a reasonably prudent and cautious person would exercise under the same conditions in approaching and passing over railroad tracks. The jury was also instructed that if it found from a preponderance of the evidence that defendant railroad had erected gates at 115th street and was operating them in the customary manner on the approach of trains, as a warning to persons approaching the track; and if it further found from a preponderance of the evidence that Kreuchunis was walking over the track at 115th street in the exercise of ordinary care for his own safety, and the defendant failed to lower the gates or to give reasonable warning of the approach of the train, as the result of which deceased was mortally injured, then the verdict should be for the plaintiff. And by another instruction the jury was told that if it found from a preponderance of the evidence that defendant operated the train in question over 113th street crossing at a speed of 20 miles or more per hour, and that such speed was dangerous and unsafe, and if it further found that defendant railroad company did not have on the forward end of a certain box car a conspicuous light on the front, or north, end of the car, and defendant was thereby negligent, and deceased was in the exercise of due care for his own safety, and that the gates were not lowered as the train approached the crossing, as a result of which deceased was mortally injured, then it should find defendant guilty.

From the foregoing it appears both plaintiff and defendant introduced evidence tending to show on the one hand that the ordinances had been violated, and on the other hand that they had not been violated; and since the jury was instructed to passon these controverted questions of fact, on the theory that the ordinances were in force and effect, and since the court is now required to take judicial notice of such ordinances, we think plaintiff is not in a position to say he has not had a fair trial. Lyons v. Kanter, 285 Ill. 336. In that case the court said there was an essential allegation of plaintiff's statement of claim omitted, but as this element was brought into the case by defendant's pleading and the issue tried out, the judgment would not be disturbed. The court said (p. 339): "The issue was introduced by the defendants instead of the plaintiff, but we will not, with the whole record before us, reverse the judgment for the purpose of letting the parties raise in a more formal way an issue of which they have already had the benefit of a full trial." So in the instant case, if there was any error on the part of the trial courtin its ruling, both parties have had the "benefit of a full trial," and the judgment will not be disturbed for any such claimed irregularity.

The judgment of the Superior court of Cook county is affirmed.

JUDGMENT AFFIRMED.

Matchett, P. J., and McSurely, J., concur.

was mortally injured, then the verdict should be for the plaintiff. And by another instruction the jury was told that if it found from a preponderance of the evidence that defendant operated the train in question over 115th street crossing at a speed of 30 miles or more per hour, and that such speed was dangerous and unsafe, and if it further found that defendant railroad company did not have on the forward end of a certain box car a conspicuous light on the front, or north, end of the car, and defendant was thereby negligent, and deceased was in the exercise of due care for his own safety, and that the gates were not lowered as the train approached the crossing, as a result of which deceased was mortally injured, then it should find defendant guilty.

From the foregoing it appears both plaintiff and defendant introduced evidence tending to show on the one hand that the ordinances had been violated, and on the other hand that they had not been violated; and since the jury was instructed to pass on these controverted questions of fact, on the theory that the ordinances were in force and effect, and since the court is now required to take judicial notice of such ordinances, we think plaintiff is not in a position to say he has not had a fair trial. Lyons v. Porter, 288 Ill. 356. In that case the court said there was an essential allegation of plaintiff's statement of claim omitted, but as this element was brought into the case by defendant's pleading and the issue tried out, the judgment would not be disturbed. The court said (p. 359): "The issue was introduced by the defendants instead of the plaintiff, but we will not, with the whole record before us, reverse the judgment for the purpose of letting the parties raise in a more formal way an issue of which they have already had the benefit of a full trial." So in the instant case, if there was any error on the part of the trial court in its ruling, both parties have had the "benefit of a full trial," and the judgment will not be disturbed for any such claimed irregularity.

The judgment of the Superior court of Cook county is affirmed.

JUDGMENT AFFIRMED.

Matchett, P. J., and McSurely, J., concur.

38921

ELLA WILSON,
Appellee,

vs.

THE NATIONAL LIFE AND ACCIDENT INSURANCE COMPANY, a Corporation,
Appellant.

APPEAL FROM MUNICIPAL COURT OF CHICAGO.

8/17

286 I.A. 617[1]

MR. PRESIDING JUSTICE MATCHETT DELIVERED THE OPINION OF THE COURT.

Plaintiff, Ella Wilson, brought suit as the beneficiary named in two life insurance policies issued by defendant on the life of her brother, John L. Robinson. The statement of claim alleged that the death of the insured occurred September 16, 1928. In one of the paragraphs of the statement plaintiff averred that the insured was legally dead, in that he had disappeared from his last known abode on or before September 16, 1928, and had not returned nor communicated with plaintiff, his only relative; that inquires and search had been made without avail, etc.

Defendant in its amended affidavit of merits denied that John L. Robinson died September 16, 1928; denied that the premiums on the policies had been paid as provided therein; and affirmed that no sufficient proof of death was furnished to the defendant as required by the terms of the policies.

The cause was tried by the court. There was a finding for the plaintiff in the sum of $321, on which the court entered judgment.

Plaintiff offered in evidence the insurance policies and the certificate of the registrar of vital statistics of the State of Florida, for the City of West Palm Beach, showing the birth there on September 16, 1884, of John L. Robinson, who the certificate stated was a male, colored, and single, and that he died September 16, 1928, as the victim of a hurricane.

Plaintiff testified that John L. Robinson, the insured, was her brother, and that there were no other relatives; that she last

saw him at 3451 Federal street in Chicago, where she lived with him and which place was his abode and domicile; that he left there in August, 1928, and that she had no word from him at all for seven years; that shortly after he went away she had a post card from him from Pellican Bay, Florida; that she lost the card when she was moving. She also identified the premium books and stated she paid the premiums, and that she had the two policies, which were for the total amount of $321. She further testified that she heard of her brother's death in October or the last of September, 1928; that she notified the insurance company and turned in the policies, the premium book and the death certificate; she also had an investigation made through the Red Cross; she went to the office of the Red Cross on Michigan avenue; letters received by the Red Cross concerning the matter were identified and offered in evidence but were excluded. It was admitted that the premiums were paid up to September 16, 1928. The witness said that after her brother's disappearance she lived in the house at Federal street over a year and then moved to East 54th street, Chicago. Her brother did not return to Chicago and she heard nothing from him afterward except by the post card.

Roger Moss testified that he knew John L. Robinson in Florida during his lifetime; that on September 16, 1928, he was with him all day and particularly that evening until a hurricane came up. At that time they were in a shack in Pellican Bay, a little shanty, and a hurricane came up and blew the roof off the shack. Before they could get out a heavy beam fell down and hit Robinson on the head; the witness ran out; when he came back the shack was dilapidated and he, with others, went out and got refuge in another low shack, "But John never showed up." When the storm was over the police came and the place was blocked off. Witness said he couldn't get work there and left the next night and came back to

Indiana. The witness also said that John L. Robinson talked to him about his sister in Chicago, and that she lived on Federal street; that he had been there several times, so when he came back he went there but couldn't find the sister and afterward happened to meet her at a dance at Forum Hall on 43rd street. Plaintiff testified that she did not give the name John L. Robinson to the officers who made out the certificate. We hold this evidence was prima facie sufficient to show the death of the insured on September 16, 1928.

Defendant contends that the court erred in admitting the certificate of death and cites Henninger v. Interocean Casualty Company, 217 Ill. App. 542. The case cited does not sustain the contention. The court there did not hold that the certificate was inadmissible, but only that it was not sufficient to establish certain "mere conclusions based upon hearsay." We hold that the certificate was admissible and with other evidence was prima facie sufficient to establish the death of the insured on September 16, 1928. The evidence as to continued absence of the insured for seven years, and of unavailing search by his only relative, strongly corroborates the certificate. The defendant offered no evidence, although the hearing was adjourned to give it the opportunity. The defendant argues, assuming without warrant, that plaintiff's case is based entirely upon the presumption of death, arising from an unexplained absence of seven years; that the premiums were not paid on the policies up to the end of these seven years; and that for this reason plaintiff as a matter of law could not recover. Plaintiff's case does not rest upon the presumption theory. Moreover, defendant cites no authority holding that in such cases the presumption of death does not arise until the expiration of seven years. However, we think the general rule is that the presumption of the duration of life ceases only at the expiration of seven years from the time when the person was last known to be living, and only

at the end of that period does a presumption of death arise. Bouvier's Law Dictionary, vol. I, page 777. However, there are well considered cases where it has been held that a presumption of death may be raised from absence for a shorter period, and the period in which the presumption of continued life ceases may be shortened by proof of facts and circumstances as submitted to the test of experience, which would produce a conviction of death within a shorter period. The authority above cited says:

"Though there is controversy on the point, the better opinion is that there is no presumption as to the time of death; Davie v. Briggs, 97 U. S. 628, 24 L. Ed. 1086; Chamb. Best Ev., 305; 2 Brett, Com. 941; 2 M. & W. 894; and the onus is on the person whose case requires proof of death at a particular period; Howard v. State, 75 Ala. 27; Whiteley v. Assurance Society, 72 Wis. 170, 39 N. W. 369; Spencer v. Roper, 35 N. C. 333; 8 U.C. Q. B. 291."

Here, we think, the court was justified in holding that plaintiff had proved by a preponderance of evidence that the insured died in Florida on September 16, 1928. The evidence shows that after the death of insured plaintiff took the policies to defendant and made claim thereunder. Defendant gave her a written receipt for the policies and retained them. We think the proofs of loss were sufficient under Anderson v. Interstate Business Men's Accident Assoc., 354 Ill. 538.

Plaintiff urges that she is entitled to recover interest, citing Knight Templars & Masons v. Clayton, 110 Ill. App. 648. Section 2 of chap. 74 of the Statutes. See Illinois State Bar Stats. 1935, chap. 74, sec. 2, page 1939. Plaintiff, however, did not demand interest in her complaint, and the judgment as entered is therefore affirmed.

AFFIRMED.

O'Connor and McSurely, JJ., concur.

at the end of that period does a presumption of death arise. Bouvier's Law Dictionary, vol. 1, page 777. However, there are well considered cases where it has been held that a presumption of death may be raised from absence for a shorter period, and the period in which the presumption of continued life ceases may be shortened by proof of facts and circumstances as submitted to the test of experience, which would produce a conviction of death within a shorter period. The authority above cited says:

"Though there is controversy on the point, the better opinion is that there is no presumption as to the time of death; Davie v. Briggs, 97 U. S. 628, 24 L. Ed. 1086; Chamb. Best Ev., 305; 2 Brett, Com. 941; 2 A. & E. 654; and the onus is on the person whose case requires proof of death at a particular period; Howard v. State, 75 Ala. 27; Whiteley v. Assurance Society, 72 Wis. 170, 39 N. W. 369; Spencer v. Roper, 35 N. C. 333; 3 C. B. 291."

Here, we think, the court was justified in holding that plaintiff had proved by a preponderance of evidence that the insured died in Florida on September 15, 1925. The evidence shows that after the death of insured plaintiff took the policies to defendant and made claim thereunder. Defendant gave her a written receipt for the policies and retained them. We think the proofs of loss were sufficient under Anderson v. Interstate Business Men's Accident Assn., 354 Ill. 538.

Plaintiff urges that she is entitled to recover interest, citing Knights Templars & Masons v. Clayton, 110 Ill. App. 648. Section 2 of chap. 74 of the Statutes. See Illinois State Bar Stats. 1935, chap. 74, sec. 2, page 1939. Plaintiff, however, did not demand interest in her complaint, and the judgment as entered is therefore affirmed.

AFFIRMED.

O'Connor and McSurely, JJ., concur.

38947

METROPOLITAN TRUST COMPANY, a Corporation, as Administrator of the Estate of KAZMIEZ OLSZOWKA, Deceased,
Appellant,

vs.

E. LEQUATTE, HELEN HOFFMAN and LINTON O. HOFFMAN,
Appellees.

APPEAL FROM CIRCUIT COURT OF COOK COUNTY.

824

286 I.A. 617[2]

MR. PRESIDING JUSTICE MATCHETT DELIVERED THE OPINION OF THE COURT.

November 21, 1933, plaintiff's intestate, a boy fourteen years of age, died as a result of injuries sustained by him in an accident at the intersection of 47th street and Racine avenue in Chicago. This action is brought by the administrator for the benefit of the next of kin against the defendants, Lequatte, Helen and Linton O. Hoffman, and Guy Richardson, receiver of the Chicago City Railway company, on account of whose negligence plaintiff avers the deceased received the injuries from which he died. The complaint contained the usual material averments required in such cases. The answer of the defendants denied these allegations. The cause was dismissed as to Guy Richardson, receiver of the Chicago City Railway Company. Plaintiff presented its evidence against the other defendants, and at the close of plaintiff's evidence the court, on motion of defendants, instructed the jury to return a verdict against plaintiff and in favor of the defendants, upon which the court, overruling plaintiff's motion for a new trial, entered judgment. The controlling question upon this appeal is whether the court erred in instructing a verdict for defendants and entering judgment on the verdict as returned. It is not argued that the Hoffmans are liable. The question is, therefore, whether the instruction was proper as to Lequatte.

The complaint was in two counts, the first of which charged defendants with negligence generally, while the second charged that they were guilty of wanton and wilful negligence. The rule applicable where a motion for an instruction is requested in favor of a defendant in an action of this character has been often stated. The question of whether a defendant was negligent or whether its negligence has been wilful and wanton is ordinarily a question of fact to be determined by the jury if there is any evidence from which the jury can reasonably find for the plaintiff upon the issue. Plaintiff cites Brown vs. Illinois Terminal Co., 319 Ill. 326, 331; Streeter v. Humrichouse, 357 Ill. 234, 238; Snedden v. Illinois Cent. R. Co., 234 Ill. App. 234, 242; Mantonya v. Wilbur Lumber Co., 251 Ill. App. 364, 369; with similar cases. The cases cited state the general rule, which is not, however, without limitations, as will appear from an examination of Bartlett v. Wabash R. R. Co., 220 Ill. 163; I. C. R. R. Co. v. O'Connor, 189 Ill. 559; Gavurnik v. Miller, 283 Ill. App. 472; in which it has been held that where after considering the evidence in the light most favorable to plaintiff, there is no evidence from which the jury could reasonably find for plaintiff that a motion by defendant for an instructed verdict should be granted. The case last cited recognizes the difficulty of stating a precise rule as to wilful and wanton negligence, holding that wilful negligence is as difficult to define as negligence itself.

The evidence shows without contradiction that the deceased, at the time he received the injury resulting in his death, was stealing a ride upon a truck of defendant driven by defendant's servant. There is abundant authority in this and other States to the effect that where the deceased is such a trespasser the only duty owed by defendant to him is the duty to refrain from wilfully and wantonly injuring him. Bartlett v. Wabash R. R. Co., 220 Ill.

163; I. C. R. R. Co. v. O'Connor, 189 Ill. 559; Hebard v. Mable, 98 Ill. App. 543; Kerins v. Anderson, 175 Ill. App. 377; Rasimas v. Chicago Rys. Co., 223 Ill. App. 288; McGhee v. Birmingham News Co., 90 So. Rep. 492; Gamble v. Uncle Sam Oil Co., 163 Pac. Rep. 627.

It therefore becomes necessary to examine the evidence in order to ascertain whether the jury could reasonably find therefrom that the servant of defendant, at the time and just prior to the accident, was guilty of negligence which as a matter of law could be found wilful and wanton.

There is practically no conflict in the evidence as to material facts. The accident in question occurred on the morning of November 21, 1933, at the intersection of 47th street and Racine avenue in Chicago; 47th street is a public highway extending east and west; Racine avenue is a public street extending north and south; each of the streets was about 33 feet wide from curb to curb; two street railway tracks were laid in 47th street; east bound cars ran over the south track and west bound cars over the north track; just north and to the west of these tracks were the Union Stock Yards of Chicago; street car tracks were also laid in Racine avenue south of 47th street; northbound cars ran over the east track and southbound over the west track. The accident occurred about eight o'clock in the morning; rain had been falling and the streets were wet and slippery; the intersection was a busy corner both in morning and evening, and there was an officer stationed there to direct traffic; there were no lights at the intersection; the pavement was in good condition; it was a brick pavement with granite stones between the tracks.

Defendant Lequatte, who lived in Illinois City, Illinois, is engaged in business as a livestock broker and in general trucking; he owned a Dodge semi-trailer truck; the tractor of the

163; I. C. R. R. Co. v. O'Connor, 189 Ill. 559; Hebard v. Mabie, 98 Ill. App. 543; Kerins v. Anderson, 175 Ill. App. 577; Hastings v. Chicago Rys. Co., 223 Ill. App. 288; McGhee v. Birmingham News Co., 90 So. Rep. 492; Gamble v. Uncle Sam Oil Co., 165 Pac. Rep. 627.

It therefore becomes necessary to examine the evidence in order to ascertain whether the jury could reasonably find therefrom that the servant of defendant, at the time and just prior to the accident, was guilty of negligence which as a matter of law could be found wilful and wanton.

There is practically no conflict in the evidence as to material facts. The accident in question occurred on the morning of November 21, 1933, at the intersection of 47th street and Racine avenue in Chicago; 47th street is a public highway extending east and west; Racine avenue is a public street extending north and south; each of the streets was about 33 feet wide from curb to curb; two street railway tracks were laid in 47th street; east bound cars ran over the south track and west bound cars over the north track; just north and to the west of these tracks were the Union Stock Yards of Chicago; street car tracks were also laid in Racine avenue south of 47th street; northbound cars ran over the east track and southbound over the west track. The accident occurred about eight o'clock in the morning; rain had been falling and the streets were wet and slippery; the intersection was a busy corner both in morning and evening, and there was an officer stationed there to direct traffic; there were no lights at the intersection; the pavement was in good condition; it was a brick pavement with granite stones between the tracks.

Defendant Regnetter, who lived in Illinois City, Illinois, is engaged in business as a livestock broker and in general truck had a three-man cab enclosed with doors and windows; the trailer was called a "stock rack," the sides being composed of six inch slats or boards spaced about three inches apart. The height of the truck was 11 feet 6 inches from the ground; in back of the cab was a glass window but with a trailer attached, one looking from the cab through the window could see only the board front of the trailer. This truck, loaded with hogs, was sent in to Chicago on the day in question, driven by one of defendant's servants, Ray Thomas; the truck was loaded with a double-deck load of hogs and was being driven east on 47th street. For several miles west of Racine avenue school boys of various ages climbed on this truck; they were on their way to school and were stealing rides on the truck and rode on it without the knowledge or permission of the driver. The deceased, Olszowka, boarded the truck at California avenue, an intersecting street about two miles west of Racine avenue. A number of boys were riding on the truck which approached the place of the accident at a speed of not more than 23 miles an hour; as this truck approached the intersection at a distance of from two to three hundred feet, there was a Racine avenue car standing on the south side of 47th street for the purpose of discharging passengers, after which it, as usual, proceeded, turning east onto the track in 47th street. Mrs. Hoffman, one of the defendants, at the same time approached the intersection from the north, driving a Pontiac automobile going south on Racine avenue; she had driven her husband to the Stock Yards that morning and was returning to her home, from which she would go to meet a social engagement in the afternoon; Joseph Cadigan, police officer, was standing in the middle of the street intersection, and Mrs. Hoffman, as she drove her automobile, was on the right hand side of Racine avenue about in the south bound track. Cadigan says that the automobile was standing right on the north curb; it had moved past the gates; it was between

the gates and the north curb of 47th street and was standing there; there was no traffic going east in front of it, and there was no traffic between this automobile and the truck, which was then two or three hundred feet away; the way was perfectly free and clear and open from Racine avenue for two or three hundred feet to the truck; the truck came on eastward without slackening its speed; the policeman motioned with his arm, indicating to Mrs. Hoffman that she should come across, which she proceeded to do; the policeman did not watch her go across but turned around and walked southward to the curb; at the same time apparently the street car moved and the next thing that happened was a crash in which the right rear fender of the truck scratched the automobile; the truck, in order to avoid a crash, had swerved to the north about 15 feet, and Cadigan says (though other witnesses say to the contrary) that the truck hit the street car; at any rate, the truck tipped over onto the eastbound track, and plaintiff's intestate received injuries resulting in his death almost immediately.

Plaintiff argues that it is apparent that the driver for defendant did not have the truck under control; that he totally disregarded the approaching danger, and as he approached the intersection took a chance that the Pontiac car would cross the intersection before he approached its path, and that taking into consideration the slippery condition of the streets, the fact that he swerved to avoid hitting the automobile and continued on in a northeasterly direction with such speed as to overturn the truck, was conduct from which the jury might reasonably infer wanton and wilful negligence.

The difficulty of defining with precision the conduct which, from a legal standpoint, may amount to wilful and wanton negligence, has often been considered by the courts of this State. In Streeter v. Humrichouse, 357 Ill. 234, our Supreme court said that ill will

was not a necessary element of a wanton act, but that "to constitute an act wanton, the party doing the act or failing to act must be conscious of his conduct, and, though having no intent to injure, must be conscious, from his knowledge of the surrounding circumstances and conditions, that his conduct will naturally and probably result in injury. An intentional disregard of a known duty necessary to the safety of the person or property of another, and an entire absence of care for the life, person or property of others, such as exhibits a conscious indifference to consequences, makes a case of constructive or legal wilfulness." Jeneary v. Chicago and Interurban Traction Co., 306 Ill. 392. In Heidenrich v. Bremner, 260 Ill. 439, the court also said that it was not necessary to prove ill will; that

"An entire absence of care for the life, person or property of others, if such as exhibits indifference to consequences, makes a case of constructive or legal willfulness, such as charges a person whose duty it was to exercise care with the consequences of a legal injury."

In Brown v. Illinois Terminal Co., 319 Ill. 326, the court in substance said that wilful and wanton misconduct "imports consciousness that an injury may probably result from the act done and a reckless disregard of the consequences." In Farley v. Mitchell, 282 Ill. App. 555, this court said:

"A great deal of language has been used in many cases in the attempt to define with mathematical certainty the difference between ordinary negligence and wilful and wanton negligence. More recent cases have held that this is virtually impossible; that whether an act is wilful and wanton depends upon the particular circumstances of each case."

In McGuire v. McGannon, 283 Ill. App. 293, the court said that courts of last resort have indicated generally that the subject of wilful acts is to be considered from the standpoint of the evidence in each particular case, "but analogous cases may be applied to shed some light and to be helpful in determining whether the defendant's agent acted wilfully and with wanton

recklessness at the time of the accident." In Gavurnik v. Miller, 283 Ill. App. 472, the Appellate court of the Second district quoted with approval the opinion of this court in Farley v. Mitchell, 282 Ill. App. 555, and reversed a judgment entered by the trial court where a sixteen year old bicyclist was killed when struck by an automobile which overtook him on a slippery highway in broad daylight. It happened that the motorist, driving about 45 miles an hour, saw the deceased three hundred yards in front of him, on the right hand side of the road, and when about one hundred to one hundred and fifty feet from him sounded a horn without, however, slackening his speed, and turned into a left lane of the highway in order to pass the bicyclist, who swerved over to the left side of the road in front of the motorist, who struck him. The court said that a more skillful driver might have avoided the accident; that a more careful driver would have slackened his speed and sounded a warning sooner, but that a failure to do these things was not, under the circumstances, more than negligent omission of duty, "and do not show an indifference to consequences, nor are they equivalent to a wilful and wanton act."

We believe it will appear from an examination of cases that a judgment for a wilful and wanton negligence will not be sustained in the absence of showing of intentional negligence or an indifference amounting to recklessness and indicating conscious wrongdoing on the part of defendant Lequatte. Such evidence is absent from this record. We hold, therefore, that the court properly directed a verdict for the defendant and the judgment of the trial court is therefore affirmed.

AFFIRMED.

O'Connor and McSurely, JJ., concur.

38825

MICHAEL BIERUT,
Appellant,

vs.

WLADYSLAW SETLAK and
MARY SETLAK,
Appellees.

APPEAL FROM CIRCUIT COURT
OF COOK COUNTY.

83 A

286 I.A. 617[3]

MR. JUSTICE McSURELY DELIVERED THE OPINION OF THE COURT.

Plaintiff filed his complaint to foreclose a trust deed signed by defendants purporting to secure their promissory note for $2500; defendants answered, alleging that the execution of the note and trust deed was procured by the fraud and deceit of plaintiff; they also filed a cross complaint alleging that they were misled into signing the trust deed and notes by the fraudulent misrepresentations of plaintiff and his lawyer, and asked that the trust deed and notes be cancelled; the cause was referred to a master in chancery who took evidence and reported, sustaining the allegations of the cross complainant, recommending a decree in accordance with its prayer and that the bill of complaint be dismissed; objections and exceptions were filed, which the chancellor overruled, entered a decree in accordance with the recommendations of the master, and plaintiff appeals.

As reported by the master, a number of witnesses testified to the transaction, and the testimony of witnesses for plaintiff is in many instances in direct conflict with the testimony of witnesses for the defendants. The transaction centered around the imprisonment of Tillie Wasik, wife of Julius Wasik, in the Rockford jail under the charge of shoplifting, and an attempt to have her released.

The evidence offered on behalf of plaintiff was to the effect that he was approached on several occasions by Julius Wasik, a Mr. Piontek and defendant Setlak and requested to advance ap-

proximately $2000 to secure the release of Tillie Wasik from jail. Plaintiff was an experienced real estate broker and a friend of Julius and Tillie Wasik and also godfather of one of their children. Plaintiff says he first refused to help Mrs. Wasik, but on November 15, 1931, both defendants, with Julius Wasik and Piontek, came to his home and offered to give him a first mortgage on the Setlak property in consideration of his advancing approximately $2000 to secure the release of Tillie Wasik; that he agreed to this and made an appointment with Frank Kuta, his lawyer, who prepared the papers, and on November 15th the parties met at Kuta's office where the defendants executed and delivered the trust deed and notes in question; that Kuta explained to defendants in the Polish language the nature of the documents they were signing and advised them that if they did not repay the $2000 to plaintiff the mortgage would be foreclosed. The evidence of plaintiff, if accepted, tended to show that defendants understood they were signing notes and a mortgage.

The testimony offered by defendants was to the effect that Wladyslaw Setlak was a brother of Mrs. Piontek; that the Pionteks and Wasiks were friends; that on November 15, 1931, Julius Wasik and plaintiff came to the home of the Pionteks seeking to obtain their assistance in procuring the release of Tillie Wasik from jail; Mrs. Piontek told them they had no money or property but that her brother, Wladyslaw Setlak, had some property and might be willing to help; thereupon plaintiff, Wasik and Mr. Piontek went to defendants' home; Wasik asked Setlak to bail his wife out of jail by signing a bond for $1200 for sixty days; plaintiff also joined in the request, telling defendants not to be afraid, that he was a real estate man and would bring their papers back to them in sixty days. The parties then went to the home of plaintiff's attorney, Kuta, where plaintiff told Kuta that Setlak would sign a bond for $1200 for Tillie Wasik; Setlak consented to this as plaintiff assured him proximately $2000 to secure the release of Tillie Wasik from jail. Plaintiff was an experienced real estate broker and a friend of Julius and Tillie Wasik and also godfather of one of their children. Plaintiff says he first refused to help Mrs. Wasik, but on November 15, 1931, both defendants, with Julius Wasik and Piontek, came to his home and offered to give him a first mortgage on the Betlak property in consideration of his advancing approximately $2000 to secure the release of Tillie Wasik; that he agreed to this and made an appointment with Frank Kuta, his lawyer, who prepared the papers, and on November 18th the parties met at Kuta's office where the defendants executed and delivered the trust deed and notes in question; that Kuta explained to defendants in the Polish language the nature of the documents they were signing and advised them that if they did not repay the $2000 to plaintiff the mortgage would be foreclosed. The evidence of plaintiff, if accepted, tended to show that defendants understood they were signing notes and a mortgage.

The testimony offered by defendants was to the effect that Wladyslaw Betlak was a brother of Mrs. Piontek; that the Pionteks and Wasiks were friends; that on November 15, 1931, Julius Wasik and plaintiff came to the home of the Pionteks seeking to obtain their assistance in procuring the release of Tillie Wasik from jail; Mrs. Piontek told them they had no money or property but that her brother, Wladyslaw Betlak, had some property and might be willing to help; thereupon plaintiff, Wasik and Mr. Piontek went to defendants' home; Wasik asked Betlak to bail his wife out of jail by signing a bond for $1200 for sixty days; plaintiff also joined in the request, telling defendants not to be afraid, that he was a real estate man and would bring their papers back to them in sixty days. The parties then went to the home of plaintiff's attorney, Kuta, where plaintiff told Kuta that Betlak would sign a bond for $1200 he would have no trouble and the papers would be brought back to him in sixty days; Kuta then said it would be necessary to have Mrs. Setlak's signature, and she was brought to the lawyer's office and defendants signed the notes and trust deed. Neither defendant can read or write English or Polish. They were advised by both Kuta and plaintiff that they were signing a bond for Tillie Wasik.

The evidence tends to show that the following day plaintiff met two men named Brown and Horowitz, and a Mrs. Olszewski, a friend of the Wasiks and Pionteks, and plaintiff delivered to Brown and Horowitz $1500 in currency, and Mrs. Olszewski gave them $500. The $2000 was to be used by Brown and Horowitz for the purpose of making restitution to complainants in the charge of shoplifting against Tillie Wasik. There is no evidence that defendants, when they executed the notes and trust deed, received any moneys or other property. They both testified that they did not know Brown or Horowitz and gave no instructions to plaintiff to pay them any money.

Within a few days thereafter it appears that the efforts to make restitution were unsuccessful and plaintiff and Mrs. Olszewski went to Brown and Horowitz to recover back the $2000; Brown and Horowitz claimed they had spent $500 and tendered back $1500, which plaintiff and Mrs. Olszewski refused to take, demanding the return of $2000; thereafter they had Brown and Horowitz arrested and on a hearing of the case apparently restitution was promised and $800 was paid in open court. There is some dispute as to how this $800 was divided; Tillie Wasik, who was at this time out of jail, testified that plaintiff got $500 and a lawyer named Goldstein $300.

It was also in evidence that plaintiff gave a lawyer named Konkowski a check for $500 which was to be used to help get Tillie Wasik out of jail. Setlak denied that he ever instructed plaintiff to pay any money to Konkowski. Konkowski testified that when he received this check he represented one Podraza who, with plaintiff, he would have no trouble and the papers would be brought back to him in sixty days; Kuta then said it would be necessary to have Mrs. Setlak's signature, and she was brought to the lawyer's office and defendants signed the notes and trust deed. Neither defendant can read or write English or Polish. They were advised by both Kuta and plaintiff that they were signing a bond for Tillie Wasik.

The evidence tends to show that the following day plaintiff met two men named Brown and Horowitz, and a Mrs. Olszewski, a friend of the Wasiks and Piéntaks, and plaintiff delivered to Brown and Horowitz $1500 in currency, and Mrs. Olszewski gave them $500. The $2000 was to be used by Brown and Horowitz for the purpose of making restitution to complainants in the charge of shoplifting against Tillie Wasik. There is no evidence that defendants, when they executed the notes and trust deed, received any moneys or other property. They both testified that they did not know Brown or Horowitz and gave no instructions to plaintiff to pay them any money.

Within a few days thereafter it appears that the efforts to make restitution were unsuccessful and plaintiff and Mrs. Olszewski went to Brown and Horowitz to recover back the $2000; Brown and Horowitz claimed they had spent $500 and tendered back $1500, which plaintiff and Mrs. Olszewski refused to take, demanding the return of $2000; thereafter they had Brown and Horowitz arrested and on a hearing of the case apparently restitution was promised and $800 was paid in open court. There is some dispute as to how this $800 was divided; Tillie Wasik, who was at this time out of jail, testified that plaintiff got $500 and a lawyer named Goldstein $300.

It was also in evidence that plaintiff gave a lawyer named Konkowski a check for $500 which was to be used to help get Tillie Wasik out of jail. Setlak denied that he ever instructed plaintiff to pay any money to Konkowski. Konkowski testified that when he received this check he represented one Podrasa who, with plaintiff, was interested in securing the release of Tillie Wasik and one Joseph Coziol from jail, and that arrangements had been made to have a surety company sign a bond for their release, and that the surety company required $1000 to be deposited to indemnify it against loss on the bond; $500 of this was advanced by Coziol's wife and $500 by plaintiff, and that some days later Tillie Wasik and Coziol were released on this bond.

The master found that plaintiff was a friend of the Wasiks and a godfather of one of their children; that he was an experienced real estate broker; that defendants were unable to read or write either the English or Polish language; that as requested, they signed the papers in question for the release of Tillie Wasik from jail upon the assurance of plaintiff that there would be no trouble and that the papers would be returned to them within sixty days; that at that time plaintiff knew it was contemplated to pay $2000 to Brown and Horowitz in an effort to make restitution in the case of Tillie Wasik and to secure her release, but did not disclose this fact to defendants but led them to believe they were signing a bond for the release of Tillie Wasik, and that defendants signed the papers to secure her release from jail.

The master also found that defendants did not at any time direct or authorize plaintiff to pay $2000 or any other sum to Brown or Horowitz and did not authorize plaintiff to pay $500 or any other sum to Konkowski to obtain Tillie Wasik's release. The master further found that the signatures of defendants to the trust deed and notes sought to be foreclosed were obtained by fraud and misrepresentation, recommended that they be held for naught and that a decree be entered in accordance with defendants' cross complaint ordering the cancellation of the documents.

This is a case where conclusions must be based upon the credibility of the witnesses. It is axiomatic in such cases that was interested in securing the release of Tillie Wasik and one Joseph Coziol from jail, and that arrangements had been made to have a surety company sign a bond for their release, and that the surety company required $1000 to be deposited to indemnify it against loss on the bond; $500 of this was advanced by Coziol's wife and $500 by plaintiff, and that some days later Tillie Wasik and Coziol were released on this bond.

The master found that plaintiff was a friend of the Wasiks and a godfather of one of their children; that he was an experienced real estate broker; that defendants were unable to read or write either the English or Polish language; that as requested, they signed the papers in question for the release of Tillie Wasik from jail upon the assurance of plaintiff that there would be no trouble and that the papers would be returned to them within sixty days; that at that time plaintiff knew it was contemplated to pay $2000 to Brown and Horowitz in an effort to make restitution in the case of Tillie Wasik and to secure her release, but did not disclose this fact to defendants but led them to believe they were signing a bond for the release of Tillie Wasik, and that defendants signed the papers to secure her release from jail.

The master also found that defendants did not at any time direct or authorize plaintiff to pay $2000 or any other sum to Brown or Horowitz and did not authorize plaintiff to pay $500 or any other sum to Konkowski to obtain Tillie Wasik's release. The master further found that the signatures of defendants to the trust deed and notes sought to be foreclosed were obtained by fraud and misrepresentation, recommended that they be held for naught and that a decree be entered in accordance with defendants' cross complaint ordering the cancellation of the documents.

This is a case where conclusions must be based upon the credibility of the witnesses. It is axiomatic in such cases that the master, who sees the witnesses and hears them testify, is better qualified to pass upon their credibility than is the reviewing court. While the report of a master is merely advisory and is not given the same effect as a verdict of a jury, yet the facts found by him are entitled to due weight. Keuper v. Mette, 239 Ill. 586. The cases are numerous which hold that where the master heard and saw the witnesses a court of review should be slow in disturbing his conclusions upon the facts unless it can be said that the master's conclusions were clearly contrary to the probative force of the evidence. Gruenenfelder Lumber Co. v. Golden, 260 Ill. App. 313, and cases there cited. See also Kahn v. Rasof, 253 Ill. App. 546; Argus Press, Inc. v. Lindhout, 268 Ill. App. 465, and Wechsler v. Gidwitz, 250 Ill. App. 136. And this is especially true after the chancellor approves the master's report.

From a consideration of the entire evidence we are of the opinion that the conclusions of the master and of the chancellor were justified. It is evident that plaintiff, because of his friendship with the Wasiks, was active in seeking to obtain Mrs. Wasik's release from jail. Apparently he had funds of his own which might be used to effect this, but he sought to protect himself by securing from defendants their note and mortgage. There is no evidence that defendants were especially interested in the Wasiks, and they received no money or other consideration for signing these papers. Mrs. Piontek, sister of Setlak, was a friend of the Wasiks, and it was through her and plaintiff that defendants were persuaded to sign what they thought was a bond for the release from jail of Tillie Wasik.

It is significant that plaintiff sought to recover from Brown and Horowitz the $2000 he paid them. He prosecuted them in his own name. There is no evidence that plaintiff considered any part of this money as belonging to defendants.

Tillie Wasik testified that she paid plaintiff $300 for going on her bond. She also testified that plaintiff told her that if she did not "stick with him" in the case he would "throw off my bonds."

Counsel for plaintiff make a vigorous attack upon the testimony in behalf of defendants and upon the findings of the master, but these criticisms are not convincing.

The decree is affirmed.

AFFIRMED.

Matchett, P. J., and O'Connor, J., concur.

Tillie Wasik testified that she paid plaintiff $300 for going on her bond. She also testified that plaintiff told her that if she did not "stick with him" in the case he would "throw off my bonds."

Counsel for plaintiff make a vigorous attack upon the testimony in behalf of defendants and upon the findings of the master, but these criticisms are not convincing.

The decree is affirmed.

AFFIRMED.

Matchett, P. J., and O'Connor, J., concur.

38848

WALKER W. TACKETT,
Appellee,

vs.

WILLIAM C. TACKETT et al.,
Appellants.

APPEAL FROM SUPERIOR COURT OF COOK COUNTY.

84A

286 I.A. 617[4]

MR. JUSTICE McSURELY DELIVERED THE OPINION OF THE COURT.

Plaintiff filed his complaint seeking an accounting from his older brother, William C. Tackett, defendant; the master heard the evidence and reported, recommending that the complaint be dismissed; the chancellor sustained exceptions to the report and decreed that plaintiff was entitled to an accounting, and defendant appeals.

Plaintiff's complaint asserted that he inherited $32,000 from his father's estate; that he was entirely unskilled in business, while his brother, the defendant, was experienced; that defendant suggested that he could better manage plaintiff's affairs and urged plaintiff to permit him to handle plaintiff's money; that on March 5, 1924, an agreement in writing to this end was prepared by Charles F. Hough, the family attorney, which was signed by both parties; that in consequence of this agreement the distributive share of plaintiff in his father's estate was retained by defendant, who was administrator of the estate; that plaintiff's share in the hands of defendant was $32,000, subsequently increased to $33,300; that after defendant took possession of these funds plaintiff took no further interest in their management; that from time to time thereafter plaintiff received from defendant certain moneys; that in 1929 plaintiff requested that defendant render an account of these moneys and finally agreed to accept the word and assurance of defendant with reference to the account, and on March 13, 1929, plaintiff was told by defendant that all that remained of the trust was $755.18, and that it was necessary to terminate the trust and execute a re-

lease; that believing defendant's statements, plaintiff executed a release. Plaintiff charged that defendant did not manage said trust funds for the benefit of plaintiff, but on the contrary made use of the moneys for his personal gain and for the entichment of himself and his partner, Harry L. Drake; that plaintiff first knew of this in July, 1932, and retained a lawyer; that an audit was made by certified accountants of the books of Tackett & Drake in connection with certain property purchased by a syndicate composed of defendant, Drake and Hough; that this audit disclosed a net profit to the syndicate of $550,000, and that there was due a further profit of $200,000. The complaint also alleged that the syndicate had received a loan of $375,000, secured by this property, which had been invested in other deals with great resultant profits; the complaint charged that defendant made no investment for plaintiff but kept and used the funds of plaintiff in defendant's own affairs and for his personal profit. The complaint prayed that the release executed by plaintiff be annulled and that defendant be required to render a true and perfect account.

The so-called trust agreement executed March 5, 1924, is attached to the complaint. It recites that William Tackett was the administrator of the estate of the father and that $32,000 is in his hands which descends by inheritance to Walker Tackett; that Walker is 21 years of age and has no business experience, and has, by carelessness, mistake or fraud on the part of outside interests, placed himself in a position that he stands to have a loss, and that it is believed his brother William should handle his business affairs; it recites the turning over to William Tackett, trustee, of $32,000, who shall have full power to invest it as he may deem fit. William agrees to pay to the beneficiary, Walker, monthly, a sum not to exceed the rate of 8% per annum upon the amount in the trustee's hands; it provides that on or before April 1, 1927, the trustee may terminate the trust or continue same, as he sees fit.

The money received by the trustee was to be identified as the "Business Trust of Walker W. Tackett." It was agreed that the beneficiary should have no power or control over the trust fund, but the trustee should handle the money as he should see fit, without regard to the desire of the beneficiary. It was also agreed that any bank account or funds should be carried in the name of William C. Tackett without reference to the trust. There was also a provision that upon the death of the trustee the $32,000 with the accrued interest thereon shall be payable to the beneficiary.

Defendant's answer in substance admitted the receipt of the $33,300, admits that he and Drake and Charles Hough formed a syndicate for the purchase of 131 acres of land, in which he permitted plaintiff to invest $4000; he denies that he ever delayed giving a statement to plaintiff and states that he gave plaintiff's attorney a statement of the trust account and furnished a complete account showing the debits and credits of the trust fund up to and including January 1, 1929; that plaintiff's attorney called at defendant's office and examined the account and also an account covering plaintiff's investment of $4000 in the 131 acres, and alleges that thereupon, on March 13, 1929, plaintiff executed the release referred to in plaintiff's complaint and received the full balance due him under said trust agreement. Defendant denied that he used any part of plaintiff's money for his own personal gain, states that plaintiff had full and complete knowledge of the account when he executed the release on March 13, 1929, and alleges that plaintiff always received his full share of any profits arising out of the purchase of the 131 acres.

There is considerable argument as to the nature of the agreement signed by the parties on March 5, 1924, plaintiff asserting it is a simple trust agreement whereby defendant was obligated to account to plaintiff for all the profits accruing from the trust funds. Defendant argues that the document was primarily executed

to protect from creditors plaintiff's share in his father's estate, and that the transaction partook more of the nature of a loan to defendant.

Plaintiff had received $8000 from his father's estate, and had expended $4000 of this in furnishing an apartment for himself and wife whom he had just married; the balance of $4000 was invested in a bumper business with the Ward-Jones company, which business proved to be a failure and there was apprehension that the creditors of the company would have recourse against the interest of plaintiff in his father's estate on the ground that he was a partner in the Ward-Jones company. Plaintiff's mother testified that he talked to her about this unfortunate investment and she told plaintiff that if they could get him out of this trouble she wanted him to let defendant handle plaintiff's money; that plaintiff said he was willing to do this if defendant would pay him 8 per cent, that if defendant would do so he could do whatever he pleased with the money. The mother further testified that after this conversation they met with defendant, telling him she and plaintiff had talked over the matter and plaintiff wished defendant to handle his money and pay plaintiff 8 per cent interest. Defendant at first objected to paying such a large amount of interest, saying he could get all the money he wanted at the bank at 5 or 6 per cent. The evidence indicates that both the mother and plaintiff argued at some length with defendant, plaintiff saying again that all he wanted was 8 per cent on his money and that defendant could do whatever he pleased with the money, as he, plaintiff, wanted to go ahead with his art work. Plaintiff and defendant told their attorney, Hough, of the proposal and Hough advised defendant to have nothing to do with it.

Plaintiff had in the meantime brought suit against the Ward-Jones company to recover his $4000 investment, and the company set up as a defense that plaintiff was obligated to the extent of

$25,000. After discussion Hough suggested that a very simple form of trust be drawn to keep the Ward-Jones company or its creditors from garnishing or attaching plaintiff's money. Hough testified that the agreement was drawn for the purpose of protecting plaintiff from his creditors and also to protect him against his own inability to handle money.

Counsel for plaintiff argue that there was no legal reason why plaintiff should apprehend any proceeding by creditors of the Ward-Jones company against him. Whether or not this apprehension had any real basis in fact or law is not important. The agreement might well have been drawn for the purpose of avoiding any such attempt by creditors.

It is difficult to characterize this document. In one aspect it appears to be an ordinary trust conveyance, but the fact that defendant therein agreed to pay plaintiff a very large rate of interest, together with other provisions, tends to negative the simple trust idea. However, we do not think it is necessary to determine definitely the character of the agreement, for the decision of this case turns upon what took place after its execution and the receipt by defendant of $33,300 of plaintiff's money.

The master found that after the execution of this agreement plaintiff received from defendant monthly a sum in excess of 8 per cent, and that the amounts paid over and above this 3 per cent were credited against the principal amount of $33,300. This is amply supported by the evidence. Plaintiff during this time was living in Europe - in Rome, Nice and Paris; he made frequent demands upon defendant for advances, and defendant, by letters and statements, called plaintiff's attention to the fact that his withdrawals greatly exceeded the 8 per cent interest defendant had agreed to pay, and remonstrated with plaintiff about his extravagance. In one letter, dated June 1, 1927, defendant wrote:

"If you draw any more drafts on me, I will refuse to honor them and will turn your money over to the Chicago Title & Trust Company to handle, who will give you five per cent interest instead of eight that you receive from me. ** I am only handling your account as a favor to you because I can borrow all the money I want from the banks at five per cent interest. **/

I do not like to be hard-boiled with you but if you are going to continue to be so foolish, somebody has to step on you along the line."

The evidence shows that from the year 1924 to 1928, inclusive, there was a yearly withdrawal from the principal of amounts in excess of 8 per cent, aggregating $32,284.65. We do not understand that these amounts are questioned.

The master found that on March 13, 1929, at plaintiff's request defendant gave him a statement accounting in full for the $33,300, plus interest at the rate of 8 per cent per annum, and that plaintiff, being fully satisfied with the statement of account, upon advice of his attorney executed a release, stating therein that he had received all moneys, both principal and interest, required to be paid by defendant to plaintiff under the terms of the agreement executed March 5, 1924.

Plaintiff's counsel earnestly argue that when plaintiff executed this release he did not know all of the facts. There is abundant testimony to the contrary. A number of witnesses, as well as plaintiff's own attorney, Harold Fein, gave testimony tending to prove beyond question that plaintiff was fully informed of all the facts at the time he executed the release.

There is an item of $4000 charged against plaintiff's account which is significant. Defendant testified that he, Drake and Hough had purchased the 131 acres called the Westchester subdivision. He testified that plaintff in January, 1925, talked with him about this, plaintiff saying that inasmuch as another brother, Marvin, had invested $4000 in this purchase, he wanted to put in an equal amount; defendant told plaintiff to consult his mother about the matter and expressed a willingness to let plaintiff come

in upon the understanding that the investment was a gamble; accordingly, on March 13, 1929, upon advice of plaintiff's attorney, another agreement was entered into between plaintiff and defendant wherein it was recited and agreed that $4000 had been withdrawn from the principal sum of $33,300 and invested in the Westchester subdivision, and that plaintiff ratified, confirmed and approved this investment. This Westchester purchase was profitable and plaintiff, up to May 31, 1929, received over $26,000 as principal on his $4000 investment. June 1, 1932, plaintiff placed the management of his interest in the Westchester subdivision with the Chicago Title and Trust Company and since that time he has continued to receive an income on his $4000 investment.

This transaction tends to support defendant's claim that plaintiff was not to participate in any profits from the use of his money except as to this specific $4000 investment.

The master found that plaintiff has received from his $33,300 turned over to defendant a total amount of between $70,000 and $80,000.

Plaintiff also says that this syndicate consisting of William Tackett, Hough and Drake, borrowed $375,000, secured by a trust deed on the Westchester subdivision, $65,000 of which was used to pay a purchase money mortgage, $37,500 to pay commissions, and the balance went to Drake, Hough, and William C. Tackett. The evidence shows that plaintiff was not a member of this syndicate but had merely a $4000 interest in William Tackett's share, and is therefore not entitled to an accounting of the proceeds of the loan.

Moreover, the master found, and the evidence supports the finding, that upon investigation by plaintiff's attorney it was found that the investment of the share of William Tackett in the proceeds of the loan was a total loss, and that if plaintiff shared

such investment made by defendant, plaintiff's loss would be betweem $18,000 and $19,000.

Defendant in handling the Westchester subdivision made a written contract with Walter Blow wherein defendant agreed to pay him 20 per cent of the net proceeds derived from the purchase and sale of the property. The master found that these payments to Blow were proper expenses chargeable against the Westchester subdivision; that in making up the account plaintiff's interest was not charged with his proportionate share of this expense, but he received a credit in excess of what he was entitled to in the amount of $5000, and that defendant was entitled to recover this amount from plaintiff. The master also found that there were three items aggregating $2300 in the final account rendered by defendant to plaintiff on March 13, 1929, which are disputed, and the master found that Walker was entitled to have this amount of $2300 set off against the $5000 found due to defendant on account of the Blow expenses.

There is some argument with reference to an item of $1000 on the so-called Newell check which plaintiff claims was given by him to defendant. The preponderance of the evidence shows that this check was not received by defendant.

Plaintiff made Drake one of the defendants to his complaint and argues that as Drake had knowledge of the existence of the trust and the useof the trust funds in his business ventures with William Tackett he is legally liable to account for the same to plaintiff. The evidence shows that while Drake was a partner of defendant William Tackett from July 1, 1924, the arrangements for the investments under dispute were made by plaintiff with William Tackett alone; that plaintiff had no contractual relationship of any kind with Drake, and that when William Tackett acted on behalf of plaintiff in any investment he acted as an individual and not

as a partner of Drake. The master found that Drake was not accountable in any manner to plaintiff in connection with any of the invesments in dispute.

The master found that plaintiff was not entitled to an accounting by defendant Tackett or Drake, and that plaintiff had received all moneys due him under the contract of March 5, 1924, and had given an acquittance and release of all liability for the principal and interest on the investment of $33,300, and that plaintiff has received more than his share out of the investment of $4000 in the Westchester subdivision. We are in accord with this conclusion, which is abundantly supported by the evidence.

The master further recommended that inasmuch as defendant Tackett had agreed to release and waive his right in and to the $5000 credit due him on account of overpayment to plaintiff, arising out of the Blow expenses in connection with the Westchester subdivision, and providing plaintiff waives any controversy concerning the items in the account of March 13, 1929, aggregating $2300, no order or decree be entered respecting these amounts; and the master further recommended that the complaint of the plaintiff be dismissed for want of equity. We are of the opinion that the evidence justifies this recommendation and that it was error to sustain exceptions to the report.

To note in detail all the points made by respective counsel would unduly lengthen this opinion. In brief, the record presents the case of a young man, inept in business, inheriting money and persuading his experienced older brother to take his money and guarantee him a fixed income - a situation potential of danger to both parties; the young man goes abroad and regularly receives the income agreed upon, but his extravagance requires withdrawals from the principal of his estate until it is nearly exhausted; one special venture managed by the older brother results in large

profits to the younger; encouraged by this he imagines his brother has also other large profits in which he can share and commences suit, although, with full knowledge, he has released all claims upon his brother. This litigation should never have been commenced.

The decree is reversed and the cause is remanded with directions to enter an order in accordance with the recommendations of the master's report.

REVERSED AND REMANDED WITH DIRECTIONS.

Matchett, P. J., and O'Connor, J., concur.

profits to the younger; encouraged by this he imagines his brother had also other large profits in which he can share and commence suit, although, with full knowledge, he has released all claims upon his brother. This litigation should never have been commenced.

The decree is reversed and the cause is remanded with directions to enter an order in accordance with the recommendations of the master's report.

REVERSED AND REMANDED WITH DIRECTIONS.

Matchett, P. J., and O'Connor, J., concur.

38913

JACOB MICHALIK, Administrator of the Estate of STANLEY MICHALIK, Deceased,
Appellee,

vs.

CITY OF CHICAGO, a Municipal Corporation,
Appellant.

APPEAL FROM SUPERIOR COURT OF COOK COUNTY.

85 A

286 I.A. 617[5]

MR. JUSTICE McSURELY DELIVERED THE OPINION OF THE COURT.

Stanley Michalik, hereafter called plaintiff, eleven years old, was run over by a trailer used in hauling waste and junk attached to a motor truck or tractor owned by defendant, and received injuries which resulted in his death; the administrator brought suit and upon trial had a verdict for $2100; defendant appeals from the judgment entered.

Defendant was engaged in filling in the Illinois-Michigan canal at a point in the neighborhood of 36th street and Homan avenue in Chicago; trailers drawn by motor trucks and loaded with garbage and junk would come in the morning from various parts of the city to this dumping place; the junk would be dumped at the canal bank and then forced by a leveler into the canal; men and boys came to this dumping ground every day to pick bottles and other articles which they might find among the rubbish, and at times, when the trailers stopped or moved slowly, they would get on top of the trailers.

On the morning of the accident a truck hauling three trailers stopped momentarily at the entrance to the dumping ground; it was toward the end of a line of trailers that were slowly moving toward the canal. Plaintiff climbed up on top of the last of the three trailers; he was not noticed by the driver of the tractor, although he was seen by the driver of a following truck.

38913

JACOB MICHALIK, Administrator of
the Estate of STANLEY MICHALIK,
Deceased,
Appellee,

vs.

CITY OF CHICAGO, a Municipal
Corporation,
Appellant.

APPEAL FROM SUPERIOR COURT
OF COOK COUNTY.

286 I.A. 617

MR. JUSTICE McSURELY DELIVERED THE OPINION OF THE COURT.

Stanley Michalik, hereafter called plaintiff, eleven years old, was run over by a trailer used in hauling waste and junk attached to a motor truck or tractor owned by defendant, and received injuries which resulted in his death; the administrator brought suit and upon trial had a verdict for $2100; defendant appeals from the judgment entered.

Defendant was engaged in filling in the Illinois-Michigan canal at a point in the neighborhood of 36th street and Roman avenue in Chicago; trailers drawn by motor trucks and loaded with garbage and junk would come in the morning from various parts of the city to this dumping place; the junk would be dumped at the canal bank and then forced by a leveler into the canal; men and boys came to this dumping ground every day to pick bottles and other articles which they might find among the rubbish, and at times, when the trailers stopped or moved slowly, they would get on top of the trailers.

On the morning of the accident a truck hauling three trailers stopped momentarily at the entrance to the dumping ground; it was toward the end of a line of trailers that were slowly moving toward the canal. Plaintiff climbed up on top of the last of the three trailers; he was not noticed by the driver of the tractor, although he was seen by the driver of a following truck.

Plaintiff's complaint alleged that defendant permitted him, with others, to climb upon the trailers and did not order them to get off, and that the truck drawing the trailer on which plaintiff was, suddenly jerked and started in motion without any warning or signal that it was about to start, and by reason of this plaintiff was violently thrown to the ground from the trailer so that the wheel ran over him, crushing him.

Even conceding that plaintiff while on defendant's trailer was a licensee rather than a trespasser and that the defendant would be liable if through its negligence plaintiff was injured, yet the evidence fails to show any negligence in the operation of the truck and trailers which resulted in injury to the plaintiff. No witness testified that the truck and trailers started with a jerk. One of plaintiff's witnesses testified that they were standing still, "it started up to move slowly, not jerked." The only witness who saw the occurrence was a truck driver following immediately after the trailer from which plaintiff fell. He testified that when they stopped he saw some boys on top of this last trailer and when the truck pulled forward the boys started jumping to the ground; that plaintiff apparently did not try to jump off but laid down on his stomach, threw his legs over the side and started to climb off; that apparently his foot or his hands slipped and he fell to the ground and was under the wheel. The evidence demonstrates that plaintiff was injured not because of any jerking of the trailer or of any failure to sound any warning before it started, but solely because as he was sliding to the ground over the edge of the trailer "he lost his grip and went off," as the eye-witness described it.

The theory of counsel for plaintiff seems to be that the driver was bound to know of the presence of plaintiff on the

Plaintiff's complaint alleged that defendant permitted him, with others, to climb upon the trailers and did not order them to get off, and that the truck drawing the trailer on which plaintiff was, suddenly jerked and started in motion without any warning or signal that it was about to start, and by reason of this plaintiff was violently thrown to the ground from the trailer so that the wheel ran over him, crushing him.

Even conceding that plaintiff while on defendant's trailer was a licensee rather than a trespasser and that the defendant would be liable if through its negligence plaintiff was injured, yet the evidence fails to show any negligence in the operation of the truck and trailers which resulted in injury to the plaintiff. No witness testified that the truck and trailers started with a jerk. One of plaintiff's witnesses testified that they were standing still, "it started up to move slowly, not jerked." The only witness who saw the occurrence was a truck driver following immediately after the trailer from which plaintiff fell. He testified that when they stopped he saw some boys on top of this last trailer and when the truck pulled forward the boys started jumping to the ground; that plaintiff apparently did not try to jump off but laid down on his stomach, threw his legs over the side and started to climb off; that apparently his foot or his hands slipped and he fell to the ground and was under the wheel. The evidence demonstrates that plaintiff was injured not because of any jerking of trailer and should not have moved forward until he had alighted safely. Cases are cited involving railroad cars placed where children were accustomed to go under the cars or in other positions of danger, and where any movement of the cars would almost inevitably injure them. This is quite different from a truck with trailers where the driver, unaware of the presence of a young boy on the trailer, slowly moves forward. In Kasimas v. Chicago Railways Co., 223 Ill. App. 288, where a boy was injured while riding, by permission, on a street car as it was being switched in and out of the car barn, it was held that whether the boy was a trespasser or licensee, the defendant owed him no duty except to refrain from wantonly and wilfully injuring him. There was no evidence whatever of such negligence in the instant case and, as we have said, neither was there any evidence of a lack of due and ordinary care in the operation of the truck and trailers.

Plaintiff's second count was drawn on the theory of an attractive nuisance and charges defendant with the duty of fencing or guarding the dumping ground and of guarding trucks and trailers so as to prevent children from climbing on them. An attractive nuisance has been defined as things which are of such a character as appeal to childish curiosity and instincts, and, left unguarded, are said to hold out an implied invitation to children who, without judgment, are likely to be drawn by childish curiosity into places of danger. The evidence in this case negatives the attractive nuisance theory. The witnesses testified that their purpose in entering the dumping grounds or mounting the trailers was to pick bottles and other articles from the junk which they might sell. The brother of plaintiff testified that they were not playing when they went on the dump but went to pick up certain articles to sell and make money, and that his brother, the plaintiff, was there for the same purpose. The element of attraction

through childish curiosity is completely lacking. The boys went to the place for the purpose of salvaging articles which might be sold.

In many cases it has been held that machines and vehicles in actual use at the time of the injury are not ordinarily recognized by the courts as attractive nuisances, and that the doctrine of attractive nuisance has been restricted to things not in use, to things at rest. Purcell v. Degenhardt, 202 Ill. App. 611; Donaldson v. Spring Valley Coal Co., 175 Ill. App. 224; Scott v. Peabody Coal Co., 153 Ill. App. 103; Newman v. Barber Asphalt Paving Co., 190 Ill. App. 636. Even if this rule were not applicable to the instant facts, there was no evidence tending to support the attractive nuisance theory.

Counsel for defendant says that in removing garbage by the operation of trailers the City is engaged in a governmental function which is the exercise of a police power, consequently the doctrine of respondeat superior does not apply. We are asked to reconsider our former holdings on this question. In Wasilevitsky v. City of Chicago, 280 Ill. App. 531, and Schmidt v. City of Chicago, 284 Ill. App. 570, we considered this question at considerable length. We there held that in the removal of garbage and the operation of trucks and trailers for that purpose the city was not engaged in a governmental function and therefore was not exempt from obligation for negligence of its employees. We see no reason to depart from that ruling.

Defendant complains of an instruction given at the request of the plaintiff embodying a statute limiting the length of tractors and trailers, and telling the jury that if defendant violated this statute the jury should consider this in determining whether defendant was guilty. The evidence showed that the truck with the three trailers exceeded the length prescribed by the statute. The instruction should not have been given. There was no suggestion through childish curiosity is completely lacking. The boys went to the place for the purpose of salvaging articles which might be sold.

In many cases it has been held that machines and vehicles in actual use at the time of the injury are not ordinarily recognized by the courts as attractive nuisances, and that the doctrine of attractive nuisance has been restricted to things not in use, to things at rest. Purcell v. Degenhardt, 202 Ill. App. 611; Donaldson v. Spring Valley Coal Co., 175 Ill. App. 224; Scott v. Peabody Coal Co., 155 Ill. App. 103; Newman v. Barber Asphalt Paving Co., 190 Ill. App. 636. Even if this rule were not applicable to the instant facts, there was no evidence tending to support the attractive nuisance theory.

Counsel for defendant says that in removing garbage by the operation of trailers the City is engaged in a governmental function which is the exercise of a police power, consequently the doctrine of respondeat superior does not apply. We are asked to reconsider our former holdings on this question. In Vasilevitsky v. City of Chicago, 280 Ill. App. 531, and Schmidt v. City of Chicago, 284 Ill. App. 570, we considered this question at considerable length. We there held that in the removal of garbage and the operation of trucks and trailers for that purpose the city was not engaged in a governmental function and therefore was not exempt from obligation for negligence of its employees. We see no reason to depart from that ruling.

Defendant complains of an instruction given at the request of the plaintiff embodying a statute limiting the length of tractors and trailers, and telling the jury that if defendant violated this statute the jury should consider this in determining whether defendant was guilty. The evidence showed that the truck with the three trailers exceeded the length prescribed by the statute. The instruction should not have been given. There was no suggestion in the evidence that the length of the unit had any relation to or connection with the accident.

There was no evidence to go to the jury tending to show any negligent operation of the truck and trailers and there was no evidence supporting plaintiff's contention of an attractive nuisance. At the close of all the evidence the defendant moved the court to instruct the jury to find the defendant not guilty. This was denied. The motion should have been allowed and its denial was reversible error.

For the reasons above indicated the judgment is reversed without remanding the cause.

REVERSED.

Matchett, P. J., and O'Connor, J., concur.

38924

NELLIE RAMSEY, Appellee,

vs.

DR. J. FRANK ARMSTRONG, Appellant.

APPEAL FROM MUNICIPAL COURT OF CHICAGO.

286 I.A. 618[1]

MR. JUSTICE McSURELY DELIVERED THE OPINION OF THE COURT.

Defendant appeals from a judgment for $1900 returned on a verdict for plaintiff in an action brought by her on an alleged oral promise made by defendant to plaintiff that he would support and maintain a child born to her provided plaintiff would not institute bastardy proceedings against defendant, alleged to be the father. Defendant denies he made any such promise and denies that he is the father of the child.

This case has been tried before three juries. The first trial resulted in a judgment against defendant for $1000; appeal was had to this court and on December 24, 1934, (case No. 37529) an opinion was rendered reversing the judgment and remanding the case for another trial on the ground that the verdict was against the manifest weight of the evidence. Upon the second trial plaintiff had a verdict for $825 and the trial court granted a new trial, in which the verdict was again for plaintiff. We are asked to reverse the present judgment on the ground, among other things, that the evidence for plaintiff upon this trial is substantially the same as it was upon the trial reviewed by us where we reversed the judgment. Examination of the record shows that the present testimony for plaintiff is substantially the same as in the prior review, and the testimony for defendant much stronger.

Briefly stated, plaintiff says that in October, 1928, her name was Nellie Young; that she was 18 years old and unmarried; that she was troubled with pains in the lower part of her abdomen;

that a girl friend recommended defendant as a physician and she went to his office for treatments; that he treated her on three occasions; that on the first two visits nothing improper occurred; that the last visit was on November 12th at 8 o'clock in the evening; that she went with her little sister to the Doctor's office, where there were other patients in the reception room; that when she went into the Doctor's private office he had sexual intercourse with her; that about three days thereafter she telephoned him that she had not menstruated, and he subsequently gave her some pills to take; that about January 29th she told the Doctor that she was pregnant and that he then promised that if she would not tell anyone he would take care of the baby when it was born; that the baby was born July 27, 1929, and that about two months thereafter she called with the baby at the office of defendant, who admitted he was the father and promised to support the child; that defendant gave her no money at any time. In June, 1932, she was married and her present name is Ramsey.

Defendant testified that he was a married man, a practicing physician in Chicago for more than twenty years and for twenty years had been connected with the Board of Health of Chicago as a school health officer; that plaintiff first called upon him in his office on October 20, 1928; that she complained of pains in the lower part of her abdomen; that he made a vaginal examination and found some tenderness over the left ovary and the mouth of the womb was red, inflamed and inclined to be purplish, indicating congestion; that he gave her electrical treatments by what is known as a vaginal electrode; that her next visit was on October 24, 1928, when the treatment was repeated; that the third and last visit was on November 8, 1928, when plaintiff complained that the treatments had not done any good, that they had not made her menstruate, and defendant told her that the treatments were not for that purpose;

that plaintiff paid $2 for this visit and was angry, threatening to get even with the Doctor. Defendant testified that he never had sexual intercourse with plaintiff on November 12th or at any other time. Defendant's testimony as to the time and number of visits is supported by the records he kept, showing the last visit to be on November 8th.

There was also evidence that plaintiff kept company with a "boy friend"; that she told this friend that she was pregnant and that she did not want him to get in trouble on this account and told him to disappear, which he did. As we said in our former opinion, there is other evidence which we do not think it necessary to detail. The entire record impels to the conclusion that plaintiff failed to prove her claim by the greater weight of the evidence.

There was also additional evidence offered by defendant which completely negatives plaintiff's testimony in one important respect. She testified that nothing out of the way happened on her first and second visits to defendant's office; that she is positive her third visit, on which the alleged intercourse took place, was on November 12, 1928, and that she arrived at the office about eight o'clock in the evening with her little sister; she was positive she had never had sexual intercourse at any other time or place with defendant except on this date, November 12th.

Defendant introduced convincing evidence that he was not in his office at the time specified by plaintiff. Dr. Stanley, a dentist sharing a suite of offices with defendant, testified that he was in the office on the evening of November 12, 1928; that at about six o'clock two men came in and asked for Dr. Armstrong, who identified himself; they said they were detectives and had a subpoena for Dr. Armstrong, read the subpoena to him and left him a copy; that defendant left the office at about six o'clock and did

not return that evening; that witness remained in the office until about nine o'clock or shortly thereafter, and did not see the plaintiff at all that evening.

Defendant testified as to the service of the subpoena on him, requiring him to appear before the grand jury of the Criminal court of Cook county at seven o'clock that evening. The copy of the subpoena is in evidence and commands defendant to appear in room 540 Otis building on November 12, 1928, at seven o'clock p.m. to give testimony in a certain pending cause. Defendant testified that upon receipt of the subpoena he left his office about 6:20 p. m., arriving at the Otis building about seven o'clock, where he remained until nine or 9:20 o'clock; that he was accompanied by a Mr. Hatchett, that they were together all the evening, arriving home about 9:30. Mr. Hatchett testified, confirming in every way the testimony of defendant in this respect. Sheridan Brosseaux testified that he was a special investigator for the grand jury in November, 1928, with his office in room 540 Otis building; that he issued the subpoena which contains his initials; that he saw Dr. Armstrong in his office at about a quarter to seven on the evening of November 12th; that he was examined as a witness and left at about nine or 9:15 o'clock.

Counsel for plaintiff call attention to the testimony of the night watchman in the Otis building, who keeps a register of persons entering the building after seven o'clock in the evening. A photostatic copy of the register is in the record; it does not contain defendant's name as having entered the building on that evening. However, the watchman further testified that a number of persons went to room 540 of the Otis building on business there with a "crime commission," and that he would let these persons go up without interference from him. The photostatic copy of the register kept by the watchman shows the rooms in the building to

which persons went after seven o'clock p. m., but fails to show that anyone went to room 540, where the witnesses were summoned to appear before the grand jury, and yet it is not denied that ten or more people went to this room on that evening. The evidence sufficiently demonstrates that defendant was not in his office at the time plaintiff testified defendant had intercourse with her.

There was persuasive evidence that when plaintiff first visited defendant and was examined by him she was already pregnant and that she hoped to obtain from defendant medicine which would cause her to menstruate.

As plaintiff failed to produce convincing evidence that defendant is the father of her child, it follows that there was no consideration for the alleged promise by defendant to support it even if we should accept plaintiff's version as to what defendant said in this respect.

Defendant testified that after the visit on November8, 1928, he never saw plaintiff or had any telephone conversation with her until she called upon him on September 20, 1932, - a period of nearly four years; that in the interval she had never threatened to take him into the bastardy court, he never knew she had a baby, and had made no promise to contribute to its support; that the first he knew of any claim that he was the father of the child was upon this visit in September, 1932; that he had entirely forgotten her, and that when she referred to "our baby" he asked her what had put it into her head to bring this charge, and that she replied that the depression was on and she had to have money; that he replied that he was in no way responsible for the child and was not going to do anything about it; that when she left she asked defendant not to say anything about it, saying, "I don't want anybody to know I have spoken to you about it."

Other points are made which it is not necessary to note. A

re-examination of the evidence, and especially the additional evidence given on behalf of defendant, impels the conclusion that the verdict of the jury must have been through sympathy for plaintiff. The verdict, both as to the paternity of the child and as to the alleged promise of defendant to support it, is manifestly against the weight of the evidence and a court of review cannot, in the exercise of its duty, permit a judgment based upon such a verdict to stand.

Counsel for defendant argue that under provision 3 of section 68 of the Civil Practice act, a motion for a directed verdict made at the close of all the evidence raises a question of law for the court to decide. This provision has no application to the instant case where only questions of fact were presented for determination.

If we had the power to pass upon the weight of the evidence we would enter judgment in this court for the defendant. But this we cannot do. For the reasons indicated the judgment is reversed and the cause remanded.

REVERSED AND REMANDED.

Matchett, P. J., and O'Connor, J., concur.

38943

PEOPLE OF THE STATE OF ILLINOIS, ex rel. OSCAR NELSON, as Auditor of Public Accounts of the State of Illinois,
Complainant,

vs.

UNION BANK OF CHICAGO, a Corporation,
Defendant.

LEWIS M. WILLIAMS,
Appellee,

vs.

JAMES S. RODIE, Receiver of Union Bank of Chicago, a Corporation,
Appellant.

APPEAL FROM CIRCUIT COURT OF COOK COUNTY.

87 A

286 I.A. 618[2]

MR. JUSTICE O'CONNOR DELIVERED THE OPINION OF THE COURT.

By this appeal the receiver of the Union Bank of Chicago, a corporation, seeks to reverse a decree of the Circuit courtof Cook county allowing petitioners' claim for $7890 as a general claim.

The record discloses that the bank was being liquidated in a proceeding brought by the Auditor of Public Accounts, and a petition was filed in the proceeding praying that an order be entered allowing petitioners' claim as a preferred claim against the assets of the bank. The receiver answered the petition, denying liability, the matter was referred to a master in chancery, who heard the evidence, made up his report and recommended that the claim be allowed as a general claim. The receiver's objections to the report were overruled and a decree was entered in accordance with the master's report.

December 28, 1928, Harriet K. Williams entered into a written agreement with the Union Bank of Chicago by which the bank agreed to act as trustee for certain of her property, real

and personal; only the latter is involved in this proceeding. Under the agreement she deposited $30,000 with the bank. The bank from time to time invested the money in certain securities, among which were 70 shares of the preferred stock of the Middle West Utilities Company and three bonds of the Southern Cities Public Service Company, which are involved in the case before us.

Petitioners' claim, as set up in their verified petition, is that the bank refused and neglected to sell the stock and bonds as requested by Lewis M. Williams, a beneficiary of the trust estate and one of the petitioners; that the market value of the securities rapidly declined and the bank was liable for the loss.

The trust agreement entered into between the bank and Harriet K. Williams, who was the mother of the petitioners, provided that the bank should "hold, manage, care for and protect the Trust Estate. It shall invest and reinvest the same from time to time as circumstances shall require and good judgment dictate, with the written consent, however, of LEWIS M. WILLIAMS. *** The Trustee shall have full power to sell and convey any or all of the Trust Estate, *** and any investments or reinvestments thereof from time to time for such prices and upon such terms as it shall see fit, provided, however, that they shall first secure the written consent of LEWIS M. WILLIAMS, *** the Trustee shall have full power and discretion in the management of the Trust Estate that it would have as an individual, if it were the absolute owner thereof, subject only to such restrictions as hereinbefore mentioned."

Lewis M. Williams, named in the trust agreement, was the son of the settlor, Harriet K. Williams. He testified that about three or four weeks prior to September 2, 1931, he called at the bank and talked with Mr. M. A. Bierdemann, of the Trust Department, to whom he had been referred by an official of the bank, that he told Bierdemann he had been advised and wished to dispose of the

stocks and bonds; that Bierdemann said he would bring the matter to the attention of the committee of the bank which attended to such matters and would later furnish the witness with a letter for his signature, in accordance with the provisions of the trust agreement; that at that time he told Mr. Bierdemann the stock was selling at $90 a share and the bonds at $530 a bond; that a few days later, not having heard from the bank, he called Bierdemann on the telephone and inquired about the matter and was advised that the committee of the bank had not yet met but that the matter would be attended to shortly; that two days later he had a similar conversation with Bierdemann; that he was ill for a short time, but on his recovery again called the bank on October 17, and again saw Biedermann, who said that nothing had been done about the matter; that thereupon witness stated he would hold the bank responsible for the loss sustained; that at that time he told Biedermann the stock was then quoted at $69 a share and the bonds at $460 a bond; that at that time Bierdemann said the banking situation in Chicago was very uncertain and that it had been impossible to get the bank committee together to take up the question of the sale of the securities, and Bierdemann also spoke of the pending merger between the Union Bank and the Chicago Bank of Commerce.

Bierdemann, called by petitioners, testified that he was an attorney at law and in 1931 was employed in the Trust department of the Union Bank; that some time prior to September 2nd he was called on the telephone by Lewis M. Williams about the sale of the stocks and bonds, and that on September 2nd Williams called at the bank and spoke about the matter, and "I informed him the investments were all right and should not be sold"; that on September 2nd Williams said he wanted the stock and bonds sold and witness replied that he would "report it to the committee, and would deliver to him the report of sale and the necessary instructions for signature;" that after Williams left he talked to the vice-president of the bank, who was

in charge of the Trust Department, and advised him of Williams' request, and the vice-president said he would take the matter up before the committee. The witness further testified that in October Williams again called and inquired about the matter and became very angry when informed that the securities had not been sold; "I explained the action of the bank was not deliberate, but simply the banking situation at that time; that the officers of our bank were occupied with their conferences, one thing and another, without calling the trust committee together." He further testified corroborating the testimony of Williams as to the price at which the stocks and bonds were selling.

It further appears from the record that the bank acted as trustee from the date of its appointment, December 28, 1928, until the bank was closed by the Auditor of Public Accounts June 24, 1932, and that the receiver was appointed June 28, 1932, by the Auditor, whose action was later confirmed by the Circuit court of Cook county. It is further stated in the record that Lewis M. Williams, in a suit instituted in the Circuit court of Cook county apparently by the beneficiaries named in the trust agreement, was appointed successor-trustee in lieu of the bank, and it is repeatedly stated in the record and briefs that he was appointed such successor-trustee January 9, 1932. Apparently this is an error, because if the bank acted as trustee until June 24, 1932, the appointment of Williams as successor-trustee would not be until after that date. However the date is not important. What ultimately became of the stocks and bonds does not appear and is somewhat of a mystery.

In their brief counsel for the receiver say that "Where the trustee is vested with absolute authority and discretion in the management of the trustee estate, the trustee is not required to sell upon the direction or request of a beneficiary and a refusal to sell on such request is not a breach of the fiduciary relation;"

and that "A trustee and others standing in a fiduciary relation are held only to the exercise of reasonable, diligent and ordinary prudence and caution, and such fiduciary is not liable for loss to the trust estate occasioned by an unforeseen occurrence." And in support of these contentions say that under the trust agreement the power to sell the securities was vested in the absolute discretion of the trustee, and the failure or refusal of the trustee to sell the securities upon the request of Lewis M. Williams did not constitute a breach of the fiduciary relation. The trust agreement did not vest absolute discretion in the trustee, but expressly provided that before securities could be sold the trustee must secure the written consent of Lewis M. Williams, one of the beneficiaries. But counsel further say that even if the trustee did not have absolute discretion in the sale of the securities but its authority to sell was subject to the consent of Lewis M. Williams, he could defeat a sale but had no power to compel the trustee to sell. We agree with this contention, but it is of little or no importance because the uncontradicted evidence shows that the securities were not sold by the trustee because it thought it was inadvisable to do so at the time it was requested, but that they were not sold because the committee of the bank did not have the time, on account of the chaotic conditions of banks in Chicago, including the Union Bank itself, to take the matter up and sell them. Obviously, this action of the banks falls far short of carrying out the provisions of the trust agreement; the law requires a trustee to exercise reasonable diligence and ordinary prudence and caution.

But counsel for the receiver further contend that the trust agreement expressly makes the trustee liable only "for its own wilful omissions or misconduct;" that there is no evidence that the trustee deliberately intended to do wrong and, therefore, the trust agreement was not breached by the trustee. The difficulty with

this contention is that the case was not tried on that theory. The master found that at the time Lewis M. Williams requested the bank to sell the securities the market for such securities was rapidly declining, and that the bank, under the facts disclosed by the evidence, was negligent in failing to sell the securities, and that petitioners suffered loss as the result of such negligence because the trustee did not exercise reasonable care and caution under the circumstances. The receiver filed objections to the master's report, in which no objection was made that the receiver would not be liable unless he was guilty of "wilful omissions or misconduct;" on the contrary, one of the objections was that the master had failed to find the trustee was obligated to exercise only "that degree of care and caution in the *** affairs of its trust as an ordinary prudent man would exercise in the administration of his own affairs." After taking that position before the master and the chancellor, the receiver will not now be permitted to shift his position in a court of review.

The receiver further contends that the burden was on the petitioners to prove the amount of their damages and that there is no proof of any substantial damages. The verified petition alleged that on September 2, 1931, when Lewis M. Williams requested that the securities be sold, the stock was selling for $90 a share and the bonds for $530 each; that on October 17, 1931, when Williams again called the bank, the stock was selling at $69 a share and the bonds for $460 each. The petition was filed February 7, 1934, and it was further there alleged that at the time of the filing of the petition the stock was of no value and the bonds quoted at $100 a bond. The receiver, in its answer, neither admitted nor denied the allegation as to the value at the time of the filing of the petition but called for strict proof, and there is not a scintilla of evidence in the record on the question. Moreover, Lewis M. Williams, one of the

petitioners and a beneficiary, was appointed trustee succeeding the bank on January 9, 1932, (probably 1933) and presumably the securities were turned over to him. What disposition was made of them does not appear. The master, in computing the damages, did so as of September 2, 1931, giving the value of the stock as $90 a share and of the bonds as $530 each, and this was approved by the master. We think the question of damages was properly saved by the receiver. In one of his objections filed to the master's report the receiver complained that the court had erred in assessing the damages at $7890. The record failing to show the amount of damages sustained by the petitioners as a result of the trustee's negligence, the decree must be reversed as to the $7890 and the cause remanded.

The decree of the Circuit court of Cook county is reversed and the cause remanded.

REVERSED AND REMANDED.

Matchett, P. J., specially concurring: I agree that the decree should be reversed but doubt very much whether defendant is at all liable under the facts.

McSurely, J., concurs.

AT A TERM OF THE APPELLATE COURT,

Begun and held at Ottawa, on Tuesday, the fifth day of May, in the year of our Lord one thousand nine hundred and thirty-six, within and for the Second District of the State of Illinois:

Present -- the Hon. BLAINE HUFFMAN, Presiding Justice.

Hon. FRANKLIN R. DOVE, Justice.

Hon. FRED G. WOLFE, Justice.

JUSTUS L. JOHNSON, Clerk.

RALPH H. DESPER, Sheriff.

286 I.A. 618[3]

BE IT REMEMBERED, that afterwards, to-wit: On SEP 3 1936 the opinion of the Court was filed in the Clerk's Office of said Court, in the words and figures following to-wit:

Gen. No. 9057 Agenda No. 3

IN THE APPELLATE COURT OF ILLINOIS

SECOND DISTRICT

MAY TERM, A. D. 1936

THE PEOPLE OF THE STATE OF ILLINOIS,

Defendant in Error

vs.

IRA PAGE,

Plaintiff in Error.

Error to the Circuit Court, Ogle County.

HUFFMAN - P.J.

This writ of error is prosecuted by plaintiff in error to review his conviction for assault. He was indicted by the grand jury of Ogle county for the crime of assault with a deadly weapon, with intent to do bodily injury. Upon a trial, the jury found him guilty of simple assault. The court assessed a fine of $50 upon the verdict.

The evidence shows that on October 6, 1934, one Frank Simone and two companions went out squirrel hunting. About mid-day they entered a certain woods which belonged to plaintiff in error. In this woods they shot one squirrel. The plaintiff in error upon hearing the shot, immediately proceeded to the place. Upon reaching the hunters, plaintiff in error began using strong and offensive language, and ordered the hunters from the premises. The evidence shows that the hunters made no resistance and interposed no objections to leaving the premises of plaintiff in error. However, the plaintiff in error seized the shot gun of the said Simone and undertook to take the same away from him. The gun was discharged in the scuffle, but no one was hurt. The parties proceeded to go toward the road with a constant argument and exortation taking place on the part of plaintiff in error, with threats to have the hunters arrested for trespassing.

The evidence of Ira Page, the plaintiff in error, discloses that

when he heard the shot back in the timber, he immediately got in his car and proceeded to the place in question; that he hurried over to where the hunters were; that he asked them what they were doing, to which they responded they were hunting. He states that he called them thieves, whereupon they insisted they were not thieves; that he went up to the largest one, Frank Simone, and told him he was under arrest, and to give him the gun; that he thereupon grabbed the gun and endeavored to take the same away from Simone. This is the time the gun was discharged. Plaintiff in error states that they started for the road; that when they reached the road he called to one Fassler, who was with him and who had remained in the car, to bring him "the club." It appears the said plaintiff in error was furnished with a club, and that when he was handed the club, the said Simone jerked loose from him, went over the top of the fence and fell into the ditch on the outside. During the time they were approaching the fence, plaintiff in error had hold of Simone. He states that after Simone fell over the fence into the ditch that he went under the fence with the club under his right arm, and again took hold of Simone; that Simone in endeavoring to pull away from him, again fell in the ditch, and plaintiff in error claims that when Simone fell this time, the stock of the gun struck the ground, causing the barrel to fly up and hit Simone over the right eye knocking him unconscious. Plaintiff in error claims that this was the manner in which Simone received the blow complained of, instead of being hit with the aforesaid club, by plaintiff in error.

It is claimed on the part of the defendant in error that plaintiff in error struck Simone over the head with the club in question, knocking him unconscious. The evidence is hopelessly in dispute, and therefore, is not susceptible of being reconciled. It demonstrates a persistent belligerent spirit on the part of plaintiff in error. There is nothing to indicate that the hunters after being order to leave, in any way delayed or refused to do so. However, the plaintiff in error entered into an argument and scuffle with these three parties

le unit, doubtlessly based upon the fact that they had
is premises without his consent. His conduct was directed
em as a whole, and his laying hold of them was not confined
. The jury heard the evidence and saw the witnesses. There
g appearing in the record which we consider indicates in
hat the verdict of the jury was the result of passion or
, or prompted by improper motives. The mere fact that the
is conflicting and in dispute as between the witnesses for
f in error and those of defendant in error, does not of
ustify a position that the verdict is against the weight
vidence. Unless from a review of the record the court so
t will not substitute its judgment for that of the jury.
considered the other objections argued by plaintiff in error,
not consider them sufficient to warrant us in disturbing
ct.

judgment will therefore be affirmed.

Judgment affirmed.

STATE OF ILLINOIS, }ss.
SECOND DISTRICT

I JUSTUS L. JOHNSON Clerk of the Appellate Court, in and for said Second District of the State of Illinois, and the keeper of the Records and Seal thereof, do hereby certify that the foregoing is a true copy of the opinion of the said Appellate Court in the above entitled cause of record in my office.

In Testimony Whereof, I hereunto set my hand and affix the seal of said Appellate Court, at Ottawa, this ________ day of ________ in the year of our Lord one thousand nine hundred and thirty-________

____
Clerk of the Appellate Court

(73815—5M—3-32)

and held at Ottawa, on Tuesday, the fifth day of May, in
e year of our Lord one thousand nine hundred and thirty-six,
thin and for the Second District of the State of Illinois:

nt -- the Hon. BLAINE HUFFMAN, Presiding Justice.
Hon. FRANKLIN R. DOVE, Justice.
Hon. FRED G. WOLFE, Justice.
JUSTUS L. JOHNSON, Clerk.
RALPH H. DESPER, Sheriff.

286 I.A. 619[1]

BE IT REMEMBERED, that afterwards, to-wit: On SEP 3 1936
opinion of the Court was filed in the Clerk's Office of said
t, in the words and figures following, to-wit:

Gen. No. 9063 Agenda No. 6

IN THE APPELLATE COURT OF ILLINOIS

SECOND DISTRICT

MAY TERM, A. D. 1936

VIOLA RAPSON, ELIZABETH EMERY, and SYDNEY GEDDES,

Appellees,

vs.

SILVER CROSS HOSPITAL, a corporation,

Appellant.

Appeal from County Court, Will County.

HUFFMAN, P.J.

This is an appeal from the judgment of the county court of Will County in favor of appellees. They instituted suit against appellant for a balance claimed due for unpaid services. The cause was heard without jury. The court gave judgment in favor of Viola Rapson for $376.85, in favor of Elizabeth Emery for $532.31, and in favor of Sydney Geddes for $138.25. Miss Rapson started work for appellant hospital in 1931. She was a night supervisor. Miss Emery began work in 1932. She also was a night supervisor. Mr. Geddes began work in 1927, as an assistant in the kitchen.

Appellant became financially embarrassed. Its monthly cash receipts were insufficient to pay operating expenses. Prior to June 1, 1932, appellees had received and accepted two reductions in salary. In this case it is claimed by appellant that appellees agreed they would accept a salary which was to be determined upon a percentage basis, after June 1, 1932. Appellants explanation of this wage scale was, that the monthly cash receipts were to be marshaled, the bills first paid, and that the balance, if any, was to be divided among the employees of the hospital, based upon a pro rata division, according to the relationship between their monthly salary and the fund to be divided. This scheme of payment was subject to a further variation

between those who received full time keep at the hospital, and those who did not. There is nothing to show to what extent this condition was to affect the above method of division of the monthly receipts. Appellees maintain that although the above situation existed, yet there was no contract, understanding, or agreement that they should reduce their wages to such a monthly contingency. They claim that such payments as they received under the above plan were to be taken and considered as advancements upon their monthly salary, and that it was definitely understood and agreed they should receive any deficiency that might accumulate in their monthly wages, as fast as the hospital was able to pay same. This is the only question in the case, whether appellees agreed to waive all fixed salary and to accept whatever division came to them at the end of each month from the cash receipts, or whether such divisions were payments being made upon their salary by the hospital during such financial stringency.

Appellant urges the weight of authority supports the rule that a promise by debtor to pay as soon as financial circumstances permit, or as soon as he can, when relied upon as an original promise, makes it incumbent upon the creditor to show that the condition has been fulfilled. The cases relied upon by appellant are distinguishable from the case at bar. In those cases cited by appellant there either existed no promise at all, or the condition was one to be performed by the payee, and not performed, or payment was to be made from and out of a certain fund. Here the evidence on behalf of appellees tended to show a definite promise to pay, that the services were performed, and that a certain amount remained due. If there was a definite promise to pay, that part of the agreement to pay as soon as possible, merely indicates a convenient and seasonable time. Under such contracts payment must be made after the lapse of a reasonable time. Allen v. Estate of Henry P. Allen, 217 Ill. App. 260, 268.

Appellant attributed the necessity of making the reductions in appellee's salaries, and its inability to pay such reduced salaries, to the fact that it was unable to collect for services rendered tothe

people using the hospital. In October, 1933, appellant made an attempt to secure sufficient funds to pay its outstanding indebtedness, by soliciting donations from the citizens of Will County. Advertisements appeared in the newspaper in which were listed a part of the financial status of appellant institution. The advertisement soliciting funds contained the following:

"Silver Cross Hospital Needs Your Help!!

This is no ordinary call for help. It is an appeal bornof ABSOLUTE NECESSITY.

Silver Cross Hospital, after serving the people of Will County for 38 years, is face to face with a financial crisis.

This crisis has been brought about through the tremendous increase in UNPAID FOR service rendered by this hospital during the past three years.

During the past 12 months alone, the UNPAID FOR service amounted to $20,000. This was financed as follows:

1.	Funds from County Board for County Patients ...	$4,000.00
2.	Funds from Relief Commission for County Patients	1,800.00
3.	Tag Day, October, 1932, after allowance for cost of new well	500.00
4.	Interest from Endowments (over $5600 retained for interest on bonded indebtedness)	4,000.00
5.	Unpaid Pay Roll..	9,500.00
		$19,800.00"

The record in this case is rather large, being comprised of four volumes, having a combined thickness of more than a foot. The testimony is conflicting. We have examined the same and are not disposed to disagree with the trial court on the judgment rendered. On controverted questions of fact, a court of review can determine only whether the evidence fairly tends to support the judgment. Sullivan v. Ohlhaver Co. 291 Ill. 359; Mayer v. Gersbacher, 207 Ill. 296, 306. A verdict or judgment rendered on conflicting evidence will not be

as it appears that it is manifestly against
se. Johnson v. Mutual Trust Life Ins. Co.
Seiffe v. id. 267 Ill. App. 23.
trial court is therefore affirmed.

Judgment Affirmed.

} ss.

I, JUSTUS L. JOHNSON, Clerk of the Appellate Court, in and the State of Illinois, and the keeper of the Records and Seal thereof, do hereby a true copy of the opinion of the said Appellate Court in the above entitled cause

In Testimony Whereof, I hereunto set my hand and affix the seal of said Appellate Court at Ottawa, this________________day of ________________in the year of our Lord one thousand nine hundred and thirty-____________

____

Clerk of the Appellate Court

AT A TERM OF THE APPELLATE COURT,

and held at Ottawa, on Tuesday, the fifth day of May, in
year of our Lord one thousand nine hundred and thirty-six,
thin and for the Second District of the State of Illinois:

it -- The Hon. BLAINE HUFFMAN, Presiding Justice.
Hon. FRANKLIN R. DOVE, Justice.
Hon. FRED G. WOLFE, Justice.
JUSTUS L. JOHNSON, Clerk
RALPH H. DESPER, Sheriff.

286 I.A. 619

IT REMEMBERED, that afterwards, to-wit On Oct. 8 1936
pinion of the Court was filed in the Clerk's Office of said
, in the words and figures following, to-wit:

Gen. No. 9082 Agenda No. 21

IN THE APPELLATE COURT OF ILLINOIS,

SECOND DISTRICT

MAY TERM, A. D. 1936

WILLIAM L. O'CONNELL, Receiver of Home Trust and Savings Bank, Elgin, Illinois, etc.,

Appellant,

vs.

FELTON CLINIC OF ELGIN, Inc., a Corporation, etc.,

Appellee.

Appeal from the Circuit Court, Kane County.

HUFFMAN - P.J.

This was an action by appellant against appellee upon an alleged guarantee. The cause was heard by the court and judgment rendered in favor of appellee. Appellant appeals.

The evidence consisted of a stipulation of facts and the testimony of three witnesses who had been in the services of the Home Trust and Savings Bank of Elgin, prior to its failure. It appears that appellee was a corporation of this state organized for profit, and by its charter, licensed to "establish, equip, operate and maintain a general medical, surgical and dental clinic; also clinical, pathological, medical, surgical and dental research and other laboratories, and also hospitals for the treatment and care of those requiring medical, surgical and dental attention." The corporation was organized under date of January 8, 1930. One of the owners, C. L. Felton, Jr., died and his interest in the enterprise passed to his widow, Julia B. Felton. J. Donald Milligan was a physician living in the City of Elgin, and had been associated with the Felton Clinic since 1921. Prior to its incorporation, it had operated as a common law trust. Dr. Milligan was desirous of purchasing the interest in said corporation that was held by said

PIERSON CLINIC OF ELGIN, Inc., a
Corporation, etc.,

Appellee.

BRISTOW - P.J.

This was an action by appellant against appellee u[illegible]
alleged guarantee. The cause was heard by the court [illegible]
rendered in favor of appellee. Appellant appeals.

The evidence consisted of a stipulation of facts an[illegible]
testimony of three witnesses who had been in the service
Home Trust and Savings Bank of Elgin, prior to its fail[illegible]
appears that appellee was a corporation of this state o[illegible]
for profit, and by its charter, licensed to "establish,
and maintain a general medical, surgical and dental clin[illegible]
clinical, pathological, medical, surgical and dental r[illegible]
other laboratories, and also hospitals for the treatment
of those requiring medical, surgical and dental attendance
corporation was organized under date of January 8, 1920.

deceased. He consummated such desire by purchasing same from the widow, Julia B. Pelton. He borrowed the money necessary to purchase this stock, from the Home Trust and Savings Bank of Elgin, giving therefor his promissory note under date of Februry 14,1931, in the principal sum of $12,000. Upon the back of the note given by Dr. Milligan was the following endorsement: "For value received we hereby guarantee the payment of the within note, at maturity or at any time thereafter, with interest at 6 per cent. per annum after date, until paid, and agree to pay all costs and expenses paid or incurred in collecting the same and hereby waive demand of payment and notice of non-payment." This endorsement was signed: "The Pelton Clinic of Elgin, Inc." "O.L. Pelton, Sr., Pres., B.L. Gabay, Vice-Pres. and J. Donald Milligan, Director." The above bank suspended business on January 12, 1932. Dr. Milligan defaulted in the payment of the note and this suit resulted against appellee.

There is nothing in the record tending to show that any consideration moved to appellee corporation by the execution of the note by Dr. Milligan to the bank. He used this money to purchase from the widow of O.L. Pelton, Jr., deceased, the interest in the corporation held by said deceased at the time of his death. It is undisputed that the money was secured by Dr. Milligan from the bank for the above purpose, that the officers of the bank so understood the transaction, and that they considered the endorsement by the appellee corporation upon the back of the note as a guarantee for the payment thereof. The evidence fails to support any claim that any part of the consideration for the giving of the note went to appellee. It demonstrates however that it was purely a private transaction on the part of Dr. Milligan in buying an interest in the corporation from the holder thereof. Under such circumstances, the appellee must be considered as an accomodation signer. A similar situation, which is considered controlling here, was before this court in the case of Culhane v. Swords Co. 281 Ill. App. 185, 200, 201, wherein it was held that a corporation suchas the one involved herein, has no implied power to indorse notes for the mere accommodation

when such transaction is foreign to the objects for
orporation was created. Such an act subjects the assets
ration to risks wholly different from that for which it
Where there is no power to make the contract, there
wer to ratify it. In addition to the authorities referred
ords Case supporting the rule above announced, is that of
well Belting Co. 134 Ill. 574.
gment of the Circuit Court is affirmed.

Judgment affirmed.

}ss.
I, JUSTUS L JOHNSON Clerk of the Appellate Couıt ın and of the State of Illınoıs, and the keepeı of the Records and Seal thereof, do hereby ; ıs a true copy of the opınıon of the saıd Appellate Court ın the above entıtled cause

In Testımony Wheıeof, I hereunto set my hand and affix the seal of saıd Appellate Couıt, at Ottawa, thıs ____________ day of ____________ ın the year of our Lord one thousand nıne hundıed and thırty-____________

____
Clerk of the Appellate Court

AT A TERM OF THE APPELLATE COURT,

.d at Ottawa, on Tuesday, the fifth day of May, in
of our Lord one thousand nine hundred and thirty-six,
l for the Second District of the State of Illinois

ie Hon. BLAINE HUFFMAN, Presiding Justice.
Hon. FRANKLIN R. DOVE, Justice.
Hon. FRED G. WOLFE, Justice.
JUSTUS L. JOHNSON, Clerk
RALPH H. DESPER, Sheriff. 286 I.A. 619[3.]

EMBERED, that afterwards, to-wit. On SEP 2 1936
of the Court was filed in the Clerk's Office of said
e words and figures following, to-wit·

Gen. No. 9108 Agenda No. 33

IN THE APPELLATE COURT OF ILLINOIS

SECOND DISTRICT

MAY TERM, A. D. 1936

C. A. WIDMAN and SAMUEL TWAIT,

Appellees.

vs.

PEOPLES TRUST AND SAVINGS BANK OF OTTAWA, et al. (The First National Bank of Ottawa, Illinois, Executor of the Last Will and Testament of Patrick J. Mahoney, deceased, and Robert Carr,

Appellants.

Appeal from Circuit Court LaSalle County.

HUFFMAN- P.J.

This case comes to this court by transfer from the Supreme Court. (Widman v. Peoples Trust and Savings Bank, 363 Ill. 345). It is an action by the creditors of a defunct bank to enforce stockholders liability under sec. 6 of Article XI of the Constitution. Only two points are urged by appellants for reversal, namely, the Statute of Limitations, and Laches. It was strenuously argued by counsel for appellants that defendants in actions of this character may avail themselves of the defense of the Statute of Limitations. They refer to no such case in this state. However, the question received the consideration of the Supreme Court in the case of Sanders v. Merchants State Bank, 349 Ill. 547. In this respect the court in that case, at pp. 559, 560 of its opinion, has the following to say: "In regard to the application of the Statute of Limitations, the appellees contend that no question of the Statute of Limitations arises on the record, because, while the debt of the bank to its creditor and the liability of the stockholder accrue at the same time - that is, at the time the indebtedness is incurred by the bank - yet no cause of action accrues against either

the bank or the stockholder until the debt or liability becomes due; that the cause of action accrues against both at the same time, and that time is when the bank becomes insolvent, suspends payment, closes its doors and quits business. On the other hand, it is argued on behalf of the appellants that the bank's liabilities in large part are barred by the Statute of Limitations; that the argument of the appellees applies only to deposits payable on demand and subject to check, and not to liabilities evidence by promissory notes executed or indorsed by the bank, drafts accepted or indorsed by the bank, certificates of deposit payable at fixed dates, breaches of contracts, or covenants in deeds or leases, torts, deceit, misrepresentation or fraud, or other forms of obligation or liability upon which no demand is necessary before the bringing of suit. Upon such liabilities the cause of action accrues against the bank upon the breach of its contract, the commission of the tort or fraud or the making of the misrepresentation, and an action may be begun at once against the bank for such breach, and against the stockholder at the same time upon his constitutional liability."

In further dealing with this question, the court in the above case on pp. 562, 563, 564 of its opinion, uses the following language: "The questions argued in regard to the Statute of Limitations are, whether the five-year or the ten-year Statute of Limitations applies in favor of the stockholder, and, When does a cause of action accrue in favor of the creditor? An answer to these questions would require a division of each, dependent upon the character of the creditors' claims. The decree makes no distinction in this respect among the creditors. Every finding of the court is a general finding of the total liabilities of the bank to all its creditors, without any distinction. The total amount of all the bank's liabilities at the date of the decree was found to be $740,000. It cannot be assumed that this amount was all due to depositors, and, even if this could be assumed, it cannot be assumed that all these deposits were subject to check. Usually a bank has savings deposits, which are subject to

a certain number of days' notice before payment may be demanded. Certificates of deposit are also issued, sometimes payable on demand, sometimes on fixed dates. Besides liabilities to its depositors, banks become liable on their own promissory notes for money borrowed, on bills re-discounted upon the bank's endorsement, on cashier's checks, for rent, the salaries of its officers, and other current expenses and other forms of liability, besides its liability to its depositors. Among the liabilities of this bank may be claims of the character of each of the forms of liability which have been mentioned and of other forms, and to some of them the five-year Statute of Limitations may be appropriate and to others the ten-year Statute, and the Statute of Limitations may begin to run against some at a different date from others. A plea of the Statute of Limitations must apply to a particular claim or class of claims. Each stockholder or class of stockholders may file pleas of the statute against any creditor or class or creditors who may be subject to its operation. It is manifest that there are probably many creditors against whose claims no plea of any statute of limitations could be truthfully made. It is equally probable that against some of the claims a statute of limitations may properly be pleaded and sustained. Under the stipulation that all questions involved in the litigation which may be raised upon the record have been duly raised by appropriate pleas, we may not decide upon the validity of those pleas which we have not seen and cannot see. Neither the character of any item of indebtedness found to have accrued during any one of these periods, nor the particular date when it accrued or when it became due, can be ascertained from this record. The decree finds only that each debt accrued between the two dates of the purchase of stock and its sale. The date when any item became due, if it became due at any time before the bank's suspension, cannot be ascertained unless it is held that the debt being due from the bank on demand became due at the time the liability arose. This

cannot be true of the deposits. The contract of the bank with each depositor is to pay the money deposited on demand made at its banking house, in such sums, at such times and to such persons as the depositor may direct. ****Until demand, the depositor can maintain no action against the bank and therefore has no cause of action. The stockholder is liable to the same extent as the bank-that is, to pay upon demand made of the bank in such sums, at such times and to such persons as the depositor may direct. He can be held on no other terms, and no action can be maintained against him until demand made on the bank. The stockholder is under no stricter liability than the bank, but under the constitution his liability is identical with the liability of the bank during the time he remains a stockholder and not something different. The Statute of Limitations is an affirmative defense, and the burden of proving it rests upon the party pleading it. **Where part of the plaintiff's demand is barred and part is not, the defendant is required to prove the part which falls specificially within the protection of the statute. ***Since no distinct, individual item of liability or class of items is pointed out in the argument as having accrued during the ownership of any particular shares of stock and no date for the beginning of the running of the Statute of Limitations for any particular debt or class of debts, there is no basis for holding that any statute of limitations applies to any debt included in the decree, and the questions of limitation of actions which have been argued are mere moot questions which do not constitute a basis of adjudication in this case."

It will be observed in the foregoing excerpts from the Sanders case, the court states that the question as to when the liability of any stockholder terminated, with reference to the claim or cause of action of any creditor, required a division of the question based upon the character of the creditor's claim against which the statute was sought to be interposed. In this respect, it will be observed that the court there states: "The decree makes no distinction in this respect among the creditors. Every finding of the court is a general

finding of the total liabilities of the bank to all its creditors, without any distinction." It will be further observed that the court stated: "A plea of the Statute of Limitations must apply to a particular claim or class of claims." And further, "The Statute of Limitations is an affirmative defense, and the burden of proving it rests wholly upon the party pleading it. Where part of the plaintiff's demand is barred and part is not, the defendant is required to prove the part which falls specifically within the protection of the statute."

Statutes of limitation are based on the theory of laches. However, there is no absolute rule as to what constitutes laches. It must be determined from the facts of each particular case. The length of time which must pass in order to constitute laches varies with the peculiar circumstances of each case and thereforein this respect is unlike the matter of limitations, which is subject to an arbitrary rule. Schultz v. O'Hearn, 319 Ill. 244. This court must review a case upon the record as presented. People v. Sucenish, 277 Ill. 290; People v. Darst, 265 Ill. 354; Soule v. People, 205 Ill. 618. The record in this case contains nothing except the pleadings, the decree, and the various papers necessary to be filed in the trial court in order to perfect an appeal. There is no evidence in the record. Under such circumstances, it is impossible to determine the question of Statute of Limitations, or any other affirmative defense. This likewise disposes of the contention of laches. The plea of the statute as made is in the most general terms possible, and under the observations as set out in the Sanders case, would not suffice. Such pleas are not directed toward the claim of any creditor, nor any class of claims or creditors. Appellant Mahoney, set up that he had disposed of his stock more than ten years before the bank closed, and for this reason was entitled to the benefit of the plea. This contention cannot be sustained under the following

}ss. I, JUSTUS L. JOHNSON, Clerk of the Appellate Court, in and of the State of Illinois, and the keeper of the Records and Seal thereof, do hereby ; is a true copy of the opinion of the said Appellate Court in the above entitled cause

In Testimony Whereof, I hereunto set my hand and affix the seal of said Appellate Court, at Ottawa, this__________day of __________in the year of our Lord one thousand nine hundred and thirty-__________

____

Clerk of the Appellate Court

ERM OF THE APPELLATE COURT

, on Tuesday, the fifth day of May, in
one thousand nine hundred and thirty-six,
cond District of the State of Illinois

NE HUFFMAN, Presiding Justice.
KLIN R. DOVE, Justice.
G. WOLFE, Justice.
JOHNSON, Clerk
DESPER, Sheriff.

286 I.A. 619[4]

---

it afterwards, to-wit: On SEP 3 1936
was filed in the Clerk's Office of said
figures following, to-wit·

GEN. NO. 9069 AGENDA NO. 11

IN THE

APPELLATE COURT OF ILLINOIS

SECOND DISTRICT

May Term, A. D. 1936.

VIRGIL J. MORTON, as Executor of the estate of William H. Edwards, deceased, Appellant, vs. LEON A. WILSON and EDNA I. WILSON, Appellees. Consolidated with VIRGIL J. MORTON, as Executor of the Estate of William H. Edwards, deceased, Appellant, vs. LEON A. WILSON, EDNA I. WILSON, MARY E. SPOHR, as Trustee under trust deed recorded as document No. 332,017, GEORGE CLIFFORD REID and BEULAH S. REID, Appellees.	APPEAL FROM THE CIRCUIT COURT OF DuPAGE COUNTY.

DOVE, J.

On September 14, 1934, a judgment by confession was rendered by the Circuit Court of Du Page County in favor of Virgil J. Morton as executor of the estate of William H. Edwards, deceased, and against Leon A. Wilson and Edna I. Wilson upon a note dated December 5, 1932, for the principal sum of $5,250.00, the note being payable in installments of $40.00 each on the 5th day of each month. On September 27,

1934, the said Morton, as such executor, filed his complaint to foreclose a trust deed upon certain premises in Du Page County, said trust deed being executed by the said Leon A. Wilson and Edna I. Wilson and given to secure the payment of the note upon which judgment was rendered by confession on September 14, 1934. On November 23, 1934, upon the motion of the defendants, an order was entered opening up the judgment rendered by confession and ordering that that judgment should stand as security during the pendency of the proceedings and transferred that cause from the law side to the equity side of the court and consolidated the law case with the foreclosure proceeding. The complaint for foreclosure was in the usual form and set forth that the defendants Leon A. Wilson and Edna I. Wilson were justly indebted to William H. Edwards in his lifetime in the sum of $5,250.00 and alleged that in consideration thereof they made their note and executed the trust deed to Mary E. Spohr, trustee, copies of which were attached to the complaint. The complaint then set forth the death of Edwards on November 9, 1933, the appointment of plaintiff as executor of his estate, the rendition of judgment on the note on September 14, 1934, avers several defaults in the provisions of the trust deed and made the Wilsons and Mary E. Spohr parties defendant. Thereafter the defendants Leon A. Wilson and Edna I. Wilson filed their answer, in which they neither admitted nor denied the indebtedness to the plaintiff, and neither admitted nor denied practically all of the other allegations of the complaint. They set up, however, by their answer, that on the day of the execution of the note and trust deed, the said William H. Edwards wrongfully and illegally charged and retained the sum of $1500.00 as a commission for making a loan of $3750.00, which commission was in addition to the interest charge of seven per cent, that the said charge of commission and interest constituted usury and was unlawful and contrary to the

provisions of the statute of this state. The complaint did not waive an answer under oath and this answer was signed and sworn to by the defendants Leon A. Wilson and Edna I. Wilson. Subsequently an amendment was filed to the complaint and an amendment to the answer was also filed, in which it was alleged that the unlawful commission charged by Edwards when the loan was made was $1250.00 instead of $1500.00 and that the amount of the loan was $4,000.00 instead of $3750.00. After the issues had been so made up, a hearing was had before the court which resulted in a decree finding that the true consideration for the note and trust deed was $4,000.00, that $1250.00 was retained by Edwards as commissions, that this commission, in addition to the interest reserved amounted to usury and that therefore the plaintiff is entitled to collect no interest whatever. The decree found that the ten payments of $40.00 each had been paid by the defendants during the lifetime of Edwards and that therefore there was due from the defendants to the plaintiff the sum of $3600.00, together with costs and attorneys' fees, making a total of $4,030.80. The decree then vacated the judgment rendered by confession on September 14, 1934, and provided that unless the defendants paid said sum of $4,030.80 within five days from the date of the decree, that the premises should be sold by the Master-in-Chancery, who was directed to execute the decree. It is from this decree that the plaintiff below, Virgil J. Morton, as executor of the estate of William H. Edwards, deceased, prosecutes this appeal.

It is insisted by appellants that it was error for the court previous to consolidating the causes to open up the judgment by confession, that the finding of the court as to usury is not supported by the evidence, that if it was and the decree was correct in finding the amount due, that then the portion of the decree which vacated the plaintiff's original judgment in the law case was unwarranted as the plaintiff was entitled to have his judgment lien preserved even though it be for a smaller amount.

We are of the opinion that there is no merit in any of appellant's contentions. The order entered by the trial court opening up the judgment was not a final appealable order and appellant does not complain of the order consolidating the causes. While the plaintiff had a right to pursue both his legal and equitable remidies at the same time, the trial court likewise was justified in consolidating the causes and disposing of them by one decree. The Court ordered that the petition filed by appellees to open up the judgment entered by confession should stand as an answer by appellees to the Narr of the plaintiff. The issue thus made in the law proceeding was whether or not plaintiff's testate had exacted usury in negotiating the loan with the defendants. Practically the only issue made by the pleadings in the foreclosure suit was the same and it was eminently fitting and proper to consolidate the law proceeding with the equity one and it is not pointed out wherein appellees' rights were in any way prejudiced by so doing. Rule 26 of the Supreme Court provides that if the motion to open up a judgment by confession is sustained "either as to the whole of the judgment or as to such part thereof as a good defense has been shown, the case shall thereafter proceed to trial, and the complaint, motion and affidavit, and counter-affidavits shall constitute the pleadings. * * * * The issues of such case shall be tried by the court without a jury unless the defendent or plaintiff demand a jury. * * * The original judgment shall stand as security, and all further proceedings shall be stayed until the further order of the court, but where the defense is only as to part of such original judgment, such judgment shall stand as to the balance and execution issue thereon". The record here does not disclose that either party ever demanded a jury in the law case, but does show that both parties proceeded to a hearing of the foreclosure suit after the order of consolidation was entered without any objection and we are of the opinion the decree as rendered is supported by the law and the evidence which is found in this record.

Upon the hearing, counsel for appellant offered in
and requested the court to take judicial notice of the judgme
against appellee by confession on September 14, 193, and of
tion issued thereon, whereupon counsel for appellees inquired
for appellant whether he was intending to press his suit on
or whether he was going ahead with the foreclosure, to which
for appellant replied, "Both". The Court thereupon stated, "
consolidated for hearing and he is simply now introducing the
and calling the court's attention to them and asking the cour
judicial notice of their existence. That is as far as it has
far". Without objection then the judgment and proceedings or
side of the court, together with the original note showing te
of $40.00 each endorsed thereon, together with the original t
were offered and admitted in evidence. Appellant also offere
evidence a deed executed by Leon A. Wilson and Edna I. Wilson
George Clifford Reid and Beulah E. Reid, which is not abstrac
which was received in evidence without objection. Appellant
proved the death of Mr. Edwards on November 9, 1933, appellan
pointment as executor and that no payments had been made sinc
death of Mr. Edwards and rested. Appellees called appellant
Section 60 of the Civil Practice Act and he produced a check
December 10, 1932, drawn on the Continental Illinois Bank & T
Company for $4,000.00, payable to the order of George C. Reid
by W. H. Edwards, and bearing the endorsement of Reid and als
Egermann and Lambe by E. J. Lambe. This check was paid on De
1932, by the bank upon which it was drawn and was offered in
by appellees and admitted without objection. E. J. Lambe te
behalf of appellees that he was in the insurance and loan bu
Wheaton, Illinois, and that he had a business transaction in
appellees were interested at the home of William H. Edwards
Grove in December, 1932. That at that time William H. Edwar

Spohr, Hjalmar Lund, George C. Reid, C. A. Carlson, a lawyer, and himself were present. Upon this occasion this witness signed and delivered a partial release of a mortgage in which he was named as trustee and which covered the premises described in the trust deed which is being foreclosed in this proceeding. It was at this time that this witness first saw the $4,000.00 check of Mr. Edwards, which had been produced upon the hearing by appellant. This witness further testified that Edwards was making a loan upon this property, that he saw no other monies passed and while he recalled that something was said about the note/being in excess of the amount of the check, he did not recall what was said. He further testified that of this $4,000.00 he was to get $2,000.00 plus the accumulated interest upon the trust deed of which he was trustee, that he went there for the purpose of delivering a partial release of that trust deed in consideration of obtaining that amount from Mr. Edwards, that he brought the release deed with him, that Mr. Edwards appeared ill at the time and was in a wheel chair, that Miss Spohr assisted him and wrote the check and he, Edwards, signed it and gave it to the witness, who left the Edwards home with Mr. Reid, Mr. Lund and Mr. Carlson and they went to Naperville, where the check was endorsed and cashed on December 14 and the proceeds thereof were distributed in accordance with the arrangement he had with Mr. Reid.

C. A. Carlson testified on behalf of the appellees that he is an attorney-at-law residing at Downers Grove and was at the Edwards home in December, 1932, upon the occasion testified by Mr. Lambe. That Mary E. Spohr, George C. Reid, E. J. Lambe and Hjalmar Lund were the others who were present. That Edwards inquired of him whether he had the note and he answered that he had and produced the note and trust deed involved in this proceeding and handed them to him. That he, Edwards, took them and examined them. That Edwards then was advised

arties the $4,000.00 check. That thereupon the wit
r. Reid "That check is only for $4,000.00", that Re
he witness then said "The note of Mr. Wilson is for
s the rest of the money?". That Reid then said "Th
et", and the witness then inquired, "Are you going
oney on this note?" and Reid answered "No, this is
Edwards) is charging us $1250.00 commission for lo
nd he wants a $5,250.00 mortage to give us $4,000.0
eid took the check and he and Mr. Lambe went to Re
hat there was no money changed hands at the time of
nd that the check was the only consideration for th

Miss Mary E. Spohr testified that she had
Edwards about thirty-five years and had resided in
wenty-seven years. That she recalls what happened
December 14, 1932, but did not recall all of the co
ook place at that time. She testified that she pr
$4,000.00 check and gave it to Mr. Edwards, who sig
then saw Mr. Edwards give it to Mr. Reid. She also
trust deed involved in this proceeding and testifie
check was the consideration for this note and trust
understood it, that she did not know it if Mr. Edwa
monies in addition to the $4,000.00. She further t
Edwards usually charged a commission for making lo
mortgages but that she did not remember whether the

charged upon this particular loan or not.

The foregoing evidence warranted the court in finding that this transaction was tainted with usury and that in return for the $5,250.00 note and trust deed involved in this proceeding, appellees received from appellant's testate the sum of $4,000.00. The evidence is further and the credits on the note so show that prior to the time this judgment was taken and this foreclosure proceeding instituted, appellees had paid $400.00, and the chancellor, in accordance with the provisions of the statute, very properly credited appellees with that sum. Chap. 74 Ill. Bar Stat. 1933, Sections 5, 4, 6.

The only decree that could have been entered upon the evidence as it appears in this record was rendered and it is accordingly affirmed.

DECREE AFFIRMED.

STATE OF ILLINOIS, } ss.
SECOND DISTRICT }

I JUSTUS L JOHNSON, Clerk of the Appellate Court in and for said Second District of the State of Illinois, and the keeper of the Records and Seal thereof, do hereby certify that the foregoing is a true copy of the opinion of the said Appellate Court in the above entitled cause of record in my office.

In Testimony Whereof, I hereunto set my hand and affix the seal of said Appellate Court at Ottawa, this______________day of ______________in the year of our Lord one thousand nine hundred and thirty-__________

____
Clerk of the Appellate Court

(73815—5M—3-32)

68 H

AT A TERM OF THE APPELLATE COURT,

Begun and held at Ottawa, on Tuesday, the fifth day of May, in the year of our Lord one thousand nine hundred and thirty-six, within and for the Second District of the State of Illinois:

Present -- The Hon. BLAINE HUFFMAN, Presiding Justice.

Hon. FRANKLIN R. DOVE, Justice.

Hon. FRED G. WOLFE, Justice.

JUSTUS L. JOHNSON, Clerk

RALPH H. DESPER, Sheriff.

286 I.A. 619[5]

BE IT REMEMBERED, that afterwards, to-wit. On the opinion of the Court was filed in the Clerk's Office of said Court, in the words and figures following, to-wit·

Gen. No. 9073 Agenda No. 14

IN THE
APPELLATE COURT OF ILLINOIS
SECOND DISTRICT

May Term, A. D. 1936

ALICE EAGLESTON,

Appellee

vs.

ILLINOIS POWER AND LIGHT CORPORATION, a corporation,

Appellant.

Appeal from the Circuit Court of Peoria County.

DOVE, J.

This case is brought to this court upon appeal from a judgment of $900.00 entered by the Circuit Court of Peoria County on a verdict of the jury in favor of the plaintiff, Alice Eagleston, and against the defendant, Illinois Power & Light Company, a corporation.

The complaint consisted of one count, which alleged that on July 27, 1934, appellee was riding as a passenger on an electric trolley bus operated by appellant in the City of Peoria. That appellant stopped the trolley bus for the purpose of allowing appellee and other passengers to alight therefrom and while appellee was in the exercise of ordinary care for her own safety and in the act of alighting from said electric trolley bus, the defendant, by its servants, caused the said bus to be jerked, swayed and moved, by reason whereof appellee was thrown violently against said bus and from it to the pavement and severely and permanently injured.

The answer of the defendant denied the allegations of due care and negligence and avers that the plaintiff tripped or caught her foot or the heel of her shoe in some manner not due to any negligence or fault of the defendant and thereby sustained the injuries complained of.

It appears from the evidence of appellee that at the time of the accident she was a married woman, forty-six years oa age, and about noon on July 27, 1934 she had boarded the trolley bus of appellant in the downtown part of Peoria, her destination being Haungs Avenue.

At the intersection of Spitznagel and Adams Streets, which was a block before Haungs Avenue was reached, she signalled the bus driver to stop at Haungs Avenue and as the bus approached Haungs Avenue, appellee arose, and when the bus stopped, the exit door opened and she started to alight. On direct examination she stated that she was on the bottom step of the bus and felt the sensation of the bus jerking, and right after that she fell. Her counsel then asked if the bus was moving as she fell or stumbled off and she answered that she couldn't say. On cross-examination she testified: "I don't know whether I was on the step or the platform or on the ground when I fell. The parcels that I had I was carrying under or in one arm and holding on with the other. I don't know which arm I had the parcels under---I don't remember. The right heel came off my right shoe and the left heel came off of my left shoe. The one heel wasn't on the shoe very tight or it wouldn't have dropped off." She was then asked: "Now where were you standing on the bus or what part of it, when you think it moved forward?", and she answered: "I don't know." She further testified that within a few days after the accident she told appellant's claim agent that when she went to get off the bus, either that she caught her heel on the metal strip or that the bus jerked, but that she thought the bus jerked and threw her. She further testified that after she fell the motorman got off from the bus to help her and she did not say to him that the bus had started while she was getting off.

Appellee further testified that for four months she had been in the hospital prior to this accident, suffering from a nervous breakdown, but had also been out of the hospital for that length of time and had recovered. That while she had been to a physician's office the morning of the accident, it was not for the purpose of receiving any medical treatment.

Ruth Kidder testified on behalf of the appellee that she was a passenger on this motor bus on the day in question, was sitting on the seat just back of the driver and looking out of the window, that

that she doesn't remember whether the bus had stopped and that then the jerk occurred or not and in reply to the question of appellee's counsel: "Was it the ordinary jerk that you feel on a bus?" she answered: "Well you get them on the bus all the time." She further testified that when she first observed appellee, she (appellee) was "right down by the steps and I can't remember whether she was touching any part of the bus or whether she was on the ground." She further testified that she did not see appellee fall and in a statement made shortly after the accident, she stated she did not know what caused appellee to fall.

On behalf of the appelant, Mrs. Henry Mishler testified that she was a passenger sitting on the second seat from the front on the right side (being the side of the exit used by appellee) of appellant's bus on the day in question and saw appellee standing up just before she got off the bus, did not see her fall, but did observe her as she was being held up after she had fallen and was positive on direct examination that the bus did not jerk or sway or move from the time the bus stopped until this witness observed appellee being held up by someone on the pavement. On cross-examination she said there was nothing unusual or in particular to attract her attention as to the movement of the bus as to whether it jerked or not.

Katherine Cullen was also a passenger and testified on behalfof appellant to the effect that she was sitting in the third seat from the front, that the bus stopped and she saw appellee fall and observed that the motorman helped her up and saw the heel of appellee's shoe on the lower step. This witness was also positive that the bus did not move after it stopped to discharge passengers. On cross-examination this witness also testified that there was nothing unusual about the movement of the car when it stopped or at any time to particularly attract her attention to the accident.

Lucille Mishler, a daughter of Mrs. Henry Mishler, was with her mother as a passenger on appellant's bus on the day of the accident and she testified on behalf of appellant, corroborated her mother's testimony and was likewise positive that the bus stood still after it came to a

stop and until after she observed that appellee had fallen and was being helped up by someone.

M.C. Pennington was also a passenger on appellant's bus on the day in question and testified that he was sitting right at the door on the right hand side of the bus, remembered that the bus stopped, the door opened and that appellee "stepped off right at the door and caught her heel and I saw the heel which was detached from her shoe on the step. The bus was standing still after the door was opened and she started to get off and (the bus) didn't move at all at any time after she started to get off or after the doors were open."

Frank Croom was the motorman on the bus on the day in question and he testified that at Haungs Avenue he made the ordinary stop there and then opened the exit doors, that two or three parties got off the bus prior to appellee, who was the last one to leave the bus. That when appellee left the bus she had several packages in or under one of her arms and in getting off the bus she took hold of the upright rod or bar with the disengaged hand, which he thought was her right hand, and as she stepped down caught her heel on the edge of the step, pulling her heel off and that she then turned to the right, that she did not fall to the street and was not on the street until this witness and others helped her from the steps. This witness further testified that the door which appellee passed through in leaving the bus folded outward from the steps, are air controlled and that he operated them by a lever on his left hand side.

Margaret Carroll also testified on behalf of appellant that she was a passenger of appellant sitting about midway in the bus on the day of the accident. She further testified that she did not see the accident but was positive that the bus stood still from the time it came to a stop at Haungs Avenue until after the accident, and that it did not jerk. It further appeared from the evidence that the step of the bus is fourteen inches from the ground and the distance from the step to the floor of the bus is thirteen inches.

Upon the trial, the shoes worn by appellee, with their detached heels, were offered and admitted in evidence and have been by the trial

court certified to this court inspection. We have examined them and have read the evidence in this record with care and the foregoing is a fair resume of all the evidence. It is not insisted that any prejudicial error occurred upon the trial, either with reference to the admission or rejection of evidence or in the giving or refusing of instructions, but it is argued that the verdict is manifestly against the weight of the evidence and for that reason the trial court erred in refusing to grant appellant's motion for a new trial. We are inclined to agree with this contention. It is to be noted that after appellee fell and the motorman went to her aid, nothing was said by her to the effect that her fall was due to any act of the motorman and upon her cross-examination she admitted that a few days after the accident she accounted for it by stating that as she was alighting from the bus, either the bus jerked or she caught the heel of her shoe on the metal strip. The weight of the evidence in this record is that appellee's injuries were not due to the alleged negligent act of appellant's motorman in starting the bus while appellee was attempting to alight therefrom. The weight of the evidence is that the bus was not in motion and did not jerk or sway, but was stopped in the ordinary and usual manner by the motorman who opened the door and that while the bus was so standing motionless, appellee, while attempting to alight therefrom, fell from a cause or causes not in any way connected with the management or operation of the bus.

The instant complaint alleged that appellee had expended and become liable to expend $600.00 for hospital expenses, nursing and doctor's fees and sought to recover $15,000.00 for the injuries sustained. The proof is that she was rather severely injured and that immediately following the accident she was taken home and later the same day to the Methodist Hospital in Peoria, where she remained until the 28th of August following, that as a result of the accident she sustained a fractured tibia of the left leg, starting two inches below the knee and extending into the knee joint. That she expended approximately $375.00 in hospital and nursing bills and doctors' fees.

It is significant that the jury only awarded her $900.00, which indicates that the award was possibly made to her more on account of sympathy than anything else.

For the error of the trial court in overruling appellant's motion for a new trial, the judgment of the Circuit Court is reversed and the cause remanded.

REVERSED AND REMANDED.

}ss.

I JUSTUS L. JOHNSON, Clerk of the Appellate Court, in and the State of Illinois, and the keeper of the Records and Seal thereof, do hereby a true copy of the opinion of the said Appellate Court in the above entitled cause

In Testimony Whereof, I hereunto set my hand and affix the seal of said Appellate Court at Ottawa this________________day of ________________in the year of our Lord one thousand nine hundred and thirty-____________

____

Clerk of the Appellate Court

69 H

AT A TERM OF THE APPELLATE COURT,

nd held at Ottawa, on Tuesday, the fifth day of May, in
year of our Lord one thousand nine hundred and thirty-six,
in and for the Second District of the State of Illinois:

; -- The Hon. BLAINE HUFFMAN, Presiding Justice.
Hon. FRANKLIN R. DOVE, Justice.
Hon. FRED G. WOLFE, Justice.
JUSTUS L. JOHNSON, Clerk
RALPH H. DESPER, Sheriff.

286 I.A. 6

IT REMEMBERED, that afterwards, to-wit On SEP 3 1936
inion of the Court was filed in the Clerk's Office of said
in the words and figures following, to-wit:

GEN. NO. 9061 AGENDA NO. 20

IN THE

APPELLATE COURT OF ILLINOIS

SECOND DISTRICT

May Term, A. D. 1936

CHARLES N. STEELE, et al, Appellees,	)	
vs.	)	APPEAL FROM THE CIRCUIT COURT OF LAKE COUNTY.
KATHERINE E. MOHRMANN, et al, Appellants.	)	

DOVE, J.

On August 20, 1929, Katherine Mohrmann, Anna J. Mohrmann, Emily L. Mohrmann, Elizabeth M. Brewer and Joseph Leo Mohrmann executed their note payable to bearer, three years after date, for the sum of $9,000.00, bearing 6% interest. This note recited that it was secured by a trust deed of even date therewith to the First National Bank of Waukegan, trustee, on certain therein described premises. On the same day the makers of this note executed a trust deed, conveying to the bank the premises involved herein to secure the payment of said note. The note having matured and not being paid, Charles N. Steele and the First National Bank of Waukegan, as trustee, filed on November 4, 1933, their bill to foreclose said trust deed. The bill was in the usual form and alleged that the complainant Charles N. Steele was the legal owner and holder of the principal note secured by said Trust deed and the bank, as trustee, joined with him as a complainant. The defendants, on April 4, 1934, filed their joint

answers denying or calling for strict proof of every allegation of the bill and averred that "the indebtedness alleged in said bill and the notes and mortgage therein referred to arose out of a transaction with the First National Bank of Waukegan, Illinois, by which on or about the 20th day of August, A. D. 1929, these defendants obtained from said bank the sum of $8,000.00 and in return therefore executed and delivered said notes and mortgage: that said bank was at that time transacting and conducting in the State of Illinois the business of buying and selling and supplying to those engaged in trade and commerce and others gold, gold coin, money, currency and legal tender used and in use in the United States of America as necessary commodities and media of exchange, for a price: that at the time of the execution and delivery of said notes and mortgage, the said premises had a market value of to-wit: $60,000.00: that said bank was at the time of the execution and delivery of said notes and mortgage a member of a secret conspiracy and agreement with the member banks of the Federal Reserve System, including the plaintiff, by which it was understood and agreed by and between said banks that certain restrictions in the purchase and sale of gold, gold coin, money, currency and legal tender would be observed by said banks, which said restrictions were designed to bring about the fixing or limiting of the amount or quantity of said gold, gold coin, money, currency and legal tender sold in all the states of the United States, including the State of Illinois, for the purpose of depressing the value of real assets upon which contracts for the delivery of said gold, gold coin, money, currency and legal tender held by said banks were secured and obtaining the ownership of said real assets, for said banks, through foreclosure of said security, at an extremely small outlay of either gold, gold coin, money, currency or legal tender on the part of said banks; that among said restrictions it was agreed by said banks that, after

restricting the sales of gold, gold coin, money, currency and legal tender and causing an artificial scarcity of said commodities of gold, gold coin, money, currency and legal tender necessarily bringing about defaults in the performance of said contracts generally, no further contracts, extensions of the performance of contracts or renewals of contracts calling for the delivery of gold, gold coin, money, currency or legal tender, the performance of which are to be secured by liens or mortgages on real property, would be consummated by said banks; that on or about, to-wit: the month of January, A. D. 1932, some of said banks, including the plaintiff herein, pursuant to the design and conspiracy aforesaid, believing that defaults in the payment of principal and interest were so generally prevalent as to amount to a practical destruction of realty values and to present an unparalled opportunity for recouping past losses and garnering huge profits, placed said plan into operation by uniformally refusing to extend, make or renew said contracts as aforesaid, the performance of which are and were to be secured by liens or mortgages on real estate and proceeded to foreclose said existing liens and mortgages; that said conspirators controlled and control the bulk of the commodities in general use as necessary media of exchange, namely: gold, gold coin, money, currency and legal tender used or in use in the United States; that by virtue of the aforesaid control, regulation and fixing, by said conspirators, one of which was the plaintiff herein of the price of said gold, gold coin, money, currency and legal tender, together with the adopted policy of refusing to make, extend or renew said contracts, it was, became and is impossible for these defendants to refinance, liquidate or secure sufficient gold, gold coin, money, currency or legal tender to fulfill the contract

obligations alleged in complainant's bill of complaint; that said agreement and conspiracy on the part of the plaintiff herein is in direct violation of an Act of the General Assembly of the State of Illinois entitled: 'An Act to Provide for the Punishment of Persons, Co-partnerships or Corporations Forming Pools, Trusts and Combines, and Mode of Procedure and Rules of Evidence in Such Cases,' Laws of Illinois 1891, Page 206, and under and by virtue of said Act, particularly Section 6, that these defendants are not liable to the complainant for the matters alleged in complainant's bill of complaint.

"These defendants further answering say that on or about the 20th day of August, A. D. 1929, the First National Bank of Waukegan was a corporation organized under the laws of the United States and transacting business in the State of Illinois; that on said date said bank was a member of a secret conspiracy, understanding and agreement with the member banks of the Federal Reserve System, including the plaintiff, under and by which said bank conspired, understood and agreed with the said member banks of the said Federal Reserve System that the price of gold, which is the standard of value of the currency system of the United States, should be regulated and fixed according to the progress of subsequent events so as to afford said banks the most advantageous and facile means of securing the highest possible profit to themselves; that on or about to-wit: the month of January, A. D. 1929, in order to bring about the fixing and regulation of the price of said gold coin, said banks entered into a secret agreement, pool and confederation for the purpose of fixing and limiting the amount of said gold and gold coin sold in all the States of the United States including the State of Illinois; that on or about, to-wit, the 20th day of August, A. D. 1929, in

pursuance of said plan to fix and limit the amount or quantity of said gold coin, said First National Bank of Waukegan entered into a contract with these defendants, who, without knowledge of the aforesaid plan, agreed to deliver to said bank $9,000.00 of the then currency of the United States aforesaid on the respective dates as evidenced by the contracts exhibited in said bill of complaint and, in addition thereto, these defendants agreed to deliver to said bank $9,000.00 in said currency on the respective dates and in the respective amounts as set forth in said bill; that said bank, further pursuing said conspiracy, required these defendants to execute and deliver to it the mortgage described in said bill to secure the performance by these defendants of the delivery of said currency knowing full well that the performance of the delivery of said currency on the part of these defendants would be impossible; that said contracts being made pursuant to said combination and confederation are absolutely void under and by virtue of the laws and statutes of the State of Illinois in such cases made and provided."

A replication to this answer having been filed, the cause was on April 26, 1934, referred to the Master to take the proof and report his findings of law and of fact. On June 11, 1934, by leave of court, Bertha Steele was made a party complainant and the original bill was amended to so show and by alleging that she was at that time the holder and owner of said principal promissory note, secured by said trust deed. The evidence was heard by the Master and on July 2, 1935, he notified the solicitors for the respective parties that he had prepared his report and that any objections thereto would be heard on July 9, 1935. Objections to said report were filed, by the defendants, which were overruled by the Master and on November 12, 1935, the Master's report was filed and on the 19th of the same month an order was entered that the objections filed to the Master's report

should stand as exceptions and leave was granted defendants to file additional exceptions. On December 7, 1935, the cause was heard by the court, all exceptions to the Master's report were overruled, the report of the Master was approved and a decree of foreclosure and sale was rendered. On the same day the defendants moved the court for leave to amend their answer and to re-refer the cause to the Master. This motion was denied. On December 20, 1935, the formal decree of foreclosure and sale was presented to the court and ordered filed as of the date the Chancellor announced his findings, which was December 7, 1935. From this decree and from the order of the court denying them leave to amend their answer and re-refer the cause to the Master, the defendants bring the record to this court for review.

Appellees filed in this court their motion to dismiss this appeal on the ground that the notice of appeal was filed January 3, 1936, and the record on appeal was filed in this court more than thirty days thereafter. This motion was taken with the case. Rule 36 of the Supreme Court and Rule one of this court provides, among other things, that in appeals taken to this court the appellant shall, within ten days after the notice of appeal has been filed, prepare and file a praecipe with the clerk, in which appellant shall designate what parts of the trial court record are to be incorporated in the record on appeal and that all parts of the record so designated shall be incorporated in the record on appeal by copies certified by the clerk, provided the original of the Master's report may be incorporated in the record on appeal by stipulation of the parties. This rule further provides that as soon as the necessary copies or originals of all the records and documents specified in the praecipe are in possession of the clerk, he shall make up the record on appeal, which shall be transmitted to the reviewing court. That when the praecipe does not specify any proceedings at the trial, the record on appeal shall

be transmitted to the reviewing court not more than thirty days after the notice of appeal has been filed, but if the praecipe does specify any proceedings at the trial, the record on appeal shall be transmitted to the reviewing court not more than thirty days after the report of the proceedings has been filed. In the instant case the parties hereto, on March 3, 1936, filed in the lower court their stipulation to the effect that the transcript of proceedings not of record certified to by the Chancellor and filed in the lower court on February 13, 1936, and the report of the Master, together with the report of the proceedings taken before him might be incorporated by the clerk in the record for appeal. The proceedings certified by the chancellor on February 13, 1936, were filed in the lower court on that date. While it is true that on February 6, 1936 the lower court entered an order extending the time to February 16, 1936, in which to present and have filed such proceedings, yet, inasmuch as such proceedings were certified to by the chancellor and actually filed in the lower court on February 13, 1936, it thereupon became the duty of appellants to transmit to this court the record on appeal not more than thirty days after the report of such proceedings had been filed in the lower court. The record was not filed in this court until March 16, 1936. No application was made to this court to extend the time within which to file the record and under Rule 36 of the Supreme Court and Rule one of this court, it is mandatory upon this court to dismiss the appeal.

We might add that we have considered the errors relied upon by appellants for the reversal of this decree and in our opinion there is no merit in any of them. While the answer sets forth that appellants' misfortunes were caused by an economic depression brought about by a conspiracy of banks and bankers, including Charles N. Steele, then president of the trustee bank, still there is no evidence to sustain this charge and even if there was,

r the trustee bank or its president
appellants borrowed, but it was the
Steels. Leave was properly granted this
y complainant and the chancellor did not
enying appellants' motion to amend their
ause. The case was pending before the
year and the decree which was rendered
evidence and law would have warranted.

APPEAL DISMISSED.

STATE OF ILLINOIS, } ss.
SECOND DISTRICT

I, JUSTUS L. JOHNSON Clerk of the Appellate Court, in and for said Second District of the State of Illinois, and the keeper of the Records and Seal thereof, do hereby certify that the foregoing is a true copy of the opinion of the said Appellate Court in the above entitled cause of record in my office.

In Testimony Whereof, I hereunto set my hand and affix the seal of said Appellate Court, at Ottawa, this________________day of ________________ in the year of our Lord one thousand nine hundred and thirty-__________

____
Clerk of the Appellate Court

(73815—5M—3-32)

)F THE APPELLATE COURT,

on Tuesday, the fifth day of May, in

e thousand nine hundred and thirty-six,

id District of the State of Illinois:

HUFFMAN, Presiding Justice.

IN R. DOVE, Justice.

. WOLFE, Justice.

OHNSON, Clerk.

SPER, Sheriff.

286 I.A. 620[2]

704

---

afterwards, to-wit On SEP 3 1936

was filed in the Clerk's Office of said

igures following, to-wit:

GEN. NO. 9085 AGENDA NO. 23

IN THE

APPELLATE COURT OF ILLINOIS

SECOND DISTRICT

May Term, A. D. 1936.

J. E. HEALY, Appellee, vs. JOHN A. ROSS, Appellant.	APPEAL FROM THE CIRCUIT COURT OF LAKE COUNTY.

DOVE, J.

In August, 1925, one J. E. Corbett purchased lot six in block sixty, Lincoln Subdivision in Dade County, Florida, from the Beach Holding Company. As a part of the purchase price, Corbett, on August 15th of that year executed his three notes, one for $1316.67 due in one year, one for $1316.67 due in two years and one for $1316.66 due in three years after date and to secure the payment of the same he executed a mortgage on the property purchased. In the following year the plaintiff herein, a resident of Miami Beach, Florida, loaned the Beach Holding Company $20,000.00 and the Corbett notes were endorsed by the then president of that company and with the accompanying mortgage, together with other securities, were delivered to the plaintiff as collateral security for that loan. No formal assignment of the mortgage was made by the Holding Company, but such an assignment was executed on April 27, 1933. In September, 1925, the defendant herein, Ross, a farmer living in Barrington, Lake County, Illinois, went to Florida, became interested in the purchase of said lot six and went to one Dooly, the vice-president

of the Meyer-Kiser Corporation and purchased said lot six. On November 13, 1925, the defendant signed a mortgage, the provisions of which recited that it was given to secure a note of $8,000.00 payable to the order of the Meyer-Kiser Corporation one year after date, with 8% interest. This mortgage conveyed said lot to said Meyer-Kiser Corporation and obligated the mortgagor to pay the principal and interest evidenced by said note therein described, together with all taxes, assessments, liabilities and incumbrances of every nature on said mortgaged property.

In December, 1934, this suit was instituted. The complaint consists of two counts. The first count sets forth the execution by Corbett of the said several notes on August 15, 1925, together with the mortgage to secure the payment of the same, the assignment thereof by the mortgagee to the plaintiff, the purchase of the lot described in the mortgage by the defendant on November 13, 1925, evidenced by a warranty deed and charges that in and by said deed, said defendant assumed and agreed to pay the Corbett mortgage. This count concludes by demanding judgment for the principal of said notes, together with interest and attorney fees. The second count of the complaint re-alleges most of the averments of count one and after averring the purchase of the lot by the defendant from Corbett, avers that to secure a balance of the purchase price thereof, defendant executed his mortgage deed by which he conveyed said lot to the Meyer-Kiser Corporation and thereby agreed to pay all the taxes, assessments and encumbrances thereon. Attached to the complaint were copies of the several notes, mortgages, assignment and deed. The answer of the defendant neither admitted or denied the execution by Corbett of the several notes and mortgage, the assignment thereof to the plaintiff and the purchase of the lot by the defendant. He denied, however, that he assumed and agreed to

pay the mortgage described in the complaint and averred that in and by the contract of purchase the agreement of the parties thereto was that such conveyance was to be made subject to the encumbrances and that defendant was not to assume or pay the same or any part thereof, but that by mistake of the parties the deed contained an assumption agreement; that defendant never at any time accepted any deed containing any assuption clause, that the assumption agreement, if made, was without consideration, that such clause was not in writing signed by the defendant and under the statutes of the State of Florida is unenforcible. The answer denied that in the mortgage set forth in the complaint he consented and agreed to assume the indebtedness represented by the several notes held by the plaintiff and avers that under the laws of both Illinois and Florida he is not personally liable to the plaintiff. After the issues were made up, a trial was had, resulting in a verdict finding the issues for the defendant. The court granted plaintiff's motion for a new trial and it is from this order that defendant appealed.

This case was, on July 7, 1936, argued orally in this court and submitted to the court upon the petition of appellant for leave to appeal and upon the answer to said petition under Rule 3 of this court. On July 22, 1936, counsel for appellee filed with the clerk of this court, without leave so to do, a motion to dismiss this appeal, basing his motion upon the ground that appellant failed to incorporate in his petition, which under said rule 3 stands as his brief in this case, the errors relied upon for reversal. With his motion he filed certain suggestions and on the same day appellant filed counter suggestions. This motion will not be considered. It was filed after the case had been submitted upon oral argument, petition for leave to appeal and reply thereto. It comes too late, The People v. C. B. & Q. R. R. Co., 253 Ill. 100, and inasmuch as it

was filed by the clerk without leave so to do, said motion, suggestions and counter suggestions will be stricken from the files.

It is first insisted by counsel for appellant that the trial court erroneously granted appellee's motion for a new trial because the order was entered upon appellee's oral motion while Sec. 196, Chap. 110, Ill. Bar Statutes, 1935, provides that if either party desires to move for a new trial he shall, before final judgment is entered, file his points in writing particularly specifying the grounds of such motion. The record discloses no objection was made by appellant in the trial court to the fact that appellee's motion was oral and not written and having proceeded in the lower court to a hearing upon appellee's oral motion for a new trial without objection, appellant is in no position in this court to take advantage of appellee's omission. This court is at a disadvantage because we are not advised of the reasons insisted upon by appellee upon his motion and also because the record does not disclose the reasons which prompted the trial court in awarding a new trial.

Counsel for appellant further insist that the record discloses that there is no likelihood that any new, additional, undiscovered or rejected evidence would have changed the verdict in this case and that the verdict did substantial justice between the parties and is sustained by the evidence. We have read the evidence as the same appears in the abstract furnished by appellant and the additional abstract, filed by appellee. Appellee's evidence consisted of the testimony of himself and John B. Reid, both by deposition. Reid testified that in 1925 and since then he has been engaged in the real estate business in Miami Beach, Florida, and in 1925 and 1926 was president of the Beach Holding Company. That he knew J. W. Corbett to whom the Beach Holding Company sold said lot 6, that Corbett received a deed for that lot and as part payment therefor executed the notes which he identified and which

are the ones described in the complaint. He further testified that he endorsed the notes and in May, June or July, 1926, sold and delivered them, together with the mortgage given to secure their payment, to the plaintiff. He further testified that he thought the mortgage had been assigned to the plaintiff in 1926 but finding that no formal assignment had been made, he did, as president of the Holding Company, execute an assignment thereof in 1933 and this assignment he identified and it was offered and admitted in evidence. Appellee, the plaintiff below, testified that he had loaned the Holding Company $20,000.00 and when he learned that this company claimed it was insolvent, he took these notes, with others, as collateral security for his loan. That he is the owner of them and has been since the Spring of 1926. That he, at this time, also received the mortgage given to secure the payment thereof, but misplaced it. That he made every possible effort to find it, but has been unable to do so. A properly certified and exemplified copy of this mortgage was offered and admitted in evidence without objection. Certified copies of the record of the deed from Corbett to appellant and of the mortgage executed by appellant to the Meyer-Kiser Corporation were offered and received in evidence. Appellee further testified that his mortgage was a junior lien on the premises described therein, that the first mortgage had been foreclosed and a sale had but he had received nothing from that sale, that he had made an effort to locate appellant and finally did so through the efforts of his attorney a few months prior to the time he instituted this suit. In his own behalf, appellant testified in person to the effect that he was a resident of Lake County, a farmer and contractor, and that during the last week in September, 1925, he went to Miami because of the real estate boom there, although he was not experienced in the real estate business. That a Mr. Reddington took him out and showed him the lot described in the complaint and that he bought it.

That when he purchased the lot, Mr. Dooly, Mr. Reddington and himself were present and over the objection of counsel for appellee, he detailed at length the conversation he had with these parties in which they assured him that they would deliver this property to him free of any encumbrances, and that they so sold it to him, that he did not recall ever signing any mortgage, nor did he recall how much he paid for the lot, never saw any deed and never had possession of the lot. Fred M. Dooly also testified in person on behalf of appellant that he was a real estate broker and had been for thirty years and in 1925 was Vice-President of the Meyer-Kiser Corporation in Miami, which was an affiliate of the Meyer-Kiser Bank of Indianapolis, that he knew Corbett, who was clerk and assistant salesman of the Meyer-Kiser Corporation and that he knew Reddington, who was a real estate broker. That the lot sold to the defendant belonged to Grace B. Jamison, a Vice-President of the corporation. That the legal title thereto was placed in Corbett's name and he thereupon executed a deed leaving the name of the grantee blank and when the property was sold, the name of the purchaser was inserted therein. Over the objection of appellee, Dooly testified that prior to the time the deal with appellant was closed, he, Ross, came to the office of the witness with Reddington and Ross there said that he didn't want to get tied up in any promises or mortgages or anything of that kind. That thereupon the witness explained to appellant that there were two ways in which the matter could be handled, one by taking title to the property and paying cash for whatever he was going to pay and subject to the encumbrances thereon and by so doing there would be no liability upon his part. That appellant then said "all right under those conditions then, I will go ahead, but I do not want to be tied up in any responsibility". That this witness recalls that the deed was to be made so that no mortgage was to be assumed by Ross. That he also thinks that the mortgage Ross signed was also

in blank, that his recollection was that it was a blank mortgage which Ross signed. That the deed to Ross was never sent to Ross to his knowledge. That he, the witness, told Mr. McClung, who was the office manager of the Meyer-Kiser Corporation and the scrivener who filled in the deed from Corbett to Ross, what to insert in the deed and that he did not tell him to put therein the clause, "subject to mortgage dated May 25, 1925, for the sum of $6551.00, which the party of the second part assumes and agrees to pay". He, Dooly, was further permitted to testify that the first time he knew such a clause was in the deed was when someone told him that Ross was being sued. Many of the questions asked this witness on direct examination were leading and objections thereto for that reason should have been sustained, for example, counsel for appellant asked Mr. Dooly in his direct examination this question: "Did you instruct McClung as to the contents of the deed, what was to be put in it?", over counsel's objection the witness answered, "Well, I directed it". Again on direct examination counsel asked Dooly, "Did you so instruct McClung, the scrivener, who wrote the deed to insert in it the clause, subject to mortgage dated May 25, 1925, for the sum of $6551.00, which the party of the second part assumes and agrees to pay?" and the witness answered, "No, sir". Again this question was asked Mr. Dooly, "Ross signed the mortgage in blank?" and the witness answered "That is my recollection of it" and the court denied counsel for appellee's motion to strike the answer and stated, "I will let it stand". The record further discloses that counsel asked Mr. Dooly, while he was testifying on direct examination, this question, "Who was Grace B. Jackson?" and the witness answered, "Grace B. Jackson was the vice-president of the Meyer-Kiser Corporation and the deed was in blank when it was executed by Mr. Corbett. That was the custom of the office". Counsel for appellee then said: "I object to that and move that it be stricken

estion" and the court overruled the
rect examination of appellant, his
g to the lot in question and described
take possession of this property, this
sel's objection he was permitted to
uestion called for the conclusion of
hereto should have been sustained.
said, it is apparent that upon the
les of evidence were violated and
y prejudiced by the rulings of the court
trial. Furthermore appellant admitted
d admitted that his signature appears
executed in the presence of James M.
and which appears to have been duly
He denies that any deed was ever
ce was introduced to the effect that
the deed (McClung who did not testify
ed for) violated the instructions of
claim to own the lot. How much credence
ony of the several witnesses was a
e for the jury and then for the trial
tion for a new trial. A court of review
tute its judgment for that of the trial
pears there was an abuse of discretion
ce with the trial court that the issues
to another jury. The order appealed from

ORDER AFFIRMED.

} ss.

I JUSTUS L JOHNSON, Clerk of the Appellate Court in and the State of Illinois, and the keeper of the Records and Seal thereof, do hereby a true copy of the opinion of the said Appellate Court in the above entitled cause,

In Testimony Whereof, I hereunto set my hand and affix the seal of said Appellate Court, at Ottawa this________________day of ________________in the year of our Lord one thousand nine hundred and thirty-____________

____

Clerk of the Appellate Court

AT A TERM OF THE APPELLATE COURT,

ld at Ottawa, on Tuesday, the fifth day of May, in of our Lord one thousand nine hundred and thirty-six, nd for the Second District of the State of Illinois:

the Hon. BLAINE HUFFMAN, Presiding Justice.

Hon. FRANKLIN R. DOVE, Justice.

Hon. FRED G. WOLFE, Justice.

JUSTUS L. JOHNSON, Clerk.

RALPH H. DESPER, Sheriff.

744

286 I.A. 620[3]

EMEMBERED, that afterwards, to-wit: On SEP 3 1936 n of the Court was filed in the Clerk's Office of said the words and figures following, to-wit:

GEN. NO. 9090 AGENDA NO. 29

IN THE

APPELLATE COURT OF ILLINOIS

SECOND DISTRICT

May Term, A. D. 1936

CHARLES D. HENRY, Jr., Appellee,	)	
vs.	)	APPEAL FROM THE CIRCUIT COURT OF KANKAKEE COUNTY.
THE FEDERAL LAND BANK OF ST. LOUIS, a Corporation, Appellant.	)	

DOVE, J.

Plaintiff is a lawyer and was employed by the defendant to assist its staff of attorneys in prosecuting foreclosure suits in Kankakee County. On April 4, 1931, the defendant, from its St. Louis office, wrote the plaintiff in connection with securing his services in part as follows: "I am, therefore, writing to know whether it would be satisfactory with you to have you follow the calendar, file the pleadings, make proof before the Master and prove up the usual attorney fee, while in turn we would prepare all pleading here. For your services we would expect to pay a nominal amount of $50.00 and whatever actual fee could be thereafter realized from the foreclosure of the farm; that is, to the extent of the collection of any fee, the entire amount would be remitted to you. Also the nominal amount is fixed on the presumption that there will be no contest. Please let me know whether such or similar arrangement will be satisfactory". The plaintiff accepted the offer of employment and thereafter appeared for an represented the defendant in sixteen foreclosure

proceedings. On November 19, 1931, defendant forwarded to the plaintiff the original and copy of a bill to foreclose a mortgage executed by John Lewis, together with a supplemental abstract of title and a check for the filing fee. Thereafter, on December 24, 1931, said bill was filed, resulting in a decree of foreclosure and sale on April 12, 1932. The Master's sale was held on May 14, 1932, at which time there was due the defendant, under the decree, the sum of $24,212.35, which amount included an attorney fee of $800.00. At the sale the premises were sold to the defendant for $23,000.00 and on August 19, 1933, there being no redemption, the Master executed a deed to the defendant. Thereafter the defendant sold the premises for $27,000.00 and conveyed them to the purchaser by a deed dated March 1, 1935, The defendant paid the plaintiff $100.00 as attorney fees and refusing to pay any more, this suit was instituted. After the issues were made up, a trial was had before the court, a jury being waived, which resulted in a judgment for the plaintiff for $700.00 and the record is before this court for review.

Counsel for appellant insist that by the terms of the contract of employment, appellee is only entitled to receive the attorney fee assessed in the foreclosure suit to the extent that it was actually collected by it over and above any sum due it for its mortgage debt prior to the expiration of the statutory period of redemption, that in the instant case it did not sell the farm until after the period of redemption had expired and therefore appellant is not liable.

It will be noted that in the letter, which forms the basis of the contract, appellant, after stating that appellee would be paid a nominal fee, added, "and whatever actual fee could be thereafter realized from the foreclosure of the farm, that is, to the extent of the collection of any fee, the entire amount would be remitted to you". The actual fee in the instant case is the $800.00 which was made a part

of the decree of foreclosure and added to the amount then found to be due appellant under its note and mortgage. This sum of $800.00, according to the wording of appellant's letter, would be paid appellee if it "could be thereafter realized from the foreclosure of the farm". There is nothing said which can be construed to mean that this amount must be realized within fifteen months following the day the farm was sold and to construe these words as appellant contends would be to insert something therein that does not appear. As a result of the foreclosure proceeding, title to the farm became indefeasably vested in appellant. After owning the farm for eighteen months, it sold it and realized therefrom an amount far in excess of the amount of its mortgage debt and costs.

It is a familiar principle of the law of the construction of contracts that where the parties thereto have interpreted its terms, that then, in the event of subsequent litigation, the court will adopt such construction as the parties themselves have placed upon it. As stated, after appellee had accepted employment according to the terms of the letter of appellant of April 4, 1931, he represented appellant in numerous foreclosure proceedings and on October 20, 1932 appellant wrote appellee with reference to the Rivard foreclosure in which appellant acknowledged the receipt from appellee of the Master's deed, the period for redemption having expired and in reference to the attorney fee of appellee in that case had this to say: "I am reminded, however, that there was a solicitor's fee of $540.00 allowed you on account of which we have paid you $50.00, the balance of which is to be paid to you in the event of a prompt sale of this farm without loss to the bank". And the evidence is that on March 30, 1933, appellant sent appellee $490.00, which was stated by it to be the balance due appellee on account of his solicitor's fee allowed in the Rivard foreclosure suit. In appellant's letter, in which it remitted this balance of $490.00, it stated that although "the subsequent

sale of the property did not quite pay us out, we realize that you were instrumental in finding this purchaser and therefore make payment in full, all of which I trust you will find satisfactory". Counsel for appellant in endeavoring to explain why this payment was made to appellee long subsequent to the time the Master's deed was issued, when, under its interpretation of the contract, its liability ceased at the time the Master's deed was issued, says that apparently appellee was overpaid and further that in that particular case, appellee actually found a buyer for the farm, but the reason appellant gives in its letter for paying appellee any further sum other than the $50.00 it had paid was not because appellee found a purchaser but because of the fact that he did find a purchaser appellant paid him the entire balance of $490.00 even "tho the subsequent sale of the property did not quite pay us out".

In explanation of why appellant paid appellee $100.00 in the instant case instead of $50.00 referred to in the letter of April 4, 1931, it appears that subsequently there was some other reference to solicitor fees in the correspondence of the parties and on May 12, 1932, appellant wrote appellee in part as follows: "Your fees will, of course, be determined according to the arrangement now existing between yourself and Mr. Kircher, which I understand is that you shall receive a fee of $50.00 in all default cases where the amount involved does not exceed $15,000.00 and $100.00 in each default case where the indebtedness is in excess thereof."

In our opinion, under the pleadings and evidence found in this record, the trial court was warranted in rendering the judgment appealed from and that judgment will be affirmed.

JUDGMENT AFFIRMED.

}ss. I, JUSTUS L. JOHNSON Clerk of the Appellate Court, in and .he State of Illinois, and the keeper of the Records and Seal thereof, do hereby a true copy of the opinion of the said Appellate Court in the above entitled cause

In Testimony Whereof, I hereunto set my hand and affix the seal of said Appellate Court, at Ottawa, this __________ day of __________ in the year of our Lord one thousand nine hundred and thirty-__________

____

Clerk of the Appellate Court

72 H

AT A TERM OF THE APPELLATE COURT,

Begun and held at Ottawa, on Tuesday, the fifth day of May, in the year of our Lord one thousand nine hundred and thirty-six, within and for the Second District of the State of Illinois:

Present -- The Hon. BLAINE HUFFMAN, Presiding Justice.

Hon. FRANKLIN R. DOVE, Justice.

Hon. FRED G. WOLFE, Justice

JUSTUS L. JOHNSON, Clerk.

RALPH H. DESPER, Sheriff. **286 I.A. 620**[4]

BE IT REMEMBERED, that afterwards, to-wit: On SEP 3 1936 the opinion of the Court was filed in the Clerk's Office of said Court, in the words and figures following, to-wit:

Gen. No. 9093 Agenda No. 32

In the Appellate Court of Illinois

Second District

May Term, A. D. 1936.

Ditha M. Weber,

Appellant,

vs.

Ora K. Weber,

Appellee,

Appeal from the Circuit Court of Warren County

DOVE, J.

On January 29, 1935, the Circuit Court of Warren County rendered its decree, which divorced the parties hereto. This decree found that the parties were married in 1926 and awarded the custody of Ralph Weber, then six years of age, and Lloyd Weber, then about four years of age, the sons of said parties, to the mother during the school year and directed the father to pay for their support and maintenance during the period while they were in the mother's custody, the sum of Nine Dollars on the fifth and a like sum on the twentieth of each month. The decree also found that both the father and mother were fit and proper persons to have the custody of said children and awarded their custody during the summer months to the father. On November 6, 1935, the mother filed in said cause her petition alleging that there had been a change in her own circumstances and in the circumstances of her husband since the decree was granted and charging that it cost more then to maintain the children than it did when the decree was granted and sought, by the petition, to have the provisions of the former decree modified and the amount increased which the husband was directed to pay her to enable her to properly support the children. The respondent answered the petition and filed a cross petition asking that the court award him the custody of the children during the school year, and that she be given the custody of the children during the summer

should be for the summer months only. After the issues were made up, a hearing was had, resulting in the court entering an order denying the prayer of both the petition and the cross petition, but directing that the husband pay to the clerk of the court for the use of his wife, the sum of Fifty Dollars to enable her to pay her attorney for his services in resisting the cross petition. It is from this order that the petitioner, Mrs. Weber, has prosecuted this appeal.

The evidence discloses that at the time the original decree of divorce was rendered, appellee was in the employ of the John Deere Plow Company. He did not own any property except his household furniture and an Essex automobile. His sole income at that time was his salary, which amounted to seventy five dollars per month. There seems to have been an amicable settlement of property rights between the parties, the wife receiving all of the household furniture and the husband retaining the automobile, which he sold shortly thereafter for seventy five dollars. As provided by the decree, appellee paid appellant's attorney's fee, amounting to fifty dollars, and he has regularly paid the semi-monthly installments of nine dollars each as provided by the decree. In March, 1935, at the direction of his employer, he went to Carthage and at the time of the hearing was conducting John Deere Traction Days in various parts of western Illinois, eastern Iowa and southern Wisconsin. In addition to his monthly salary of seventy five dollars, he is receiving a further sum of forty dollars a month, but he testified that the particular work which he was doing at the time of the hearing would be completed on March 18, 1936, and he had no definite agreement as to salary after that date. On March 22, 1935, appellee re-married and was living with his second wife and step-children at the time of the hearing. Appellant, at the time the original decree was rendered, was conducting a beauty shop in the business district of Monmouth, but shortly

thereafter moved the location of her beauty shop to her home and according to her testimony the new location is not as desirable as her former one and her earnings have decreased materially from what they were at the time the decree was rendered. It further appears from the record that appellant refused to deliver the children to appellee on June 1, 1935 and appellee was compelled to employ an attorney and file a petition in this cause before appellant surrendered them to appellee in accordance with the provisions of the original decree. It further appears that while, at the time of the hearing he was receiving from his employer one hundred and fifteen dollars per month, he had been unable to save any money, had no property of any kind or character and no income from any source other than his salary. He testified and it is not contradicted, that in January of this year he voluntarily paid $35.15 for expenses incurred by reason of Ralph's (one of the boys) illness and that during the summer of 1935 while the boys were with him he expended more than $20.00 for sweaters, caps, pajamas, underwear and play suits for them, and this clothing, together with shoes and other articles of clothing which appellee's father and mother had bought the children, were delivered to their mother when they were returned to her in the fall.

Counsel for appellant insist that since the decree was rendered, appellee has had a fifty-three per cent increase of salary and this fact, taken in connection with her decreased earnings, would have warranted the court in increasing the amount appellee was ordered to pay from $18.00 to at least $27.54 a month, and that when all the equities are considered, appellee should be required to pay appellant to enable her to support the children not less than $45.00 per month.

determining alimony are the ages of the parties, their condition of health, the property and income of the husband, separate property and income, if any, of the wife, the station in life of the parties as they have heretofore lived, and whether or not there are any children dependent upon either for support, and also the nature of the misconduct of the husband. It was never intended that the allowance of alimony shall be used as a means of visiting punitive damages upon the husband in favor of the wife for the husband's misconduct, but, guided by the different phases, heretofore mentioned, of the situation of the parties, such allowance is to be made as may furnish the wife support or contribute to her partial support. Gilbert v. Gilbert, 305 Ill. 216. If the circumstances of the parties change, upon proper showing the court may increase or decrease the amount of alimony as conditions may warrant". In the instant case only nine months had elapsed from the time the original decree was entered until appellant filed her petition to modify the same. It is true that during that time appellee had received an increase in salary and that appellant's income from her business had decreased, but her decreased earnings were due to the fact that she moved from the business district to a residential neighborhood and while she says she was prompted by a desire to be in a position to give more time and attention to her children, the change was a voluntary one upon her part and the consequences of such a move were undoubtedly foreseen by her. The statute wisely provides that the court may, on application, from time to time, make such alterations in the allowance of alimony and maintenance, and the care, custody and support of the children as shall appear reasonable and proper, and under the authorities such an application is addressed to the judicial discretion of the Chancellor and the inquiry is directed to ascertain whether any sufficient cause has intervened since the original decree as should, in the application of equitable principles, authorize a change in the allowance. While the Chancellor might have been justified in

making a slight increase in the amount which appellee was directed to pay appellant, we are clearly of the opinion that there was no such abuse of judicial discretion as would warrant this court in substituting its judgment for that of the Chancellor who heard the case. The order appealed from is therefore affirmed.

ORDER AFFIRMED.

}ss.

I, JUSTUS L. JOHNSON, Clerk of the Appellate Court, in and he State of Illinois, and the keeper of the Records and Seal thereof, do hereby a true copy of the opinion of the said Appellate Court in the above entitled cause,

In Testimony Whereof, I hereunto set my hand and affix the seal of said Appellate Court, at Ottawa, this ________________ day of ________________ in the year of our Lord one thousand nine hundred and thirty-____________

____

Clerk of the Appellate Court

AT A TERM OF THE APPELLATE COURT,

gun and held at Ottawa, on Tuesday, the fifth day of May, in the year of our Lord one thousand nine hundred and thirty-s within and for the Second District of the State of Illinois

esent -- the Hon. BLAINE HUFFMAN, Presiding Justice.

Hon. FRANKLIN R. DOVE, Justice.

Hon. FRED G. WOLFE, Justice.

JUSTUS L. JOHNSON, Clerk.

RALPH H. DESPER, Sheriff. **286 I.A. 6**

BE IT REMEMBERED, that afterwards, to-wit On SEP 3 1936 the opinion of the Court was filed in the Clerk's Office of said Court, in the words and figures following, to-wit:

Gen. No. 9041 Agenda No. 1

IN THE
APPELLATE COURT OF ILLINOIS
SECOND DISTRICT

FEBRUARY TERM, A. D. 1936.

KANE COUNTY BANK & TRUST
COMPANY,
Plaintiff and Appellee

vs.

ELLA WINTERHALTER,
Defendant and Appellant

Appeal from Circuit Court,
Kane County.

Wolfe, J.

This is an appeal from an order of the Circuit Court of Kane County, denying the motion of Ella Winterhalter to quash the levy made under an execution issued on a judgment, entered in said Court by confession in favor of the plaintiff, and against the defendant, and from the finding of said Circuit Court that it had no authority to quash said writ in a law case.

The appellant was the defendant and the appellee the plaintiff in the trial court and in this opinion, the parties will be designated as plaintiff and defendant.

On March 21, 1935, the plaintiff filed its complaint and cognovit in said court and obtained by confession, a judgment against the defendant for the sum of $2,037.14. The debt was evidenced by two notes secured by a deed of trust on certain real estate in Kane County, Illinois, which was in the name of John Winterhalter, the husband of the defendant. An execution was issued on the judgment and levy made upon the separate real estate of Ella Winterhalter and the sheriff advertised such real estate for sale. On July 15, 1935, the defendant filed her written motion in which she asked that the levy under the execution be quashed. Her motion, stated in substance, that the notes in question were personal obligations of her husband and not of herself; that said notes were secured by a trust deed to C. L. Morris, as trustee, upon the interest of the

said John Winterhalter in a farm of 228 acres; that the defendant signed said notes as an accomodation; that the notes in question and others of the same series were a first lien to the extent of the interest of John Winterhalter in said farm, and that said interest was of greater value than the principal of all the notes secured thereby with interest thereon; that all the interest was paid as and when due; that John Winterhalter died intestate June 28, 1932, and his estate is in process of administration; that the sheriff, by virtue of the execution, has levied upon the realestate owned by the defendant, and that the said real estate is not the land described in the trust deed; that the judgment was entered and the levy made for the purpose of oppressing the defendant to compel her to pay the obligations of her husband and thereby relieve the mortgage premises of the trust deed obligation, so that thereby the defendant's property might be brought into the estate of John Winterhalter, deceased, and be subject to the payment of his unsecured debts; that if the levy is permitted to stand, it will in effect, make the separate property of the defendant subject to payment of the unsecured debts of John Winterhalter, deceased, and that the defendant is not indebted to the unsecured creditors of John Winterhalter and is under no legal obligation to pay the same. This motion to quash was verified by the affidavit of the defendant.

An order was entered to stay further proceedings under the executionuntil further order of the Court upon the hearing of the motion to quash. On September 27, 1935, there was a hearing before the Court on which evidence was submitted on the part of both parties to the suit, and the Court overruled the motion to quash and an appeal was perfected from such order.

In the Appellant's brief she has incorporated a statement of the trial judge in overruling the motion to quash. The statement is as follows: "It appears to the Court that there are no decisions

allegations to obtain relief in a proceeding in equity; that here is a judgment conceded to be a valid judgment, upon which an execution was regularly issued and the Court does not feel that it can grant the relief asked in a law case, and therefore denies the motion to quash."

The only error relied upon for reversal is: "That the finding of the trial court that said Court had no authority, under the law, to quash said writ, but that recourse must be had in equity."

It is conceded by both parties that this is a valid and existing judgment and that the execution was duly issued as provided by law. This was a proceeding at law and under the law the appellee has the right to pursue as many remedies as it desires in collecting the note which it held. As indicated by the trial court in his statement, it might be that the appellant by proper proceedings in a Court of equity could cause the appellee to first resort to the security pledged for the payment of its debt, before subjecting the unsecured lands of appellant to sale--but that is not the case before us to decide. The motion to quash raised a purely legal question of the sufficiency of the judgment and the execution thereon. It is our opinion that the trial court properly found that the motion to quash could not be sustained.

The judgment of the Circuit Court of Kane County is hereby affirmed.

Affirmed.

STATE OF ILLINOIS, } ss.
SECOND DISTRICT

I, JUSTUS L. JOHNSON Clerk of the Appellate Court, in and for said Second District of the State of Illinois, and the keeper of the Records and Seal thereof, do hereby certify that the foregoing is a true copy of the opinion of the said Appellate Court in the above entitled cause, of record in my office.

In Testimony Whereof, I hereunto set my hand and affix the seal of said Appellate Court at Ottawa, this ______________ day of ______________ in the year of our Lord one thousand nine hundred and thirty-______________

____
Clerk of the Appellate Court

(73815—5M—3-32)

AT A TERM OF THE APPELLATE COURT,

ld at Ottawa, on Tuesday, the fifth day of May,
of our Lord one thousand nine hundred and thirt
nd for the Second District of the State of Illin

the Hon. BLAINE HUFFMAN, Presiding Justice.
Hon. FRANKLIN R. DOVE, Justice.
Hon. FRED G. WOLFE, Justice.
JUSTUS L. JOHNSON, Clerk.
RALPH H. DESPER, Sheriff. 286 I.A.

MEMBERED, that afterwards, to-wit: On SEP 8 19
. of the Court was filed in the Clerk's Office o
he words and figures following to-wit:

Gen. No. 9060 Agenda No. 4.

IN THE
APPELLATE COURT OF ILLINOIS
SECOND DISTRICT

MAY TERM, A. D. 1936

MARIA McGUIRE,
(Complainant) Appellee

vs.

JAMES J. McGUIRE,
(Defendant),

Appeal from Circuit Court of LaSalle County.

THE RETIREMENT BOARD OF THE POLICEMEN'S ANNUITY AND BENEFIT FUND OF CHICAGO,
(Intervening Defendant) Appellant

Wolfe, J.

In 1910, Maria McGuire filed a bill for divorce in the Circuit Court of LaSalle County, against her husband, James A. McGuire. On January 6, 1911, a hearing was had and a decree entered granting Maria McGuire a divorce. At this time James J. McGuire, the husband, was a member of the Chicago Police Force. On January 15, 1930, he resigned from said Police Force and was granted a pension. On September 28, 1934, James J. McGuire died. On January 18, 1935, Maria McGuire filed in the original divorce proceedings of LaSalle County, her petition praying that the decree of divorce granted her in January 6, 1911, be vacated and set aside on the ground that at the time the divorce was granted, she was an insane person. On February 2, 1935, leave was granted to the Retirement Board of the Policemen's Annuity Benefit Fund of Chicago, the appellant, to file an intervening petition. On February 16, 1935, the defendant filed in the said court an amended petition, and on February 23, 1935, an order was entered granting appellant leave to intervene. On July 8, 1935, a hearing was had on said petition and an order was entered striking the answer of the appellant's and vacating the order granting leave to intervene. The Court also vacated and

set aside the decree of divorce on January 6, 1911. On August 5, 1935, the entire order of January 8, 1935, was set aside and the decree for divorce entered January 6, 1911, was vacated. It is from this order of August 5, 1935, that the appellant, the Retirement Board of the Policeman's Annuity and Benefit Fund of Chicago, brings the record to this Court for review.

In a very recent case of Bernero vs. Bernero, reported in Volume 302, Illinois Supreme Court Report at page 329, the Supreme Court of this State had under consideration the identical question presented by this record and was there held that the Retirement Board had no legal rights which would permit it to intervene in a proceeding of this character. The appeal, therefore, in this case must be dismissed.

Appeal dismissed.

STATE OF ILLINOIS, }
SECOND DISTRICT } ss.

I JUSTUS L JOHNSON, Clerk of the Appellate Court, in and for said Second District of the State of Illinois, and the keeper of the Records and Seal thereof, do hereby certify that the foregoing is a true copy of the opinion of the said Appellate Court in the above entitled cause of record in my office.

In Testimony Whereof, I hereunto set my hand and affix the seal of said Appellate Court, at Ottawa, this ________________ day of ________________ in the year of our Lord one thousand nine hundred and thirty-____________

____

Clerk of the Appellate Court

(73815—5M—3-32) 7

Lord one thousand nine hundred and thirty-six,

,he Second District of the State of Illinois:

. BLAINE HUFFMAN, Presiding Justice.

. FRANKLIN R. DOVE, Justice.

. FRED G. WOLFE, Justice.

TUS L. JOHNSON, Clerk.

PH H. DESPER, Sheriff. **286 I.A. 621**[3]

ED, that afterwards, to-wit On SEP 3 1936

e Court was filed in the Clerk's Office of said

ds and figures following, to-wit:

No. 9065 Agenda No. 7

IN THE
APPELLATE COURT OF ILLINOIS
SECOND DISTRICT

MAY TERM, A. D. 1936

JOHNSON & CARLSON, a Corporation,
(Plaintiff) Appellee

vs.

PIONEER BREWING COMPANY, A Corporation,
(Defendant) Appellant

Appeal from Circuit Court, Will County.

Wolfe, J.

Johnson & Carlson, a Corporation, started a suit of replevin in the Circuit Court of Will County on June 6, 1935, against the Pioneer Brewing Company et al., to recover possession of nine fermenters. On June 25, 1935, the sheriff returned the writ unexecuted with a notation that he was unable to find said property in his county. On July 2, 1935, the plaintiff filed its declaration in trover in said court. The defendants filed their answer to the declaration in trover. The case was submitted to the Court without a jury on the declaration and the defendant's amended answer. The Court found for the plaintiff and against the Pioneer Brewing Company and assessed the plaintiff's damage at $1,941.00. The defendant entered a motion for a new trial and in arrest of judgment, both motions were overruled. Judgment was entered for the plaintiff for the sum of $1,941.00, and the case is brought to this Court for review.

From the evidence, it appears that on June 18, 1933, the Johnson & Carlson Company submitted a written proposition to the Hillside Brewing Company of Joliet, Illinois, to install in the brewery of said company certain fermenters, which are the subject matter of the present suit. The offer was accepted and the fermenters were installed in said brewery. Later, the Hillside Brewing Company

went into bankruptcy and a trustee was appointed to take charge of the bankrupt property. On May 11, 1934, the schedule of the Hillside Brewing Company was filed in the bankruptcy proceeding, which designated the plaintiff as a secured creditor for $2,189.39, held under conditional sales contract. The trustee in bankruptcy was directed to sell the brewery property. When the plaintiff learned that the assets of the Brewing Company were about to be sold, it filed in the District Court its reclamation, claiming to own said fermenters. As far as the record discloses, this petition was never acted upon by the Court. The property was sold for $15,000.00. The court approved the sale and directed the receiver to deliver his deed and bill of sale to the purchaser, upon the payment of said $15,000.00, and the surrender of the receiver's certificates. The latter part of said order of sale and confirmation thereof recited that the sale is made subject to mortgage on the real estate, and quoting, "All conditional sales contracts, all chattel mortgages in existence and mechanic's liens."

The appellant now insists that the trial court erred in admitting in evidence the conditional sales contract as between the plaintiff and the Hillside Brewing Company, the bankruptcy schedule Exhibit A 2, and the plaintiff's intervening petition in bankruptcy of the Hillside Brewing Company. We find no merit in this contention, as the plaintiff had a right to introduce these exhibits for the purpose of establishing its chain of title to the fermenters in question.

The second assignment of error avers that the Court's opinion is contrary to the evidence and contrary to the law of the case. The evidence clearly establishes the fact that the fermenters were sold upon a conditional sales contract. The trustee in bankruptcy did not sell the fermenters and the title did not pass to the defendants when they purchased the brewery. It is our conclusion that the Court's finding, the issues in favor of the plaintiff, is in accordance with the facts and the law applicable to the case.

The fourth assignment of error is that the Court erred in overruling defendant's motion for a new trial and in arrest of judgment and in entering judgment for the plaintiff in view of the fatal variances in the allegations and the proof. It is a well established principle of law that a plaintiff cannot recover upon a state of facts different from that alleged in his pleadings. It has been a long established rule of practice in replevin and trover actions to aver that the plaintiff casually lost the articles in question and that the defendants found and reduced them to its possession, the defendants well knowing that the chattels were the property of the plaintiff, and converted them to their own use. The evidence in this case, we think, clearly establishes the fact that the title to the fermenters in question never passed to the defendant; that title always remained in the plaintiffs; that the plaintiff made demand upon the defendants for the return of the property, which they refused, and claimed them as their own. Under the law, the plaintiffs were then entitled to either possession of the fermenters or damages for their wrongful detention. The Court has found the value of the converted property to be $1,941.00, and we think, this is a fair estimate of their value.

We find no reversible error in this case and the judgment of the Will County Circuit Court is hereby affirmed.

Affirmed.

STATE OF ILLINOIS, }
SECOND DISTRICT } ss.

I JUSTUS L. JOHNSON, Clerk of the Appellate Court in and for said Second District of the State of Illinois, and the keeper of the Records and Seal thereof, do hereby certify that the foregoing is a true copy of the opinion of the said Appellate Court in the above entitled cause of record in my office.

In Testimony Whereof, I hereunto set my hand and affix the seal of said Appellate Court at Ottawa this __________________ day of __________________ in the year of our Lord one thousand nine hundred and thirty-____________

____
Clerk of the Appellate Court

(73815—5M—3-32) 7

AT A TERM OF THE APPELLATE COURT,

ıt Ottawa, on Tuesday, the fifth day of May, in
›ur Lord one thousand nine hundred and thirty-six,
›r the Second District of the State of Illinois:

Hon. BLAINE HUFFMAN, Presiding Justice.
Hon. FRANKLIN R. DOVE, Justice.
Hon. FRED G. WOLFE, Justice.
JUSTUS L. JOHNSON, Clerk
RALPH H. DESPER, Sheriff.

76

286 I.A. 621[4]

ERED, that afterwards, to-wit: On SEP 8 1936
the Court was filed in the Clerk's Office of said
ords and figures following, to-wit:

Gen. No. 9076 Agenda No. 16

IN THE
APPELLATE COURT OF ILLINOIS
SECOND DISTRICT

TO THE MAY TERM, A.D. 1936

SOMONAUK STATE BANK, a Corporation, AUGUST MARCO, Individually and as Administrator of the Estate of INGERBORG NESS, Deceased, JOSEPH H. STANDART, Receiver of the Ottawa Banking & Trust Company of Ottawa, Illinois, and JOHN G. SCHUMACHER, Receiver of the Serena State Bank of Serena, Illinois,
Appellees

vs.

BARTEL B. HAGEN, ARTHUR NESS, FRESENIUS NESS, ISABELLA O. UGLAND, ADA GRANDGEORGE, ELMA O. BERNARD, HANNAH M. MUNDORF, BURT M. THOMPSON, Trustee of the Estate of ARTHUR NESS, Bankrupt, ALEXANDER LUMBER COMPANY, a Corporation, THE FIRST NATIONAL BANK OF SHERIDAN, ILLINOIS, a Corporation, and the CO-OPERATIVE GRAIN & SUPPLY COMPANY OF SERENA, ILLINOIS, a Corporation,
Appellants.

Appeal from Circuit Court of LaSalle County, Illinois

Wolfe, J.

This case came before us at a former term of Court and is reported in a memoranda decision in 276, Illinois, Appellate page 608, at which time the case was reversed and remanded to the trial court. The case was again heard on January 20, 1936. The Court entered an order in conformity with the prayer of the bill, as directed in our former opinion.

STATE OF ILLINOIS, }
SECOND DISTRICT } ss.

I JUSTUS L. JOHNSON, Clerk of the Appellate Court in and for said Second District of the State of Illinois, and the keeper of the Records and Seal thereof, do hereby certify that the foregoing is a true copy of the opinion of the said Appellate Court in the above entitled cause, of record in my office.

In Testimony Whereof, I hereunto set my hand and affix the seal of said Appellate Court, at Ottawa, this__________day of __________in the year of our Lord one thousand nine hundred and thirty-__________

____

Clerk of the Appellate Court

(73815—5M—3-32)

AT A TERM OF THE APPELLATE COURT,

at Ottawa, on Tuesday, the fifth day of May, in our Lord one thousand nine hundred and thirty-six, for the Second District of the State of Illinois:

Hon. BLAINE HUFFMAN, Presiding Justice.

Hon. FRANKLIN R. DOVE, Justice.

Hon. FRED G. WOLFE, Justice.

JUSTUS L. JOHNSON, Clerk

RALPH H. DESPER, Sheriff.

286 I.A. 621

MBERED, that afterwards, to-wit: On

f the Court was filed in the Clerk's Office of said words and figures following, to-wit:

Gen. No. 9033 Agenda No. 22

IN THE
APPELLATE COURT OF ILLINOIS
SECOND DISTRICT

MAY TERM, A.D. 1936.

A. P. KANNAPEL,

Plaintiff-Appellant, Appeal from Circuit Court,

vs. Peoria County.

THE GOODYEAR TIRE & RUBBER
COMPANY, INC., (a corporation),
Defendant-Appellee.

Wolfe, J.

A. P. Kannapel started suit in the Circuit Court of Peoria County, against the Goodyear Tire & Rubber Company, a corporation, and E. H. Eager claiming damages for injuries sustained by him as a result of a collision of the automobile of the defendant Rubber Company, which was being driven by Eager, its agent, with the plaintiff while he was walking on West Washington Street within the corporate limits of the City of East Peoria, Illinois, November 6, 1933. The collision occurred on State Bond Issue Highway No. 8, just south of the Tazewell County entrance to the lower free bridge leading from East Peoria to Peoria. The complaint consists of several counts charging the defendants with different forms of negligence, by reason of which the plaintiff was injured. The petition alleges that the plaintiff just before and at the time of the accident in question was in the exercise of due care and caution for his own safety. The defendants filed their answer to the amended complaint in which they denied that the Goodyear Company was the owner of the automobile in question and that E. H. Eager was driving the same as their agent. The defendants were granted leave to file an amendment to their answer, which was filed. They admitted the ownership of the automobile in question and that

E. H. Hager was driving it as agent of the Goodyear Company, but denied that the agent of the defendant was driving the automobile in a negligent manner. The case was tried before a jury who found the issues in favor of the defendant. The plaintiff entered a motion for a new trial, which was overruled and judgment was entered on the verdict in favor of the defendant. The appeal is from that judgment to this Court.

The appellant in his errors relied upon for reversal, has stated 6 reasons, 5 of which are that the Court erred in giving certain instructions to the jury. The 6th is, "The verdict and judgment are against the law."

The appellant seriously insists that the Court erried in giving the jury any instruction relative to the due care and caution of the plaintiff, because they claim that is not a converted question under the pleadings in this case. The original answer of the defendant put that question in issue as it denied that the plaintiff was in the exercise of due care and caution for his safety. The defendant filed an amendment to the answer which consists of two paragraphs, and designated as, "Amended Answer." It is contended by the appellant that this is the only answer that the appellee has on file, and it does not relate in any way to the negligence of the plaintiff, but only puts in issue the negligence of the defendant in the operation of the automobile. The appellee filed in this Court its written motion together with an additional abstract of record and asked leave to file the same. This additional abstract shows the original answer filed by the defendants in the case. Leave was granted to file the additional abstract. It is the conclusion of the Court that the pleading marked, 'amended answer' is but an amendment to the original answer and the amendment and original answer should both have been in the appellee's abstract as part of the pleadings in the case. It is the substance of a paper or pleading that is filed that governs its legal effect. It is the substance of the plea or answer that controls and the nature of the pleading is

determined by the allegations and averments that appeal therein and not what the paper may be designated or labelled.

The court on behalf of the plaintiff, give the second and third instructions which are devoted wholly to the due care and caution that the plaintiff was required to exercise in such cases and the case was evidently tried on the theory that the original answer of the defendant was a part of the pleadings in the case.

The evidence shows that this accident happened on a very busy street in the City of East Peoria, Illinois; that it was in the evening of November 16, when, as the witness described it, "It was not quite dark." The plaintiff crossed diagonally across the street, ~~not at the intersection~~, and the defendant's car struck him and knocked him down. Mr. E. H. Hager, the driver of the defendant's car said that the plaintiff as he was crossing the street was walking or running, at a rate of speed as was what he had commonly heard called a dog trot. Doctor Kammapel, in his testimony says, that he was "Walking briskly, or rushing, or a slow run." Albert J. Cohen, a witness for the plaintiff and an eye witness to the accident, in response to a question of what part of the defendant's car struck the plaintiff, said, "The part of the car, that came in contact to him was the end of the door." Doctor Kammapel said, "The contact between the car and myself was near the door, first, with the fender and then with the post of the door, if I can recall correctly." E. H. Hager, the driver of the car, in his evidence states, "The plaintiff came in contact with my car I would say, just behind the front door on the left side of the car."

The evidence further shows that the plaintiff was a practicing physician living in the City of Peoria, but had formerly lived in the City of East Peoria and still had a large practice in East Peoria; that he travelled this street very frequently, practically every day, and was well acquainted with the street and the enormous amount of traffic that it carried; that the defendant's car was a Ford two door sedan; that at the time the collision occurred, the

driver of the car had the front wheels off or nearly off the pavement trying to avoid an accident with the plaintiff and the uncontradicted evidence is that the plaintiff walked or ran into the side of the defendant's car.

The appellant criticizes several of the given instructions that were offered by the defendant, especially instruction No.2, in which it states that, "Before the plaintiff can recover he must establish by the greater weight of the evidence that the defendant is guilty of the negligence charged in some count of the declaration, etc." A similar instruction has been severely criticized by the Appellate Court of the 4th District and no doubt this instruction is subject to criticism, but from the conclusion we have reached in regard to the evidence, we do not deem it reversible error for the Court to give this instruction. We realize that no one can tell what was the controlling factor in a jury's verdict,but from the evidence in this case, we do not see how the jury would be justified in rendering a verdict in favor of the plaintiff, as it appears to us that the plaintiff was grossly negligence in crossing the street at the time and place he did and that if he had exercised ordinary and reasonable care, for his own safety, he could easily have avoided the accident.

The appellee has filed a cross-appeal. The appellant contends that the same cannot be considered by this Court, as the cross-appeal is not perfected in the manner provided for in the Practice Act. An examination of the record discloses that the appellees have not proceeded in accordance with the Statute. The failure to do so is jurisdictional and the appellee's cross-appeal cannot be considered by this Court.

We find no reversible error in the case and the judgment of the trial court is hereby affirmed.

Affirmed.

S, }ss.

I, JUSTUS L JOHNSON, Clerk of the Appellate Court, in and of the State of Illinois, and the keeper of the Records and Seal thereof, do hereby g is a true copy of the opinion of the said Appellate Court in the above entitled cause

In Testimony Whereof, I hereunto set my hand and affix the seal of said Appellate Court, at Ottawa, this __________ day of __________ in the year of our Lord one thousand nine hundred and thirty-__________

____

Clerk of the Appellate Court

AT A TERM OF THE APPELLATE COURT,

Begun and held at Ottawa, on Tuesday, the fifth day of May, in the year of our Lord one thousand nine hundred and thirty-six, within and for the Second District of the State of Illinois:

Present -- The Hon. BLAINE HUFFMAN, Presiding Justice.

Hon. FRANKLIN R. DOVE, Justice.

Hon. FRED G. WOLFE, Justice.

JUSTUS L. JOHNSON, Clerk

RALPH H. DESPER, Sheriff.

286 I.A. 622

78

BE IT REMEMBERED, that afterwards, to-wit On

the opinion of the Court was filed in the Clerk's Office of said Court, in the words and figures following, to-wit

GEN. NO. 9087 AGENDA NO. 25.

IN THE

APPELLATE COURT OF ILLINOIS,

SECOND DISTRICT.

May Term, A. D. 1936.

MARTHE WILLGEROTH, Administratrix of the Estate of ALFRED O. WILLGEROTH, Deceased, Appellant, vs. SUSIE W. MADDOX, Administratrix of the Estate of WILLIAM A. MADDOX, Deceased, Appellee,	Appeal from Circuit Court, Winnebago County

WOLFE, J.

This case was before this Court at the May Term, 1935, at which time it was reversed and remanded to the Trial Court. It was again tried in the Circuit Court before a jury and a verdict rendered in favor of the plaintiff for the sum of $7,500.00. The defendant, through her attorney, filed a motion for judgment notwithstanding the verdict. This motion was granted and the Circuit Court entered judgment for the defendant notwithstanding the verdict. From this judgment, the case comes to this Court for review. With the exception of the proof relative to the heirship of Alfred O. Willgeroth, deceased, in this case the evidence is nearly identically the same as in the former case, and we approve and confirm our former opinion which is

William A. Maddox. The complaint alleged that on August 10, 1933, William A. Maddox was driving his automobile and Alfred O. Willgeroth was riding with him as a passenger; that Maddox was driving said automobile on State Route No. 70, known as the Meridian Highway; that said highway runs north and south, and about one mile east of Davis Junction crosses the railroad track of the Chicago, Milwaukee, St. Paul & Pacific Railroad Company; that the automobile was being driven in a southerly direction; that as the car was approaching the crossing, Maddox then and there wilfully, wantonly and recklessly ran, managed, operated, and drove said automobile, and that on account of said wilful, wanton and reckless conduct of defendant's intestate, said automobile was caused to and did collide with a railroad train on said railroad track at said crossing and the plaintiff's intestate, Alfred O. Willgeroth, then and there received injuries from which he thereafter died. The complaint also sets forth the heirship of Alfred O. Willgeroth.

To this bill of complaint the defendant filed an answer admitting part of the allegations of the petition, but denying that William A. Maddox was guilty of wilful and wanton conduct in the management and operation of the automobile just prior to and at the time of the collision which caused the death of the plaintiff's intestate. The case was tried before a jury which rendered a verdict in favor of the plaintiff and against the defendant in the sum of $5,000.00. The defendant entered a motion for a judgment notwithstanding the verdict, which was overruled. After a motion for a new trial was entered and overruled, the defendant was then granted leave to file an amendment to her answer which charges, "That the plaintiff's intestate, Willgeroth, then and there, was guilty of wilful and wanton conduct, and that said wilful and wanton

conduct contributed as the proximate cause to his own injury and death, without which the accident would not have occurred;" and (b) also charged "that plaintiff's intestate, Willgeroth, before and at the time of the accident in question, had the same opportunity to observe the oncoming train which defendant's intestate, Maddox, had, and that plaintiff's intestate, Willgeroth, was guilty of the same degree of wilful and wanton conduct of which defendant's intestate, Maddox, was guilty, if any, which wilful and wanton conduct on the part of plaintiff's intestate, Willgeroth, contributed as the proximate cause of his own injury, and death, and without which it would not have occurred;" and (c) also charged "that plaintiff's intestate, Willgeroth, had equal opportunity to observe the approach of the railroad train with the opportunity which defendant's intestate, Maddox, had, and that nevertheless in wilful, wanton and reckless disregard of his duty in that behalf, and with utter disregard of consequences, the plaintiff's intestate, Willgeroth, wilfully, wantonly and with wilful, wanton and reckless disregard of his duty in that behalf, and with a willingness to accept the chance of injury to himself, wilfully, wantonly and with reckless disregard either failed to observe the coming of said train, or having observed the coming of said train, and knowing of its approach, and with a conscious willingness to incur injury to himself failed to do anything to protect himself and failed to do anything to warn the said Maddox of the approach of said train, and the said Willgeroth wilfully and wantonly, and with reckless disregard of his own safety, left a place of safety, and rode in front of said approaching train, and was struck by said train, which wilful, wanton and reckless conduct of the said Willgeroth, contributed as the proximate cause of his own injury and death, and which it would not have occurred."

To this amended answer the plaintiff filed a replication denying that the plaintiff's intestate was guilty of any wilful, wanton and reckless conduct which was the proximate cause of his injuries.

The first point urged by the appellant for a reversal of the judgment is that the plaintiff failed to prove that she was the widow and next of kin of the plaintiff's intestate. There may be, and probably is, some merit in this contention but as the case will have to be reversed and remanded for other reasons, we do not decide this pointin this appeal.

There is very little, if any, dispute in regard to the evidence in this case. The main witness for the plaintiff, Mr. Ross C. Wheat of Bensenville, Illinois, a locomotive engineer employed by the C. M. St. P. & Pac. Railway Company, testified that he was in charge of the engine on August 10, 1933, at the time of the accident in question; that he was driving the engine at approximately 50 miles per hour; that the bell was ringing and that he blew the whistle as he approached the crossing where the accident occurred; that he first observed the automobile coming in a southerly direction about 700 feet north of the intersection of the highway with the railroad track; that in his opinion the automobile was traveling approximately at a rate of 60 miles per hour; that the driver of the automobile was looking straight ahead until he approached within two or three hundred feet of the crossing when he turned his head to the west; also, that the man who was riding with him did the same thing; that within a few seconds they faced ahead again and kept coming on at the same rate of speed until they got within 75 or 100 feet of the track, when the automobile slowed down and the driver just as he got in front of the engine looked at the engine and that was the last that he, the engineer, saw of the automobile until the engine struck it; that when the driver and the passenger in the automobile first looked at the engine they were

perhaps 15 feet from the crossing and the engine was about the same distance away.

Other witnesses testified relative to the speed at which the automobile was being driven and that neither of the deceased parties in the automobile appeared to have any knowledge of the approach of the freight train. The fireman on the engine, testified that because the automobile was stuck on the front of the engine another engine was procured from the station a short distance west of the scene of the accident and that they had that engine come up and pull the automobile loose from the engine which struck the automobile. This witness also testified that the engine that came to pull the automobile from the other engine was being used for switching purposes near the station at the time of the accident.

The jury by their verdict evidently thought that Maddox at the time he was driving the automobile in question was guilty of wilful and wanton conduct which caused the injuries to the plaintiff's intestate. The appellant seriously contends that the evidence does not justify such a finding, and if it does, that the plaintiff's intestate is guilty of the same wanton and wilful conduct as Maddox, and therefore, the plaintiff is barred from a recovery.

It is hard to distinguish between negligence and wanton and wilful conduct. In the case of Lake Shore & M. S. Ry. Co. v. Bodemer, 139 Ill. 596, the Supreme Court in discussing this matter use the following language: "What degree of negligence the law considers equivalent to a wilful or wanton act is as hard to define as negligence itself, and in the nature of things, is so dependent upon the particular circumstances of each case as not to be susceptible of general statement." In Illinois Cent. R. Co. v. Godfrey, 71 Ill. 500, we said that where a trespasser is injured,

the railroad company is liable for "such gross negligence as evidences wilfulness." We said the same thing in Blanchard v. Lake Shore & M. S. Ry. Co., 126 Ill. 416. What is meant by "such gross negligence as evidences wilfulness?" It is "such a gross want of care and regard for the rights of others as to justify the presumption of wilfulness or wantonness." "It is such gross negligence as to imply a disregard of consequences, or a willingness to inflict injury." In Harlem v. St. Louis, Kansas City & N. Ry. Co., 65 Mo. 22, it was said: "When it is said, in cases where plaintiff has been guilty of contributory negligence, that the company is liable, if by the exercise of ordinary care it could have prevented the accident, it is to be understood that it will be so liable if, by the exercise of reasonable care, after a discovery by defendant of the danger in which the injured party stood, the accident could have been prevented, or if the company failed to discover the danger through the recklessness or carelessness of its employees, when the exercise of ordinary care would have discovered the danger and averted the calamity."

The evidence in this case shows that William A. Maddox and Alfred C. Willgeroth had been friends, and for several years were employed at the same place; that they had been together frequently, that as they were riding they evidently were attracted by the freight train which was switching west of the road on which they were traveling, that they were both looking in the same direction toward this engine; that neither of them gave any indication whatsoever that they were aware of the approach of the freight train which caused their deaths. That each of these parties was guilty of the grossest negligence in not discovering the approaching freight train is beyond question. From the evidence in this case we are of the opinion that Maddox and Willgeroth were guilty of

negligence or wilful and wanton conduct to the same degree, as they both had equal opportunity to observe the approaching train. It is further our opinion that the plaintiff has failed to prove that defendant's intestate was guilty of wilful and wanton misconduct that was the proximate cause of defendant's intestate's injury that caused his death.

Assuming that both Maddox and Willgeroth were guilty of wilful and wanton conduct in not discovering the approach of the freight train, the question then arises whether that is a defense to the action of the plaintiff in this suit. It is conceded that contributory negligence is not a defense to an action for the personal injuries, when it is charged that the acts were done wilfully and wantonly. The Supreme Court of Michigan in the case of Redson v. Michigan Cent. R. Co., 120 Mich. 671, 79 N. W. p. 939, had occasion to pass on this question, and in their opinion say: "Plaintiff saw this train coming. He was just in the act of hitching onto a log. Instead of immediately removing his horses, which, it is evident, he had then ample time to do, and taking them out of danger, he ordered the log rolled up onto the car, and before he could then get his horses removed, both the horses and his partner, Wentworth, in charge of them, were killed. Had injury resulted to the train, or to the trainmen, it might just as well have been charged that he (the plaintiff) was guilty of intentional wrong, as to charge that the engineer was guilty of it. It would then be gross negligence against gross negligence, wilful misconduct against wilful misconduct, and intent against intent; and in such case the law leaves both parties where they have placed themselves, and gives recovery to neither."

In the case of Hinkle v. Minneapolis, A. & C. R. Co., 162 Minn. 112, 202 N. W. 3, the Supreme Court of the State of

Minnesota defines what is wilful and wanton conduct, and defenses to such actions and in their opinion say this: "Wilful and wanton negligence is reckless disregard of the safety of the person or property of another by failing, after discovering the peril, to exercise ordinary care to prevent the impending injury. One is liable for negligence only when such negligence is the proximate cause of the injury. When a defendant is charged with ordinary negligence, contributory negligence is a good defense. Why? The answer is founded in proximate cause. In the absence of the doctrine of comparative negligence they are equally to blame. When two persons are equally at fault in producing the injury, the law leaves them where it finds them. Contributory negligence is not a defense to wanton and wilful negligence, for the very simple reason that the parties are not equally delinquent in the violation of duty. In such case the negligence of the defendant is the proximate cause of plaintiff's injury while his negligence is no more than a remote cause.

"The theory of these variations of negligence leads to but one logical conclusion, and that is that the same basic reason which causes contributory negligence to prevent a recovery in an action sounding in ordinary negligence also prevents a recovery by one who is guilty of wilful and wanton negligence. Such negligence is just as efficient to offset the defendant's negligence of the same character as contributory negligence offsets ordinary negligence. There can be no more comparative wantonness than there can be comparative negligence. When both parties are guilty of such negligence neither can be selected as that which is the proximate cause, and hence the law must leave both where it finds them. The conclusion is inevitable, even though its application be fraught with difficulties."

The case of Osteen v. Atlantic Coast Line R. Co., 119 S. C. 438, 112 S. E. 352, holds that "contributory negligence on the part of the plaintiff is a defense to negligence on the part of a defendant, and contributory wilfulness, wantonness, or recklessness on the part of the plaintiff is a defense to wilfulness, wantonness or recklessness on the part of the defendant."

In the case of Spillers v. Griffin, 109 S. C. 78, 95, S. E. p. 133, the Supreme Court of South Carolina uses this language: "Again, contributory negligence is not a defense to wilfulness, because the parties are not equally to blame. Apply that same rule here, and we find that when a plaintiff wilfully contributes, as the proximate cause to his own injury, he cannot recover, even though the defendant was wilful. If the parties were equally, in the same class, to blame in producing the injury, neither can recover."

It is our opinion that where the plaintiff charges the defendant with wilful and wanton misconduct as being the proximate cause of injury to him, and the defense charges that the plaintiff was also guilty of wilful and wanton misconduct which was the proximate cause of the injury, then the same is a good defense, and bars the action if proven."

In the former opinion there is a slight error in the statement of facts, in which we state: "That when the driver and the passenger in the automobile first looked at the engine, they were perhaps 15 feet away from the crossing and the engine was about the same distance away." There is no evidence that the passenger in the automobile looked at the engine at that time, as the engineer stated, he could not see the passenger in the car when it was that close to the engine.

The only questions presented by this appeal is whether the deceased, William A. Maddox, was guilty of wilful and wanton conduct in driving his car, which caused the death of the plaintiff's intestate; assuming that Maddox was guilty of such wilful and wanton conduct, was plaintiff's intestate guilty of the same wilful and wanton conduct; would the same be a good defense to this suit. As stated in our former opinion the evidence shows that each of these parties was guilty of gross negligence in not discovering the approaching freight train, but we do not believe the evidence was sufficient to show that Maddox was guilty of wilful and wanton conduct as described by our Courts. We further stated that Maddox and Willgeroth were guilty of negligence or wilful and wanton conduct to the same degree as they both had equal opportunities to observe the approaching train.

It is our opinion in this case that the evidence does not show that William A. Maddox at the time and place in question was guilty of wilful and wanton conduct, and the plaintiff cannot recover in this suit. If it can be said, that William A. Maddox at the time and place in question was guilty of wilful and wanton conduct in the management of the car, then the plaintiff's intestate was clearly guilty of the same wilful and wanton conduct. This would be a bar to the action and the plaintiff could not recover.

It is our opinion that the trial court properly sustained the motion for a judgment notwithstanding the verdict and the same should be affirmed.

AFFIRMED.

STATE OF ILLINOIS, } ss.
SECOND DISTRICT

I, JUSTUS L. JOHNSON, Clerk of the Appellate Court in and for said Second District of the State of Illinois, and the keeper of the Records and Seal thereof, do hereby certify that the foregoing is a true copy of the opinion of the said Appellate Court in the above entitled cause, of record in my office.

In Testimony Whereof, I hereunto set my hand and affix the seal of said Appellate Court, at Ottawa this ______________ day of ______________ in the year of our Lord one thousand nine hundred and thirty-______________

____
Clerk of the Appellate Court

(73815—5M—3-32)

AT A TERM OF THE APPELLATE COURT,

Begun and held at Ottawa, on Tuesday, the fifth day of May, in the year of our Lord one thousand nine hundred and thirty-six within and for the Second District of the State of Illinois.

79

Present -- the Hon. BLAINE HUFFMAN, Presiding Justice.

Hon. FRANKLIN R. DOVE, Justice.

Hon. FRED G. WOLFE, Justice.

JUSTUS L. JOHNSON, Clerk.

RALPH H. DESPER, Sheriff.

286 I.A. 6

BE IT REMEMBERED, that afterwards, to-wit: On SEP 3 1936 the opinion of the Court was filed in the Clerk's Office of said Court, in the words and figures following to-wit:

Gen. No. 9089 Agenda No. 23

IN THE
APPELLATE COURT OF ILLINOIS
SECOND DISTRICT

MAY TERM, A.D. 1936.

THE GRUNDY COUNTY NATIONAL BANK,
and WARREN E. BULL, Trustee,
Appellees

vs.

FRANK SANFORD, EMMA P. SANFORD
and JAMES GRONER,
Appellants.

Appeal from Circuit Court, Grundy County.

Wolfe, J.

The Grundy County National Bank brought suit in the Circuit Court of Grundy County to foreclose a trust deed. It made Frank Sanford, Emma P. Sanford and James Groner parties defendant to the suit. Groner defaulted, but the Sanfords filed answers to the original and amended bill of complaint. The case followed the usual procedure and was referred to the master to take proofs, etc., a decree of foreclosure and sale was signed by the Court. The land in question is situated in Cook, Grundy and Iroquois County. The decree of sale ordered that the property be advertised for sale on September 1, 1932, in each of the counties. On account of a mistake of the date of sale in the advertisement in one of the counties, this Court set aside the former order of sale and reversed and remanded the case with direction for the trial court to order the master to advertise a sale of said property according to the original decree of the Circuit Court of Grundy County.

The case was again heard before said court and the decree entered in conformity with the mandate of this court. The appellants, Frank Sanford and Emma P. Sanford, filed their motion to vacate the decree of foreclosure and dismiss the bill of complaint

as to the lands located in Cook and Iroquois County, because the Circuit Court of Grundy County did not have jurisdiction of the subject matter of the suit, and has not now jurisdiction of the land located in Cook and Iroquois County; that the trust deeds referred to in the bill of complaint were separate and distinct trust deeds and neither of them had any lands of Grundy County described in any or either of them. The Court overruled the motion to dismiss and entered the decree as above stated. The Sanfords have again perfected an appeal to this Court.

In the case of Belding vs. Belding 281, Illinois Appellate, page 351, there was a similar question presented to this Court in which we said, "Where a judgment is reversed and the case remanded with directions as to the decree or judgment to be entered in the trial court, it is the duty of that Court to follow such instructions and it cannot err in doing so. Upon appeal from the decree of the lower court so entered, the only question presented by such appeal, is whether the decree entered, is in accordance with the mandate and directions of the Court of review." The appellants do not seriously question this rule of law, but contend that the question they have raised, is one of jurisdiction and such may be raised at any time.

The appellants insist there are three separate and distinct deeds of trust securing a series of notes involved in this suit. An examination of the record discloses that this was one transaction. The notes and deeds of trust were all signed and acknowledged on the same date. When the original decree of foreclosure was prepared, it was presented to the attorney representing the appellants, who gave it his approval by marking it, "O.K.--Reardon." The Court and attorneys at that time, treated it as one deed of trust. The Court in its decree finds, among other things, that it has jurisdiction of the subject matter and the parties to this case. It is our conclusion that the Court properly found that the notes and trust deeds in question, constituted a single transaction, or one deed of trust

and that it did have jurisdiction of the subject matter of the suit and the parties thereto.

There is a well settled rule of law that where questions could have been raised on a former appeal and were not raised on such appeal, such questions will not be considered upon the second appeal thereof. Morgan Creek Drainage District. v. Hawley, 255, Ill., 34; Stringer vs. Berrington 198, Ill., 121. The trial court in its original decree states expressly that it had jurisdiction of the subject matter and the parties to the suit. This question could and should have been raised in the former appeal. For this reason alone this appeal cannot be maintained.

The decree of the Circuit Court of Grundy County, is hereby affirmed.

Affirmed.

}ss. I JUSTUS L JOHNSON, Clerk of the Appellate Court, in and of the State of Illinois, and the keeper of the Records and Seal thereof, do hereby ; is a true copy of the opinion of the said Appellate Court in the above entitled cause

In Testimony Whereof, I hereunto set my hand and affix the seal of said Appellate Court, at Ottawa, this ______ day of ______ in the year of our Lord one thousand nine hundred and thirty-______

______

Clerk of the Appellate Court

ract

PUBLISHED IN ABSTRACT

John R Bradshaw, Appellee, v. Sallie A Bradshaw, Appellant

Appeal from Circuit Court of Macon County

APRIL TERM, A D 1936

Gen. No 8967 **Agenda No. 3** 286 I.A. 622[3]

MR JUSTICE DAVIS delivered the opinion of the Court

This is an appeal from a decree entered in the circuit court of Macon county, Illinois, on April 4, 1935, in favor of John R Bradshaw, plaintiff, on a complaint in chancery, praying that the defendant, Sallie Brad shaw, wife of plaintiff, be decreed to surrender and deliver up to plaintiff certain government bonds claimed by plaintiff to be held by his wife for the purpose of paying certain mortgage indebtedness on lands in Macon county, Illinois, which were owned by said Bradshaw

In his complaint plaintiff claims the ownership of four tracts of land situated in Macon county, Illinois, and a dwelling house in Decatur, all of which were alleged to be encumbered by mortgages He also alleged the ownership of a 250-acre farm in Kentucky, which was unencumbered and which he decided to sell and apply the proceeds towards the liquidation of the mortgages on the Illinois land He further alleged that his wife, Sallie A Bradshaw, refused to sign a deed to said Kentucky farm unless the proceeds were turned over to her for safe keeping, and that he had entered into a verbal contract with his wife to receive and hold in trust for him the proceeds from the sale of this Kentucky farm until the same could be used to liquidate the mortgages on the Illinois land He further alleged that the Kentucky farm and the live stock thereon were sold for a total of $29,000 00, all of which was turned over to his wife and by her converted into Government Bonds

He further alleged that his wife, after the purchase of said bonds, signed a certain statement in writing in reference to the same, a copy of which is attached to the complaint, and marked Exhibit "K" He further alleged that he made arrangements with the holders of the mortgages to accept the payment thereof, but that the defendant refused to carry out the trust al-

leged by him to have been created, and prayed that the court upon a hearing order and decree that the defendant, Sallie A Bradshaw, surrender up and deliver to him said bonds in order that he might use the same to satisfy said mortgage indebtedness in Illinois

The bonds in question were alleged to have been kept in a safety deposit box in the Milliken National Bank, it being made a defendant but defaulted The defendant answered and also filed amended answers by leave of court, and the defense which was interposed and finally relied upon by said defendant was that the whole transaction involving the proceeds as to the Kentucky farm was a gift between husband and wife, and that the conveyance was in fraud of creditors and that the defendant did not come into court with clean hands and could not recover the money

From the evidence it appears that the plaintiff, John R Bradshaw, and Sallie A Bradshaw, the defendant, were married in Kentucky in 1870, and lived there for a period of about three years, when they came to Illinois and lived on a farm for sometime, and finally lived in Decatur, Illinois The plaintiff for a good many years bought and sold lands, and he also was a real estate auctioneer At the time in question he was owner of a farm known as the Gerber farm, of 228 acres, and encumbered by a mortgage for $15,000 00, securing his personal notes, a farm of 160 acres, known as the Pritchett farm, encumbered by a mortgage securing a note for $9,000 00 executed by himself and wife He also owned at this time an unencumbered 80 acre farm and a homestead in the city of Decatur Although the complaint alleges that the farm of 80 acres and the homestead were each encumbered by a $2,000 00 mortgage, yet at the time in question there was no mortgage encumberance on either of the two places At this time, however, Bradshaw was indebted to the Milliken Bank in the sum of $4,000 00 which was later secured, $2,000 00 on the 80 acre farm and $2,000 on their homestead

In 1932 Bradshaw was obligated on two mortgages, each for $32,000 00, payable to the Aetna Life Insurance Company, and secured on lands in Illinois formerly owned by him and which he sold to Jacob Reich, upon which Reich had made a payment of $3,000 00 He also purchased what is known as the Clifton farm, subject to a mortgage of $31,000 00 which he assumed and agreed to pay under the terms of an extension agreement made in December, 1928, and which amount was still unpaid

Bradshaw had a farm in Boyle county, Kentucky, of 250 acres which he obtained from his brother, Walker Bradshaw His brother owed him some money, the amount of which the plaintiff was unable to say, but he testified that his advances to Walker did not run a half or a third of a $100,000 00 Walker and his wife moved off of the farm and the plaintiff moved on about April 1, 1932, and he and his wife arrived back in Decatur Christmas eve of the same year

During the months of November and December of that year the plaintiff and his wife had various talks about selling the Kentucky farm She asked what he was going to do with the money, and he told her he was going to pay off the mortgages on our Macon county real estate, and plaintiff testified my wife said to me she was afraid I would buy more land and lose more money on land deals, and he told her he did not want to buy more land, and said to her, the lands in Illinois that he would pay the mortgage on is splendid income property, and that they had better sell and go home and spend our honeymoon in our old days well fixed

His wife said she was afraid he would spend the money buying more land and lose it on the land like he had lost so much money The plaintiff told her he would not but that he wanted to pay off that eucumbrance Plaintiff testified his wife objected and said she would get Agnes, their daughter, down and that Agnes came and they talked Plaintiff had received an offer from a Mr Simpson for the land, and there was a conversation between plaintiff and his wife and Simpson, and she said she didn't know about it until she talked with Agnes Plaintiff testified that a few days before Thanksgiving Simpson had offered $25,000 00 for the land,—$15,000 00 cash and two notes of $5,000 00 each After Simpson went away he talked with his wife and told her he wanted her to sign the deed and make the sale Plaintiff further testified that she finally said that if I would let her hold all the money in her box in Decatur until Horace McDavid and I could make arrangements to get the people to take the money on the mortgages she would sign the deed, and she asked me if I would put it into the contract of sale that I would pay her the cash down payment and the deferred payments would go to her, and I agreed

A contract was entered into, after the daughter had been there, between Mr Simpson, the plaintiff and his wife There was paid, in cash, $15,000 00 and two

notes were prepared for $5,000 00, each, and the deed was executed The notes were payable to Mrs Bradshaw, and the plaintiff sold the cattle for $3,000 00, which was given to the wife of the plaintiff, together with the $15,000 00, and some other personal property was sold, amounting to about $1,000 00, all of which was given to Mrs Bradshaw

Plaintiff testified that a check for $18,000 00 was given his wife in the settlement, and bonds were purchased to the amount of $15,000 00 for which plaintiff testified he paid a premium of $750 00 or $800 00 After the money was turned over to Mrs Bradshaw, plaintiff testified some of it was used by her to make payments on notes, on indebtedness of plaintiff in Illinois Although the complaint alleges that plaintiff was indebted on the Noble farm in the sum of $2,000 00 and on the homestead in the sum of $2,000 00, being the indebtedness due the Milliken Bank, yet the mortgages were not placed upon said tracts until after the parties had returned to Illinois and was not indebtedness secured by the mortgages on the Macon county land prior to the date of the sale of the Kentucky farm, and that after they returned, instead of using the money that Mrs Bradshaw had received from the Kentucky land, the mortgages were placed on said tracts to secure said notes in the bank The two mortgages were both dated December 14, 1932 On the same day plaintiff put a $17,000 00 mortgage on all his property in Macon county, in which a B S McGaughey was named Trustee and for which plaintiff testified there was no consideration, and that the same was made at the request of his wife, and the notes and mortgage and the release thereof were given to her to be put in a box Mrs Bradshaw had in the bank

Plaintiff produced Exhibit "K", which purported to have the signature of Mrs Bradshaw attached, and which is dated August 10, 1933, written on a letterhead of plaintiff in his own handwriting, and was an acknowledgment that the bonds were held by her for her husband, and in which it is stated she agreed that they were to be converted into money to pay off the mortgage indebtedness on all property in Macon county, owned by the plaintiff

The plaintiff in this connection testified that his wife signed this exhibit on a desk in the living room of their home in Decatur, that his wife said as soon as she made a trip to Hot Springs she would unlock the box and get the bonds and settle all encumbrances The plaintiff also testified that he wanted her to wait until

their boy came in to witness the signature before she signed, but that Mrs Bradshaw said "If you are going to let him know about it, I will not sign it" And plaintiff said, All right, let it go anyhow, and she signed it

Mrs Bradshaw testified that she lived with her husband up to the time that he served the summons on her in this lawsuit, and that they came to Illinois to live a few months before their son, Noble, was born Mr Bradshaw first bought a farm near Decatur, and since then has owned a number of farms in Illinois Mr Bradshaw gave her $5,000 00 to sign the deed to a farm he wished to sell He had the Powers farm, and I did not want to sell that as I thought he was selling too cheap and begged him not to do it, and he said he would give me $5,000 00 if I would sign the deed, but he never did He traded a great deal in farming The Powers farm is the same property as the Clifton farm He gave me all of the proceeds of the Kentucky farm, —telling me that it should be mine There was a lot of talk about the Kentucky farm, and he said, if I did not give up, the Iroquois heirs and the Cliftons would take it away from me, and that a half a loaf would be better than being left without any bread I finally said, Well, if you will give me all of that for my part I will do it, and he said, I give it all to you for your part, for when I go back to Decatur I can make all of the money I need, I have made money and I can make all I need, when I get back to Illinois

We were living on the Kentucky farm at that time He promised me, before I left Decatur, I should never have to move any more, that it should always be my home He kept after me to sell the Kentucky farm and said the creditors would take his property from him. I begged him to go to Illinois and sell in place of selling the Kentucky farm He said those creditors are going to come in and take what I have got away, I don't want to leave you penniless

Mr Bradshaw told me that he had made an agreement to sell the farm to Mr Simpson for $100 00 per acre I told him, You are fooling the farm away, let us keep the farm and give up the Illinois property, this is my home and let us stay where we can have a home I told him when he kept telling me he was going to lose his property and everything,—I said, sell the Illinois property, let us keep the Kentucky farm and make a deed to me, and then entail it to the two children The only thing he ever talked to me about was to get rid of the farm and give me the proceeds, and we could go back to Illinois

I was in Mr Lamer's office, when the papers were drawn up to sell the Kentucky farm My husband said the money was to go to me, that it was mine After the deed was signed certain moneys were paid over it me I received a draft for $18,000 00, I also got two notes for $5,000 00, each I did buy Government Bonds, one for $10,000 00 and one for $5,000 00 I had to pay premium on the bonds The money I had left, after I bought the bonds, I put away in the safety deposit box It is $2,900 00 I turned over a part of the money to my husband

During the spring of 1933 my husband and I had a number of conversations about the purchase of more land Later on, in August, my husband had a conversation with my brother, Jesse, and asked him to talk to me about paying off the mortgages She further testified she had never seen Exhibit "K", dated August 10, 1933, but once before and that was when Mr Stenning showed it to me in Judge Baldwin's office, after the suit was brought I never signed it The signature looks like mine, but it is not, I never signed it The mortgages I signed, after I returned from Kentucky and before I went back there and bought the bonds, were one on the home for $2,000 00, I believe, and one on the eighty acres for $2,000 00 I never heard of the $17,000 00 mortgage that I signed, covering various farms and the home He would have the mortgages laid out in front of me and would tell me to sign there, and I would sign; but what they were I did not know If I signed a $17,000 00 mortgage on the same date I signed the $2,000 00 mortgages, it was done always when Mr Bradshaw would tell me what to sign I did not make a statement to my husband, just before the Kentucky farm was sold,—unless he would let me hold the money in my box in Decatur until Horace McDavid and he could make arrangements to get those people to take the money on the mortgages, that I would not sign the deed My husband did not make the statement,—I would let her hold those bonds to pay off the encumbrance I was willing for her to hold them and invest the money in bonds and put them in the Milliken bank The defendant denied all of the testimony of plaintiff in reference to the bonds, and denied she told plaintiff in Kentucky, I will hold the bonds that way and will release them when you and McDavid get things in shape to pay off the mortgages, release a few bonds to pay all of the mortgages on the Macon county real estate She denied that she said, As soon as I make a trip to Hot Springs we will

unlock the box and get the bonds and settle up the mortgages Defendant also denies that she had any conversation with her husband in the presence of either of her grandchildren

Agnes Allen, daughter of the parties, testified she visited her father and mother in Kentucky on Saturday before Thanksgiving Father told me, in the presence of my mother, that they would sell the farm, and whatever cash was realized was to be converted into bonds and turned over to mother to clear up the property in Macon county, and mother said, I will not sign a deed to the place until that is the way it is done The daughter also testified that the signature to Exhibit "K" was that of her mother A grandson, Edwin Allen, said he remembered the trip to Kentucky in 1932, that he heard the conversation in the evening between his grandfather and grandmother and mother, that the grandfather said he would sell the farm and give the money to grandmother, she was to put the money in the bank box, and they were to come back and grandmother on a certain date was to take the money and pay off the mortgages on the land in Macon county Several signatures of Mrs Bradshaw were admitted in evidence for comparison purposes, at the instance of the plaintiff

Ralph Salmon, a witness on behalf of the defendant, after testifying to the characteristics of the various letters composing the name, Sallie A Bradshaw, gave it as his opinion that she did not write the signature on Exhibit "K".

Enoch Downs, a witness on behalf of the defendant, testified that he was in the real estate business and sold the Kentucky farm for plaintiff, and that every time he talked about the sale Bradshaw said he had to see Mrs Bradshaw, he said, The money goes to her. I was present when the $15,000 00 was paid over and the two notes were made to Mrs Bradshaw

Ad Lanier, an attorney at Danville, Kentucky, drew up the contract of sale for the Kentucky land He testified that Bradshaw told him to make the two notes of $5,000 00, each, payable to Mrs Bradshaw He told me the money belonged to her, and for that reason he wanted them payable to her The deed was signed in his presence Simpson gave Bradshaw a check for $15,000 00 and the two notes, for $5,000 00 each, payable to Mrs Bradshaw The two notes were handed to Mrs Bradshaw, and the check to Mrs Bradshaw I think, and the deed to Mr Simpson Mr Bradshaw stated that he owned property in Illinois and he owed

some money and wanted to sell out and get away from Danville I know the values of lands in Boyle county and have an opinion of the fair cash, market value of Bradshaw's land, and think on December 1st, 1932, it was worth from $125 00 to $150 00 per acre

E W Cook, of Danville, Kentucky, president of the Citizens National Bank, testified that on about December 6, 1932, Mr Bradshaw stated that he wanted to turn over the money he was getting from Mr Simpson, which was $15,000 00 and some other money he sold the cattle for,—$18,000 00, to Mrs Bradshaw, and that he had some notes in the North West which he endorsed, and was afraid they would come back on him and he wanted to put the money in his wife's name. Mrs Bradshaw was present on that occasion

The circuit court found that Mrs Bradshaw received $25,000 00 in Government Bonds from the sale of the Kentucky farm to be held by her in trust, and by her, as trustee, applied in payment of the mortgage indebtedness upon the real estate owned by said parties in Macon county, Illinois, and that defendant refused to carry out said trust, and ordered that Sallie A Bradshaw be removed as such trustee and the Citizens National Bank of Decatur, be appointed successor in trust, and that the defendant pay over to said successor all of said $25,000 00 in bonds and that the Citizens National Bank execute the trust

It appears from the evidence that plaintiff and defendant are husband and wife, and that the plaintiff voluntarily transferred all of the funds received from the sale of the Kentucky farm, live stock and other personal property to his wife, the defendant

The plaintiff, John R Bradshaw, contends that the funds were paid over in trust for the purpose of paying off all of the incumbrances which were on the lands owned in Macon county, Illinois, and his wife, Sallie A Bradshaw, contends that the funds were a gift to her from her husband While it is true that a trust in personal property may be created and proven by parole, the inquiry is as to whether from a preponderance of the evidence the moneys was received by the defendant in trust for the purpose contended for by plaintiff

We are of opinion that the determination of this question will be decisive of this case, although other questions are raised by appellant The same rule applies in the case of a transfer of personal property as in real estate

It is held that when a husband has bought property and had the title transferred to his wife or a parent has bought property and had the title transferred to his child, a resulting trust is not shown to exist unless it is established that it was not intended that the wife or child should take a beneficial interest in the property, because under such circumstances there is a presumption that the property was transferred to the wife or child as a gift or an advancement This presumption is not conclusive but may be rebutted by proof, and whether or not a resulting trust arises in such a case is purely a question of intention. The burden of proof is upon the party seeking to establish a resulting trust, and the evidence to be effective for that purpose must be clear, unequivocal and unmistakable, and if it is doubtful or is capable of reasonable explanation upon any theory other than the existence of a trust it is not sufficient *Kartun* v *Kartun,* 347 Ill 510, 180 N E 423

While it is true that when a conveyance is made to a person occupying a relation of trust and confidence to the grantor which confers a beneficial interest on the grantee it is presumed that it was obtained through fraud or undue influence, and the burden of the proof is upon the grantee to rebut the presumption, however, this doctrine has no application to the relation of husband and wife And when a husband voluntarily conveys land to the wife or procures its conveyance to her by a third person, a presumption arises that he intended to make an absolute gift to her, and to overcome this presumption it must appear that there was an obligation on her part to hold the property in trust for him *Delfosse* v *Delfosse,* 287 Ill 251, 122 N E 484.

There is no charge of fraud or undue influence in the complaint and no evidence that the defendant in any way exercised any undue influence upon her husband or practiced any fraud upon him to obtain the proceeds of this farm and personal property

The evidence instead of being clear, unequivocal and unmistakable that a trust was created is doubtful and is capable of reasonable explanation upon the theory that the money is a gift to his wife

Aside from the testimony of the plaintiff and defendant it is clear that the contract of sale provided that the two $5,000 00 notes should go to Sallie A Bradshaw, and the statement of Bradshaw to Lamer, Cook & Downs shows that the money belonged to his wife, and when the notes were paid she received the money And when they arrived back in Decatur, instead of

Mrs Bradshaw using the money to pay indebtedness to the Milliken bank, Bradshaw placed two additional mortgages on the unencumbered real estate to secure his notes and also executed the $17,000 00 trust deed upon all his property. The two notes for $5,000 00 each were endorsed to Jesse Noble, a brother of Mrs Bradshaw, at the suggestion of Mr Bradshaw, and remained a lien upon the farm in his name, and after they were recorded he turned them over to his sister These notes were paid the following February The draft came in the name of Jesse Noble, and he got the letter at Mr Bradshaw's residence, and Bradshaw said, Take it and go buy bonds His sister and he and lawyer McDavid went to buy the bonds After this draft was paid over they were looking at farms to buy Bradshaw told Noble where some of the farms were He said he thought they were a good buy

We are of opinion that the plaintiff has failed to prove his case by a preponderance of the evidence, and the decree of the circuit court is therefore reversed

Reversed.

(Thirteen pages in original opinion)

Published in Abstract

2

A

Viola C. Drake, Plaintiff and Appellee, v Charles B. Wood, Defendant and Appellant, Amy M Wood, Frank J Cimral, Receiver of the Bowmanville National Bank of Chicago, and William L O'Connell, Receiver for Baldwin State Bank of Delevan, Counter Defendants and co-parties

Complaint at Law, No 11376.

Harry C Roberts, Executor of the Last Will and Testament of John P Roberts, Deceased, Plaintiff and Appellee, v. Charles B Wood, Defendant and Appellant, et al.

Complaint at Law, No 11378

286 I.A. 623'

George H Jeckel, Plaintiff and Appellee, v. Charles B Wood, Defendant and Appellant, et al

Complaint at Law, No. 11379

Hazel L. Hanna, Plaintiff and Appellee, v. Charles B. Wood, Defendant and Appellant, et al.

Complaint at Law, No 11380.

William T Kunkel, Guardian of William D Kunkel, Plaintiff and Appellee, v. Charles B. Wood, Defendant and Appellant, et al.

Complaint at Law, No 11381

Appeal from Circuit Court of Tazewell County.

April Term, A D 1936

Gen. No 8982 **Agenda No. 9**

Mr Justice Davis delivered the opinion of the Court

This is an appeal from the circuit court of Tazewell county by Charles B Wood, appellant, from a judgment entered in said court in this case in favor of Viola C Drake and against appellant, and by stipulation of the parties from judgments entered in the cases of *Roberts, Exec.*, v *Wood,* No 11378, *Jeckel* v *Wood,*

No 11379, *Hanna* v *Wood,* No 11380, and *Kunkel, Gdn*, v *Wood,* No 11381, all entered in said circuit court of Tazewell county.

The complaint of appellee, Viola C Drake, consisted of two counts, in one of which it is alleged that Charles B Wood, appellant, made and delivered a certain mortgage note for the principal sum of $2000 00, payable to bearer, with interest thereon at the rate of five percent per annum, payable annually, according to the five interest coupon notes

The second count alleges that appellant made and delivered his certain mortgage note in writing for the sum of $1,000 00, payable to bearer, with interest thereon at the rate of five percent per annum, payable annually, as evidenced by the coupon interest notes attached, and that she is the owner of said notes and demands judgment against defendant-appellant for the aggregate sum of said two promissory notes and the interest coupons attached, in the total sum of $3,782 32

On the 10th day of June, 1935, appellee, Viola C Drake, filed her motion for a summary judgment and filed her affidavit in support thereof, in which affidavit appellee alleges that she is the legal holder and owner of said mortgage bonds, that they were purchased by her and her husband, David R Drake, from the Baldwin State Bank, of Delavan, Illinois, on or about the first of March, 1928, for which they paid $3,000 00, and that the $2,000 00 note was purchased in the name of her husband and the $1,000 00 mortgage note was purchased in her name, that her husband died on or about the 16th day of September, 1933, leaving a last will and testament, which was admitted to probate in the County court of Tazewell county on November 20th, 1933, and that by the terms of which he bequeathed all of his personal property to her absolutely, and that said $2,000 00 note was a part of the personal property and personal estate of her said husband, and that his estate has been fully administered and said note was taken and accepted by appellee as part of the personal estate of her said husband, and that she is now the owner and holder of the same, and that no part of the principal of said mortgage notes or the interest on said notes from the first day of March, 1931, has been paid, and that there is now due and remains unpaid from the said Charles B Wood to appellee on said principal note and interest coupons with interest thereon the sum of $1278 05, after allowing to said appellant all just deductions, credits and set-offs, and prays that judgment be ordered for her against the defendant- appellant for the sum of $1,278 05

She also filed an affidavit in support of her motion, made by W W Crabbs who was engaged in the banking business in the city of Delavan and had seen Charles B Wood write his name on various occasions and was acquainted with his signature, who states that he has examined the $2,000 00 note and coupons attached, and has also examined the signatures on the $1,000 00 note, dated March 1st, 1928, and the coupons attached and that, in his opinion, judgment and belief, the signature Charles B Wood to each of said mortgage notes and coupons is the genuine signature of said Charles B Wood

Appellant, Charles B Wood, filed an answer in said cause and counterclaim by which he admitted certain allegations of certain paragraphs of the complaint, but denied that at the time of his death said David R Drake was the owner and holder of the promissory note upon which Count 1 is based, and for defense alleged that on March 1st, 1920, one Garretson borrowed from the Baldwin State Bank of Delavan, Illinois the sum of $21,000 00 to apply on the purchase price of a farm in said county, and gave and executed 21 promissory notes for the principal sum of $1,000 00 each, payable to bearer, that said notes, shortly after their execution, were sold by said bank to divers customers, that Garretson was unable to pay the mortgage notes at maturity, and the holders of said notes authorized Frank B Shelton, Trustee, to execute written extension agreements extending the maturity of said mortgage notes, that on March 1, 1927, Garretson, being still unable to pay, agreed to convey said mortgaged premises to the bank so that the same could be sold and the obligations paid, and that, in carrying out this agreement, it was thought best to keep the title of said farm in the name of an individual and appellant was asked to and consented to receive and hold the title of said premises as agent of all the parties concerned until such time as said premises could be sold, and that said premises were conveyed to appellant on or about the 28th of March, 1927

On March 1st, 1928, said farm had not been sold An agreement was made between the holders of the notes and the officers of the bank whereby the bank was to obtain title to said farm and pay all the interest due on the notes and secure new notes for like amounts, due in five years with five per cent interest, that, in carrying out the provisions of this agreement, the officers of said bank requested appellant to retain title to said premises in his name, as agent or trustee for it,

and to execute new notes and a trust deed, and appellant consented to and did execute new notes, dated March 1, 1928, sixteen in number, for the aggregate sum of $21,000 00, each payable to the bearer on the first day of March, 1933, and to secure the payment appellant and his wife, Amy M Wood, executed, acknowledged and delivered to said bank a trust deed conveying said premises to E R Rhoades, trustee, that said notes were executed without the payment or advancement of any money, credit or anything of value to appellant by said bank or any other person, and without any benefit of any kind to him, that he was induced to execute said notes solely upon the express promise and agreement of said bank, made to and with him by all of the officers, that said bank would pay said notes on or before maturity thereof, cancel and return the same to him, and that he should not become personally liable for any payment or expense in connection with said notes or in connection with the holding of the title to said premises, that said notes, after execution, were entruster to said bank for delivery in exchange for said Garretson mortgage notes on condition that said bank assume the payment thereof and hold the appellant free and clear from any and all personal liability

After the execution of said mortgage notes they were by the officers of said Baldwin State Bank, of Delavan, exchanged for past due mortgage notes of said Garretson, and when so delivered all of the mortgage notes, signed by said Garretson, were surrendered by the holders thereof to the officers of the bank, cancelled and returned to the maker, and the trust deed securing said notes released, and said bank paid said holders all interest due, that when said mortgage notes executed by appellant were delivered to the holders by said bank each of said holders knew said notes were secured by mortgage or trust deed upon said Garretson farm, and that appellant had or claimed no personal interest in said farm but held title solely as the agent or trustee of said bank, and that appellant had not been paid, lent or advanced any money, credit or anything of value by them or either of them, or any other person, or by said bank on account of signing said notes, that as further protection to said bank and the holders of said notes signed by appellant and as a further assurance he claimed no further interest in said farm he and his wife, at the time of the execution of said notes and trust deed, conveyed said premises to said bank and said deed was held by said

bank and placed on record at the time of closing thereof, that said bank paid all the interest when due on said notes

John H Shade was appointed receiver of said bank about January 25, 1932, and acted as such until the appointment of William L O'Connell, on April 3, 1935, as successor, and he is now acting as receiver, that upon the closing of said bank appellant sought to have a claim allowed against the assets of said bank, in the hands of the receiver, on account of said mortgage notes signed by him, that a suit was started on or about April 20, 1932, by the holders of all said mortgage notes signed by appellant against the receiver of said bank to enforce against said receiver the claims on said notes, which suit is still pending

That the note executed by appellant and delivered to Mary M Wood is now held by Amy M Wood, and the note delivered to Emma Gilmore is now held by Emma Rubien, and the holders of all said notes, with the exception of Amy M Wood and Emma Rubien, have brought suit against appellant on said notes, and their rights are identical or similar to those who have brought suits and should be adjudicated herein, and appellant is informed that Frank J Cimral, receiver for the Bowmanville National Bank has, or claims some interest in said note of Emma Rubien, that appellant is not indebted to appellee upon the notes held by her, that said notes were executed wholly without consideration, of which appellee and her husband, David Drake, were well aware at the time the same were negotiated to them

Appellant makes Amy M Wood, Emma Rubien and Frank J Cimral, receiver for the Bowmanville National Bank, parties defendant, and by way of counterclaim against them re-alleges the affirmative defense of his answer and requests judgment be entered herein finding appellant is not indebted to them, or either of them, by reason of the mortgage notes executed by appellant, and further makes William L O'Connell, receiver for the Baldwin State Bank of Delavan, an additional party defendant, and by way of counterclaim re-alleges the affirmative defense of the answer and asks that his alleged defense as against further carrying out the obligations of said bank in connection with said mortgage notes executed by appellant be inquired into, and that, in case appellant be found personally liable in this cause upon any of said notes, judgment be entered finding that, as between the defendants and said bank, the bank was the principal

debtor and that the receiver should exonerate him by paying him and discharge such personal liability of the defendant in so far as the assets of said bank will ratably reach in the course of liquidation

Appellant also demands a trial by a jury, and requests the clerk to issue a summons directed to the additional defendants, Amy M Woods, Emma Rubien, Frank J Cimral, receiver, and William L O'Connell, receiver, returnable on the third Monday of August, 1935

The affidavit of Carter J Harrison, who was bookkeeper in the Baldwin State Bank from April, 1924, until the closing of the bank in July, 1932, was filed in support of the answer of appellant and verified the matters set forth in said answer

Appellee filed her motion to strike the answer of appellant and the affidavit in support thereof and for summary judgment, and for reasons alleged that plaintiff filed her motion for summary judgment, and that said defendant has not filed his affidavit of merits as required by statute, and that the defense alleged in the answer and in the affidavit in support thereof does not show that appellant has a sufficient and good defense on the merits to appellee's claim

Appellant filed an amendment to his answer and also filed the affidavits of William W Garretson and W. O Pendarvis in support of his answer

Frank J Cimral, receiver, and Amy M. Wood filed answers and counterclaims

The cause coming on to be heard upon motion of Viola C Drake, plaintiff-appellee, for summary judgment it was ordered that she have and recover from the defendant-appellant, Charles B Wood, her damages of $3928 23 and costs

Judgment in the sum of $1309 41 was entered in favor of Frank J Cimral, receiver, and judgment for $1309 41 in favor of Amy M Wood was entered.

On motion of William L O'Connell, receiver, the counterclaim of Charles B Wood as against the Baldwin State Bank, of Delavan, and William L O'Connell, receiver, was dismissed, and leave was given said defendant, Charles B Wood, to file a counterclaim and amended answer

It was stipulated between all of the parties, plaintiff and defendant, that Cases Nos 11376, 11378, 11379, 11380 and 11381, of the Circuit Court of Tazewell County, Illinois, be consolidated for the purpose of appeal from the judgments in all such cases

The defendant, Charles B Wood, gave notice of appeal to the Appellate Court for the Third District and

among other things from the judgments entered in said causes of action in the Circuit Court of Tazewell County on November 4, 1935, and prayed that the reviewing court would reverse the aforesaid judgments of the said Circuit Court of Tazewell County, Illinois, and remand said causes to said court with instruction to enter an order, in each of said causes of action, vacating and setting aside the judgments for the plaintiff heretofore entered

While appellant gave notice of appeal from causes, Numbered 11376, 11378, 11379, 11380 and 11381, in the circuit court of Tazewell County, and although the record shows that upon stipulation of all the parties, plaintiff and defendant in said causes, it was ordered that the said above causes be consolidated for the purpose of appeal from the judgments in all such cases, yet the record fails to show anything in relation to said cases except in case numbered 11376 of the circuit court of Tazewell county, being case numbered 8982 of this court The record on appeal fails to contain any of the matters, required by Rule 1 of the Rules of Practice of the Appellate Court, in any of such cases other than in case numbered 8982, *Viola C Drake* v *Charles B Wood* There is nothing in the record filed relating to such cases. In the abstract of the record it was recited that at the same time judgment was rendered in the case of *Drake* v *Wood,* No 8982, that similar judgments were entered in each of the cases consolidated in that case for appeal, each of which cases is based upon one or more notes of the same issue as sued upon in this case, and the pleadings of which are identical with this case There is nothing in the record to even show that final judgments were ever entered in any such cases

In order to confer upon an Appellate Tribunal jurisdiction to hear and determine a cause appealed to such court, there must be a record of the proceedings in the court from which such appeal was taken, and there being none in the case of *Roberts, Exec*, v *Wood, Jeckel* v *Wood, Hanna* v *Wood, and Kunkel, Gdn*, v *Wood,* the court not only has nothing from which to determine the issues in said causes and no jurisdiction to enter any judgment therein In the case before us, No 8982, *Viola C Drake* v *Wood,* appellee made a motion for a summary judgment, and supported the same by her own affidavit and that of one W W Crabb.

Appellant answered the complaint denying liability and setting forth a defense of want of consideration, and in his answer he alleges that Amy M Wood held

one of the notes executed by appellant and that Emma Rubien held one of said notes and that the holders of all of said notes, with the exception of said two parties, had brought suit against appellant in said court to enforce liability, and that the rights of said two note holders are identical or similar to those who had brought suits and should be adjudicated in this case, that Frank J Cimral, reeeiver, claimed some interest in said note of said Emma Rubien

Appellant by his answer makes Amy M Wood, Emma Rubien and Frank J Cimral, receiver, additional parties defendant, and by way of counterclaim re-alleges the affirmative defense of defendant and requests judgment finding the defendant is not indebted to them, or either of them, on account of the mortgage notes now held by them, and by his answer further makes William L O'Connell, Receiver of the Baldwin State Bank of Delavan, an additional defendant, and by way of counterclaim re-alleges the affirmative defense of his answer and asks that, in case he be found personally liable in this cause upon any of said notes, judgment be entered that said bank was the principal debtor and that the receiver should pay and discharge such personal liability

The counterclaim of appellant against said additional defendant, William L O'Connell, Receiver, was dismissed

While none of the additional parties except William L O'Connell, receiver, made any objection to being made parties to said litigation, yet we are of the opinion they were not properly brought in the case of *Viola C Drake* v *Charles B Wood* So far as that case is concerned a complete determination of the controversy in said case could properly be had without the presence of these additional parties There were several suits pending to recover judgments against appellant on some of the various notes executed by him and secured by trust deed, and the addition of two more of the note holders to the suit on trial would not assist in any way in a settlement of the whole controversy between appellant and the various note holders and the receiver of the Baldwin State Bank The additional parties were in no way interested in the matters alleged in the complaint of appellee The record fails to show that the summons issued for the additional parties was pursuant to an order of said court

A counterclaim is any demand by one or more defendants against one or more plaintiffs, or against one or more defendants, and may be treated as a cross demand in any action.

The counterclaims filed by appellant against the additional parties defendant, Amy M Wood, Emma Rubien and Frank J Cimral, receiver, were founded upon the defense against the claim of appellee and the relief sought was a judgment of the court finding the defendant not indebted to them, or either of them, on account of the mortgage notes alleged by appellant to be held by them

Neither of said additional parties defendant, so far as the record in this case shows, had asserted any claim against appellant, and he sought by his answer and counterclaim to inject into the suit between Viola C Drake and himself questions in which appellee was in no way interested, and which would only tend to confuse the matters at issue between the parties, and the court should have, of its own motion, dismissed out of said suit said additional parties

The principal contention between appellee and appellant is as to whether the court erred in granting the motion of appellee for a summary judgment On the part of appellant it is contended that appellee did not make a sufficient showing, and on the part of appellee that appellant's affidavit of merits was not sufficient and that the court did not err in granting such motion of appellee and in entering judgment in her favor

Sec 57 of the Civil Practice Act, chap 110, par 185, sec 57, Ill State Bar Stats, 1935, chap 110, sec 181, Smith-Hurd Ann Stats provides, in part, that if the plaintiff shall file an affidavit of the truth of the facts upon which his complaint is based and the amount claimed over and above all just deductions, credits and set-offs (if any), the court shall, upon plaintiff's motion, enter a judgment in his favor for the relief so demanded unless defendant shall, by an affidavit of merits filed prior to or at the time of the hearing on said motion, show that he has a sufficiently good defense

One of the requirements that plaintiff must comply with is that he state the amount claimed over and above all just deductions In her affidavit in support of her motion for a summary judgment she alleges there was due her the total sum of $1278 05, and prayed judgment against appellant for said sum of $1278 05 Her affidavit filed in support of a summary judgment did not warrant the court in entering judgment in her favor and against appellant for the sum of $3928 23, and the court erred in so entering said judgment

The appeal of appellant in the cases of *Roberts, Exec*, v *Wood, Jeckel* v *Wood, Hanna* v *Wood* and *Kunkel, Gdn*, v *Wood,* are dismissed

The judgments of the circuit court entered herein in favor of Frank J. Cimral, receiver, and against appellant and the judgment in favor of Amy M. Wood and against appellant are reversed and remanded

The judgment in favor of appellee and against appellant for the sum of $3928 23 is reversed and said cause is remanded to the circuit court of Tazewell county for a new trial, and the court is directed to dismiss from said cause the additional defendants, Amy M. Wood, Emma Rubien, Frank J Cimral, receiver, and William L O'Connell, receiver

Reversed and remanded with directions

(Thirteen pages in original opinion)

17

PUBLISHED IN ABSTRACT

Josephine M Blumb, Administratrix of the Estate of Frank W Blumb, Deceased, Plaintiff-Appellee, v Ben Getz, Defendant-Appellant.

Appeal from the Circuit Court of Tazewell County.

APRIL TERM, A D 1936 286 I.A. 623

Gen No 8987 **Agenda No 12**

MR JUSTICE DAVIS delivered the opinion of the Court

This is an appeal by defendant-appellant, Ben Getz, from a judgment of the circuit court of Tazewell County in the sum of $3,000 00 in favor of plaintiff-appellee, Josephine M Blumb, Administratrix of the Estate of Frank W Blumb, deceased

The complaint consisted of two counts, in the first of which it was charged that Ben Getz was operating and managing a motor vehicle in his own behalf, and as agent and servant of Ross C Adams, on State Highway No 9, between the cities of Pekin and Morton in Tazewell County, that plaintiff's intestate was walking along said highway in a westerly direction and was in the exercise of due care and caution for his own safety, that the defendant, Ben Getz, carelessly, wrongfully and negligently suffered and permitted said automobile to run against the deceased and knock him down upon the highway, causing fatal injuries from which he died on December 2, 1933

The second count alleges that plaintiff's intestate was walking on said public highway with due care and caution for his own safety and stopped to pick up his glove which he had dropped on said highway, when Ben Getz in his own behalf and as the agent of the defendant, Ross C Adams, then and there approached plaintiff's intestate and negligently, carelessly and unlawfully failed to give any reasonable warning of his approach, failed to stop his automobile before striking plaintiff's intestate and failed to use every reasonable precaution to avoid injuring plaintiff's intestate, but approached so rapidly that plaintiff's intestate was unable to remove himself from the path of the automobile, contrary to Sec 40 of the Illinois Motor Vehicle Act, that as a result of said negligence plaintiff's intestate was struck and fatally injured

The defendants, Ben Getz and Ross C Adams, answered and denied each and all of the allegations

of the complaint, and alleged that the death of intestate was due to his own carelessness and negligence At the conclusion of the plaintiff's case, upon her motion Ross C Adams was dismissed as a party defendant, leaving Ben Getz as the sole defendant

It appears from the testimony that the accident which resulted in the death of plaintiff's intestate took place on State Highway No 9, which is a hard surfaced road between the cities of Pekin and Morton, Illinois

John Nord, a brother-in-law of deceased, lived on the north side of Route 9, and about 600 feet east of his home there is a bridge over the hard road The road ran straight in front of Nord's house 160 rods each way The deceased was at Nord's home on the morning of November 28, 1933 He and Nord left his home to go hunting about 12 00 o'clock, noon They went east on the hard road towards the bridge They had stopped in one place and deceased lit a cigarette and dropped one of his gloves They proceeded on east a short distance before he discovered he had lost his glove He started west after his glove, and John Nord proceeded on east After deceased started on west an automobile passed Nord, going west Nord walked about 40 feet and then turned and looked west and he saw the car swaying from right to left, and at that time Nord saw an object in the middle of the road and he started back and, before he got to the place, Mr Strubhar was there He was the first one to get to the object in the road Mr Blumb was taken away before Nord got there He had been taken to the oil station He was unconscious and bleeding from his mouth and the right side of his head The oil station was 130 feet west from where Blumb was lying on the pavement The jury, that heard the cause, returned a verdict in favor of plaintiff in the sum of $3,000 00 and, after a motion for a new trial was overruled by the court, judgment was entered on the verdict of the jury

Apellant assigned, as one of the errors for reversal of the judgment, that the court erred in refusing to direct a verdict at the close of plaintiff's case on motion of defendant

A motion to instruct the jury to find for the defendan is in the nature of a demurrer to the evidence, and the rule is the evidence so demurred to, in its aspect most favorable to the plaintiff, together with all reasonable inferences arising therefrom, must be taken most strongly in favor of the plaintiff The evidence

is not weighed, and all contradictory evidence or explanatory circumstances must be rejected The question presented on such motion is whether there is any evidence fairly tending to prove plaintiff's declaration In reviewing the action of the court of which complaint is made we do not weigh the evidence,—we can look only at that which is favorable to appellant *Yess* v *Yess*, 255 Ill 414, *McCune* v *Reynolds*, 288 *id*, 188, *Lloyd* v *Rush*, 273 *id* 489, *Hunter* v *Troup*, 315 Ill 293-297

It was alleged in each count of the complaint that appellee's intestate was, at the time and place in question, in the exercise of due care and caution for his own safety This is a material allegation of the complaint, and plaintiff-appellee was required to prove the same by a preponderance of the evidence before she could recover

The witness, John Nord, testified that when plaintiff's intestate left him, as they were walking east on Route 9, to go and get his glove that he walked east alone and Blumb walked west in the direction of my house After plaintiff's intestate started back west an automobile passed me going west Nord testified that after the car passed him he walked about 40 feet and then turned and looked west and saw the car, and it was swaying back and forth on the road, going west The car was over the black line on the north side Blumb walked down on the shoulder on the north side The last I saw Blumb he was on the shoulder, walking west

Raymond Strubhar testified that at the time in question he was working for John Nord, he was in the barn yard doing the chores, that he saw Nord and deceased going away about 12 00 o'clock, at the time of the accident he was just leaving the barn, headed towards the house, he was about 200 feet from the concrete highway where the accident occurred, he saw Blumb before the accident Blumb took a couple of steps and was bending over, he was facing southwest, he was walking slow and kind of cater-cornered southwest, he saw him take two or three steps, and then he stooped down, he was bending over just as if he was going to pick something up, he saw the automobile when he saw Blumb take those steps and bend over, it was a distance of 20 or 25 feet away from Blumb, the automobile was going west, after that he saw Getz turn over to his left, he saw the running board strike Blumb and knock him down, Blumb was picking up his glove when he was struck, the lower hinge on the

front door on the right side also came in contact with Blumb's head

Helen Hocker, a daughter of John Nord and who lives with him, was in the house at the time of the accident The windows in the house were open She heard a thud and ran to the window and looked east and south, she saw a car traveling west, the wheels of the car were about the middle of the road on the concrete, the car was about 20 feet from the object on the pavement when she saw it

This is all of the evidence concerning the accident, and the witness, Strubhar, seemed to be the only eye witness

We are of opinion that there was no evidence fairly tending to prove due care on the part of plaintiff's intestate, and for that reason the circuit court should have sustained the motion of appellant at the close of plaintiff's case to direct a verdict in his favor

The judgment of the circuit court of Tazewell County is reversed

Reversed

Upon consideration of petition for rehearing the opinion is modified and a rehearing denied

(Five pages in original opinion)

(14588—10 36) 14

abstract.

R... ... 3, 1936
denied - Oct. 6 1936

PUBLISHED IN ABSTRACT

Josephine M Blumb, Administratrix of the Estate of Frank M Blumb, Deceased, Plaintiff-Appellee, v. Ben Getz, Defendant-Appellant.

Appeal from the Circuit Court of Tazewell County

APRIL TERM, A D 1936

Gen No 8987 **Agenda No. 12**

MR JUSTICE DAVIS delivered the opinion of the Court

This is an appeal by defendant-appellant, Ben Getz, from a judgment of the circuit court of Tazewell County in the sum of $3,000 00 in favor of plaintiff-appellee, Josephine M Blumb, Administratrix of the Estate of Frank W Blumb, deceased

The complaint consisted of two counts, in the first of which it was charged that Ben Getz was operating and managing a motor vehicle in his own behalf, and as agent and servant of Ross C Adams, on State Highway No 9, between the cities of Pekin and Morton in Tazewell county, that plaintiff's intestate was walking along said highway in a westerly direction and was in the exercise of due care and caution for his own safety, that the defendant, Ben Getz, carelessly, wrongfully and negligently suffered and permitted said automobile to run against the deceased and knock him down upon the highway, causing fatal injuries from which he died on December 2, 1933

The second count alleges that plaintiff's intestate was walking on said public highway with due care and caution for his own safety and stopped to pick up his glove which he had dropped on said highway, when Ben Getz in his own behalf and as the agent of the defendant, Ross C Adams, then and there approached plaintiff's intestate and negligently, carelessly and unlawfully failed to give any reasonable warning of his approach, failed to stop his automobile before striking plaintiff's intestate and failed to use every reasonable precaution to avoid injuring plaintiff's intestate, but approached so rapidly that plaintiff's intestate was unable to remove himself from the path of the automobile, contrary to Sec 40 of the Illinois Motor Vehicle Act, that as a result of said negligence plaintiff's intestate was struck and fatally injured

The defendants, Ben Getz and Ross C Adams, answered and denied each and all of the allegations of the complaint, and alleged that the death of intestate was due to his own carelessness and negligence At the conclusion of the plaintiff's case, upon her motion Ross C Adams was dismissed as a party defendant, leaving Ben Getz as the sole defendant

It appears from the testimony that the accident which resulted in the death of plaintiff's intestate took place on State Highway No 9, which is a hard surfaced road between the cities of Pekin and Morton, Illinois

John Nord, a brother-in-law of deceased, lived on the north side of Route 9, and about 600 feet east of his home there is a bridge over the hard road The road ran straight in front of Nord's house 160 rods each way The deceased was at Nord's home on the morning of November 28, 1933 He and Nord left his home to go hunting about 12 00 o'clock, noon They went east on the hard road towards the bridge They had stopped in one place and deceased lit a cigarette and dropped one of his gloves They proceeded on east a short distance before he discovered he had lost his glove He started west after his glove, and John Nord proceeded on east After deceased started on west an automobile passed Nord, going west Nord walked about 40 feet and then turned and looked west and he saw the car swaying from right to left, and at that time Nord saw an object in the middle of the road and he started back and, before he got to the place, Mr Strubhar was there He was the first one to get to the object in the road Mr Blumb was taken away before Nord got there He had been taken to the oil station He was unconscious and bleeding from his mouth and the right side of his head The oil station was 130 feet west from where Blumb was lying on the pavement The jury, that heard the cause, returned a verdict in favor of plaintiff in the sum of $3,000 00, and, after a motion for a new trial was overruled by the court, judgment was entered on the verdict of the jury

Appellant assigned, as one of the errors for reversal of the judgment, that the court erred in refusing to direct a verdict at the close of plaintiff's case on motion of defendant

A motion to instruct the jury to find for the defendant is in the nature of a demurrer to the evidence, and the rule is the evidence so demurred to, in its aspect most favorable to the plaintiff, together with all reasonable inferences arising therefrom, must be taken

most strongly in favor of the plaintiff The evidence is not weighed, and all contradictory evidence or explanatory circumstances must be rejected The question presented on such motion is whether there is any evidence fairly tending to prove plaintiff's declaration In reviewing the action of the court of which complaint is made we do not weigh the evidence,—we can look only at that which is favorable to appellant *Yess* v *Yess,* 255 Ill 414, *McCune* v *Reynolds,* 288 *id*, 188, *Lloyd* v *Rush,* 273 id 489, *Hunter* v *Troup,* 315 Ill 293-297

It was alleged in each count of the complaint that appellee's intestate was, at the time and place in question, in the exercise of due care and caution for his own safety This is a material allegation of the complaint, and plaintiff-appellee was required to prove the same by a preponderance of the evidence before she could recover

The witness, John Nord, testified that when plaintiff's intestate left him, as they were walking east on Route 9, to go and get his glove that he walked east alone and Blumb walked west in the direction of my house After plaintiff's intestate started back west an automobile passed me going west Nord testified that after the car passed him he walked about 40 feet and then turned and looked west and saw the car, and it was swaying back and forth on the road, going west The car was over the black line on the north side Blumb walked down on the shoulder on the north side The last I saw Blumb he was on the shoulder, walking west

Raymond Strubhar testified that at the time in question he was working for John Nord, he was in the barn yard doing the chores, that he saw Nord and deceased going away about 12 00 o'clock, at the time of the accident he was just leaving the barn, headed towards the house, he was about 200 feet from the concrete highway where the accident occurred, he saw Blumb before the accident Blumb took a couple of steps and was bending over, he was facing southwest, he was walking slow and kind of cater-cornered southwest, he saw him take two or three steps, and then he stooped down, he was bending over just as if he was going to pick something up, he saw the automobile when he saw Blumb take these steps and bend over, it was a distance of 20 or 25 feet away from Blumb, the automobile was going west, after that he saw Getz turn over to his left, he saw the running board strike Blumb and knock him down, Blumb was picking up his glove

when he was struck, the lower hinge on the front door on the right side also came in contact with Blumb's head

Helen Hocker, a daughter of John Nord and who lives with him, was in the house at the time of the accident The windows in the house were open She heard a thud and ran to the window and looked east and south, she saw a car traveling west, the wheels of the car were about the middle of the road on the concrete; the car was about 20 feet from the object on the pavement when she saw it

This is all of the evidence concerning the accident, and the witness, Strubhar, seemed to be the only eye witness

We are of opinion that there was no evidence fairly tending to prove due care on the part of plaintiff's intestate, and for that reason the circuit court should have sustained the motion of appellant at the close of plaintiff's case to direct a verdict in his favor

The judgment of the circuit court of Tazewell county is reversed and the cause remanded for a new trial.

Reversed and remanded

(Five pages in original opinion)

ct

PUBLISHED IN ABSTRACT

44

Kaywin Kennedy, Plaintiff-Appelle, v. Grace H. Lang, Defendant-Appellant, Lucy H Darst, Defendant-Appellee, Rolla M. Darst, Intervening Petitioner Appellee.

Appeal from Circuit County, McLean County

APRIL TERM, A D 1936 **286 I.**

Gen No 8976 **Agenda No. 7**

MR JUSTICE ALLABEN delivered the opinion of the Court

This case arises out of a bill of interpleader brought by Kaywin Kennedy, trustee, against Lucy H Darst and Grace H Lang, to determine the ownership of two real estate mortgage bonds in the amount of $2,000 each Grace H Lang filed her answer to the bill, alleging ownership of the bonds Lucy H Darst filed an answer stating that she claimed the bonds as her own, but that she was acting for her husband, Rolla M Darst, that he was the owner of and entitled to the bonds An intervening petition was filed by Rolla M Darst, by leave of court, alleging that he was the husband of Lucy H Darst, and father of Grace H Lang, that the bonds were his individual property, that whoever had possession of them held them in trust for him

Grace H Lang filed a demurrer to the intervening petition, which was overruled, then filed exceptions to the intervening petition, which the court had previously ordered to stand as an answer These exceptions were overruled, and Grace H Lang then filed exceptions to the answer of Lucy H Darst, which were sustained Defendant appellant then moved for judgment in her favor on the pleadings, which motion was denied The intervening petitioner had filed a general replication to the appellant's answer, and appellant filed a special reply to the intervening petition The intervening petitioner then moved that appellant's special replication stand as a general replication only, which motion was allowed

Appellant then by leave of court filed an amendment to her answer which in addition to the matters set up in the original answer alleged that Rolla M Darst was guilty of laches, and that he was barred by the five-year statute of limitations The intervening petitioner's exceptions to this amendment were sustained An in-

terlocutory decree was entered, and by order of court reference was made to the master By the interlocutory decree the chancellor dismissed the original bill as to Lucy H Darst, because by her answer it appeared that her interest was identical with that of her husband, Rolla M Darst, intervening petitioner

After a hearing before the master, the master filed his report, finding that the equities of the cause were with the intervening petitioner, that a trust resulted in favor of Rolla M Darst for said bonds, that a decree be entered awarding the bonds in question to the said Rolla M Darst, that the cost of the action be taxed against the defendant, Grace H Lang

Objections were filed to the report of the master, which were ordered to stand as exceptions The chancellor overruled the exceptions to the report and approved it, entering a decree finding the equities in accordance with the master's report, and directing that the bonds in question be turned over by the clerk of the circuit court to Rolla M Darst, and taxing the costs against the defendant, Grace H Lang From this decree this appeal is taken

The evidence shows that the bonds in question were purchased by Lucy H Darst, the wife of the intervening petitioner, in January of 1925, with money given to her by her husband, Rolla M Darst, that Lucy H Darst, wife of Rolla M Darst, regularly transacted his financial affairs, since he worked in Springfield, and was only home for short intervals It further shows that the bonds were bought from the First Trust and Savings Bank of Bloomington, it being shown on the books of the bank that they were purchased in the name of Grace H Lang, with interest payable to Lucy H Darst, that Grace H Lang was on the road, travelling, selling books, and knew nothing of the purchase of the bonds at the time they were paid for, and paid nothing on the purchase price The evidence further shows that Rolla M Darst at no time authorized the purchase of the bonds in his daughter's name, that Grace H Lang in December of 1925 returned home and while there was told of the purchase of the bonds

From 1926, until July, 1933, the interest on said bonds was collected both by Lucy H Darst and Grace H Lang, being paid over to Lucy H Darst to use as she saw fit in the maintenance of the family When the bonds were purchased they were put in a box at the bank, which was rented by Lucy H Darst, where they were kept until August, 1927, when the box was

given up, at which time they were given into the possession of Grace H Lang by Lucy H Darst, and after which they were kept in her deposit box in the bank by Grace H Lang, until April or May of 1933, and then they were taken to the Darst home and turned over to Lucy H Darst at her request, and kept there until July of 1933, when they were delivered by Lucy H Darst to Kaywin Kennedy, trustee, in whose possession they remained until the filing of the bill of complaint Thereafter, by order of court, they were deposited with the clerk of the court

It is contended by appellant that since the bonds were purchased with Rolla M Darst's money, and entered on the books of the bank at the time they were purchased, in the name of his daughter, Grace H Lang, that such action creates a strong presumption that they were transferred to the daughter as a gift, and appellant cites a number of cases showing that where property, both real and personal, is transferred by a parent to a child such a presumption arises These cases, however, appear to be different from the case at bar in that the bonds in question were bearer bonds, and not made out in the name of the appellant, or transferred to her, the only reference to her being a notation on the books of the bank that she was the purchaser, whereas, in the cases cited by appellant the transfer was by a deed or bill of sale, directly to the person claiming the transfer as a gift

We believe the correct rule to be that the burden is upon the donee to prove by clear and convincing evidence the delivery of the property in question by the donor to the donee with intent to pass title, and that the law never presumes a gift (*Bolton* v *Bolton,* 306 Ill 473, *Cusack* v *Cusack,* 253 Ill App 288, *Fanning* v *Russell,* 94 Ill 386, *Telford* v *Patton,* 144 Ill 611)

There are many complaints made by the appellant on the rulings of the court over the various pleadings filed by the various parties in connection with the intervening petition Without going into detail, we believe that the trial court was correct in every ruling, except for one technical mistake in one of the orders, which is so plainly apparent it is of no consequence It seems to us that appellants do not understand the purpose or function of a bill of interpleader The plaintiff in such a bill sets up that he holds property to which he has no claim, avers that there are several claimants, and he does not know to whom the property in his hands should go, and that there is no collusion between himself and any of the parties defend-

ant The purpose is to determine the ownership of the property involved, which the plaintiff offers to tender into court It is appellant's complaint that one who is not named as a party defendant can not ask and be given leave to become a party defendant where he claims the property to be his There is no merit in this complaint, and the court properly permitted the defendant, Rolla M Darst, to intervene (*Wightman* v. *The Evanston Yaryan Company,* 217 Ill 371) It appears to us to hold otherwise would reach a ridiculous result Appellant complains because she says she was not permitted an opportunity to plead the statute of limitations, and laches An examination of the pleadings discloses that this is not true, but that the defense of the statue of limitations, or laches, could not successfully be maintained as to intervening petitioner, Rolla M Darst, because same would not commence to run until he had knowledge that there was some one claiming title to this property other than himself, and this he did not know until two days before the filing of the bill.

Intervenor, Rolla M Darst, claims that he furnished the money with which the bonds were purchased There is no evidence to the contrary, and the court was correct in so finding His wife testified that she received the money from him for the specific purpose of buying these bonds for him, and that she had no other authority.

It is contended that the wife should not have been permitted to testify in this case In our opinion, on the authority of Section 5, Chapter 51, Cahill's Revised Statutes, as construed by our appellate court in *Kirman* v *Hutchinson,* 254 Ill App 469, no error was committed by the trial court in permitting her to testify, since she was the agent of her husband in that transaction (Also *Sargeant* v *Marshall,* 38 Ill App 642) In any event this ruling was not assigned as error for reversal and can not be questioned on appeal. (*Brown* v *Higgins,* 259 Ill App 34)

It is further contended by the appellant that she gave up a position whereby she earned $100 a week, on the representation that she would be taken care of; and that the gift to her of these bonds was the method by which she was "taken care of " However, it appears that property valued at $9,000 was given to her, and that a mortgage of $2,000 which was on it, was later removed So, certainly, it was not necessary that Rolla M Darst divest himself of all his property in

order to fulfill the promise to take care of this daughter

There is some evidence which seems to bear out the contention that some bonds, whether the bonds involved in this litigation, or not, were diverted to this appellant without the knowledge of Rolla M Darst, and that much secrecy was maintained concerning them.

A great deal of the abstract and much of the argument is devoted to detailing some very unfortunate, one might almost say "scandalous" acts by various members of this family, but we do not see that they in any way prove or disprove anything concerning this particular transaction, or are at all pertinent to the issues

There are a number of matters concerning which the testimony can not be harmonized In all of these cases the master, who heard the testimony, had the opportunity of observing the witnesses, their candor or lack of it, their opportunity of knowing the facts concerning which they testified, and we see no reason why this court should disturb his findings of fact, which were confirmed by the trial court

It seems to us that the manner in which appellant, Grace H Lang, treated these bonds, as if placed in her box for safe keeping (Lucy H Darst and Rolla M Darst having surrendered their own safety deposit box) does not comport with a belief on her part that she was the sole owner Some of the interest was collected by Lucy H Darst, all of the balance which was collected by Grace H Lang she immediately turned over to Lucy H Darst In the spring of 1933 she took these bonds out of her box, brought them to her mother's home, and gave them to her mother, at her mother's request Her mother kept them in her home for several months, and then turned them over to the plaintiff in this suit It might well be noted that at the same time these bonds were taken out of the box of Lucy H Darst and Rolla M Darst, and turned over to Grace H Lang to be placed in her box that there were numerous other papers accompanying them to which apparently Grace H Lang makes no claim

All of this is as consistent with the theory that they were turned over to her merely for safe keeping as with the theory that they were turned over to her as a gift Complaint is made that Rolla M Darst made no inquiry concerning the bonds or what had become of them, and that he should have been put on notice to

investigate. He knew that the bonds had been purchased; that his wife was receiving the income. So long as that was the situation he had no occasion to make inquiry.

For the reasons heretofore set forth it is our opinion that there is no reversible error in this record, and that the decree of the trial court should be affirmed.

Decree affirmed.

(Eleven pages in original opinion)

PUBLISHED IN ABSTRACT

Louise Lavin, Plaintiff Appellee, v. Yellow Cab Co., a Corporation, Springfield Yellow Cab Co., Inc., a corporation, Defendant-Appellant. Carl R. Ferguson, doing business under the style and firm name of Ferguson Grocery Company, Defendant

286 I.A. 623[4]

Appeal from Circuit Court, Sangamon County.

APRIL TERM, A D 1936.

Gen No 8995 **Agenda No 19**

MR JUSTICE ALLABEN delivered the opinion of the Court.

This case is an appeal from the judgment entered by the circuit court of Sangamon county in an action for alleged personal injuries sustained by plaintiff appellee in a collision between a taxi cab and a delivery truck in Springfield, Illinois The complaint, consisting of four counts, alleged that the plaintiff was a passenger in a taxi cab of the defendant appellant, and that the cab and the delivery truck of the co-defendant, Carl R Ferguson, collided in the 900 block in South Second street, Springfield, Illinois The first count charged both of the defendants with driving and operating their motor vehicles negligently The second count charged the carelessness and negligence of the drivers was due to the high rate of speed at which they were travelling The third and fourth counts charged that the defendants drove their vehicles out of the regular line of traffic, and attempted to pass other vehicles Each of the said counts alleged due care on the part of the plaintiff and contained an ad damnum of $4,000

Defendants filed separate answers to the complaint, denying the allegations of the respective counts The case was tried before a jury, and a verdict was returned in the sum of $1,000 against the defendant appellant, but found the Ferguson Grocery Company, the co-defendant, not guilty Motion for new trial was filed, and denied The court entered judgment in accordance with the verdict From this judgment and the denial of the new trial this appeal is prosecuted

From the evidence in the case it appears that the plaintiff, Louise Lavin, was a passenger for hire in the taxi cab owned and operated by a servant of the de-

fendant appellant; that the said taxi cab was being driven south on South Second street in the 900 block, in the city of Springfield, Illinois; that a commercial delivery truck owned by Carl R Ferguson, and operated by his agent was proceeding north on the same street, and in the same block; that a collision occurred approximately in the north quarter of the block; that after the collision the cab was out of control, proceeded in a southeasterly course, over the curb, side-walk, and yard of a dwelling house, at 918 South Second street, and came to a stop after striking the lower portion of the foundation of the house, breaking some of the bricks in the foundation The delivery truck after colliding with defendant appellant's vehicle, collided with a cab, Ford car, and a parked car Mrs Lavin, the plaintiff, testified that the cab turned to pass another car, that she noticed an increase in speed just before the crash with the delivery truck of Ferguson There was testimony that the cab was travelling at from 45 to 50 miles an hour after the crash, and that before the collision it was running at from 30 to 35 miles an hour The driver of the taxi cab testified that he was behind a truck, that there were cars parked on both sides of Second street, that traffic was fairly heavy, that except to try the foot brake he did nothing to stop or slow down the speed of the taxi cab

One of the exhibits offered and admitted in evidence was a photograph showing the tire tracks of the cab, showing deep imprints in the ground which the tires had made after the cab had gone over the curb It further appears from the evidence that when the cab struck the foundation of the house, some distance beyond the curb, it broke the bricks, that the doors on the right side of the cab could not be opened, that the seat of the cab was pushed out of place, glass broken, fly wheel housing broken, and the radiator smashed some

Mrs Lavin was stunned, and her mother suffered a broken leg Further testimony showed that plaintiff was in good health prior to the accident, that after the accident she lost weight, that she was suffering from traumatic neurosis, which the physicians stated is always due to a shakeup or severe blow on the head or spinal column, that she was improving slowly; that she would recover from her injury in two years, that her condition was not permanent, but was considered as having an effect of mental depression, resulting in loss of sleep, appetite and weight, that if such condition progresses it developes into nervous deterioration, and lowers the resistance of the body

In reciting the errors relied upon an appeal appellant complains that the court admitted improper, incompetent and highly prejudicial evidence No reference is made to this alleged error in appellant's brief of authorities, and it is only discussed indirectly in appellant's argument, where attention is called to the fact that certain witnesses did not see the accident occur, and that the witness, Dr Rosen, diagnosed the illness of the plaintiff as traumatic neurosis, which he testified was based on the fact that she had been involved in an accident Arguing from this the defendant appellant says there is no basis or justification for the amount of the verdict However, if facts and circumstances are proved, which lead to a conclusion that other facts and circumstances are true, such conclusions based upon circumstantial evidence may be accepted and acted upon by the jury (*Mahlstedt* v *Ideal Lighting Co*, 271 Ill 154) In many instances circumstantial evidence is all that exists, and is frequently as satisfactory in drawing a conclusion as to the existence or occurrence of a fact, as direct evidence (*Wilkinson* v *Aetna Life Insurance Co*, 144 Ill App 38, *Kennedy* v *Aetna Life Insurance Co*, 148 Ill App 273) This should be particularly true where there is no evidence given to controvert the circumstantial evidence offered Even where the evidence is conflicting a reviewing court will not reverse the finding of a jury in relation to disputed questions of fact unless the finding of the jury is manifestly against the greater weight of the evidence (*Lyons* v. *Stroud,* 257 Ill 350, *Noyes* v *Heffernan,* 153 Ill 339)

Appellant complains that the court refused proper instructions, and admitted improper instructions No discussion of the improper instructions is made by the appellant and we, therefore, deem it unnecessary to discuss this question As to the improper instructions which were refused the defendant appellant refers to the instruction offered which referred chiefly to the degree of care required in sudden and apparent danger, and cites the case of *Letush* v *New York Cent R R.*, 267 Ill App 526, from which appellant quotes the statement "The law does not require of a common carrier 'unreasonable or impracticable vigilance' " It is insisted by appellant that such an instruction was necessary because the court had given an instruction regarding the fact that the defendant appellant was a common carrier, and that the jury evidently misunderstood or was not informed as to what the legal responsibility of a common carrier was The instruc-

tions given on that point were more favorable to appellant than to appellee and we, therefore, feel that the failure to give the requested cautionary instructions did not constitute error

Defendant appellant's brief of authorities and argument is partially devoted to the contention that the plaintiff must show by affirmative proof that she was in the exercise of due care for her own safety just before and at the time the accident occurred However, there is no showing on the part of the plaintiff appellee of any want of due care, and it is obvious that the plaintiff and her mother could not have been guilty of any want of due care and contributory negligence when they were passengers in a common carrier Such due care can be established as any other fact by circumstantial evidence (*Chicago & E I R Co* v *Beaver,* 199 Ill 34) The allegation of due care on the part of the plaintiff we think was substantiated by the evidence adduced in her behalf The other errors relied upon by appellant, to-wit The alleged improper admission of exhibits, that the verdict was a result of passion and prejudice, that it was erroneous in finding the issues against the defendant appellant, and not against the defendant, Carl R Ferguson, in denying the motion of defendant appellant to set aside the verdict, are without merit, as the jury is the sole judge of the facts The alleged improper admission of the exhibits is not argued, and no authorities are cited in connection with the ruling on the motion For the reasons given the judgment of the trial court is affirmed

Judgment affirmed

(Eight pages in original opinion)

PUBLISHED IN ABSTRACT

Erma Templeman, Appellant, v U. G. Usher, Nick Kish, Appellees.

Appeal from Circuit Court, Sangamon County

APRIL TERM, A D 1936 286 I.A. 624

Gen. No 8970 **Agenda No. 5**

MR JUSTICE FULTON delivered the opinion of the Court

This is an action of replevin brought by the Appellant, Erma Templeman, against the Appellees U G Usher, a constable and Nick Kish proprietor of a garage for the possession of an automobile On April 20th, 1922, one Marie Phillips recovered a judgment in a Justice of the Peace Court against J W Templeman, husband of Appellant, for the sum of $375 00 An execution was issued out of said Court and on February 11th, 1934, Appellee Usher, as constable, seized a Chevrolet coach on said execution and placed the same in the garage of Appellee Kish On February 14th, 1934, the Appellant, claiming to be the sole owner of said automobile, filed her replevin suit before a Justice of the Peace to recover possession of the automobile The case was tried before the Justice, who found the issues for the defendants An appeal was taken to the Circuit Court of Sangamon County where the case was tried before a jury and a verdict returned for the defendants The present appeal is from a judgment upon said verdict

It is the contention of the Appellant that she was the sole owner of the automobile in controversy, subject to the payment of a balance due to the General Motors Acceptance Corporation, and that her husband, J W Templeman had no interest or legal title to the car The evidence shows that J W Templeman, husband of the Appellant, bought a Chevrolet coupe in May 1934 as his own individual property, that he purchased a new Chevrolet coach on September 20th, 1934 and traded the old coupe in on the new car for which he was allowed the sum of $430 00 in trade The balance remaining unpaid on the new coach was the sum of $180 66 and in order to finance this balance the Appellant and J W Templeman entered into a conditional sales contract with the Company from whom they purchased the car The instrument was signed

by both Appellant and her husband J W Templeman The automobile company then assigned to J W Templeman and Erma Templeman the certificate of title which assignment was approved by and filed with the Secretary of the State of Illinois The conditional sales contract dated September 20th, 1934, was payable in six monthly installments of $30 11 each, and was assigned and sold to the General Motors Acceptance Corporation Appellant testified that she had made three payments on the car amounting to $85 33, as part payment under the conditional sales contract, for which she presented receipts showing such payment The certificate of title from the Secretary of State was issued to J W Templeman and Erma Templeman jointly

There is further testimony showing that the car was driven without any license plates attached thereto, that the car was used by J W Templeman for both business and pleasure and that the Appellant could not drive and did not drive the car in question, that J W Templeman told the proprietor of the garage that the car was his property Appellant testified that the Chevrolet coach was her own property because she had paid off a judgment to the Wayne City National Bank in the sum of $525 00 where she was co-signer or surety on a judgment note of her husband The judgment on this note was taken by confession against both J W Templeman and the Appellant in the Circuit Court of Sangamon County on August 5th, 1931 An issue of fact was therefore presented to the jury as to whether or not the Appellant was the sole owner of the car replevined or whether she owned a joint interest with her husband, J W Templeman On this question the jury found in favor of the Appellee and there being sufficient evidence to support their finding this Court would not be warranted in disturbing such finding In order to maintain replevin Plaintiff must show title, special property interest, or right of possession *Horn* v *Zimmer,* 180 App 232 A party bringing an action of replevin must either be the owner or the person entitled to the possession of the property sought to be replevined *Swain* v *First National Bank,* 100 App 31 Replevin cannot be maintained by one partner against an officer levying upon the interest of the other partner *Weber* v *Hertz,* 188 Ill 68 *Shoe* v *Webb,* 87 App 522 In this case the jury having found adversely to the Appellant it follows that J W Templeman had a substantial interest in the automobile in question and a right to the possession thereof and

an officer with an execution based upon a judgment against J W Templeman was authorized to make a levy upon Templeman's interest in the property

Appellant also objects to one instruction given by the trial Court as not stating the law correctly but under Rule 8 of this Court and Rule 38 of the Supreme Court the Appellant was required to prepare and file a complete abstract in accordance with the rules in order to have the instructions considered which they failed to do It has been repeatedly held that questions on instructions will not be considered by the reviewing Court where the complete series is not abstracted for the benefit of the Court on review *Reavley* v *Harris,* 239 Ill 526

The Appellant further urges that Appellees were not entitled to a trial by a jury because no request or demand was made by either of the parties in writing before the trial On and after the June Term, 1935, Rule 24½ of the Supreme Court provided that in cases of appeal from a Justice of the Peace, where a trial by jury may be permitted, either party desiring a trial by jury shall, before trial, but in any event not later than the second return day following the filing of a transcript on appeal, file a written demand for a jury trial This cause however, was tried during the month of April 1935, prior to the passage of such rule At that time there was no provision in the New Practice Act or in the rules of the Supreme Court which required the filing of a written demand for a jury trial and it was therefore not error for the trial Court to permit a trial by jury to either of the parties to this cause.

We believe that the main question in this case was one of fact which has been determined by the jury upon competent evidence to support the verdict and finding no substantial error in the record the judgment of the Circuit Court of Sangamon County is affirmed

Affirmed

(Four pages in original opinion)

.ract

PUBLISHED IN ABSTRACT

Elizabeth Bailey, Appellant, v H B Keck, Sheriff of Logan County, Appellee.

Appeal from County Court Logan County

APRIL TERM, A D 1936. 286 I.A. 624[2]

Gen No 8993 Agenda No 17

MR JUSTICE FULTON delivered the opinion of the Court

On the 31st of October A D 1935, Appellant filed her complaint in the County Court of Logan County against the Appellee as Sheriff of said County In her original complaint the Appellant claims from the Appellee the sum of $225 00 which she alleged Appellee had in his hands as Sheriff The original complaint was dismissed on motion of the Appellee and leave given Appellant to file an amended complaint The amended complaint was also dismissed on motion of the Appellee as not stating a cause of action, and judgment for costs entered against the Appellant The sole issue in the case was whether or not the amended complaint contained sufficient facts to state a cause of action

Paragraph two of the amended complaint alleges that Appellee had in his hands $225 00 belonging to the Appellant, that said money was paid to the Appellee, as Sheriff of Logan County, by Jess A Bailey to have and to hold said money at the direction and assignment of said Jess A Bailey, that no other person had any interest in said money except Jess A Bailey and that said money had been furnished to Jess A Bailey by the Appellant out of the proceeds of her business Paragraph three of the amended complaint alleges an assignment from the said Jess A Bailey to the Appellant and paragraph five alleges that the Appellant made a written demand on the Appellee demanding that he pay over to her the said sum of $225 00 No other facts are stated in the amended complaint tending to show upon what terms or under what circumstances the money was paid to the Appellee or attempting to show any contract, bailment or trust relation of any kind between Jess A Bailey and the Appellee All the averments of the Appellant are conclusions of the pleader and no where does the amended complaint allege facts which disclose the real basis of a claim

against the Sheriff of Logan County Such a pleading does not tend to advise a defendant of the nature of the action which will enable him to prepare a proper defense and it is hard to see how the Appellee could answer specifically the general averments and conclusions set forth in the amended complaint

While the provisions of the New Civil Practice Act require that all pleadings shall contain a plain and concise statement of the pleaders cause of action in an attempt to simplify procedure, still this court has held in *Whalen* v *Twin City Barge Co*, 280 App 596, that those substantial averments of fact heretofore necessary to state a cause of action are in no way affected by any provisions of the New Civil Practice Act Our Courts have always held that general allegations of indebtedness, without any statement of fact supporting them, are mere conclusions and are not sufficient to state a legal cause of action

An examination of the amended complaint discloses only a series of legal conclusions on the part of the pleader and the trial Court properly sustained the Appellee's motion to dismiss and the judgment of said Court should be affirmed

Affirmed

(Two pages in original opinion)

Lightning Source UK Ltd.
Milton Keynes UK
UKHW031210271218
334538UK00005B/24/P

9 780260 427601